STOCKS, BONDS

& TAXES

A Comprehensive Handbook and Investment Guide for Everybody

Textbook Edition

PHILLIP BRUCE CHUTE, EA

Textbook edition 2020

Editing: Leslie Adkison & Nenita Lariosa
Book design by: German Creative
Book Formatting: Sarah Dietz

ISBN 978-1-7328855-4-7

www.phillipbchute.com

DISCLAIMER

On December 22, 2017, President Trump signed the Tax Cuts and Jobs Act, which contained 115 new tax provisions effective in 2018. This publication will contain many of the new relevant provisions.

The book material is based on personal experiences, with a tip of the hat to Wikipedia, Wall Street Journal, Investopedia and the myriad of state and federal government agencies and public information sources available today.

Because Federal and State taxes are a constantly moving target, professional counsel is recommended before making financial decisions.

The Author, Phillip Bruce Chute, EA

ABOUT THIS BOOK

This book is a compilation of investment information about securities, stocks, bonds, insurance, and essentials for the typical investor who needs a better understanding of the mechanics of New York's Wall Street and the insurance giants of New England. The format is broken down into the type of investment, commissions or cost, FINRA compliance law, tax laws, successful strategies, charts and graph aids, trading tips, pros and cons of specific investment and financing. Notice the term "law", the foundation of all transactions, which must conform to legal parameters to be valid, and the tax effects and consequences. A glossary provides practical reference information. The scope of this book is quite broad and reaches beyond the normal investment situation encountered by an investor meeting with his/her financial planner. It is not a book of theory, but of real-life practice.

The purpose of this book is to provide the intelligent reader with enough information to be at least as knowledgeable as the stockbroker or insurance agent he/she is dealing with, and to be capable of conducting personal planning and trading with confidence. It has been the experience of the author that most people are rightly overwhelmed by the limited information presented to them by the sophisticated and highly educated sales people making presentations. Informed people who can resist sales pressure enough to comprehend what they are doing make the best investment decisions. Good investments are made when the buyer can put the sales pitch person on hold until he/she can reference a book such as this to further understand the implications of these important decisions. Because the nature of money and finance is complex and always exposed to risk, an attempt is made to simplify the text and real examples are given.

This book is not designed by the author to show you how to be rich instantly with your savings. He intended to show you the risk, costs, and mechanics of investments so you will understand your true potential in the investment business and make money the old-fashioned way...by being smart and informed. As an insurance salesperson once told him, "Sell the sizzle, not the steak."

There are also dozens of success stories, not only of dollars and entrepreneurs, but also of individuals and their successes. Included are reflective examples of our powerful American economy and how the chess pieces of character and energy move together. Success is never without hard work and diligence to a sound goal, as these real-life strategies testify.

Are worm farms a good investment? Read the real-life Horror Stories and find out what investors did with them. Also, find out why new huge tractor-trailer rigs were surprisingly delivered to the front doors of wealthy investors, why the investor's high yield Mexican bank bonds were unredeemable, or about the investor who bought unsalable common stocks in a large Long Beach bank, or why the millionaire bought worthless tax-exempt muni (municipal) bonds, etc. All investments are tax-related and focused on the Tax Code because it has become the center of all economic decisions.

Finally, questions are provided at the end of each chapter so you can practice applying your knowledge. The Application Exercises include multiple-choice and True-False items. After the Application Exercises, an answer key is provided at the back of the book.

ABOUT THE AUTHOR

Phillip Bruce Chute is an Enrolled Agent, tested, licensed, and appointed by the IRS directly. He has prepared and supervised over 25,000 tax returns over 30 years or more. These are individual, business, fiduciary, estate, corporate, partnership, and many kinds of business entities. He has also represented clients in hundreds of audits including payroll and sales tax, secured and unsecured property taxes, workman's compensation, Labor Board, IRS and FTB office and field individual taxes, corporate taxes, and estate taxes.

Phil, as his clients respectfully address him, obtained his first securities license to protect his clients, as a direct result of witnessing terrible investment machinations done by financial salespeople. As a focused, committed financial salesperson, business consultant, tax expert, and as a securities principal supervising other brokers by the National Association of Security Dealers' (now FINRA) tough rules, he has become an authority in all aspects of finance.

Aside from holding the highest credential award by the IRS by passing the Special Enrollment Examinations to become an Enrolled Agent, the author served concurrently as a supervising principal of the Office of Supervisory Jurisdiction and branch manager of various security brokerage firms for twenty years. For five years, he was the President and Registered Financial Advisor of Pacific Financial Advisors Corporation. An author of *American Independent Business*, a college-level textbook on small businesses and entrepreneurship, Phillip B Chute is listed in the *Who's Who* Marquis book on successful business professionals and won National and International writing awards for Kiwanis International.

TABLE OF CONTENTS

SECTION I   INVESTMENTS

PART 1   EQUITIES

PART 4   OTHER INVESTMENTS

SECTION II LIFE PLANNING

PART 5   FINANCIAL PLANNING

SECTION I

INVESTMENTS

PART ONE

EQUITIES

Equity capital is the stockbroker term for corporate stock issued for cash. Thus, it is outside ownership in the corporation. This interest, usually expressed as voting common shares, is sold through various financial firms that are authorized through the **Securities Exchange Commission (SEC)**. Equities are the common currency of the average citizen today. Stocks are owned by almost all pension/retirement plans, in individual portfolios, and in everyday economic discussions. Several television stations are devoted full-time to live trading and economarket discussions. Economic events such as a large company layoff or merger are transformed into headlines of stock market movements that appear in newspaper headlines or bylines on the hourly news. Equities are the stock market and woven into the fabric of daily American life. Although the top 5% of the population owns 90% of all wealth, there is enough left for trading, investment, pensions, and speculation by the typical middle-class citizen today.

Accessibility of the equity markets by individual Internet trading has expanded public awareness and participation to an extent never imagined by the cyber dreamers of these times. The Internet stocks themselves have added fuel to the fire that has driven the **NASDAQ** and **Dow Jones Industrial Average Composite (DJIA)** to unheard of levels. The swift driving forces behind modern computerized equity trading operate without historic reference to the times when the Chosen Few Bankers, behind closed boardroom doors, traded stocks until Thomas Edison invented the ticker-tape machine.

The **Financial Industry Regulatory Authority (FINRA)**, formerly **The National Association of Securities Dealers (NASD)**, is a **Self-Regulatory Organization (SRO)** in which stockbrokers and dealers pay all the dues and expenses. The organization strictly monitors the professional conduct of the **Broker/Dealer (BD)** firms and account executive representatives through their licensing and audit functions.

FINRA, under the umbrella of the Securities Exchange Commission (**SEC**), is the investigative and compliance function for security sales and trading. Their sanctions and penalties are quite harsh in comparison to other professional organizations, which tend to act fraternally for member protection. Because of the fiduciary exposure of individuals to securities representatives and their firms handling client funds, the FINRA is a welcome ally for the average investor.

CHAPTER ONE

INITIAL PUBLIC STOCK OFFERS, SECURITIES EXCHANGE COMMISSION REGISTRATION

The SEC subjects new **Initial Public Stock Offerings (IPO)** going public to the sale of their shares of corporate stock for operating capital, to intense scrutiny. The company must have been in business prior to the offer, complete registration questionnaires, disclose antecedents about the management, satisfy capital requirements, and provide certified financial statements to satisfy the SEC that the business is a viable going concern and that the offer is not fraudulent. After Registration, all corporations must file periodic form 10Q every three months to report earnings. Of course, nobody can **GUARANTEE** (that word is never used in the securities business) the real future of the company. The underwriting process is complex and expensive. Only large brokerage houses and a few specialized banking institutions handle new issues. The **UNDERWRITER** charges about 7% of the new issue and sets the price for the Initial Public Offering. This offering is a selective offering, which is sold in blocks to large brokerage firms (their other selling division) and institutional buyers such as mutual funds. These funds and firms are advised to hold the stocks, for say…a month at least, to avoid speculation. What really happens is that they **FLIP** the stock over and sell it on the secondary market for a quick profit after a minute or two.

The corporate seller usually authorizes **common voting stock**, which has **no-par** value. By not having a stated value, such as $10 per share, the stock sale price per share can vary and will be booked at the actual amount sold instead of a fixed price. If it was fixed at $10, the stock could be sold for only $10 initially, which would create corporate accounting and tax problems if the public would not pay (**cash price,** which is defined as what two unrelated parties would pay for any item in an open arms-length transaction) that much or it could be sold for more on the open market.

A **Committee on Uniform Securities Identification Procedure (CUSIP)** nine-digit alphanumeric number is assigned and noted on the left-hand top corner of the stock certificates. Every time a security (including bonds) is traded, this number is used. This agency has assigned the numbers to all North American U.S. and Canadian financial instruments since 1962.

NEW ISSUES are always a highly speculative venture and subjected to much fraud. First, why are we buying a new issue? We are speculating that the price we pay for the shares of stock will increase dramatically once offered. We are hoping it will run away and become a **Microsoft**. Therein lies the truth. We are hoping it will run away NEXT WEEK, after we buy it (**buy low, sell high**)! Now we join the line of speculators. First, is the guy who owned the **STOCK OPTIONS** of the company before it went public (**privately held**) along with his **VENTURE CAPITAL** investors. He is selling his shares or new shares (which might be restricted to one year after the IPO) that will pour money into his business and generate higher salaries and **perks** for him as well as an increase in the value of his original holdings. Next, there is the **underwriter institution** that creates a huge commission to issue the stock. The underwriter can set the initial price, which can create much speculation if it is priced under the "**perceived**" market value. Then, there is the brokerage or institutional firm who will buy an allocated block of the stock for them, unless they know it is a dog. They will control the now secondary speculative market prices, after it is first offered, by calling their list of investors and telling them how great it is. This stock is not listed on the open market yet, so the few brokerages or investment bankers really control the issue. Then, you buy the remaining public shares. Did you buy it when it was first sold on the **secondary market** at $7.50 by the initial institutional while $5 buyers were now taking their first profits, or a week later when it was at $10, when everybody was now reselling higher? Or the next month when the same shares are bidding for $23.50, or the next year when they bottomed out at $2.50? The first Broker-Dealer or institution who bought the allocated block of shares at $5 for their own account hopes to sell when the market is higher, and he is in a great position to know when to move because he is actually "**MAKING THE MARKET**" by controlling the limited and allocated issue.

The **STOCKBROKER sales rep** is not forgotten in the **FEEDING FRENZY** arrangement since he can earn a maximum commission on the deal, both when the issue is first **SOLD TO** the investor, when it is **SOLD BY** the investor and when it is **RESOLD** to another investor. He can also allocate new issues to selective clients, which enables him to sell doggy issues along with potential **"HOT ISSUES"** or set the investor off for the next new really good deal. Most market-making brokerage or investment firms are asked to hold the initial issue new stocks up to a month to discourage excessive trading and speculation, which is rarely done, because that is why the investors are there in the first place.

Most of the IPO trading traffic these days is done on **E-stocks**, which are **Internet-related speculations**. The venture capitalists deal in three basic categories leading to the IPO. These are **vertical portals, business-to-business portals**, and **e-commerce superstores**. These are not generally technology issues, but purely over-the-Internet electronic speculations.

All IPOs must be registered and approved by the **SEC** before they can be sold to the public. Many fraudulent stock offers are now appearing on the **INTERNET**. The best way to buy any stock on the Internet is to work through a broker. This is the only official control over legitimate offerings. Many new Internet HOT TIP publications can **hype** new issues with fantastic predictions. The people offering the issues may pay them off or be connected insiders, so beware. Continuous fortuitous statements issue from principals about their holdings and undisclosed options. The **SEC** receives hundreds of calls each day from investors who are concerned about dubious Internet offerings. The **SEC** filed formal charges against only one scam per month, until late 1998 when they filed 44 in one day, which is still only a fraction of the actual total. Sometimes they only order the peddler to **"CEASE & DESIST"**, which is another way of saying your money is gone forever and the bad guys are leaving on vacation. This means that you are on your own if you buy any security or investment not offered through a reputable firm. Do not invest money for any IPO that you cannot afford to lose, because IPO is another word for **SPECULATION**. Best to let it age a little while and settle down, unless you like sleeping with your eyes wide open.

There are many good companies helped by going public because they have large capital requirements for expansion, equipment or other needs besides speculation or profit-taking. Only very large issues will ultimately be accepted for sale over the New York Stock Exchange **Big Board** in public trading. **IPO's** will not be listed in the financial section of your local newspaper under **NASDAQ, NEW YORK,** or **AMERICAN** exchanges, unless they are large private companies going public. Some newer stocks are now listed in the NASDAQ Small Capital Issues section.

PLANNING TIPS

New initial stock issues should have two key points. The first is the particular **INDUSTRY** the company is located in and the second is why the company should be especially successful as a **COMPETITOR** in that industry. Gather information, if possible, on the industry (is it a **growth industry** like software or a **dying industry** using Bessemer steel furnaces?) and ask the sales rep for data on the company and its officers. He can send it by fax or e-mail if he wants to make a sale. You will not have much time because he will be working the phone, so be brief and call him back in the same day (keep in mind that they may close early because most trading halts at 4 PM New York time and these guys start early at 9:30 in the morning). Some **IPO's** are solid gold, (I sold a lot of **Tesla** at $20 when it first went public) and the stock shares are allocated to the **BD's BEST CLIENTS** (best is a term meaning large trades, sales, and commissions). Evening trading under the NASDAQ, although automated, will certainly result in much loss of sleep by brokers, as well as clients. Moreover, we all know that the more stocks are traded, the higher the price can go!

Because of intense speculation during late 1998 and early 1999 shares of stock for new issues were traded over ten times daily, some of the large brokerage firms closed out **MARGIN ACCOUNTS** (interest bearing accounts for investors which are offered by the broker firms with bank backing) for all Internet stock trades. The volatility of the prices caused too many margin calls on these accounts whenever the prices dropped.

Most stock issues are packaged with financing leverage by huge institutionalized broker firms and associated banks. They are available, like most individual stock issues, for purchase through mutual funds and investment advisor fiduciaries. Individual stocks traded over the market will sell for about 1% commissions, which is down from the traditional 5% before discount brokers took over the trading business. Some discount brokers in 2020 sell for zero commissions on stock trades. They simply make money on other security products, especially insurance related and **advisory clients** (these accounts are charged large fees based on portfolio value) which we will cover later.

Internet trading firms are now entering the IPO market and will be offering smaller offerings directly to the investor on a **Dutch auction** (each person bidding separately) basis, which will eliminate some of the excessive middleman profit taking between investment bankers and brokerage or institutional firms. It will also bring a higher price and more cash to the corporation owning the stocks that are being offered, because the price will correspond to the market, and would not be conservatively underpriced, which offers speculative opportunities especially benefiting the controlling first buyer brokerage firms and institutions. Some of these new offers will spend multimillions on advertising a software application, which may not have any value if it doesn't fly.

TAXES

All stock sales are subject to rules on profits or losses. The gains are the greater of the selling price over the purchase price. Commissions and ticket charges reduce selling prices or increase purchase costs. **SHORT-TERM GAINS**, which are sales of investments held less than one year, are taxed as **ORDINARY INCOME** (your highest tax bracket). For **LONG-TERM GAINS** of over the one-year holding period, the tax rate will be maxed out at 0 to 20% according to the applicable tax rates on an individual's tax return (which have a new high of 37%). If your taxable bracket is a lowly 10%, then the long-term capital gains tax is reduced to only 0%. All short-term and long-term losses will offset capital gains and are subject to a loss deduction limit of up to $3,000 per year against other income. Excess losses can be carried forward to future year tax returns, never backward. By now, you should know that tax laws are constantly changing, like marking the spot where your hat fell off before floating down the river. Capital Gains tax brackets at the time of printing (2020) begin at 0%, 15% and 20% depending on taxable income and filing status. Qualified dividends, which are dividends from equities--not bonds, are also taxed at capital gains rates.

TAX TABLES FOR CAPITAL GAINS AND QUALIFIED DIVIDENDS

EFFECTIVE 2020 THE BREAKPOINTS ARE:

Single Taxable Income:	
$0 to 40,000	maximum rate = 0%
40,001 to 441,450	maximum rate = 15%
441,451 and over	maximum rate = 20%
Married Filing Joint or QW Taxable income:	
$0 to 80,000	maximum rate = 0%
80,001 to 496,600	maximum rate = 15%
496,601 and over	maximum rate = 20%
Married Filing Separate Taxable Income:	
$0 to 40,000	maximum rate = 0%
40,001 to 248,300	maximum rate = 15%
248,301 and over	maximum rate = 20%
Head of Household Taxable Income:	
$0 to 53,600	maximum rate = 0%
53,601 to 469,050	maximum rate = 15%
469,051 and over	maximum rate = 20%
Estates and Trusts Taxable Income (for capital gains)	
$0 to 2,650	maximum rate = 0%
2,651 to 12,950	maximum rate =15%
12,951 and over	maximum rate = 20%

Brokerage tax statements usually list the sales of the securities or bonds and the costs. Sometimes the costs are not all identified because the securities were transferred from another broker account and the purchase amount is unknown to the new dealer. In that case, the costs are undisclosed and the clients must identify their original costs or guess to fill in the cost space. Never leave it blank because it results in taxes on the sale amount.

Stock options are issued by **management agreements** which generally allow future taxation as wages or taxable gains. They are not usually exercised (the **kill price** and dates are set at the time of employment agreement) unless there is a gain on the value of the equities. Some broker firms handling the transactions kindly note the individual wage tax treatment on the year-end broker statements at tax time. Other brokers leave it off with questionable results (because the brokerage tax statements show the sale as a taxable event), causing immense conflict between the tax preparers and clients.

TO COMPUTE TAXABLE CAPITAL GAINS PROFITS (OR LOSSES):

ORIGINAL COST OF SECURITY	$
PURCHASE COSTS (commissions, ticket charges, other)	+
REINVESTED DIVIDENDS & GAINS (which were taxed on 1099 forms)	+
NET SALE (A)	+ $
TOTAL COST (BASIS) (B)	$
SELLING PRICE	+ $
SELLING EXPENSES (commissions, ticket charges, other) *	-
TAXABLE GAIN	
(A) $_____ LESS (B) $_(_____)_	= $
	=========

(COMPUTE FOR EACH SECURITY TRANSACTION, THEN SEGREGATE ALL SHORT-TERM {under one-year holding period} FROM LONG-TERM CAPITAL GAINS OR LOSSES).

* When scheduling these items on **Schedule D** of the individual tax return, it is best to show the selling price alone (**so it will match the 1099 form with the IRS computer**) and add the selling expenses to the cost-basis purchase price.

Fortunately, all broker firms will segregate the data for you under short term, long term, income, and purchase or unallocated cost for stocks moved into their brokerage with unknown costs. Bonds are usually segregated from equities.

LEGAL COMPLIANCE

SPECULATIVE ISSUES CANNOT BE LEGALLY SOLD TO UNSOPHISTICATED (low income, uneducated, small net worth, no prior experience with stocks) or **ELDERLY INDIVIDUALS** (who do not have a stock portfolio). Some brokers also tell great stories over the phone to sell an issue, even though insider information is illegal for securities trading, so a tape recording (which could also be illegal) or another person listening to the conversation on another phone would be a great asset if the issue were misrepresented. Sales spiels are supposed to be reviewed and approved by the SEC and the broker-dealer compliance principals. If you experience a loss and feel you were misinformed (nice word meaning LIED TO), first call your sales rep to find out what happened and get the facts straight. Although a telephone complaint may be ignored or misconstrued by the sales rep, a written complaint to the broker-dealer must, by securities compliance law, always generate a serious response if you have a loss and you feel you were misinformed. If their response is inadequate and you still feel you have suffered real losses directly due to their activity and want commissions or losses repaid, then write directly to **NASD at 1735 K Street NW Washington, D.C. 20006** or their replacement **FINRA at 100 F Street, NE Washington, D.C. 20549**. These organizations are **Broker-Dealer self-financed Self-Regulatory Organizations (SRO)** who will immediately query the **BD** who will talk to the sales rep and then respond in writing both to the FINRA and you. This is a very serious business at this level and can endanger licenses, so the response is appropriate. It is also important that your complaint be accurate and documented. They will arbitrate the claim if reasonable. The **Securities Exchange Commission** will also respond to complaints of official or national importance (they are government funded).

A large brokerage firm in **Beverly Hills, California,** advertised that they would not charge commissions for trades made to certain stocks. The slick professionally prepared booklet offered many deals to new clients, who would save a ton of money by **NOT CHARGING COMMISSIONS.** Well then, how do they make enough money to pay for the beautiful advertising and overhead? The **SEC** looked into it and found that they were simply marking up the prices on some stocks (by making the market) they were buying for customers. There was a million-dollar fine connected to the cease and desist order from the audit so the firm may now need a new approach to finding new clients or making money on them. Beware of the **FREE LUNCH,** which can be very costly.

About suing the broker-dealer on the above issue. Most broker-dealers require an **ARBITRATION AGREEMENT** from clients before they will open an account. This eliminates frivolous and nuisance suits from unscrupulous lawyers and their clients. In-house broker-dealer attorneys estimate it costs over $25,000 to successfully defend any suit, no matter how small or absurd. New clients who won't sign will not become new clients. The **FINRA** would recommend an arbitration panel hearing with you if the issue remains unresolved. You will have your day in conference with their retired or independent professionals within a few short months.

Some unregulated or sparsely unregulated **Hedge Funds** or other firms acting on the edge of the law sometimes come to light as the **Bernie Madoff Ponzi Scheme** in 2008, which reached National province after the lawyers got busy and resulted in tax code changes afterward to account for losses from **clawback restitutions** paid to other investors for prior years.

SUCCESSFUL STRATEGIES

There can be no greater success story than of a person who bought **Dell Computer** when it first went public. The legend of college student Michael Dell building computers in his garage and selling them directly to consumers still holds true today as his huge firm now sells them over the Internet and by other **DIRECT SALES** methods. By building a reliable product and eliminating retail outlet costs, he capitalized on a fundamental advantage as well as maintaining close contact with his customers. Without being blinded by component manufacturing giant **IBM's** leasing philosophy, or **Apple Computer's** creating software to sell hardware, he adhered to the philosophy that a computer is a metal box filled with basic components, which can be bought on the street. The fast-changing computer component business was a challenge he was able to master by shortening the gap between customer orders and manufacturing, thus avoiding finished goods inventory buildup. By carefully crafting a selling philosophy of avoiding middlemen retailers such as Radio Shack which sold the first micro-computers (**Tandy**), he stuck to direct sales by media advertising until achieving **NIRVANA** (not a stock issue but an elevated state of being) on the Internet that connected his clients directly to him. Now his international firm literally assembles computers to the wholesale and retail seller's specifications in short order from parts manufactured overseas and south of the border. Other computer manufacturers are attempting to copy his mode of operation. An investment in a **VISIONARY** person, not just the firm, is the true test of entrepreneurial investment when the business comes out the chute as an **IPO**.

A Dell investor, careful of his small retirement savings, took advantage of his good investment luck by selling off his original investment shares (**because Dell keeps dividing like an amoeba**) periodically. Thus, he **TAKES SOME OF HIS PROFITS** out as the stock runs up the ladder. No matter what happens to the market (**a high tide raises all the boats, a low tide can beach them**), he will have covered his end if it declines. This careful person will keep most of his profits, whatever happens to the market or his investment. Instead of a **STOP-LOSS** on the price, he simply limited his holdings.

No, I will not take up too much space here talking about **Elon Musk and Tesla,** because that would be another book about the visionary's vision and risk-taking. I did sell a lot of Tesla when it went out the door at $20 and now it floats between $500 and $900 still without making any profit. Musk applied the **First Principle of Aristotle** which is to change things you have to go back to the beginning and change the old approaches to the project. Everything must be new, do not apply old solutions to new problems. And do whatever is in your power to make it work.

Elon Musk is currently the CEO and founder of several successful companies including Tesla and Space X. Elon Musk realized that nobody had an electric car and designed his Tesla from the ground up changing manufacturing, design, and sales techniques anew. He threw out the Wernher Von Braun's rocket technology used by NASA from WW II and designed his fabulous rocket program including the recovery of major components, from anew. He created the Boring Company to drill underneath Los Angeles for a limited low-cost transportation solution. This visionary is capable of starting new business concepts from the First Principles theory of tossing the accepted handed down theories and "reinventing the wheel".

ELON MUSK'S FIRST PRINCIPLES:

- **Identify and define your current assumptions.** Find your root problem.
- **Breakdown the problem into its fundamental principles.** Ask yourself powerful questions about the problem. Break it down into basic truths.
- **Create new solutions from scratch.** If you ask yourself powerful questions about your problem then a new unique solution may come to you.

ELON MUSK'S 6 HIRING TIPS FOR LEADERSHIP PRINCIPLES:

- **Move.** The ability to keep up with current trends and stay competitive.
- **Do the Impossible.** Think outside the box
- **Constantly Innovate**
- **Reason from "First Principles".** Identify root problems and solve problems

- **Think Like Owners.** Leaders should be supportive in business development like an owner would be.
- **We are all in.** Teamwork.

HORROR STORY - BAD IPO

A friend, tired of buying losing California Lotto tickets, invested his small savings into an **IPO**, which purported to generate a **KILLER PROFIT**. This fellow was in bad shape financially and based his future on this hot deal. The **IPO** went up a little, then down a little and settled on a trip to nowhere. The fellow was lucky to have relatives take him in afterward when he was between jobs and broke.

This item should be labeled **"Future Horror Story"**. There is always a loophole to every rule and law of the land because lawyers for lawyers write them. The **Securities Act of 1933 (Truth in Securities Law)**, which covers the registration of securities and new offers, had a small business registration exemption for offerings under $1 million with only minimum restrictions. This was a useful measure allowing small businesses to incorporate and issue their stock. The result, however, was a recent Fortune Magazine article that showed a small storefront retail business selling shares of stock to school children and people off the street. The article indicated that this small business focus was not to make money from operations, but was in the business of selling its stocks. Only the future will tell if the business will succeed in either, but the eye should always be set on **EARNING PROFITS**, not taking money from lenders or shareholders because there is always the day when all accounts must be satisfied and reconciled.

SECOND HORROR STORY - CRITICAL PATH INC

Another **IPO** example is **Critical Path Inc.**, which had a **market capitalization (the value of all shares outstanding at a current market price)** of $1,400,000,000 and lost $11,400,000 on sales of less than one million in 1998. What will happen if the company continues to lose money? For every dollar, in sales, they lose eleven. A corner liquor store or gas station can easily do a million dollars annually in sales. Where did the money go? How was it put to use? Why are people buying the stocks?

PROS AND CONS ABOUT IPO

- Don't speculate with money you cannot afford to lose.
- Be wary and cautious about telephone sales spiels.
- Most IPOs are old and tired by the time the general trading public gets to trade them.
- Do your homework about the new firm before you invest.
- Find out if your Broker is trustworthy.
- Brokerage firms make a market with new issues and have great control over the sales method and pricing.
- Don't use borrowed money for speculation. That is money you do not have to lose.
- Remember always that all firms must earn a profit to survive in the end that includes Tesla Motors.

TAX TIPS

- The good news is that there are no tax problems with losses.
- Tax gains or losses are not recognized until the equity is sold or exchanged so it is a good idea to sell losers before year-end (November, not December because of tax rules).
- Stocks with large gains might be sold at the same time (not same stocks) that have big losses and if the trading expenses are small, they can be bought back again later on in the next year. Be careful of exchange trading the same stock.
- Exchanges (selling a security for losses and buying it back right away) create tax problems.
- Capital losses are limited to maximum offsets of $3,000 per year against ordinary income after offsetting other capital gains. The remaining losses carry forward to future years.
- If the $3,000 capital loss cannot offset income in any year, it still reduces the loss carryforward while the losses not used that year

become a part of a Net Operating Loss, which is a separate loss to carry back or forward to other tax years.

- The Wall Street Journal lists valuable trading information and closing prices daily for the largest 1,000 companies in the USA.

CHAPTER 1: APPLICATION EXERCISES

1. Tax gains and losses are not recognized until the equity is sold or exchanged so it is a good idea to sell losers before year-end.
   ____ True ____ False

2. IPO's are always a highly speculative venture and sometimes subjected to loss or fraud. ____ True____ False

3. A CUSIP number is noted on each stock certificate.
   ____ True ____ False

4. Selling a security at a loss and buying it back within 30 days creates tax problems. ____ True ____ False

5. Which tip(s) are included in Elon Musk's leadership principals?
   ____ a. Think outside the box
   ____ b. Teamwork
   ____ c. Keep up with current trends
   ____ d. Aristotle's first principles for success
   ____ e. All of the above

6. The NASD and FINRA are:
   ____ a. Divisions of the SEC
   ____ b. Self-Regulatory Organizations
   ____ c. Funded by the U.S. Treasury
   ____ d. Managed by elected officials
   ____ e. All of the above

7. Fiduciary responsibility is:
   ____ a. The problem with on-line trading
   ____ b. Only a broker-dealer management concern
   ____ c. The sole responsibility of the Registered Representative salesperson
   ____ d. A joint responsibility of the Registered Representative and the Registered Principal representing the BD firm

8. New public stock registrations (IPO) require:
   ____ a. An underwriter
   ____ b. Certified financial statements
   ____ c. Common voting stocks
   ____ d. A viable going concern
   ____ e. All of the above

9. Margin Accounts:
   ____ a. Provide leverage
   ____ b. Are secured by the investor's portfolio
   ____ c. Enhance speculation
   ____ d. Can result in a call to close the account and sell all securities
   ____ e. All of the above

10. Securities are not taxed (check all that apply):
    ____ a. On appreciated values at year end
    ____ b. On sales gains of short term ordinary income tax tables if held less than a year
    ____ c. On sales gains of long term capital gains rates if held longer than a year
    ____ d. On gains within pension funds or IRAs
    ____ e. None of the above

CHAPTER TWO
SMALL CAPITAL STOCKS

Small company stocks, **a.k.a.** **SMALL-CAPS**, are the growth stocks. They are traded on the **National Association of Securities Dealers Automated Quotations (NASDAQ) Exchange**, which handles the newer (smaller) publicly traded issues. The initial private offering, after stabilizing and reaching a certain size, will aspire to public trading which puts upward pressure on the price and guarantees press coverage of the principals and financial activity, good or bad. An example of how large a company must be to jump into public trading and rub shoulders with **IBM** and **Microsoft**, can be found with a very large company which holds over 1/3 billion equity position in real estate and is always **THINKING** about going public. Because the company is not publicly held, I cannot disclose the name here.

Some successful firms reverse their public exposure by buying back all their shares to **go private** and take the pressure off quarterly earnings reporting and public exposure of liability and risk.

Small caps are growth-oriented. They actively seek growth capital through stock issues or alternate financing. Because they are focused on growth and capital formation, they will not pay dividends. All earnings, if any, will be plowed back into internal growth or debt reduction. These are the exciting issues, highly traded and fresh in the public mind. Microsoft is an example of how a company with intense visionary leadership under **Bill Gates**, started out by working with the giant old **Blue-Chip Company, IBM**, and grew larger than them are by focusing on **mind-ware** (software) instead of hardware. The results are in the papers every day.

The **Civil War**, over a hundred years ago, changed our economy into a manufacturing economy, leaving farming behind as the basic economic structure of the nation. A hundred years later, companies such as **Microsoft** grew out of nowhere, usurping the industrial giants in size and scope with nuclear growth unheard of in an economy where health is measured by the size of the manufacturing assets section of the balance sheet. This change was so profound that the Dow Jones Industrial average stock listing has been changed to include software and mindware such as Facebook businesses in the Industrial Index of 30 largest traded stocks.

What does it all mean? To the investor, we have companies not paying dividends, which is interest on capital related to earnings, paying investors back instead by the growth of stocks expressed by price changes in the public marketplace. In real terms, reflecting the fundamental changes in the economy, there are much greater future returns on investment in this area. This highly volatile investment area, holding huge amounts of public capital including most mutual funds and pension money, can change in value overnight on a press release or a distant world event. This is where the true focus of capitalism rests today with investor confidence leading the sum of the values to all-time highs.

Small caps are subject to **stock splits**. A stock split is created when the price of the stock has reached a very high level and the Board of Directors of the firm meet to decide that they can sell more shares if the offering price were less. Then, they do the official paperwork and issue new shares to shareholders on record and the owners now have two or more shares for every old share they held. The equity position is the same, because the transaction merely creates more certificates much like breaking a ten-dollar bill into two fives. Investors usually love stock splits because it increases the number of shares held (**a psychic satisfaction**), proves the price has been rising, and makes the stock more affordable again. These are referred to as **diluted shares** by the market. A stock that never splits is successful **Berkshire Hathaway**. Warren Buffet is the chairman and chief executive and it would take a mortgage refi to buy a share at present highs. On 12/31/19, the closing price of the Berkshire Hathaway stock was $339,590 per share.

Stocks are usually sold in **round lots** of 100 shares, so being able to buy a hundred shares for half the money definitely has an appeal to the trading public, especially small investors. Of course, investors can do a number on their uninformed collegiate when they inform their economic rivals at the Saturday party that they now own over (**1,000 or more**) shares of

XYZ company instead of the 500 they held the week before. These are **diluted shares**. That is, each share is worth only half as much as it was before the split. It also makes tracking difficult because if you own ten shares of stock, were they ten shares before they became a hundred or a thousand?

Small stocks generally do not issue preferred stock shares that guaranteed dividends. (**They act like bonds without maturity dates.**) They also issue millions of shares to distribute to management in one form or another. Different classes of stock can be divided into **voting shares and non-voting shares (a.k.a. A shares or B shares)**. Some preferred stocks can be exchanged into common shares.

The actual certificates of stock purchased can be held by the investor or at the brokerage firm. The sales rep will always ask you if you want the shares held in-house or not. It is best to leave it with the broker to save handling because if you decide to trade it later on, the certificates must be properly endorsed on the back and sent to the broker before the trade can be properly completed. The settlement time for a trade is now one business day (**T plus 1**), so there is not much time to fool with the certificates if you are a serious trader. This really brings us into the electronic age for trading. Of course, many investors hold older certificates good for pinning on the den wall, because they have no value at all. My clients leave them with me so I can wallpaper the hallway in my office. Most people without walk-in safes simply lose them and need to sign a **lost certificate affidavit** when sale day happens.

Corporate mergers create unique situations where the old certificates trade for new certificates or are bought outright. Many elderly people scramble to locate these certificates when the certified letter comes in the mail. Best to keep them in a bank safe deposit box or a home safe that is big and heavy enough to offer fire protection and also give a hernia to anybody but a professional mover. If the merger cashes out the stocks the registered owner simply gets a check in the mail and another reporting line on the tax return.

The securities' **Corporate Secretary** dutifully records all certificates in an official register. This can be automated today, instead of the black fountain pen of yesterday, and the Secretary can be located in a broker office or a bank investment department.

Trading can be monitored today while watching the television's financial channels or on your computer. This brings the market literally to the doorstep. It is incredible to watch a billion shares of stocks change hands in a single day. Sometimes the market will begin in highly negative territory and turn completely around before the day is over. The trading results are delayed by twenty minutes to slow down speculation from the media watchers. The **New York Stock Exchange** hours are from **9:30** am to **4 PM Eastern Standard Time,** three hours ahead of the Pacific Western states. **NASDAQ** hours are the same but will probably be extended into the evenings one day so that day traders can become night traders.

Stock reverse splits have been in the news recently. This is an event caused when companies issue fewer shares to replace outstanding shares. Thus if 100,000 shares were outstanding at $1 each, a one for ten would result in 10,000 new shares of stock outstanding valued at $10 each. This can be an attempt to keep the stock listed on the NASDAQ exchange by keeping the value high enough to trade. I remember when Ford Motor Company was in danger of being **delisted** and the common stock was trading at just over two dollars. Naturally, I put a lot of clients into it because I had faith in the new aerospace management, while GMC and Chrysler kept with their old management in place. I was chewed out for bringing clients into a possible bankruptcy, but saved when the shares recovered to $14 the next year.

A company can also buy all outstanding shares of stock and delist itself by going private with few founder owners again. A business buying its own stock creates **treasury stock.** This reduces the pressure to issue dividends, keeps the corporate affairs away from the public eye, reduces SEC scrutiny, and puts a wall around the company which is probably now closely held by few related family members. By not issuing dividends, required by the IRS code, the company can hoard cash although also subject to tax codes of **holding company** concerns. A holding company, according to the IRS, is a corporation that hoards cash and fails to pay taxable dividends. The management of a delisted private company can consist of fewer members who lack the normal controls for shareholder and public involvement.

Some companies sell their shares directly to the public as an effort to reduce investor load or commission expenses. These companies will handle the actual registration of the shares and issue the shares to people investing on a one-for-one basis. These are in addition to the corporations that allow shareholders to reinvest dividends without paying brokerage commissions. Be sure of the financial strength of any firm doing this because they may not be strong enough to be listed on the stock exchanges and quite risky. Any transactions away from the licensing and controls of a broker-dealer should be suspect. Naturally, they would be located on an Internet trading site.

Stock repurchasing is a rare event where a company decides, usually because of very close family or management ownership, to repurchase all the publicly held shares and become a privately owned and operated corporation. This keeps the pressure off management to appease public shareholders with short-term positive events that increase costs in the long run. A true example of bad public stewardship was a major firm near San Francisco, which traded higher present earnings for a long-term expense. They sold a large transportation terminal to boost current earnings a few cents and creating a tax liability from leasing it back unprofitably in the future.

PLANNING TIPS

Keep in mind that commissions are usually charged on every transaction, usually from 1% up to **5%** (**the legal limit**) plus ticket or delivery charges. It is true that some brokerage firms do not charge commissions but not the big reputable ones. Thus, to buy a small lot of stocks one day and sell them the next and go on a wild trading frenzy can consume the entire investment with costs and make the sales rep really happy until you disappear. Best to hold securities long enough to see if there is a trend developing rather than sell and buy at a panic or whim. Buying and selling on short notice using **arbitrage** is truly speculative, so keep in mind that there are costs involved. The larger the purchase, the smaller the commission percentage charged. Odd lot purchases of less than **100** shares have higher charges to offset trading difficulties. Discount brokers charge fewer commissions than regular brokers. Know what stock you are buying, that is, do your own research. Investors sometimes do better on their own knowledge than the sales rep on the phone exaggerating his hot deal of the day. **Insider tips are always illegal.** Most public data about corporate events are old and public before you hear about it, which leaves the average investor behind the curve. The magic trick is to be predictive, that is to see and read or feel trends, instead of history. It helps to be psychic, but reading the **Wall Street Journal** daily will help a lot.

Upon becoming a **shareholder,** many firms invite their new owners to participate in a **corporate dividend direct stock-purchasing plan**. You have now joined their mailing list. This plan allows shareholders to buy shares of stock directly from them with your cash dividends, without paying any commissions or ticket charges. This is a good way to save money on **B/D** commissions and charges in a small way if you wish to increase your holdings in the firm. Your purchases will also reflect **dollar-cost-averaging** because you will be averaging the ups and downs of the market by buying at three-month intervals.

TAXES

As with small caps, all stock sales are subject to the capital gains rules for gains or losses. Most broker-dealers are now using sophisticated software to track purchases through sales to provide **1099 B forms** at year-end with both costs and sales data for the sale. This is a lifesaver because it is very confusing to match confirmations with 1099 forms, especially on some of the trades made many years ago. Short-term gains from securities held less than one year are taxable as additional income at the highest rate on an individual's tax return. Long-term gains from securities held more than one year are taxable at more favorable tax rates.

LEGAL COMPLIANCE

Beware of the telephone solicitor. Today's hot tip of the day could be tomorrow's disaster. For this reason, every sales ticket the broker sales rep makes out is checked off for solicited (him/her advising you) or unsolicited (you tell him/her what to buy) trades. This is an important issue if there are heavy losses involved. Again, elderly and unsophisticated investors are not usually considered qualified clients for speculative stock trading. Florida land schemes are the oldest bad news, but oil wells and now gold mines are more common. I have a tax client who claims to have direct conversations with a foreign gold mine promoter and now is part of his tip-of-the-day-club with info that never pans out. This is a **penny stock** and it takes many pennies to equal $1,000.

SUCCESSFUL STRATEGIES

Timing is everything. In the securities business, there must be a buyer and a seller for every trade. Some small-cap stocks explode in value after millions of dollars are spent to complete grand expansion plans. The financial printers happily run the presses overtime to create new stock certificates. Everybody makes money except for the business. Sometimes a person needs to be psychic to know when to get off the train and take the money and run. An example of rags to riches to rags is **Boston Capital,** which went public in **1993** and built over a thousand restaurants with over a billion dollars in sales (you may have noticed that this author likes round numbers). The investors profited by the sheer size of the growth that was the entire goal, with the belief that profits would automatically follow. An investor would have made money at any time from **IPO** inception purchases at **$20** share prices to **$50** a year later, and more from a stock split that same year which further increased stock sales, as investors bid up the prices. These are only paper profits unless the stocks are sold. That was also the best time to be a seller, not a buyer.

In **1997,** the operation collapsed and the stock price fell on the **NASDAQ** to 25 cents (**pink sheet of delisted stocks**). A Chapter 11 bankruptcy was filed to sort out the business shortcomings that October to preempt a short-term bank loan coming due. An investor must watch the profitability of a firm to decide when it will succeed past the growth stage. Businesses must ultimately provide profits for investors to prove substance. A favorite **IRS** audit question for business owners deducting losses is **"are you in business to make a profit or is this a non-deductible hobby?"** **Wash Sales** are created when a sale is made on a security, mainly to take a loss for tax purposes, when the stock is replaced within 30 days. This sale is disallowed by the IRS as a capital loss because the intent is to create a tax loss while replacing the security. Most of these sales occur in December and are replaced in January. Trading brokerage firms are responsible for reporting the loss.

HORROR STORY - RECKLESS INTERNET TRADER

An unsophisticated machinist was laid up with a work-related disability. Finally, after a long period of litigation (**in California medical and insurance matters are traditionally conducted at attorney's offices instead of medical clinics or company benefit departments**), he received the big settlement check of $40,000. Then, he discovered the stock market, where he could get rich and never go back to work again. At first, he tired several local brokers for his stock trades. They were too slow for him so he bought a computer. With this marvelous machine, he was able to buy software, which put him online for stock prices and direct trading. Now he wheeled and dealt on his own with no annoying broker to interfere. He was so excited at his new occupation that he began trading more and more, buying dozens of stocks with no plan and sometimes trading the same security two or three times in the same day. After three months, he was broke and borrowing money for his trading addiction. It was all over. All he had to show for the experience was a huge box of trading confirmations. At year-end, he was also unable to reconstruct all his trades to match the sales-based 1099 forms received in January and February. All sales must be offset with purchase costs because the IRS adds the 1099 sale income forms together as taxable income. To make matters worse, he could not afford to pay a qualified tax person to prepare his taxes.

PROS & CONS ABOUT SMALL-CAP STOCKS

- The profits are there for new firms with good fundamentals (product, management, market, plan, capital, and good luck).
- Prepare to hold the new security for the long run, unless you are an unemployed day trader.
- Watch out for trading costs such as ticket charges, commissions, cash wiring costs, overnight mail, etc.
- Pay attention to the one-year threshold on capital gains taxes if the stock earns a profit and you wish to trade.
- Stocks are **delisted** from **NASDAQ** when the trading price drops to less than one dollar, so your stock could vanish from the daily newspapers if it does badly (**Chapter 7** or **11 bankruptcy territory**). A Chapter 7 bankruptcy is liquidation and bankruptcy 11 is a 5-year court-supervised recovery mode.
- It can be tax-wise profitable to sell your losers by year end December to take advantage of the tax losses. Beware of wash sales rules.
- Small-cap securities are generally newer issues or small firms. If they do not grow internally, then they may never become big-cap and could disappear altogether.
- Leave the stock certificates with the broker to facilitate trading as the handling term is only one day.
- Don't put all your money into equities. Diversify to protect against market changes.
- Review all of your investments and know where your money is. Create a schedule or ledger to do this.
- Know and understand what you are buying. There is a great risk in buying into small or new companies. Do some homework besides liking the name.
- Be cautious of Internet bulletin boards and newsletters that hype unknown stocks; they could be self-serving for individuals or brokers who are making a market in the issue and illegally promoting it for quick profits.

CHAPTER 2: APPLICATION EXERCISES

1. Management may reverse the firm's public exposure by buying back all of the shares to go private. ____ True ____ False

2. Stocks are delisted from NASDAQ when the trading price drops below one dollar. ____ True ____ False

3. Brokerage firms reduce their fees for odd lot purchases of less than 100 shares. ____ True ____ False

4. Small caps are not subject to the capital gains rules for gains or losses. ____ True ____ False

5. Small cap securities are generally newer issues or small firms. ____ True ____ False

6. Stock splits are a solution for:
    ____ a. Avoiding dilution of shares
    ____ b. Splitting dividends
    ____ c. Reducing share price to affordably attract more shareholders
    ____ d. Psychic remuneration for larger dividend payments

7. Berkshire Hathaway common stock shares:
    ____ a. Are generally the lowest priced stock listed in the Wall Street Journal
    ____ b. Are considered a speculative issue
    ____ c. Have reached a value of 1/3 million dollars per common share by being successful for many years without splitting stocks

8. Insider trading is:
    ____ a. Legal if nobody finds out
    ____ b. Allowed if management approves
    ____ c. Not scrutinized by the SEC
    ____ d. Always illegal even between family members

9. Horror Stories in this book are:
    ____ a. Mostly political
    ____ b. Satirical to a fault
    ____ c. Theoretical
    ____ d. All of the above

10. The corporate secretary:
  ___ a. Has the responsibility of recording corporate matters and BOD meetings
  ___ b. Is responsible for recording and/or certifying all stock certificates and dividends
  ___ c. Is no longer the Gregg Shorthand bearer but is the official signer of many official corporate documents
  ___ d. Maintains the corporate minute book
  ___ e. All of the above

CHAPTER THREE

BLUE CHIP STOCKS

Blue-chip stocks are generally from older established companies, which are usually included in the DJIA and listed on the New York Stock Exchange. They represent the surviving mature industrial giants and conglomerates of this industrial age. The **Dow Jones Industrials Averages (DJIA), which now include non-industrial companies**, a field of over **3,000** companies, including the **30** largest industrials of the **DJ Industrial Average (the DJIA is an adjusted value which allows for historic stock splits and dividends, times the current closing daily prices of the 30 shares**), are composed of these giants.

The **Dow Jones or Fortune 500 companies**, and the **Standard & Poor 500 companies** are the largest firms in the investment universe. They are huge compared to other businesses, the giants of the industrial (**and software-services**) world. The **Dow Jones 30 Industrials**, upon which the daily market is indexed, consisted of the following companies (**as of December 31, 2019**):

- American Express Co. (AXP)
- Apple Inc. (APPL)
- Boeing Co. (BA)
- Caterpillar Inc. (CAT)
- Cisco Systems Inc. (CSCO)
- Chevron Corp. (CVX)
- DowDuPont Inc. (DWDP)
- Exxon Mobil Corp. (XOM)
- Goldman Sachs Group Inc. (GS)
- Home Depot Inc. (HD)
- International Business Machines Corp. (IBM)
- Intel Corp (INTC)
- Johnson & Johnson (JNJ)
- Coca-Cola Co. (KO)

- JPMorgan Chase & Co (JPM)
- McDonald's Corp. (MCD)
- 3M (MMM)
- Merck & Co Inc. (MRK)
- Microsoft Corp (MSFT)
- Nike Inc. (NKE)
- Pfizer Inc. (PFE)
- Procter & Gamble Co. (PG)
- Travelers Companies Inc. (TRV)
- UnitedHealth Group Inc. (UNH)
- United Technologies Corp. (UTX)
- Verizon Communications Inc. (VZ)
- Visa Inc. (V)
- Walgreens Boots Alliance Inc. (WBA)
- Walmart Inc. (WMT)
- Walt Disney Co. (DIS)

Every day the DJIA is the sum of the values of the above companies and is used as an index of the whole market. As the prices of these thirty huge firms goes up and down, so goes the market. The Standard & Poor 500 stocks are a better guide of the market-indexed activity because it is broader than the narrow Dow 30.

These firms, all-corporate because they issued shares of stock, are addicted to growth and paying dividends. Most of them held post Second World War monopolies and oligopolies on chemicals or technology. Some are experiencing business geriatric problems to maintain market share and profit margins. Older companies acquire many layers of overhead and bureaucratic largess, like governments and the Maginot line becoming quite belligerent with the invulnerable mindset that nobody can attack their established markets or core products.

Most of the blue chips are under intense pressure to keep stock prices up because of a large amount of executive officer's options and holdings, as well as the public perception of how well they are performing. A dollar per share change in the marketplace can change the value of the total stock outstanding by many millions overnight.

One thing the blue-chip companies do quite well though is to pay dividends. Investment analysts closely scrutinize quarterly earnings reports, which are filed with the Securities Exchange Commission, because they are public information. Many pension plans and individuals are dependent on the quarterly checks every third month of the year. Earnings and losses are always expressed in terms of dollars and cents per share, and the resultant dividends to be cut, maintained, or increased. If a company is in trouble, management may find it difficult to pay dividends and need to draw down cash balances and retained earnings unless there are large reserves and they feel committed to maintaining a fixed dividend. Many executive stock option plans and bonus arrangements are based on increasing stock prices and the total values of outstanding stocks (**market capital**).

Corporate dividends are serious business with the government because they are the only way a corporation can distribute earnings after taxes. In other words, they are not deductible as an expense. A common **IRS** audit approach is to declare the **officers' salaries excessive** so they can tax the perceived excess portion as dividends. They can also tax **excess retained earnings** (usually cash or investments) as undeclared dividends. This results in the **double taxation** of any undistributed earnings. The ploy works well when the **IRS** attacks some smaller unsophisticated but highly profitable businesses. Many small businesses loan officer's money. This money is also reclassified as dividends by the IRS auditors. I won a tax court case on this excess officer salary issue.

Corporations also own other corporations through the development of new business ventures, mergers, or acquiring other businesses. Because they would be taxing their own earnings in the other businesses, the IRS tax code allows an exclusion of 70% of these **domestic internalized earnings.**

Large companies frequently own franchised branch divisions, and other businesses in foreign countries. Sometimes it is to provide raw materials for production, but it is also to secure larger marketplaces and keep the international foreign competition at bay. This globalization subjects them to foreign politics, currency exchange problems, and an exposure to the world economy. It is essential though, for large corporations to globalize for survival.

For the typical or conservative investor, blue chips are an important part of the portfolio. **Diversification** in different areas of investment dictates portfolios holding some of these stocks, which are more stable than the smaller growth stocks. They also pay dividends, which can be reinvested to acquire more shares of stock or spent as cash.

Many large firms today are reinvesting excess cash for the purchase of their own shares of stock. That reduces their cash hoard, which is tempting to outside business acquisitions or future acquisitions, concentrating the earnings per share of stocks for increased dividends. It can also increase the trading price of the remaining outstanding shares.

PLANNING TIPS

Many financial planners are recommending buying global stock funds to diversify. They correctly assumed that a proper portfolio would include other economies of this world economy. What resulted was a flood of Asian funds in everybody's portfolio. The Asian economies are on a crazy growth pattern, which is debt-driven, and in many dictators, cronyistic, government or militarily controlled economies. These often-corrupted economies and holdings did not reflect the uninformed typical investor's perception of **U.S. stock & security equivalents**. As a result, this part of the portfolio is subjected to huge waves of speculation and crashes which sometimes did a big number on the average investor.

The solution is to buy stocks in blue-chip companies, which have global operations. This results in a conservative portfolio with American management in place instead of holdings in an overleveraged dictator's nephew's business. Another alternative is to buy stocks in Western G-7 countries, which reflect our more consecutive established investment culture.

Index stock funds are an excellent alternative because they average the activity in the entire market and go with the ebb and flow of the averages. They usually offer lower commission for the buyer because of lower trading of securities.

TAXES

Corporate gains or losses on stock sales are subject to capital gains taxation. Dividends are fully taxable when recorded (**when the check is cut...not when received**) and taxed based on the investor's taxable income levels. Corporations can exclude 70% of domestic stock dividends from taxes and find it a good way to invest excess cash to increase retained earnings in the parent conglomerate.

There are two kinds of dividends. The first is **dividends paid from bond funds, which are really interest,** paid to the holder. These distributions are taxed as **ordinary income** in your tax returns. The second kind of dividend paid from corporations declaring **dividends from shares of stock** owned by the recipient. **These are Qualified Dividends** which are treated **as long term capital gains** on your tax returns. The logic is that they are paid from earnings, which could have accumulated from more than one year making them long term capital gains.

A form 1099 DIV is mailed by all payers unless less than $10 for the year. Dividends less than that are still taxable and are noticed by the IRS computer electronically, even if no form was mailed to the individual recipient. **Reinvested dividends increase the basis or cost of the issuing stocks.** Taxes have already been paid on them, so they must be added back to the original purchase amount, which should always include any commissions or fees. Many brokerage firms and mutual funds, with new software, have begun tracking these costs, which will only reflect recent year purchases. This will eliminate much guesswork at year-end tax filing time.

LEGAL COMPLIANCE

Blue-chip stocks are a reasonable investment for the elderly investor because they usually pay cash dividends, which the retired person may need to live on, and are usually more conservative than other investments, excluding bonds. Holdings in these stocks should be long-term to avoid trading costs and speculation. These stocks are **liquid current assets** in the portfolio because they can be readily sold. The list of Dow Jones Industrial 30 stocks is a trip down memory lane with many newcomers, now including Wal-Mart, McDonald's, Microsoft and others. That indicates the longevity of these large firms as successful industrial and retail-service competitors for exposure on the listing.

SUCCESSFUL STRATEGIES

Most successful businesses mosey along economically until a visionary miracle happens to strike. If the company has no visionary people at the top, they plod along like a governmental bureaucracy, until the company stumbles or dies a natural death. Shortly after the Second World War, Thomas Watson of **International Business Machines (IBM)** received a small transistor radio from a friend. The radio lacked the usual markings of "Made in Occupied Japan", because it was a product of the newly unoccupied Japan of the early 1950s, and appeared to be highly portable, cheaply made, using only a few electronic parts and small batteries. It was the dawn of the creative Japanese electronics industry, which also spawned the creative application of American science. American-made portable radios were big heavy things full of electronic tubes, many big batteries, and were a scaled-down version of the large table or console radios used in households. These new unique Japanese radios, built around transistors that amplified radio waves, converted them to stronger music, news, and commentary commercial signals.

Watson thought about the small radio he held in his hand. His company at that time was evolving to large electronic tube machines from the purely mechanical wired board and punch card reader machines that would calculate numbers or compute data. They were called computers. The machines were marginally reliable because vacuum tubes would weaken or burn out, which represented a great maintenance and reliability problem along with energy control and costs. They also filled big rooms that needed huge power supplies and air conditioning to move the heat away. Tom Watson looked at the little radio and a huge visionary bell rang in his brain. If the Japanese could substitute germanium transistors for vacuum tubes, why not do the same with the computers they were building? Tom approached his board of directors with the idea. They voted him down; after all, they had come a long way with their punch card systems for input and verification of data, and were still trying to get used to using vacuum tubes. The competitive **Univac** computing machines in use were purely mechanical wired boards, although IBM now had **reel-to-reel magnetic tape storage**, which was coming into wide use.

Tom Watson, being a tough visionary, decided to go it alone. He then changed the course of history by overriding his **BOD** to go ahead with new designs. The result was the ancient **1401** machine with only **64 K** of internal memory (**yes, only 64,000 bytes**) was born. The punched cards would live on for many years afterward though, as they were fed through vacuum trough-readers (**after being duplicated and verified**) into the **new computer that had no keyboard**.

In March of 1956, about the time the new machine was perfected, the total value of the Dow Jones Industrial Average was only 500 points. If you held one share of IBM stock at that time you would now be almost a millionaire. Some of the gains would be inflation; the rest would be the results of visionary management. If you invest in good stable companies that are about to change direction in the right way, and can leave it alone, your investment will reward you with unbelievable wealth. This is not speculation. It is investing by an economic principle also called capitalism. Having a visionary at the helm is also required.

Eventually, IBM would grow into a giant to be almost felled by the microcomputers now known as desktop computers (now downsizing into cell phone instruments). IBM made its money leasing equipment, as did Xerox with its giant copying machines, and it would almost bring the company down as small portable computers made by Dell. IBM was saved by providing software for future computer standards and Tandy computers (made in Japan while sold by Radio Shack) brought the industry to its knees.

HORROR STORY - SEARS AND ROEBUCK

Sears and Roebuck's employees used to work for the pension plan, as well as their salaries. Retail employees are not usually well paid, but the Sears **money purchase pension** plan bought company stock for the benefit of their management and employees. Steady growth all but guaranteed a healthy retirement from this 18th century conservative blue-chip company. This allowed the company to attract and hold quality people in a retail trade notorious for bad wages and equivalent help. The employees had a greater interest in the firm than their paycheck, which translates into better cooperation and productivity. A true working democracy. Then 20 years ago, the stock lost its bloom when superstore competition killers and discounters changed the retail industry. A shift to lower quality merchandise added to the loss of Sears shoppers. A century of expansion became decades of contraction including corporate earnings and stock values. Many of the younger employees who could have found better employment elsewhere felt trapped because they had only the limited paycheck to count on. This is an example of how the positive investment value of the firm affects employees. The future of any firm is the quality of the individuals are bonded directly to growth and earnings, far beyond the weekly paycheck. Sears, after continuing declines in quality goods, along with Kmart, filed for bankruptcy in 2019. I once interviewed a retired Sears's executive who stated he was the manager who introduced luxury fur coats to the Sears stores. He is now in the home care business. Sometimes the ride downhill is long but not exciting.

PROS & CONS OF BLUE CHIPS

- Blue-chip stocks are for the conservative investor, or to balance a more aggressive portfolio.
- These stocks pay dividends and because they are established and well-capitalized, they have staying power in the world economy and your portfolio.

- Blue-chips are not for speculation when compared to the Internet stocks, but will generally ride the market up and down with the economy and investor perceptions.

- Individual stocks are subject to risk depending on their individual markets and the demands of class action attorneys. Example: Philip Morris cigarettes and Colt firearms.

- Dividends are the basic reward for these conservative stocks. The check is in the mail and if the value of the stock stood still, it could be easily calculated into a percentage return the same as interest rate earnings. Real Earnings are calculated after subtracting inflation indexes.

- The Blue Chips are subject to dividend capital gains rules that can save taxes.

- They are liquid and do not require a secondary market or market maker to sell.

- A broad-based portfolio based on the Standard & Poor 500 will earn better than a narrow field such as the Dow Jones 30 Industrials.

CHAPTER 3: APPLICATION EXERCISES

1. For the typical or conservative investor, blue chips are an important part of the portfolio. ____ True ____ False

2. Qualified dividends are treated as long term capital gains.
   ____ True ____ False

3. Reinvested dividends increase the basis or cost of the portfolio stocks.
   ____ True ____ False

4. All blue chip companies are required to pay dividends.
   ____ True ____ False

5. Which company is not Blue Chip?
   ____ a. Intel Corp (INTC)
   ____ b. Caterpillar Inc. (CAT)
   ____ c. Fitbit (FIT)
   ____ d. Verizon Communications (VZ)

6. A business visionary is:
   ____ a. A person who delegates all his work and enjoys consensus in everything he does
   ____ b. Is found in government offices where every move must be approved and sanctioned politically
   ____ c. The person who can think out of the box and provide leadership in the vacuum of geriatric Management consensus

7. Blue Chip stocks are:
   ____ a. Growth stocks
   ____ b. Best for young investors interested in fast growing internet stocks
   ____ c. Mature companies always paying steady dividends
   ____ d. NASDAQ small cap issues

8. Blue Chip stocks and companies are too big to fail except:
   ____ a. Chrysler Motors
   ____ b. General Motors
   ____ c. K-Mart
   ____ d. All of the above

9. Corporate Dividends are:
   ___ a. Always taxable as ordinary income
   ___ b. Sometimes taxable as capital gains, if qualified dividends
   ___ c. The only return of capital or income from a corporate business
   ___ d. Usually paid monthly
   ___ e. All of the above

10. Appreciation of stock value as a return of capital:
   ___ a. Dividends are the only return of earnings and capital investment
   ___ b. Stock appreciation is the only return of earnings
   ___ c. Dividends are taxable to shareholders but not an expense to the corporation

CHAPTER FOUR

ADR'S & FOREIGN STOCKS, PRECIOUS METALS

American Depository Receipts (ADRs) are units of exchange for foreign stock shares and traded on the New York Stock Exchange. Therefore, instead of buying shares of **Daimler Benz (Mercedes)** in Deutschmarks, they would be available as Daimler American Depository Receipts in dollars on the Exchange. The shares of stock are bought and sold through a U.S. bank that holds the stocks of the foreign company on deposit. Daimler Benz became **Daimler Chrysler** in 1995 back to **Daimler AG** in 2009 after dropping the Chrysler shares. This example happens during international mergers. Another famous foreign company **De Beers'** trades on the NASDAQ. They deal in diamonds. Most of the African and Canadian gold mines trade as ADRs. Foreign oil companies also are ADRs.

ADRs are held in some mutual funds, as strategic funds, or other foreign funds, which sometimes hold a mixed bag of bonds, foreign stocks, and even currencies.

Since many foreign multinational conglomerates have manufacturing and sales facilities in this country, as well as American conglomerates do in theirs, investments in many ADRs would be part of a good blue-chip portfolio as long as the business is not old and declining. This is certainly true of global automobile manufacturers who have successfully managed expansion by closely working with physical plant and equipment where the customers are.

ADRs are not a specific market or investment and thus are generally considered a blue-chip investment in a foreign country. Foreign currency exchanges can affect transactions as exchange values between dollars fluctuate.

PLANNING TIPS

Foreign countries can be very restrictive and contrary when compared to our American "Capitalistic Democracy". Some of them are socialistic, monarchial, newly democratic, or ex-communistic. When considering foreign stocks, research on the **socioeconomic** treatment of business in the country would be helpful. Better yet would be some insight from a relative in Prague, who could tell you if the new Volkswagen plant is working out. Another relative might tell you about the oil wells **appropriated** in Venezuela or the devaluation of their currency and bond defaults. Note that one missed (one day) is a default which, according to the note agreements, subjects the whole note to be repaid immediately.

TAXES

Sales of ADRs would be subject to capital gains taxes, the same as domestic American stocks and securities.

LEGAL COMPLIANCE

The further a person is removed from his/her investment, the less he/she knows about it, and the greater risk to which he/she is exposed. Buying foreign stocks can be considered at the high-risk level of a blue-chip stock portfolio. International worldwide capitalization has reduced much risk for internationally operating firms but there can always be some risk in a dark corner of the firm's far-flung activities.

Large transactions and trades, especially liquidations or transfers, usually require something in writing. The letter then must be signature verified to prove that the signer is real. This is the equivalent to a notary function by the broker-dealer. He/she has a special stamp called the **Medallion Signature Stamp**, which requires his/her signature on the imprint. The stamp, which has his/her special number, costs about $50 and guaranteed by the broker-dealer through the stock exchange, which makes it official. This is an important step to protect all parties of securities transactions. The stamp is also required on the signature page of new checking accounts. I once had my own stamp as a **Registered Principal**, but now it is at the administrative level of the BD and others are at your local bank.

THE NOBLE METALS

Gold has always been revered by human society. It has been the exclusive property of kings, governments, and even used in nuclear bombs. Why? Because it is beautiful to hold and view, it will not corrode, it's so malleable that very thin gold leaf can be made of it, a great conductor of electricity, and is very dense... about 18 times as heavy as water which makes it easier to hoard or carry. Pure gold is 24 karat. Gold is diluted for strength and cheapness for jewelry and coinage by alloying it with brass, copper or silver. For centuries, it has been the standard for economic wealth and prosperity.

Now it is demonetized and our currency can no longer be exchanged. The Gold Reserve Act passed on January 30, 1934, and the US Treasury abandoned the gold standard which backed all large denomination paper notes with gold in the Treasury. An earlier executive order 6102 had the Treasury recalling all gold coinage and gold certificates from circulation on May 1, 1933, and replaced it with paper notes through the Federal Reserve banks for the real thing. They paid $20.67 per ounce for it and are today minting $50 one-ounce gold coins they sell for over $1,500 each. This is **demurrage,** profits made by the mint. Great economic esteem is still placed on the value of this metal of Kings and Gods.

All precious metals have two values. The first is the spot price from the **London Commodities Exchange**. That is for ingots, which are produced, marked, and carefully tested for purity. Gold coins today are bullion coins of pure gold if marked. Here, the gold Karat mark of 10K (40% pure), 14K (58% pure), 18K (75% pure), and pure 24K are stamped on jewelry as well. Silver is marked as Sterling if it is .925% pure with copper alloy, or pure if marked accordingly. Silver bullion coins are pure silver if marked. Beware of some Mexican Sterling jewelry, which is not always sterling.

The second value is the mark-up for coinage manufacture. A price could be $1,500 an ounce for spot gold on the London Exchange but it would cost you a few dollars more for a one-ounce coin plus delivery. Some states like California collect sales taxes on coin or bullion sales of less than a thousand dollars. Expensive gold jewelry is usually 14 Karat (58% gold) with platinum under the diamond setting to highlight the brightness. Usually, good gold jewelry is 18 Karat (75% gold), but the brass alloy of yellow gold is needed for the setting prongs to hold the stones or diamonds in place (because pure gold is soft). Gold was worth only $250 per ounce twenty years ago.

Silver backed dollar bills until 1955 when the Treasury abandoned the exchange. Silver dollars were called cartwheels because they were so large and heavy with .925% silver content and a copper alloy. In 1919 Silver traded in the $15 to $20 range, is hardly a precious metal, and is used mostly for jewelry, although the Treasury loaned out many tons of the metal during WW 11 for electrical centrifuges to refine-enrich uranium for nuclear bombs. It is available in ingots and coins. Silver was worth only $5 per ounce twenty years ago. The Silver Purchase Act of 1963 retired the use of $1 silver certificates, in response to a potential shortage of silver bullion. For the following four years, **silver certificates** were redeemable in uncoined silver "granules". All FDIC chartered banks returned to the mint all the silver dollars and one-dollar bills "Silver Certificates" were reissued with "Federal Reserve Notes". Silver redemption ceased on 24 June 1968. You now held part of the national debt in your hand instead of a redeemable cartwheel.

The English pound currency originated in the Anglo-Saxon period of English History. It was the value equivalent of one pound (16 ounces) of silver. The UK decimalized the ancient Pound Sterling on 2/15/19 and the replacement devalued pound became 100 pennies instead of 240. The Pound has always been referred to as the Pound Sterling because of the sterling silver purity basis.

Most of the world's **platinum** is mined in Africa, but the price, which used to be twice that of gold, has declined ½ because industrial uses for auto-catalytic converters have declined. Platinum is used for jewelry, coins, and can be purchased in small ingots. Palladium has replaced platinum as automobile exhaust catalytic converters and Platinum is now used for diesel truck engines. Surprisingly, due to supply and demand, Platinum prices fell and Palladium is now the metal priced higher than gold. Platinum is available in both ingots and coins.

In 1998, the Korean government faced a destabilizing economic crisis and could not stem the flow of foreign currency out of the country. There were very little precious metal reserves held by the government to exchange for dollars to stabilize the economy. Their desperate solution was to ask all the citizens to turn in their gold jewelry and coins to save the country. The results were highly patriotic and resulted in soliciting 200 metric tons of gold from the citizenry, which stabilized the monetary crisis.

Gold is subjected to the free market prices and is considered a hedge against inflation by some investors and a hedge against monetary crisis by many countries, some of which hold huge reserves. At this time, the US is reported to have 8,000 metric tons of gold held in reserves at Fort Knox. This is four times the reserve of any other country or institution such as the International Monetary Fund, which has only 2,000 tons. Yet, during World War II, gold was of no value to the war effort and all the US mines closed.

A gold mine contains an ore inventory subjected to the economic costs of removal balanced against the bullion value on the world commodities markets. When the market price is low, less metal will be mined from marginal sources as the mines shut down. Larger mines reduce operations to stockpile more inventory and sell as little as possible. The reverse happens when the price is higher. The commodity price then reflects the value of the mineable reserves and speculative hopes of profitability. The current high price of gold has resulted in diminished gold jewelry sales but a huge increase of gold-plated silver jewelry with semi-precious stones.

Diamonds are also foreign-dominated and controlled (we are still on ADRs here) by **De Beers/Anglo American**. Foreign companies, who control both inventory and prices, **cartelize** them thus the value of their stocks would relate more to the world (mostly USA) economics and consumer spending, than speculation on the stock market. Diamonds are valued using the **4Cs of Diamond color, clarity, cut**, and **weight** (by measurement). This standard is used for grading by the **Gemological Institute of America (GIA) standards**. Did you know there are 4 diamond karats to a gram? And, 28 grams to the Imperial ounce that we use. And, 31 grams for a Troy ounce, which is the gold and silver standard.

Many commodities have different quantities of exchange. Wheat is traded in bushels at 8 gallons each (now also tons Imperial short or Metric long), mercury was in 76-pound flasks, Iron in long metric tons, or short Imperial tons. Lumber in board feet, etc. They are traded on the **Chicago Commodities exchange**. Precious metals are on the **London Exchange**.

Africa is the unique center of the precious metal and gems world we live in. **Tanzanite** uniquely comes from Tanzania. Half of the gold ever mined on earth came from the 100-mile South American geological rift valley, which cuts deep into the earth and was full of top-grade ore. The mines are now over two miles deep with water incursion and heat severely restricting ore production and working conditions. The diamond center is in Africa and controlled by De Beers. Now they have problems controlling the world supply because of many other volcanic pipes of these hardest crystals in the world. You do not buy diamonds from the commodities market or ADRs, just the companies involved. Lots are sold at showings in New York, Amsterdam, and other places where the diamond cutters buy the larger stones. Synthetic-manufactured diamonds, under many names, have identical characteristics. They have evolved from industrial diamonds to compete with mined diamonds at a very high price level in the jewelry stores.

This insurance salesman investor lived very cheaply. His tired car lived twice as long as the normal 10-year life expectancy. When he went to the perfunctory weekly steakhouse dinner with the family, he carried a can of beer in his pocket. Landscaping at his home was unheard of because it used the expensive utility-water. What the investor did though, was to buy stocks in African gold mines, which mine and refine most of the world's gold. These stocks, sold as ADRs, were accumulated by him year in and year out. These mines, which are now miles deep following a fissure in the earth, are the most successful in the world and apparently very profitable. Twenty-five years later, the insurance salesman retired and is living off his multimillion-dollar portfolio of gold stocks. If you were to visit him today, there would not be a gold coin or bullion to be found in his house. The gold is all on paper. After all, the market value of the metal is reflected on the extraction value of the gold in his mining company's mines. If you visit this guy, look for the house with no lawn, now in Florida.

A **contrarian strategy** would be to disengage from the investing herd and go the opposite way. This is not as hard as it seems. When oil prices are low, the stocks of oil companies and drilling/exploratory firms go down. When the price of oil recovers and the players have reduced overhead, the price of their stock also recovers. Thus, you should be buying when everybody else is selling, which is a **contrarian outlook**. Precious metals act in the same way because, in the big overall economic picture, there is only so much capital to invest. With the stock market at all-time highs, the value of precious metals has declined in direct relation. Governments have been selling off their bullion monetary reserves at the same time. It would follow then, that when the stock market declines, the prices of precious metals should move up accordingly. This used to be the strategy with the stock prices vs bonds, but the low-interest rates have changed the game.

HORROR STORY - FOREIGN INVESTMENT

Americans have been fortunate to change presidents periodically, but fortunately, not Constitutional form of government or to devaluate our currency, except in 1933 when the country went off the gold standard and citizens were not allowed to own gold coin or bullion. In 1924, Germany was printing currency in runaway inflation which wiped out most investments. Many foreign countries undergo dramatic economic and political revolutions, which can destabilize many investments. With this in mind, the history of the country you invest in could be as important as the investment itself. The nationalization of an industry could be the end of a fine investment. Beware of oil company nationalization with socialized Venezuela and Mexico.

ANOTHER HORROR STORY - GEM MINING

A client worked for the **Gemological Lab** in Carlsbad, California. She was a curator with the esteemed position of traveling all over the world to visit mines and people who work in the gem business. Gemological was responsible for grading gems and had a large school dedicated to cutting diamonds and working with precious colored crystals of great wealth. Huge cascades of crystals in their natural stone setting greet visitors in the lobby. The work is serious with security to match as the people work quietly in laboratory settings or classrooms.

The lady was invited to visit an emerald mine in Columbia. She visited and met with the mine owners. It was a hard-rock mine reaching back hundreds of feet into the side of the mountain with footpaths used by Incan Indians for a thousand years. I personally remembered seeing a documentary of the mine with tough-looking security men toting short-barreled shotguns everywhere, at least one for every miner inside and outside the cave. The curator went into the mine and viewed the area where the emeralds were chipped out of the rocks. Suddenly, a miner took an emerald and put it in his pocket when he thought nobody was looking. A moment later, right in front of her, a security person pulled the shotgun trigger and killed the miner for stealing the gem. This was a shocking example of how precious minerals are sometimes sourced. An emerald was worth more than a man's life. She had a new appreciation of the value of her work after she returned to the beautiful weather and laboratory, high on a secluded hill overlooking the ocean in Carlsbad.

PROS & CONS OF ADR

- An ADR is simply the exchange conversion for a foreign stock to be purchased or sold in dollars. Thus, you need to be tuned in to the world economy for these investments.

- Most commodities are produced in overseas markets and are bought through ADRs. If you are interested in investing in the world economic consumption of raw materials, then you will be buying ADR stocks.

- The New World shift to overseas production of manufactured goods presents an opportunity to buy shares in newer large companies there, which might be state-controlled. Even though large and quite visible, they can be very high risk. If they were not state-controlled, they would not suddenly come into existence, yet because they are state-controlled they probably could not stay in business because they are usually not efficient. Government management is generally not competitive.

- Precious metals present ADR buying opportunities because when bullion prices are down, the stock shares are down accordingly. Hedging can be with stocks instead of bullion.

- ADRs are normal stock transactions in foreign places and present no trading difficulties.

- Sometimes **currency conversions** can be a bit calculating, like a recent broker trading account balance that had to be converted from 19 Mexican Pesos to US Dollars. (For a Federal Bank and Financial Accounts Report or **FBAR)** filing).

There are $10,000 penalties for not filing the FINCEN 114 form if you have $10,000 or more in a foreign financial account. There is a checklist on every tax return asking if you have a foreign bank account or another asking if you received money from a foreign trust and lastly if you have had 10,000 or more in it at any time of the year. I had a client who was fined $20,000 for filing the form correctly (yes, correctly). They were Canadians who started and closed a business here. I spoke to an IRS Lawyer who couldn't find them on his computer and tried reading the instruction publication to me instead. A month later, $10,000 in penalties disappeared from the client's correspondence. She closed her US bank account for good and stayed home in Canada where it was safe and sound from the tax thieves.

CHAPTER 4: APPLICATION EXERCISES

1. ADRs are normal stock transactions in foreign places and present no trading difficulties. ____ True ____ False

2. You are required to file a FinCEN 114 form if you have over $100 in a foreign financial account. ____ True ____ False

3. Sales of ADR's are not subject to capital gains taxes.
____ True ____ False

4. Investors using the contrarian strategy will sell when most investors are buying, and buy when most investors are selling.
____ True ____ False

5. Most commodities are produced in overseas markets and are bought through ADRs. ____ True ____ False

6. ADRs are the standard units of exchange and:
____ a. Are for only Asian funds and stocks
____ b. Are blue-chip investments in a foreign country
____ c. Are not subject to currency fluctuations
____ d. Knowing the socio-economic status of the foreign country is not important

7. Gold:
____ a. Is traded on the London Commodities exchange
____ b. Is considered pure if it is 18 Karat
____ c. Is the standard for all U.S. currency held in the Federal Reserve Depositories
____ d. Was once worth less than silver
____ e. None of the above

8. Silver:
____ a. Is still used in U.S. coinage and all over the world
____ b. Is no longer exchanged for paper money in the U.S.
____ c. Was used with plutonium in nuclear bombs during WW2
____ d. Was recalled with Gold coins during 1934

9. Platinum is:
____ a. Always worth more than gold
____ b. Available in ingots and pure coins
____ c. Found along gold deposits all over the world
____ d. Used in electric car catalytic converters

10. Diamonds are:
    ____ a.   Available as
    ____ b.   Not recognized by customs X-ray machines
    ____ c.   Valued by the 4Cs of quality, color, clarity, cut and weight
    ____ d.   Weighted by measurement and equal four carats to a gram
    ____ e.   All of the above

CHAPTER FIVE

OPTIONS & MARGIN ACCOUNTS, DESIGNATED SECURITIES, ETF, COMMODITIES TRADING, DISCRETIONARY TRADING, INSIDER TRADING, SPECULATION

Put options are the right, purchased for a price of course; to buy or sell stocks for a future designated amount. They is a way to protect stock holdings against losses. A stock can be insured from future losses by buying a contract for a put option, which will limit losses if the value falls. The **strike price** is the amount, above or below future markets that you want to limit your losses that will protect you. As an example, you may want to limit your losses to 10% of the present price. Then you would buy a put option, which would insure your losses if the market falls below 90%. This would save most of your investment if there were a dramatic change in the market or the stock price. Options are traded by specialists on the **Chicago Board Options Exchange**.

There are also **call options**, which allow you to own stocks for higher future prices by buying the stocks today for future delivery. Of course, in today's world, everything is on paper, so you are merely buying the right to deliver the stock at a future date. The tons of future bacon pork bellies need not be delivered to your front door unless you are in the grocery business. If you guessed the market or stock right, you have bought cheap. If not, you will lose some money. Options are particularly useful for speculating on the values of commodities, also to protect supplies and prices by manufacturers, where price swings can be dramatic. An example of this is the Gorham Silverware Company, which speculates in **silver futures** as part of their precious silver inventory needs. Options are a **Speculation** and handled by specialists in a brokerage firm. They are not for elderly people or a place for a retirement plan or trust fund. Only the most sophisticated individuals who enjoy risk-taking should indulge.

Margin accounts are used extensively by traders. The commodities trader or BD firm will borrow money from their bank at rates pegged to the prime rate. Then they will add a few points and loan it to their client. The broker is now a banker and charges about 1/10 of 1% daily for the privilege. This amounts to an annual 36-½% rate on money costing them close to prime. **Leverage** is very important in securities trading because it **multiplies the profit or loss** effects. The **margin for stock trading** requires at least 50% cash to open a margin account (**Federal Reserve Board Regulation T**) at original purchase stock-values. Before the Great Depression, the margin was more liberal and banking institutions were allowed to participate in speculative trading. The October 1929 Crash included a huge sell-off for margin calls when values collapsed. Our recent **Savings and Loan** debacle was caused by liberalized rules allowing banks to speculate internally in real estate deals instead of only loaning money out on real estate. The taxpayers, not only the S&L insurance fund that was overwhelmed and insolvent, paid for that great wasteful speculation.

Now the banks feel left out, enough that the Bank of America gave up a billion-dollar loss for their very own hedge fund speculation during 1998. **The Glass-Steagall Act of 1934** was passed by Congress to separate the banks from the Securities market. They could no longer be on both sides of the fence as lender-investor. In October 1934, The SEC was created with other legislation to keep the banks out of the stock market business. In November 1999, this was partially reversed when President Clinton allowed banks to own brokerage firms but not to use bank FDIC money to buy stocks and bonds. In other words, the financial institutions can now direct their clients to their own brokerage salespeople nearby on the floor. Banks have always struggled to loan out funds found in savings accounts and compensating checking account balances.

Once the margin account is established, the investor must maintain equity of at least 25% in his/her account. So, you buy your Amazon Common for $20,000 with $15,000 down and a $5,000 margin loan. The price falls daily, but no sweat until the day it is worth only $4,000. Then you get a **margin call** from your broker (always early in the morning) to put money in the account that same day, deposit securities of at least twice the value of the shortcoming, or he/she is obligated to **close your position** and sell off your other stocks to cover the loan. Since you might only receive $4,000 against the $5,000 loan, you will still be short and need to cover from outside funds. At any rate, the portfolio must fall to 25% of the original margin account balance, or any other arrangement, before the call is made. Some broker-dealer firms will make the call before the equity in the account reaches 25%. And, there is a short-term loss for your tax return.

Designated securities are securities which generally sell for less than $5. They are over-the-counter stocks, which are traded between dealers, and not listed on the major stock exchanges (**the Pink Sheet listing**). They are also companies with a **net worth** (retained earnings) of fewer than two million dollars. They can be the stocks of companies that have fallen from grace (bankruptcy usually Chapter 11) or new companies with uncertain economic futures but very certain cash needs. **Penny stocks** are the trade name for these securities that were once dumped hotly over the telephone. After much abuse by sales reps, first NASD, then FINRA clamped down by restricting the sale of these highly speculative securities. The sales are now restricted to strict high income/net worth suitability investor standards including experience investing in risky stocks. The broker must also explain both the offer and bid amounts and disclose his/her commission charges. The difference between the offer and bid represents the markup or spread between the wholesale (dealer) cost and the retail (investor) selling price. The dealers control the market (making the market) for these stocks, which is how monopolies and oligopolies control prices. Because you may never be able to sell the securities back and other abuses, the FINRA requires written disclosures, signatures (and probably a **DNA** sample) before they will let the broker-dealer principal approve the sale.

The **FINRA** is so tough on this subject that they offer the **800-289-9999** telephone number for you to get the disciplinary history of the salesperson or firm selling these securities. It seems that everybody knows someone else who got rich buying penny stocks, but the truth is that there are more who know poor people who once bought penny stocks.

Discretionary trading is the sales rep's dream. All it requires is a signature (actually three because the firm's principal must approve it too), and your money. In theory, because the sales rep is a professional trader and knows everything about economics, the market, finance, and securities, he/she will do the trading for you. After all, if you knew what he/she knew you would not be unsophisticated enough to not know what he/she is doing. Bankers have done this for many years while handling trust accounts for estates and trusts while charging a fat annual fee (about 1½ to 2% of the total portfolio) for placing most of it into savings accounts back into the institution. This is like portfolio management by financial advisors who manage accounts for the same annual fee. When the bank Certificate of Deposit rates fell below the fee charges these past years, this created a problem (a.k.a. loss). Not a problem of profitability, but of disclosure and how to disguise the fees from clients by burying them in the backs of tax statements and Advisory Financials.

The danger of discretionary trading is that brokers use it mostly for stock trades. Stock trades have two-way commissions. That is, you pay a commission when you buy and at the same when you sell. So, in effect, you have given your broker authority to buy and sell (actually sell to buy) stocks every time his/her rent is due, like the lawyers creating billable time when the rent is due. Very few brokers can keep their hands out of the cookie jar without some churning for commissions. Excessive trading is the common complaint of unwary investors who wonder where their money went.

Insider trading is a criminal offense. Corporate principals are required to notify the SEC in advance when large blocks of securities are issued or traded by principal shareholders. Large trades can disrupt the market and must be conducted with a certain amount of public disclosure. Insider trading is usually based on information, good or negative, concerning the firm's operations or finances privy to the management, which results in cheating the public who holds the bulk of the securities. A good deal of stock trading is based on rumors and speculation, but the problem is that if it originated inside, it is illegal, and if it originated outside, everybody else knows about it. In other words, if public information is available, it is old information, and everybody else has probably already taken advantage of it.

SPECULATION is part of every investment. We think of it as a wild investment fling, like money into the slot machines at Vegas (which have automatic 50% payout to the house). However, every investment has a speculative edge to it. There is the inherent **interest rate risk** of every CD that the savings interest rates will rise after purchase and is locked in. There is also a market risk that the new shares of your favorite stock will go down for any one of a zillion unforeseen reasons. Pure SPECULATION is when underlying economic values are ignored, you probably pay more than the sticker price for a new car, unknowingly bidding it up, because it is a new hot model, not knowing that the manufacturer will crank up production to make millions more of them before the run is over. It is speculation because you bought it to make money, not just to drive it, when the investor plans on unrealistic increases in value. SPECULATION and RISK are the same, and the best way to cope with it is to trust your financial advisor and to be knowledgeable about your situation and honest about what you are doing.

Financial advisors have a fiduciary duty to document correctly your age, income, savings, financial experience, and risk assessment. They are required not to match conservative investors with risky investments and to make their clients aware of the difference. This is the main point of contention on Broker-Dealer Sales Representative complaints for arbitration.

PLANNING TIPS

If you turn part of your portfolio over to a broker for discretionary trading, you must monitor the results. Do not turn funds over to him/her and forget about the investment. Check individual trades to see if he/she is making you money. Check your account balances to see if you are losing ground. The only test of his trading ability is for him/her to outperform the market, which is the exception, not the rule. If he/she is not successful, then you must find a better way to invest. Sometimes a broker can successfully trade for you and at a later time trade badly against the market or trade excessively for commissions. You must always be vigilant by keeping an eye on the trades and balances. After all, it is your money and if it disappears with bad or excessive commission-generating trades, then there is nobody else to blame. A bad market or bond prices will also lower all the boats at sea.

Today many brokers are using Advisory fee-based investments where as they charge the usual advisory fees of 1½-2% to manage your money. If they do discretionary trading there is a tendency to blanket the statements with masses of trades of companies, you never heard of. This is computer trading and obscures the focus and results. Some Advisors also mix mutual funds and other statements into a blend of financial data for presentation, which obscures the source of the results. The great advantage of Advisory accounts is that a stockbroker does not have to trade to earn commissions. Actually, he/she is supposed to not trade for commissions while receiving advisory fees, which average from 1½% to 2% of the total portfolio value. There has been a lot of legislation and argument about the **Fiduciary Responsibility** of advisors. The truth of the matter is that everybody dealing with other people's finances should be accountable for fiduciary responsibility. I have never been with a BD where that was not a compliance trading concern. Putting the client ahead of yourself is the mantra in a good firm regardless of the law.

TAXES

This chapter is concerned with high-risk investments and the handling of funds. Losses of this nature are capital losses and are limited to reducing other taxable income by up to $3,000 annually after absorbing any other capital gains. The remaining losses must be carried forward, never backward, until they are used up. Although everybody in the business knows there is a fiduciary responsibility for brokers to represent their clients, in truth many of them think of only their commissions and fees.

Margin account interest used to be a legitimate deduction. It was once entered on Schedule A of itemized deductions on the individual tax return. It could only be deducted, however, as an offset to passive investment income. If there is no offsetting income the unused investment expense must be carried forward to the next year. If you did not itemize, it was lost forever (thanks to the clever people you elected who create the IRS tax code). The creation on the new tax code for 2018 eliminated **Schedule A Miscellaneous** deductions, margin account interest, and investment fee expense deductions are gone forever. Along with the loss of margin account interest is the loss of deductions for advisory fees. If you have an advisory account earning only 2% last year and the broker charges an advisory fee of 2%, you have lost money after taxes, not zero. Because you can't deduct the fees you will be taxed on the 2% gains.

LEGAL COMPLIANCE

The sale of securities is a highly regulated business because it involves money and people in the same place. If you are elderly or an inexperienced investor and are receiving telephone solicitations from brokers about hot stock tips, make a note to call him/her back before agreeing to buy. This will give you time to cool off and digest the situation. If the stock is selling for less than $5, there can be legal problems with the deal. If it is for listed stocks then ask him/her for his/her sources of information. This is a solicited trade and he/she should be subjected to some scrutiny for his/her sources. E-mail or faxing data to you should give you time and information to form your own opinion. All trades require ticket approval to indicate on the ticket if the trade was unsolicited or if the client asked for it.

SUCCESSFUL STRATEGIES

In the *East of Eden* movie, Cal heard a rumor that the price of beans would go up. This was in 1917 before the US entered the First World War, which was then The Great World War, because there would be no others after this was finished. Beans were selling for 2 cents a pound at that time. Young Cal, and his advisor, correctly speculated that the price would go higher after the US declared war. They knew that governments were big buyers of commodities during wars. So, Cal borrowed $5,000 from his mother, a businesswoman of sorts, and bought a farmer's next year crop at the current 2-cent price. In due course, war was declared, and Cal made a lot of money on his leveraged speculation on beans. Uniquely, even today it takes $5,000 or more to open a commodities account with a broker.

This is true **SPECULATION** on the commodities market. It also works in reverse, sometimes very excessively. The following year's beans, bought for delivery in 1919, could have been bought for 5 cents with the expectation that the price would go higher, and the price would fall instead because the war ended in November 1918. The strategy would then backfire. This is true **SPECULATION** based on perceived events such as war, weather, or other facts. The investment would also be leveraged by using a margin account, thus more than $10,000 of beans might have been bought with the $5,000 at that time. Under that scenario, if the first price had fallen from 2 cents to one cent per pound, all the money would have been lost.

SPECULATION is always a risky business that should never be attempted with money you cannot afford to lose. It is an illegal event, by the BD and SEC, for a broker salesperson to solicit a client to borrow money against any source such as home equity or other means to buy investments. If you cannot afford to speculate, you need a business that has steady demand, is profitable, and provides a reliable service. Cal's mother, who was in the entertainment business, had a big bank account.

HORROR STORY - INSIDER TRADING

Somehow, the independent stockbrokers find the people with money, as effectively as the bank security broker sales reps that just look at the bank customer account balances or respond to the teller's call. A radio station owner-manager left $150,000 with his broker for discretionary trading. His broker would make a fortune for him. For one year, the manager didn't hear from the broker even though he kept receiving buy and sell confirmation statements in the mail. Finally, even those stopped arriving. The entire $150,000 had been traded away with losses and commissions. The huge loss lived in the individual's tax return for many years at the rate of $3,000 per year to offset other income. If the client had no other capital gains, he needed to live another 49 years to offset the losses against his wages and other income in his tax returns.

INSIDER TRADING is a commonplace hazard with investors and especially executives holding stocks in their companies. It is a crime to sell or buy stocks using internal information that is not available to the public. It is simply stealing based on an event that will be publicized, resulting in a profound change in the value of public stock prices. The most common reason is great or awful earnings or an official event such as a license or new drug approval or not. In the wonderful movie *Wall Street*, insider information that the company pension plan was overfunded and that the excess could be taken out and invested internally was one of the plots which define the corrupted Gordon Gekko and his interaction with naive Bud Fox, the new stockbroker. Later, he and Gekko, now enemies, were arrested for insider trading. "Greed is good" is the leitmotiv of the story.

INSIDE TRADING was the bane of Karl Karcher who, at the dinner table one evening, mentioned that Carl's Junior earnings had dropped dramatically. The next day, family members and an informed employee were selling their shares to avoid the bad results. This was noticed by the SEC and **INSIDE TRADING** charges were filed against the parties. The case was settled against the family for a clawback of illegal profits from the trade, plus a fine of an equal amount. The employee went for a civil trial and settled for a clawback of earnings (in a civil trial the recovered losses usually go back to the injured party "to make the aggrieved whole again" but in this case, they went to the Feds) with a fine equal to his profits resulting from the trade. Everybody was able to avoid larger fines of triple damages of the amount settled.

Martha Stewart, the beautiful smart celebrity, sold all her stock of an investment when acting on insider information from her stockbroker. The next day, the stock fell 16%. Consequently, the SEC pressed charges for securities fraud and obstruction of justice. In 2004, she was tried in a six-week jury trial and sentenced to prison and later supervised release. The usual clawbacks and fines followed. She was able to revive her business after release and is still popular and back on top again.

PROS & CONS OF MARGIN ACCOUNTS, SPECULATION & INSIDER TRADING

- Margin account interest is twice as expensive as most credit cards (not the teaser rates), so it must only be used for speculative trading where high returns are expected.

- Options for security transactions are a risky hedge, so be sure a trend is developing to bet on the future this way.

- Insider trading is illegal and the hot tip must have a reliable source. Beware of rumors.

- Penny stocks and very low-priced securities are the riskiest of all. Do not allow a broker to trade for you if you have any doubts about the risk involved. There are strict FINRA rules to protect elderly and unsophisticated people from sales pressure in this area. Many I know are in foreign countries, out of sight, out of mind, with lax regulations, foreign laws and corrupt politicians governing.

- Allowing a broker to handle your funds on a discretionary basis requires an almost religious level of trust between client and broker. It is easier to affirm or confirm unsolicited trades with your broker, than allow him/her unlimited trading authority. Check out his/her trading by matching buy and sell confirmations to see if you are making or losing money on his/her professional activities and judgment.

CHAPTER 5: APPLICATION EXERCISES

1. Designated securities are securities which generally sell for less than $5. ___ True ___ False

2. Corporate principals are required to notify the SEC in advance when large blocks of securities are issued or traded by principal shareholders. ___ True ___ False

3. A penny stock typically refers to a small company's stock that trades for less than $1 per share and has high risk and +suitability investor standards. ___ True ___ False

4. A strike price is the price at which a put or call option can be exercised. ___ True ___ False

5. Financial advisors have a fiduciary duty to correctly document the following information about their investors (check all that apply):
   ___ a. Age
   ___ b. Sex
   ___ c. Race
   ___ d. Income
   ___ e. Risk Assessment
   ___ f. All of the above

6. Put options are:
   ___ a. An offer or right to own stocks for higher future prices
   ___ b. Conservative investing
   ___ c. Good for limiting losses
   ___ d. Recommended for retirement portfolios
   ___ e. All of the above
   ___ f. None of the above

7. Call options are:
   ___ a. Stocks bought today for future delivery
   ___ b. Very speculative
   ___ c. Popular for commodities trading
   ___ d. For sophisticated trading
   ___ e. All of the above
   ___ f. None of the above

8. The Glass-Stegall Act of 1934:
   ___ a. Limited losses caused by the Great Depression
   ___ b. Allowed banks to use margin accounts for stocks and commodities trading
   ___ c. Limited margin calls for banks
   ___ d. Restricted FDIC insured banks from participating in the securities market

9. The Pink Sheet is:
   ___ a. A listing of designated securities
   ___ b. Securities which sell for less than $5
   ___ c. Securities with a net worth of less than $2,000,000
   ___ d. Penny stocks
   ___ e. Delisted securities
   ___ f. All of the above

10. Speculation is part of every investment risk except:
   ___ a. Interest rates because they can be FDIC insured
   ___ b. Changes in profitability of investments because you can make more earnings
   ___ c. Casinos because you can win big time
   ___ d. Bonds because they always pay on maturity
   ___ e. All of the above
   ___ f. None of the above

CHAPTER SIX

STOCK EXCHANGES, INTERNET TRADING, BROKER-DEALERS, SECURITIES EXCHANGE COMMISSION, NATIONAL ASSOCIATION OF SECURITY DEALERS, REGISTERED REPRESENTATIVES, & PRINCIPALS, REGISTERED INVESTMENT ADVISORS

Most securities trading is conducted on the **New York Stock Exchange** (**NYSE** The Big Board), which is the oldest exchange in the country. Because it was the first, it contains most of the blue-chip corporate issues. Trading is conducted on this exchange from 9:30 am to 4 pm Eastern Standard Time and other exchanges are pegged to this schedule, which means that the **West Coast regional Pacific Exchange** in California opens at 6 am and closes at 1 pm. A 20-minute to half-hour reporting delay is imposed during very heavy trading to slow the action down. The NYSE provides most of the stock values used in various indexes such as the **Dow Jones Industrial Average, Wiltshire 500, Standard & Poor 500**, and other trading summaries. The NYSE is the mainstay, staid indicator of the market in general. Broker/Dealer firms pay dearly to become a member to trade on this exchange. The listing fees and qualifications for corporations are also highest to trade here. Also, in New York, the New York Mercantile Board trades commodities.

The **National Association of Securities Dealers Automatic Quotation Service** (**NASDAQ**) handles trading for securities, not listed with an exchange but traded over the counter. All unlisted stocks are included in this system, which is broken up into national markets and smaller capitalized businesses. The **NASDAQ** handles newer smaller capitalized securities, mainly technological issues. This market sometimes appears non-economic in performance, with individual prices surging or declining sharply daily largely due to rumors or economic whispers.

Companies come and go here and several supernova-type stars such as **Microsoft Computer, Intel, Tesla,** or **Facebook** can lead the whole exchange with volume and values compared to the hundreds of other upstart listings. The NASDAQ is an exciting marketplace representing the fundamental changes to the new American economy, which begins and ends with the computer age. NASDAQ is broken into the large national listings and a separate listing of the small-cap issues that average only a dollar or two per share. Many companies aspire to grow big and strong enough to join the NYSE, but they all begin here or at a smaller regional exchange. The recent transformation of our economy, as it shifts inexorably from manufacturing to a more technical cerebral state with outsourced manufacturing, is that passionate speculation dominates the newer NASDAQ issues, which balance the staider blue-chip giants of the past. Excess trading can be shutdown to cut off temporarily.

The **Chicago Board of Trade** (**CBOT**) is, of course, located in Chicago. An outgrowth of the Chicago stockyards and Midwest granaries, the **CBOT**, also known as the **Chicago Mercantile Board**, has become the commodities trading center of the country (government bonds trade on this exchange as a commodity). Stock trading also takes place at a sister regional exchange. Sometimes ancient trading practices still prevail. CBOT grain prices-futures are traded by the bushel (32-quart volume). Metals such as #1 iron or copper are sold as a short ton (2,000 LBS) or long ton (2,240 LBS about a metric ton).

The **American Stock Exchange** (**AMEX**) is located in New York. Smaller National companies join this large exchange. Many **AMEX** companies will migrate over to the **Big Board** when they mature. There are smaller **regional exchanges** such as the **Pacific, Boston, Philadelphia,** and **Chicago** that handle trading for local firms.

A unique relationship exists between the Dow Jones Industrial Average, NASDAQ, and the more conservative AMEX. The sum of the NASDAQ listings is smaller than the Dow Jones Average by a multiple of four or more to one. Thus, if the New York or American Exchanges went up ten points, the NASDAQ composite, if equally traded, would go up only two points. The NASDAQ is thinner in value than the Dow Jones and appears to move slower in volume-dollars.

In November 1998, the NASDAQ merged with the AMEX, creating the combined NASDAQ-AMEX Market Group. The two units would share the NASDAQ electronic trading and Amex floor-based auction. AMEX, like the NYSE, is a single-dealer auction market in which customer orders flow to one central location. NASDAQ has a multi-dealer structure of brokers linked by computers. Corporate clients can now move from one exchange to another under central management.

Another stock market trading phenomenon is that the world is on a 24-hour clock. European markets are trading while you are sleeping, and the Asian markets are trading when you go to bed at night. The result of all this, in a truly global financial economy, is that our market opens with a big bang each day as the early-rising traders react to world events. Subsequent trading sometimes appears tame in comparison as normal trading reflects American domestic news events and our daily economic issues. This oftentimes results in huge swings in the market after the first hour of trading. A frantic hour of positive or negative trading based on world events could be offset later by six hours of opposing negative or positive trading influenced by more favorable domestic events.

The markets do not react with millions of shares traded every few minutes because of individual stockholders, such as you, buying and selling their stock picks or mutual fund shares. The institutional traders and Financial Advisors of mutual funds, who routinely trade large blocks of shares, do most of the market trading. Thus, the market activity of these few influences the holdings of many. I wanted to say "the masses", but that sounds Communistic while we are truly discussing Capitalistic activities in which most Americans are active or passive participants. And if you don't think you're invested in the market, just find out where your pension plan money is invested, or why your bank calls some of their savings plans "money market accounts". Better yet, ask your banker how their across-the-aisle securities fund or securities representative is performing or insured, compared to your **Federal Deposit Insurance Corporation** (**FDIC**) savings account balance.

Sooner or later it is worth mentioning REGULATION T, the SEC rule which requires all security trades to be settled within one working day. This means that if you have a stock certificate or bond and wish to sell it, that you must properly sign (endorse) the back and physically get it in the hands of the B/D firm's trading office, (which is usually on the opposite side of the country) all within one day of the trade date. The same rules apply for cash, as there is only one day to cover. Beginning on the second day, if the funds have not been received, the sale or trade is backed out (sold). For this reason, most stocks are held in-house at the broker/dealer firm and funds are wired electronically, if not available in your broker/dealer money market account. This is where electronic banking and swift modern financial practices come into play. Overnight delivery by a commercial carrier is also very popular with stock traders. One day clearing (T+l) is now required like clearing time for checks between banks, everything moves faster again.

The **Securities Exchange Commission (SEC)** was created in 1913 to regulate securities by requiring standards for stocks offered for public trading. This is an immense responsibility because the country, for all its political and economic ups and downs, has a truly capitalistic open market economy. Later, after the Great Depression began with the late October 1929 crash, the **Investment Advisor Act of 1934** passed, endowing the SEC with further standards to regulate the sale of securities while creating the NASD to enforce their rules of conduct. Within this framework, the SEC monitors the companies and conduct of corporate officers while the newer FINRA holds the BD firms and their sales representatives in strict compliance for fair and ethical standards. The **Registered Investment Advisor Act of 1940** passed to codify financial industry practices and procedures and to protect the investors. The FINRA holds every BD under utmost scrutiny of their own operations, requiring periodic FOCUS reports because they do some trading on their own as well as handling client's money, and the conduct of the people in the organization. Broker-Dealer operations are under close scrutiny with SEC notification required immediately for financial or administration changes even for a change of accounting firms doing the certified annual financial statements, taxes and audits.

Licensing, by FINRA examinations, exists at every level of trading and supervision. Cash requirements of the firms, because they have such a large fiduciary relationship to the clients and are holding financial instruments under their own names, require certified audited financial statements and are held to exacting standards with the **FOCUS reports**. There is also a bonding requirement, which insures clients for funds lost due to BD default, or bankruptcy. Last, of all, the worst fate is for a registered principal, Office of Supervisory Jurisdiction manager, to be found guilty of "failure to supervise" one of his/her sales reps, which holds him/her and the firm out to severe penalties for improper trading or fraudulent activities.

Worth noting is the fact that a sales rep is held open to working for only one BD firm at a time. This is a similar standard to being a realtor. The reason for this is that the BD must approve all products sold, (a process called **"due diligence"** which includes financial reviews, interviews, and visits to investment offices) as well as the individual trades. Thus, an individual selling units of his friend's worm farm venture, while licensed to sell mutual funds for a BD firm, is **"trading away"** from his firm by selling an unapproved product. This is illegal and results in the loss of the rep's security licenses as soon as it is discovered, and possibly his **Office of Supervisory Jurisdiction (OSJ)** manager, as well (I was one), depending on the outcome of the investigation. The close review of reps and dealers protects the public because only approved securities (**Selling Away** is the unauthorized deal) can be sold by the licensed rep. Although this does not guarantee the success of every security, it eliminates the worst ones and the frauds. Life or casualty insurance product sales by independent brokers are not subject to this restriction unless they combine or include securities sold as an investment, which they don't do. However, most large broker/dealer firms require all life insurance products clear through their firm so they can share in the commissions. Life insurance licenses are the licensed domain of all the 50 states. Registered representatives are insured by malpractice insurance with large deductibles.

A Registered Investment Advisor (RIA) is the cream of the investment community. He/she is the most licensed and knowledgeable of the financial industry. Any person you see on television discussing investments (I was one) must be an RIA. The RIA individual is required to be free of customer complaints, compliance problems, personally financially stable, and most of all… cleared through a separate application process directly through the SEC. He/she is also required to be a registered principal, the highest securities qualification, and clear another FINRA (Series 63) exam on the Investment Advisor Acts. Many people will practice as an RIA under the umbrella registration of another RIA and thus are not required to possess the dreaded principal license (I was a principal).

Only an RIA is authorized to perform trading and maintain client portfolios for an annual fee instead of working for sales-generated commissions. This function requires state and SEC audits because of the important fiduciary relationship with the clients. A certified audit is required for each year-end. An RIA must maintain a signed contractual relationship with his/her clients to charge any fees. Part of the contract is to give the clients an **ADV** statement. This statement, which is part of the SEC licensing process, discloses the firm's responsibilities, commission or fee structure, trading relationships, and detailed information on the principles. The managing principle must hold a general securities license (Series 7) and a principal license (Series 24) while the other people directly employed at the client level must hold general securities licenses. The ADV also discloses the business background, education and licensing particulars of each person engaged in the RIA. A registered representative cannot do any trading with other securities firms. Other securities professionals include the **Certified Financial Planner** who has completed the coursework of the College of Financial Planning, but holds no licenses from them.

Last, but not least is the Internet trading. With every securities sale, a registered representative must complete a form asking if the sale was solicited or not. If it was solicited, it means the sales rep probably asked you to buy it. An unsolicited sale indicates that the individual asked the broker to place the trade for a security he had in mind. This is a very important issue in client complaints about being sold unsuitable investment (which might lose money) when the client insists that the sales rep told him/her to buy it.

With the direct new Internet trading, the client commissions are low because the sales rep is not present, and the trade is always unsolicited. New accounts and trading information are instantaneously processed for the individual trader's computer. Unsupervised accounts are opened with a minimum of fuss and interaction. This is a marvelous opportunity to buy and sell stocks with minimum costs. You are on your own and can make your personal investment decisions. Many people can outperform the investment decisions made by sales reps on the phone exaggerating his/her favorite stock of the day, if they do some investment research. For those people who are reasonably competent about managing their own financial affairs, without further financial needs such as estate planning or diversification, this is a fine way to trade for your own portfolio. How do Internet broker-dealers make money on low commission trades, yet spend megabucks on television advertising? That is, by borrowing money at a prime rate from banks, marking it up, loaning it to customers for margin accounts, and leveraged trading.

PLANNING TIPS

When trading on the Internet, keep in mind that you are not diversifying. You will be trading stocks at your own whim and discretion but need to be doing other financial things as well. Be sure not to put all your eggs in this basket, or become stuck in a trading frenzy. If something pulls the trigger on the stock market, you could lose a lot of money in a big hurry.

There are new elements of creative high-tech fraud appearing on the Internet. Supervision is very sketchy although the SEC has an **Internet Enforcement Unit** watching the monitor, these **Cyberforce** people spend all day searching for the bad people. The FINRA also scans the Web with their **Net Watch** software. Yet, only one charge per month is filed by the SEC **cyberpolice**, even though thousands of complaints are received monthly. E-mail, offering phony fantastic quick returns, may also be sent to potential investors. To avoid losing your investment, the safest bet for purchasing stocks is to work through a broker/dealer. The firm is strictly regulated; the individual hot stock tips floating over the Web are not.

SEC CIRCUIT BREAKERS

The following is the thresholds when trading is halted market wide for single-day rapid decline in the S&P 500. The Standard & Poor 500 funds are used as the index fund stocks for Mutual Funds and other Index Funds when they mark to the market. The index funds must duplicate the S&P to get the same result.

LEVEL 1: Halts trading if the market drops 7% from the previous day closing. The market will close for 15 minutes before 3:25 p.m. EST. If after 3:25 p.m. the market will continue.

LEVEL 2: Halts trading at 13%. The market will close for 15 minutes if before 3:25 p.m. EST. If after 3:25 p.m. the market will continue.

LEVEL 3: Halts trading at 20%, at any time during the trading day, and will remain closed the remainder of the day.

SINGLE STOCK PRICE BANDS: The marketplace Limit Up-Limit Down rule prevents trades from executing out of price bands throughout the day for individual stocks and exchange-traded funds (ETFs).

SEC STUFF

SECURITIES ACT OF 1933: This was the "truth in securities" legislation that required registration of new issues and disclosure (the prospectus was created) to prevent deceit, fraud or misrepresentation in the sale of securities.

SECURITIES ACT OF 1934: This legislation focused on stricter trading and supervision of the markets and stock exchanges for publicly traded securities.

PUBLIC UTILITY HOLDING COMPANY ACT OF 1935: This legislation regulated intrastate issues of new and existing securities of giant utility companies that create or distribute electric power or natural gas across the nation. Tennessee Valley Authority and Bonneville Dam were controlled by this act.

TRUST INDENTURE ACT OF 1939: This legislation reinforced prior laws pertaining to the issuance and sales of bonds, debentures, notes, and other debts offered to the public (excluded independent states issues, or federal issues that are managed by the Federal Reserve Board, over which the SEC has no jurisdictional control).

INVESTMENT COMPANY ACT OF 1940: Mostly concerned with the registration of investment company securities (mutual funds), and public disclosure of their operations and financial data.

INVESTMENT ADVISORS ACT OF 1940: Created the standards for Registered Investment Advisors to advise and manage financial matters for the public. This includes registration, record keeping, and disclosure (ADV) statements.

CORPORATE REORGANIZATION: Allows the SEC to interact with bankruptcy proceedings of public companies where fraud might be involved.

THE SEC COMMISSION ORGANIZATION: Was created in the Act of 1934 by the Federal Trade Commission. The complex SEC maintains offices throughout the country and has a huge network of organizations below them. The principal regulatory organization is the Financial Industry Regulatory Authority (FINRA) which is a Self-Regulatory Organization (SRO). Thus, the SEC writes the rules and the FINRA polices them. The FINRA has the power to enforce the act by acting both as the judge and jury in the legal judgment of the SEC rulings.

SEC REQUIRED CORPORATE FILINGS:

- SC 13D (ownership statement)
- 11K (annual report of employee stock plan)
- 10Q (quarterly earnings report)
- 8K (report of unscheduled material events)
- SC 13GA (amended ownership statement)
- DEFA 14A (proxy statement)
- 428 B3 (prospectus change or additions)
- 10K (annual report)

TAXES

We are still working with equities, so the capital gain and loss rules still apply. Gains on securities held less than one year are taxed as ordinary income, other gains are long-term and special tax tables apply. Deductible capital losses, after offsetting all capital gains, are allowed only up to $3,000 annually with any excess carried forward to future years (never backward on amended returns as in corporate NOL's).

LEGAL COMPLIANCE

All new accounts and security trades must be reviewed and signed off by a supervising principal, OSJ branch manager. His/her job is on the line, if the trade is illegal, misrepresented, or the client does not qualify. If a serious pattern of misconduct is present, the firm can also be held responsible for the bad deals. It goes with the FINRA rules of conduct and fair-trading. Everybody in the chain of command is responsible for the conduct of the people under them. It is worth remembering that any illegal conduct should be reported, first to the BD firm, then, if there is no action or they tell you to get lost and you really have a case, go directly to the FINRA or the SEC where results will be immediate. It's important to know this because the sales rep has a fiduciary responsibility to the client when handling your funds and proper sales conduct is the standard for the business. Most people are not aware that the sales rep cannot replace or guarantee any losses you might have. But, the dealer can, if he feels his people were at fault. All new account applications contain an **arbitration clause,** which promises an arbitrated case instead of a lawsuit to settle claims or complaints between you and the BD. New clients who refuse to sign are not new clients.

Another important point to remember is that a sales rep is never allowed to handle cash for any transaction or to ever have an investment check made out to him/her. All funds must be addressed to the broker/dealer firm, or in rare cases, to the actual investment they represent. Why? Because the temptation could be too great for some sales reps to keep the money and convert it to his/her own use.

The BD is insured (errors, omissions, malpractice, lack of supervision) for client vs BD losses (not investment losses), which is mandatory. There is also a firm requirement that all sales reps be insured for malpractice, errors, and omissions from individual acts. These bonds have large deductibles and if a sales rep should ever need it for a lost case, he would probably be held responsible for at least $5,000 or more of the claim before the insurance company would kick in the remainder; another reason for the sales rep to be honest and professional because so much is at stake when handling client's funds.

The **FINRA** imposes horrible fines on individuals and their supervisors when problems arise. Fines of $10,000 to $50,000 are common and have the effect of driving the sales rep or supervising principal to a different line of employment. The FINRA usually suspends individuals from trading for a week to months, and sometimes requires them to retake the tough securities licensing exams again (after all, they should have **LEARNED** the lesson).

FINRA prefers to conduct arbitration hearings rather than engage in prolonged expensive lawsuits to settle client claims that have merit. The FINRA conducts 90% of all security industry arbitration. Sometimes clients expect too much from a sales rep. A recent arbitration case concerned a client who claimed that his sales rep should have informed him to sell when his stock price started going down. This security had been unsolicited, that is the customer had initiated the purchase. The sales rep won because he did not have discretionary control over the stock and the client should have kept track of it himself. **Day traders** have their own problems.

Arbitration process begins with the arbitration agreement that is signed by the client. Without this agreement, the broker-dealer will refuse to open the account, sometimes correctly deducing that the client MAY sue him/her over anything at all (some people LOVE to sue people and look for million-dollar opportunities). When a complaint about inappropriate trading or fraud is unresolved at the broker-dealer level and is serious enough to go to the FINRA for resolution, the complainant will be allowed to pick three arbitrators from a list of 15 names (from a pool of over 4,000 arbitrators). The arbitrators, who are paid $400 daily, are from all occupations from schoolteachers to attorneys. FINRA surveys showed that 90% of all security arbitrations were successfully settled as a favorable experience of the investor plaintiff parties and their counsel. The FINRA arbitrators, who must complete training in the security arbitration process (which provides for discovery and interpretation of securities/**SEC/FINRA** regulations), provide a highly efficient method of keeping disputes out of heavily trafficked courts, which can take up to five years to resolve a case.

SUCCESSFUL STRATEGIES

Movie actors are usually too busy to handle their own financial affairs so they find an individual or agency to manage their money. Some people have a knack for managing their personal interests, but most successful creative people are too busy to know or care about what needs professional delegation. Elvis Presley had his Colonel Parker, and was lucky to find a gifted dedicated individual who was both talented and honest, to entrust his business affairs. Many professional people are unfortunate and connect with unscrupulous nonprofessional individuals, family, or managers who waste or steal their earnings and end up in court afterward.

Registered Investment Advisors are paid a fee (usually 1½ % but can be over 2% if they can get away with it), based on the dollar size of the investment portfolio, to manage an individual or fund's investment. One Advisor had a practice that specialized in working for individual clients who were retiring from a large chemical manufacturer, which was downsizing their overhead and staff. His whole practice consisted of these customers and their referrals. The white-collar management retirees were leaving with huge pensions that needed reinvestment. The advisor earned large commissions on securities and insurance trades when he purchased investments for the rollover IRA's. Part of the investment process was to review the client's financial affairs to create a complete financial plan that encompassed the whole lifestyle of the retiree. Because the pension amounts were very large, there was no lack of compensation for the planner to spend a great deal of time, which he did, to create a very good comprehensive plan.

During the investigation process, he and his staff would constantly find problems with the clients' tax returns, their home, auto, or life insurance not matching their economic situation, and a lack of wills or other estate planning. This planner was a particularly diligent professional, and as I mentioned… well paid, so he really investigated everything he could to do a good job, far more than would normally be done.

After several years of working with these clients and finding problems everywhere, he evolved into a different plan for his business. Rather than charge fees to place securities in the new IRA pension plans, he evolved to fee-based planning whereas he would charge an annual fee, paid quarterly, based on the size of the investment. He and his staff also were preparing the client's taxes because they wanted them done correctly and wanted to **"build a proper fence"** around the client to keep bad advice away. This worked fine for a year. There was always a problem, though with different professionals doing their sales thing in a non-professional manner or just not being close enough to get the whole picture of their client's affairs. The clients were coming back to the Advisor with problems he had no control over. Then, after believing he was not doing a proper job by handling only the investments, he took the plan a step further.

His clients, now having the utmost confidence in his small organization, wanted him to handle everything. Instead of having their Advisor point out all the problems of the different professional aspects of their lives, they wanted him to control it all. An Advisor usually has licenses to sell only securities and life insurance. Some, like this Advisor, had other professional qualifications in the form of tax and accounting experience. All that was missing, was a casualty insurance license for auto and homes, and professional legal services. Therefore, the Advisor hired people with other licenses to handle these parts of the financial affairs (and the paperwork), or farmed the work out to his researched particular specifications. Then he changed his fee structure to include all of the individual's estate. This included the total sum of all savings, pensions, and equities in business and personal assets. The clients, who had larger than average estates but not wealthy individuals, were perfectly pleased to find someone professional enough to handle all of their affairs and were willing to pay to have it properly done all under one roof.

The Advisor has now limited his practice and is turning new clients away. He realized that quality has its limitations. The little practice evolved into a high-quality institution that provided services that most professional intellectual or artistic people can never find. He and his small elite professional staff have all the work they can handle. Besides, he likes to go to the Caribbean with his family to take time off under the sun.

HORROR STORY - REAL ESTATE INVESTMENT

A registered principal, OSJ, and Certified Financial Planner, who held a Ph.D. in education, had his own investment to sell. A real estate deal promised fantastic short-term profits. Unfortunately, it was only available in jumbo $100,000 units so very few clients could participate in this good opportunity, which was sure to not last very long. Somehow, the man was able to locate several wealthy business people who would take the chance. There was a great incentive for the CFP because the commissions were 10% or $10,000 per deal with no haircut from the broker/dealer. "This can't be real!" I told a tax client who showed it to me. If it is too good to be true, then it is probably not true, the age-old axiom reads. The client, whose rich friends liked it enough to buy into the deal before it was fully subscribed, bought it anyway, because investment greed overrides common sense.

Several years later, the deal proved to be a fraud. The registered principal lost his licenses because the BD had never approved or seen the investment in the first place. Everybody sued everybody else in sight and the man lost his home and everything he owned to pay off the lawyers (there was probably nothing left for customer restitution). His huge FINRA fines were probably never paid, so he would never sell securities again, if he could find a firm to hire him. He blamed his BD for the bad deals although they had no part in the illegal act. This is an example of a highly qualified professional who not only lost his job, but any opportunity to be in the business again. In retrospect, he should have known better, but commission greed had overwhelmed him. He now works in a public school.

PROS & CONS OF ALL THE ABOVE

- Internet trading brings the market to every man. Money is made or lost overnight. The commissions are cheap and investment advice is available to all on TV. It's an opportunity to be independent and take great risks. Like the machines at Las Vegas, it involves systematic hypnotic risk, so traders beware. Now, evening trading will be allowed on the NASDAQ so day traders can become night traders! There will be no sleep for these challenging people.

- The security dealer is under very close supervision. Consult with your sales rep if you feel cheated. Contact him or her in writing if there is a real problem. You can't work it out over the phone. The sales rep cannot guarantee your losses or repay you. If the broker/dealer feels you were misrepresented, he can replace your losses. He would like to avoid a FINRA complaint that he could lose and affect his insurance costs or non-renewal.

- Investment professionals have all kinds of licenses. Unfortunately, they make a living by selling investments and will sometimes place their livelihood at risk. Do not be hypnotized by the framed stuff on the wall. Just listen carefully and use good judgment for your money.

- The Dow Jones Industrial Average is the sum of the largest 30 corporations, although they represent the bulk of the trading on that exchange. This average dominates everybody's thinking about the market being up or down or whatever. Try to make individual stock picks and forget about the market. A good market could pull your stock up and a bad one could pull it down, but the real investment factor is how well the company is managed and performs within the stock market. Elon Musk of Tesla and other firms (Space X and the Boring Company) has shown that visionary leadership is the most important element of management.

- The high-flying Internet stocks pose great trading possibilities with great volatility in day-to-day trading. Ultimately, Internet companies will be required to make a net profit commensurate with the large capitalization given to them. That will be the day of reckoning. As the IRS would say, "You are in business to make money."

CHAPTER 6: APPLICATION EXERCISES

1. The Securities Exchange Commission (SEC) was created in 1913 to regulate securities by requiring standards for stocks offered for public trading. ___ True ___ False

2. A Certified Financial Planner is the most licensed and knowledgeable of the financial industry and must be cleared through a separate application process directly through the SEC. ___ True ___ False

3. The Securities Act of 1934 focused on stricter trading and supervision of the markets and stock exchanges for publicly traded securities. ___ True ___ False

4. FINRA Rules of Conduct state everybody in the trading firm's chain of command is responsible for the conduct of the people under them. ___ True ___ False

5. The SEC is not allowed to interact with bankruptcy proceedings of public companies during Corporate Reorganizations. ___ True ___ False

6. Security Broker Dealers have authority to:
    ___ a. Hire sales reps without background or fingerprint checks
    ___ b. Allow sales reps to work concurrently with other similar sales organizations
    ___ c. Terminate reps for selling away securities without due diligence by compliance
    ___ d. Avoid the scrutiny of the OSJ for client trading risk qualification
    ___ e. All of the above

7. The Registered Investment Act of 1940 created the NASD and later FINRA required BD firms to:
    ___ a. License by exam all levels of trading and supervision
    ___ b. File FOCUS reports for the SEC on operations and BD trading
    ___ c. Obtain bonds and register employees for client losses
    ___ d. Approve all products sold by the reps of the BD firm
    ___ e. All of the above
    ___ f. None of the above

8. SEC Circuit breakers halt trading:
   ___ a. At Level One for 15 minutes when the S&P 500 drops 7% from previous day closing
   ___ b. At Level Two for 15 minutes when the market drops 13%
   ___ c. At Level Three for all day when the market drops 20%
   ___ d. When limit-up and limit-down price bands on individual stocks and ETFs are exceeded
   ___ e. All of the above
   ___ f. None of the above

9. Which Act of Congress allowed the SEC to interact with public company bankruptcies for fraud:
   ___ a. The Securities Act of 1934
   ___ b. The Public Utility Holding Company Act of 1935
   ___ c. The Trust Indenture Act of 1939
   ___ d. The Corporate Reorganization Act

10. Which is not a required SEC corporate filing
   ___ a. 10-Q for quarterly earnings
   ___ b. 10-K annual report
   ___ c. Schedule D for capital gains or losses
   ___ d. 11-K Employee Stock Plan annual report

CHAPTER SEVEN

PSEUDO STOCK INVESTMENTS

Eventually, unless you are broke, somebody will offer you a deal you cannot refuse. The best one was before 1986 when the IRS code was highly favorable to investors and business people. An accountant wrote to his Congressman that his client bought a $100,000 Rolls Royce auto, and because he used it for business, he was able to expense the entire cost in three years. That woke some people up and the rules began to change. The resulting new 1986 auto tax rule, which is still with us, labeled luxury autos as things with four wheels, not including the spare, which cost barely more than $13,000. These lesser vehicles are expensed over five years with the most conservative straight-line method. Therefore, a fine business investment in tax refunds, by way of excessive deductions, invited sour tax retribution. Uniquely, Congress also created a luxury tax on all auto sales, which began on autos selling over $32,000.

All of this was changed with the new **Tax Cuts and Jobs Act of 1998** which renewed and enlarged **Section 179** (now $1 million including used equipment) and larger **accelerated first-year depreciation** deductions.

Other tax credit investments also prevailed during the predawn of the new **Great Tax Increase Code of 1986**. Investors were able to take advantage of the liberal rules to deduct huge business losses on equipment purchases and these losses flowed through non-corporate businesses to offset other income. Under the tax code anomaly, a contractor could buy a new Caterpillar crane for his business, which would create huge deductions, which might well be larger than his income for the year. Then he could offset other wages or investment income with the net business losses. The 1986 tax code prevented this with active/passive loss limitations and changes in the depreciation rules.

The new code also created a fire-breathing tax dragon called the **Alternative Minimum Tax (AMT)** a.k.a. **alternate maximum tax**, which affected both corporate and individual taxpayers. This new tax simply applied the viewpoint that if the taxpayer had a certain amount of income, then by limiting the credits and deductions, he or the business should pay a certain amount of tax anyway. In addition, of course, a completely new tax rate was established to make sure the taxpayer did not get away clean. The AMT calculations were so complicated that they tested the limits of the tax congressional manipulators, thus human intelligence, and would have been impossible without the creation of the computer, which barely existed functionally before 1986. It is highly possible that the government invented computers just to increase taxes.

Many, many years ago, the IRS published a handbook on tax deductions for business equipment. Equipment lived many years in this little book, which stated the lives of wooden aircraft, and cast-iron factory machines (50 years) and other things that were made differently than today. Then over the years, the rules changed into becoming very liberal and favoring business. Now, they have changed back again to become much more restricted.

Residential rental properties were also tax-advantaged as pseudo investments prior to 1986. In 1980 a house could be bought for a rental (not the land, just the building) and written off any arguably useful life with accelerated depreciation. Then the rules changed to 15-year life, then 18, then 19, now 27½ years with only straight-line depreciation. Eventually, rental houses disappeared as tax-advantaged investments. They were tax-advantaged simply because they lasted longer physically than they lived in the tax returns. A simple test was, did the house last longer than 15 years? If it did, as an auto lasting longer than three years, then it was a pseudo investment because it created tax refunds or reductions and could be manipulated enough to create investment opportunities built around the tax code. Investments sold with tax advantages offered with the **Internal Rate of Return (IRR)** calculations to show how much the additional tax savings enhance the return on investment. Commercial properties have a depreciable life of 39 years.

There are other types of investments as well. An interest in a small corporate business cannot be sold, except to immediate associates or family. Small businesses always need more cash and selling stock shares creates a non-bank financial source. This is frequently a business partner that the controlling business owner-managers would like to forget about soon afterward. The security rules are very strict about these types of transactions because close-held business stocks would be considered a security if held out to strangers and sold to outsiders. A Corporation, no matter how small, still has stock certificates, which are equities and subject to SEC and state restrictive rules. One of the problems with a small corporation is that after you have bought some of it, you may still not have a large enough position to have any influence on management or even any return of your capital. It could be illiquid and it might be impossible to sell your shares back. Many lawyers are busy today handling the affairs of powerless business partners who own worthless stock in going concerns.

One way around the corporate investor problem is for fraudulent promoters to sell a "working interest" in a business. One such investment, which was bold enough to be printed in color on glossy paper, was looking for people to financially share in the development of a device, which would allow autos to run on water. The inventor told people he had hired bodyguards to protect him from the Big Oil and Detroit Auto monopolies who wanted to stop him. There was a picture of a Volkswagen bug in the foldout, which was supposedly able to run on the miraculous water injection system that would soon rule out the greedy energy-dominated oil barons of the world. Naturally, all the civilized nations except Saudi Arabia, Texas, and the military were interested in the program, which needed a few more dollars to get started. By not selling shares in the Corporation or inviting people to invest in a formal partnership, the people were invited to be an active participant somehow (yet passive investor) in the scheme. This approach kept the regulators at bay. Regardless of investment form, the scheme never did well financially, perhaps because most people know that water just does not burn very well weather inside an auto engine or out.

The old tax code, which had higher tax tables before the **Tax Reform Act of 1986**, invited tax investment schemes which offered huge multiple tax write-offs up front, which returned to the tax returns years later in the deal. For instance, a person could invest one dollar and get a four-dollar reduction off his taxable income on his tax return. The promoters would argue for the time value of the invested tax savings over the period (internal rate of return or IRR) when it would return many years later. Somehow, though, in the complexity of the deal, the customers would forget about the return of the taxes. Alternatively, the sales rep would forget to tell his clients why sharks circle in the water.

PLANNING TIPS

Extreme caution should be exercised about investments that offer fantastic, outrageous, or tax-advantaged returns, especially if they somehow avoid the scrutiny of state or federal regulators. One way to keep ahead of the schemes is to contact your state department of corporations, which always has terribly unhappy and mean attorneys on staff. Their first job seems to be to increase and collect wages and more taxes but their secondary job is to investigate schemes offered to the public.

TAXES

The tax-advantaged schemes of the past still live in individual or corporate tax returns as credits and losses carried forward. These credits have been unused because of the limitations of the Alternative Minimum Tax. There have been also taxes returning in the form of deferred tax write-offs. Finally, it is because the tax code is created to be incomprehensible to all including the creators, just like Obamacare. Ask your Congressman if he understands the tax code and he will call for security or the Secret Service before he can answer. The AMT itself creates tax credit carryforwards that are offsets of the original items rejected and replaced with new AMT taxes on the applicable tax returns. Confusing? I hope so, because this could be a test for normalcy. In any case, because this area is so complicated, be sure to find a tax-consultant who isn't smart enough to charge hourly fees, then (if you really don't like him) make him sweat out a long weekend to research and explain the AMT portion of the tax code to you on a Monday.

A note about taxes on real estate rentals. Rentals, an active-passive income activity according to the IRS code, allows the flow-through of up to $25,000 in deductible losses against other income each year, if the income does not exceed certain large amounts (this moving target rested at $150,000 married and $100,000 if you're single recently). Many people like rentals, usually ex-residences, in their tax returns because they produce loss deductions. The losses help with tax refunds or reduce taxes owed. These tax-advantaged rentals are addictive, even though they create tenant or repair cash flow headaches or nightmares from time to time. What property owners forget is what happens after the sale. The depreciation expense, which created the beautiful losses on the tax returns, is recaptured as taxable income by reducing the original cost. This stroke of the pen creates a huge amount of taxable income in the year of sale. The new unsuspected gain is now taxed as Sec 1250 income (assuming you own property in California). That was the good news. The bad news is that most people borrow their equity out of the property thinking the gain is limited to the cash that flows out of the escrow sale closing. This may leave no money to pay for all the taxes. Beware of tax-advantaged investments! Learn to love your tax advisor and feel sorry for him because he has to know and explain all this to you on demand. Most of them lead terrible lives crushed as they are between the tax code and ordinary people.

Section 1244 small business stock losses are permitted up to $50,000/$100,000 without annual $3,000 business loss restrictions if qualified.

LEGAL COMPLIANCE

All legitimate security issues are reviewed for due diligence and offered by the sales reps of B/D firms. If you are offered any investment that does not appear to be represented by a B/D rep, ask your state regulators to check it out for legitimacy, or walk from the deal. Somebody must look at it, as a second opinion, for your protection. The investment risk is tremendous if nobody else reviews the deal. A state or federal regulator can also put the promoters out of business if the deal is illegal, which indirectly makes you a good citizen.

SUCCESSFUL STRATEGIES

Some great investments are not bought on the open market or Big Board. They are grown economically by entrepreneurs in very small towns. An investment in the neighborhood or family is an asset to all involved.

The Second World War enabled the Southern California economy to begin the huge expansion required for ship and aircraft military needs. The rapid expansion, which began with the War effort, continued afterward from the GI's pouring out of the Universities, now teachers instead of machine gunners. The suburbs, formerly farmland…not desert yet, began growing houses for returning GIs instead of grain or feed. Huge local unionized factories hummed with the Post War–Cold War boom that became another of America's great moments in history.

A local farmer and carpenter began building small houses for local wartime factory workers. As the years passed, he built more and more of the small two-bedroom houses, which at that time had no garages or huge up-front city planning taxes & fees. To facilitate his construction efforts, he also started his own hardware and lumber company. Business continued successfully as he also invested in his sons and daughter's college educations or by working with them in the business.

Then he did something most successful people would not do today. He built a church and gave it to the community. After all, it was his community and since he had created most of it with his hands, he felt something was missing…there was an empty place in his plan without a church nearby. Afterward, he began naming the new streets after his grandchildren, and there were many. To complete his scheme of family and community he gave many of the new little houses to his children and grandchildren. He once told me that God had given him everything he needed, and that he had a great deal of money in the bank, so he felt obligated to help his family and community. These little houses were rented and kept in repair by the family and through the family hardware store.

During our busy tax-time, he would bring in dozens of rental schedules for the family, which included income property for some children who would be filing tax returns while still in grade school. There was not a gift tax problem, even if he had paid attention to the rules when he signed the grant deeds over. The $5,000 (X 2) gift tax exemption (before 1981) easily covered the cost of land and construction of each house in those times. (The exemption is now $15,000.)

Now the city has dried up with most of the blue-collar jobs fading away or fleeing out-of-state. All the newer housing and attendant shopping has moved out of the city leaving these rows of little houses rented to poorer folks. The family has grown and expanded but as far as I know, none of the little houses were ever sold. The hardware store is gone, no longer needed since the construction needs have stopped and eclipsed by the declining local economy and retail superstores. There was an offsetting windfall for the extended family when Superfund litigation for the contaminated String fellow Acid Pits paid a dividend to the nearby property owners. However, the investment paid off, as all the family is now successful, within their personal goals, as the changing economy moved on. In addition, the big tree-lined streets still bear the first names of their owners.

HORROR STORY - WORM FARM

Eventually, there is a worm farm story. Worm farms have been offered for sale almost as long as the oldest profession. The deals vary: First, there was the Super worm, which eats radiation and created in response to the government superfund to cure the nuclear waste stockpile. Then there are Special worms that have returned by new issuers. To help you with your investment there are worm farms that can only be managed by the promoters for the huge creative response to the tremendous unknown marketplace demand for both worms and their incredible valuable byproduct…worm (poo) casings, which only the promoter knew about before he met you, his investor. All of the deals have four things in common. One is that they offer you an opportunity to own the prodigious worms, generally in the promoter's wonderful skillful care and supervision, while they help you manage the (your) business. This approach skirts the security laws because they are not offering you a partnership interest or stock in their corporation. The second is the huge and spectacular profits which are offered nowhere else in the investment universe. The third is that they control the market and will be in the middle of your deal (between you and your money). The last thing in common is that they are probably an illegal promotion.

One fellow bought $70,000 worth of worms, in $10,000 increments. The quasi-proprietorship deal offered huge quarterly cash dividends beginning in the following year. It offered a share of the huge profitable sales of his crops. There were no financial reports from operations (or the tax return statements for his taxes at year-end) sent to the investor at the end of the first year, which raised the first question of accountability. At the end of the first quarter that next year there was no check in the mail either. Finally, the investor got the sad news; El Nino, the weather disrupting influence of 1997, had caused problems back on the farm, delaying the proposed check in the mail. Then the good news, the promoters declared a dividend of more worms in place of the cash.

PROS & CONS ABOUT PSEUDO STOCK INVESTMENTS

- The best investment is education and family. The rest will follow.
- Unregulated investments involve unsupervised individuals selling investments, which have not been reviewed or qualified by authorities.
- Tax losses are not a reason to buy any investment (Tax credits will be covered in another chapter).
- Investments away from the regulated stock market or licensed brokers must be specially investigated, along with their principals, for fraud. Your state agencies maintain lists of deals and unethical promotions.
- All investments must contain substance. If this is lacking, the deal is illusionary and the money will disappear and become an illusion as well.

- Iffy tax deals invite audits which are expensive and sleep-depriving, even if they can be won, but are very bad news if they are lost.

- Highly professional people from prestigious firms put together complex tax avoidance schemes for wealthy clients that are still struck down by the IRS. Note that Arthur Anderson, the huge accounting firm, that once created and sold questionable audit and tax avoidance schemes, is no longer in the accounting business.

- Tax avoidance is sometimes fraudulently flaunted in the local papers with ads such as "pay no California taxes by incorporating in Nevada". The truth is that if the business does anything in California, a corporate return and resulting taxes will result from that economic activity, regardless of where it is incorporated. Your common sense or reliable professional counsel should prevail over the "if it's too good to be true, then it must be untrue" rule.

CHAPTER 7: APPLICATION EXERCISES

1. Unregulated investments involve unsupervised individuals selling investments, which have not been reviewed or qualified by authorities. ____ True ____ False

2. A corporation that does business in California can avoid paying California state taxes if they are incorporated in Nevada. ____ True ____ False

3. Extreme caution should be exercised about investments that offer fantastic, outrageous or tax-advantaged returns. ____ True ____ False

4. Real estate rentals are a popular way to produce loss deductions on your tax return. ____ True ____ False

5. The Great Tax Increase Code of 1986 included active/passive loss limitations and changes in the depreciation rules. ____ True ____ False

6. The Success Story is an example of entrepreneurship and American capitalism enabled by:
    ____ a. Economic local expansion of nearby Second World War Steel works
    ____ b. A farmer and his family becoming contractors to build housing on his farmland
    ____ c. Advantages of integration opportunity to build his local hardware and lumber yard
    ____ d. Building a church for his community and family as an example of returning his wealth
    ____ e. All of the above
    ____ f. None of the above

7. What is the Worm Farm Horror Story about?
    ____ a. Successful agribusiness opportunities
    ____ b. Worm farm investments
    ____ c. An opportunity to own your own business with proposed prodigious profits
    ____ d. An opportunity to take profits in inventory instead of missing tax statements showing losses
    ____ e. All of the above
    ____ f. None of the above

8. Some national accounting firms have created questionable tax shelters for their clients:

    ___ a. That defy the Tax Code to save tons of tax money

    ___ b. That cannot fail because of the collective expertise of firm lawyers and accountants

    ___ c. Which are guaranteed to fly before IRS scrutiny and audits

    ___ d. That earn huge fees for proposed tax savings for their wealthy clients

    ___ e. All of the above

    ___ f. None of the above

9. Alternate Minimum Tax (AMT):

    ___ a. Is a tax refund scheme

    ___ b. Was created in the Great Tax Act of 1986 to eliminate most passive loss tax shelters

    ___ c. Was outlawed by Congress

    ___ d. Shortened the life and increased the deductibility of real estate depreciation write-offs

    ___ e. All of the above

    ___ f. None of the above

10. Pseudo Stock investments are:

    ___ a. Sold by reputable brokerage firms

    ___ b. Offer exceptional opportunities for wealth creation

    ___ c. Usually vetted as illegal and not sold by reputable brokerages

    ___ d. Oftentimes involve marvelous tax avoidance schemes

    ___ e. All of the above

    ___ f. None of the above

CHAPTER EIGHT

DIVIDENDS, STOCK SPLITS, VOTING-NONVOTING, PREFERRED STOCKS, COMMON STOCKS & RIGHTS

We live in a society where everything has a cost. The cost of a relationship is commitment. The cost of a bank loan is interest. The cost of a corporate stock issued initially is lawyer fees and later cash dividends. If a new corporation is not paying dividends because the cash-starved young firm is striving to grow, the cash dividends, if any, from earnings are reinvested. Then how do these corporations reward investors? By increases in stock values which is a capital gain. Capitalization of a firm can be from three sources: the first is from issuing stocks, the second is by borrowing money, and the third is by reinvesting dividends. Securities capitalization is the sum value of outstanding stocks at market value.

It is nearly impossible for new firms to borrow money when they have no collateral, which comes from reinvested earnings (after taxes) and stocks issued. This leaves no choice except to keep issuing more stock, which must be legally authorized by the SEC. Cash dividends are the only way a corporation can distribute earnings to shareholders. Corporations must pay federal and state income taxes on earnings and distribute dividends from the remainder. The net amount of earnings after taxes and dividends remains in the company to increase equity capital. The company **Board of Directors (BOD)** meets quarterly to review earnings and arrive at the amount of dividends paid or retained. **10-Q** documents report to the SEC quarterly informing the public about the financial condition of the company. Stock prices bounce up and down after the earnings are publicly released.

Corporations sometimes find themselves with extra cash and favorably low (but sometimes high) prices on their stocks. If the money is not required for capital improvements or expansion, the BOD may decide to buy some of their outstanding stocks back from the shareholders. This move actually conserves cash in the future because there will be fewer stocks outstanding to pay dividends on. They could now increase the dividends per share without spending more money or increased earnings than before. The **repurchased treasury stock** increases the book value of the outstanding shares as well.

Older blue-chip corporations will sometimes pay dividends from cash reserves even when earnings are down, to maintain continuity of cash flow with shareholders who expect steady income from their investment. This also keeps the stock values higher and prevents panic-selling from some shareholders. The lack of cash can also keep corporate raiders or take overs, at bay.

Shares of stock trading in today's market tend to increase in value. As the company matures over the years, a $25 share might have edged up to $250 per share. There are two reasons for this, the first is that retained earnings increase the book value and the second is the speculative perceived value of the company's future earnings or market potential. The BOD might one day decide that the outstanding shares are priced too high for some trading, and will divide the shares up by reissuing two or more shares for every outstanding share. Thus, a five-for-one split of this stock would result in $50 shares which could put more pressure on the overall stock prices because investors could buy a round lot (100 shares) for $5,000 instead of $25,000. The result would be overall higher stock prices because of increased trading and perceived affordability. Higher stock prices always please corporate management because of their stock options, which then result in taking profits when exercised. Increased stock prices are always viewed as confirmation of corporate success within the business world. The increase in shares from the split also divides the dividends resulting in no actual increase in share values or dividends afterward. Stock prices are known to defy gravity by increasing when the businesses lose money. Examples are Facebook and Tesla.

Officers' compensations are required to be scheduled on the year-end **10-K** financial statements and SC 13D/G reports to the SEC as part of the public disclosure process. This is because the effect of hidden stock options, which are a great part of executive compensation, are now required to be reported along with other compensation. Since you need to know, the SEC Internet website is www.sec.gov and all public company information reports are posted here.

The above securities are voting common shares of stock, which is the general source of capital for corporations. These shares carry one vote per share as well because the passive shareholders technically have a voice in company management. The BOD represents these shareholders and are also elected by shareholders, themselves at the annual meetings. Shareholders are mailed a voting proxy form (**SEC form DEF 14A**) for special corporate events. Somehow, many large corporations appear divorced from shareholder interests by a self-serving BOD that ignores economic reality when it comes to excess executive compensation and other management issues. Management gets around the shareholders by creating management compensation committees that they control. Holders of large security blocks, such as state pension plans, have now taken active roles to protect their investments. If a block of stock equal to 5% or more of the outstanding shares is owned by a single party or entity, notification is required by the **SEC (SC 13G)** of all shares of stocks bought or sold, including potential acquisitions or mergers.

On rare occasions, restructuring common shares outstanding as nonvoting, creates a special class of voting shares. This dastardly act upsets common shareholders because these shares short out the control the common shareholders have, over any corporate matters or electing the BOD. Nonvoting shares are issued only when the BOD is controlled by blocks of family shareholders that limit the value of trading on the open market because they act in their own self-interest. If the nonvoting stock is issued after the common, then an economic crime has been committed by the controlling interests, which are usually active executives. This also becomes a tax issue subject to revocation. Control and ownership by shareholders should be the same. Common folk do not usually elect Kings, or especially Dictators (sometimes they are surprised afterward). The Los Angeles Times had ownership problems in this area for many years.

Recently there have been estate planning considerations to split up small business stocks into two classes or voting and non-voting but a careful review of past IRS decisions indicate that a tax court case would eventually dislodge this type of event. The old rule, if it is too good to be true, it probably will not last nor prevail.

Large corporations, as an alternative to bank financing or debentures, can issue a class of preferred stocks. The **preferred shareholder** receives a stated fixed-dollar quarterly dividend. This dividend is always paid before common stock dividends; thus, they always are paid first. If there were not enough funds to pay either dividend, then the unpaid preferred dividend would accrue as arrears (owed). A separate class of **convertible-preferred stock** can also be issued that would allow the preferred shareholder to **convert his shares** (**a right**) to common stocks under certain conditions; that is, if the strike price is achieved. This is an alternative to borrowing money from other sources. This pseudo loan can default without a call.

Generally speaking, the payment of dividends is the healthy conduit of earnings from a corporation to its shareholder owners. Growth companies that use all earnings, if any, to finance expansion and corporations which are dying, do not pay dividends. The ratio of stock price to earnings is a barometer of the underlying value of an investment. Thus, a $100 stock paying a $5 annual dividend ($1.25 per share each quarter which theoretically equals to net after-tax earnings), would have a ratio of 20/1. Companies which never pay dividends, must reward investors by increasing stock values because all capital has a cash cost.

Many new companies also have reserved shares of stock to be issued to management at designated times or values. They have zero value until exercised but represent a dilution threat for other shareholders.

Some companies have dividend reinvestment plans, especially **Employee Stock Option Plans (ESOP)**, which allow dividends automatically to be reinvested to buy more shares of stock. Because all corporations pay any costs for registration and trading for their own securities, these **ESOP** plans are always advantageous unless the company is going down.

Money market funds, which earn fluctuating interest returns on financial instruments, pay the interest out as **1099 dividends** because the Money Market funds are a security. Savings & Loans and banks lay claim to money market accounts, which are really a savings account invested in short-term interest-bearing financial instruments, and report interest income paid on **1099 Interest** forms at year-end.

PLANNING TIPS

Stock prices usually anticipate dividend values. Dividends are always paid quarterly. A stock, which is about to pay a dividend to shareholders on record would be worth more before the dividend is paid. Thus, the market price of the shares would normally be a little higher before the dividends are issued. Shares traded close to the dividend declaration date of record are traded ex-dividend, which means that the dividends go to the prior shareholder. When buying or selling shares close to dividend dates check, to be sure who gets paid the dividend.

TAXES

Dividends, like interest income, are always taxed at ordinary income tax rates, even if reinvested and not received as cash. Dividends are doubly taxed distributions because the corporation must pay taxes on the income then pay dividends out of the remaining amounts where it is taxed again to the receiving individuals. This is a great inequity of our already unfair system of taxation. Since capital gains on stock sales are not taxed at the corporate level, more investor's emphasis has recently been on growth stocks than dividend-paying blue chips.

Because dividends increase adjusted gross income in an investor's tax return, they can cause a retired investor to additionally pay taxes on his Social Security benefits by increasing his income over the exclusion threshold ($25,000 single, $34,000 married but including some of the Social Security benefits received).

The Internal Revenue Service plays a tough game of taxing "excess" salaries, rents, and benefits as converted unpaid dividends when they audit small corporations. The IRS also applies excess capital rules that allow them to tax money held in the bank as undistributed dividends. This is a terrible method of double-taxing small businesses for non-deductible corporate money or retained earnings that are then taxed to the owner-shareholders as dividends.

LEGAL COMPLIANCE

Brokers sometimes induce buyers to buy stocks immediately, "because they will soon be paying a dividend, in a day or two." In some cases, savvy investors have already devalued the stock prices before the broker gives you the good news. The smart investors or brokerage firms holding the stocks are now selling them after the date of record when the dividends are declared, but before they are paid, and you are unknowingly buying them at discounted ex-dividend values. It is illegal for a broker to advise a client to buy a stock to receive a windfall dividend if the stock price has already anticipated the windfall.

SUCCESSFUL STRATEGIES

The best investment strategy in these times is to buy and hold. If you could buy a 100-share position of a newly established firm and reinvest the dividends for ten or more years, the results would seem miraculous. To hold a position from the IPO time would be best, but there are many losers before the winner's strategies, luck, and management survive and take hold. Dell, IBM…the oldest hi-tech, Microsoft, Intel, and other pre-Internet hi-tech firms have increased share value over the years due to market pressure on stock prices, inflationary effects, dividends reinvested in growth (not declared or paid) or by shareholder reinvestment, and good visionary management.

Every five years or so most firms undergo a cyclic period of introspection during which they must reinvent substantial parts of their business to survive in the World marketplace. Layers of surplus management can suddenly disappear from corporate reorganization. Younger companies will be the best bet for the long run. This New World marketplace requires brighter and fresher managers than many older industrial giants traditionally produce. An example of stagnant growth would be the automakers, which through historic oligopolistic market, share momentum and massive investment in plant and public culture defied the logic of change to meet the marketplace and grow with it. Unions have a structural hold on efficiency and innovation. Their marketplace control forced the buyers to compromise on old designs, poor quality, and high prices. Toyota, TESLA, and the World market have now broken the spell, except at GM. Therefore, there is still money made on the old blue chips, but more money with the newer newly established firms of the future.

HORROR STORY - ILLIQUID STOCK

A client inherited a large block of stock in a large established local bank that had several branches in town. The **closely held** bank had never paid dividends since inception. Most of the original shareholders had worked for the bank at one time or another in management positions because of **SEC 144 small business rules** that the stock could not be traded over the counter, but only to people well known to the holder.

The client's inherited shares had cost $25,000 many years ago. When he tried to sell them, he found there was no market. After communicating with the President of the bank, he found that the only market for the stock would be the current bank owner-managers who could buy back shares of stock. These people were apparently unwilling to buy the stock back because they controlled the business and since they never paid dividends. They had their big salaries, benefits, and pay for monthly board meetings. It cost the banks and limited shareholders no stocks in the client's hands. The client had an investment that paid no interest and was unredeemable. The investment acted as an interest-free loan to the bank, a very ugly security position. His only hope is that the bank would be absorbed or merged into a larger institution that would purchase his shares. If not, his stock was worthless because it was **illiquid**. Last hope is a bankruptcy which would give him a tax loss. Cash is king!

PROS & CONS OF ALL THE ABOVE

- Buying stocks for steady dividends is a good bet for retired folks if the stock price to dividend ratio is decent. In today's inflated equities market many blue-chip companies would fulfill this need. Most elderly people live off their social security and dividend checks, but the stocks were purchased many years ago, when they were much cheaper. Social Security cost of living (COL) increases are always understated while the stock market (DJIA) always overstates the cost of living increases.

- Preferred stocks are a substitute for corporate bonds. Why not buy the bonds instead? For this reason, very, few corporations today issue preferred stocks and they are not generally available. (See High Yield Investments later in this book.)

- Common stocks carry the right to vote for the Board of Directors. Unfortunately, the internal events leading up to these events, are usually preempted by the internal politics of the business and their committees. Do not count on electing the next president of General Motors.

- Do not buy stocks because they are about to pay a dividend. If you know they will pay a dividend, and you are early enough, it is okay. Otherwise, just pass or buy the stock because you like the company. In any case, check the ex-dividend date to see who will get the check and then check again to see if the stock price has already risen in anticipation.

- Stock splits help sell more stocks because people get all excited about the event. Investment, in growing companies that split frequently (amoebae multiply this way), tend to be good investments over the long run.

- Investments in companies, which pay dividends steadily over the years tend to be good investments because of their stability and massive economic inertia, which helps them survive economic change. Exceptions were Chrysler and General Motors which filed bankruptcy and washed out shareholders.

CHAPTER 8: APPLICATION EXERCISES

1. A 10K is a quarterly report filed with the SEC informing the public about the financial condition of the publicly held company.
    ___ True ___ False

2. Older blue-chip corporations will sometimes pay dividends from cash reserves even when earnings are down, to maintain continuity of cash flow with shareholders who expect steady income from their investment. ___ True ___ False

3. Common stocks carry the right to vote for the Board of Directors.
    ___ True ___ False

4. A preferred shareholder receives a stated fixed-dollar quarterly dividend, paid before common stock dividends. ___ True ___ False

5. Many new companies reserve shares of stocks to be issued to management at designed times or values which may dilute the value of the stock for other shareholders. ___ True ___ False

6. Treasury Stock is:
    ___ a. Stock issued by the US Treasury
    ___ b. Special series corporate stock issues
    ___ c. Repurchased stock shares by issuer corporations
    ___ d. Subjected to capital gains by the receiver organization
    ___ e. All of the above
    ___ f. None of the above

7. Dividends from C corporations:
    ___ a. Are deductions to the corporation
    ___ b. Are not taxable to the recipient
    ___ c. Can be issued from cash reserves instead of earnings
    ___ d. Decrease earnings and dilute equity
    ___ e. All of the above
    ___ f. None of the above

8. Shareholder classifications:
   ____ a. Common stock shareholders generally have one vote per share for Officers & Directors
   ____ b. Preferred Shareholders have preferences for dividends and the issue acts as Loans to the business
   ____ c. Convertible-preferred class shareholders have a right to convert shares to common stocks
   ____ d. Non-voting issues of stocks can be issued for controlling circumstances by family ownership
   ____ e. All of the above
   ____ f. None of the above

9. Dividends in general:
   ____ a. If issued by a credit union may be interest income
   ____ b. Can be taxed as ordinary income
   ____ c. Can be taxed as capital gains if distributions from securities
   ____ d. Are usually declared by the Board of Directors and paid quarterly afterwards
   ____ e. All of the above
   ____ f. None of the above

10. Illiquid stocks:
   ____ a. Are always listed on the NASDAQ
   ____ b. Are a part of most portfolios
   ____ c. SEC Rule 144 restricted stocks which cannot be sold because there is no market
   ____ d. Can be anybody's listed corporate business on the Pink Sheet
   ____ e. All of the above
   ____ f. None of the above

CHAPTER NINE

CLOSE CORPORATIONS, SECTION 1244
SECURITIES, VENTURE CAPITAL

A **close corporation** is a privately held business that has not publicly sold its stocks. Certain differences exist between close corporations, also called C {as in Common} because they are not special corporations. All corporations must conform to the SEC strict guidelines before public sale can commence. A certified audit is not required for close corporations at year-end, except for the firms with fiduciary responsibilities, which are responsible for other people's funds. The owners choose their own board of directors, and voting proxies are not required for changes in the BOD, corporate management or on any major issues. They tend to be patriarchal (perhaps the publicly traded Ford Motor Corporation is the corporate exception here), unlike most publicly held businesses. The biggest legal issues are usually updating the minute book annually and the annual secretary of state officer and shareholder statement.

Most non-public corporations would fall into the official **Small Business Association (SBA)** definition by having sales of less than five million annually and less than 75 shareholders (there are other small business definitions such as one million or less in capitalization for close corporations used by the IRS). They are the small successful businesses in town and include a few larger national companies that have grown internally from profits, and enjoy autonomy from public eyes.

A private corporation enjoys legal protection from individual liability called the "corporate veil" unless it represents a profession such as lawyers, dentists, doctors or accountants who buy liability insurance. Since a corporation is a legal entity, it files its own tax returns and pays a salary to the owners. If you have your own Corporation you can be subject to two audits, your individual and the corporations. The government loves to reclassify salaries and rents paid to owners as dividends, paid from after-tax earnings, but are taxable (again) on the owner-executive recipient's tax returns.

Close corporations are also **SEC Section 1244** Corporations. This is a **restricted stock corporation**, which is another way of saying the shares of stock are restricted to private ownership and cannot be sold to the public (at least not on the street corner to strangers). During the incorporation process, the new stock certificates are imprinted with the company name but with a blank in the corner for the number of shares issued with each certificate. This space is completed when the shares are issued. Most of these shares have a large legend stamped or printed across the face of the document that attests that the stock is a **restricted stock** and cannot be sold publicly.

Close corps cannot issue stock options for management because the stocks are not publicly traded and there is no benchmark value. Thus, they cannot make money on upward changes in stock prices, bought at lower amounts, because nobody is buying the stuff. The alternative is the phantom stock plan. This plan rewards management for corporate performance based on internal benchmarks such as free cash, sales goals, increases in equities or retained earnings, or internalized retained profits. They establish a comparable value that would increase the stock prices if publicly traded. These long-term (10-year) performance projections create **exercisable bonus options**. This is a simple redefinition of management bonuses, to get the responsible employee to work for the company without the stock market prices in the middle of the deal.

A C-Corporation (1120) can change to a special subchapter Status (you must petition the IRS for this one), which acts as a corporation for liability protection, and would file K-1 earnings schedules (like a partnership) in addition to W-2 salary forms for taxable income. The S corporation thus does not pay income tax (1120-S) but transfers all of the income or loss to the owners. An S Corp is ideal for a start-up business that expects to produce losses for the first few years. These losses can be applied to reduce other taxable income in the individual owner's (1040) tax returns. Because they are a return on invested capital as well as owner's personal earnings, there is a tendency to fudge and avoid paying Social Security (a.k.a. self-employment tax) taxes when the K-1 merges into the owner's personal tax returns.

Since a corporation is not a publicly listed corporation, how does it obtain capital for expansion? By borrowing from a bank, which will secure all the business assets it can by filing a form **UCC-1**, or by going public. The Universal Commercial Code form 1 is a state form that was preapproved by the Federal government as a standard legal form. Generally, the institution will attach personal assets as well, if the risk is high enough. Bunker Hunt lost his Rolex to the banks when trying to corner the silver market.

Successful businesses tend to go public. Sometimes unsuccessful businesses or new businesses with successful sounding ideas also go public. For this giant step to wealth or bankruptcy, they usually need an **Angel.** An Angel is a small venture capitalist who somehow "discovers" the business and provides "seed" money to jump-start the new firm. Now, we are not talking about the huge IPO ventures that keep the public investors drooling or hair on fire until they get a chance to jump on the passing train. No, these are usually small firms selling a concept or new product and need a vehicle to take it to the public arena as an **Initial Private Offering (IPO)**. The Angels are taking the greatest investment risk of all by investing their six-or-seven figure seed money to get the idea off the ground. Sometimes the Angels or shark tank hosts on television provide hands-on experience and management on a part-time basis to protect their investment. The angels always take an equity interest, because they are not a bank. They expect an entrepreneurial good return on their capital, not interest. They are also taking long odds that the business will work because this is the dangerous stage between idea and creating a working model for the next step. **Seed money Angels** can sometimes provide enough money and expertise to take the company public but sometimes more is not better at this stage. **Hedge funds** are generally in the bidding arena for larger issues.

The next step is not necessarily the IPO, which requires much money, connections, and backing. It is for more capital, at which time the well-heeled **Venture Capitalist** knocks on the door. Now the money is in seven figures and the new equity partner represents a group or partnership of investors who will plump up the concept, prepare a bigger and better business plan, and fill out the technical and management ranks in order to wire all the connections for the expensive legal moves for the IPO. The VC will expect to earn from 3-20 times his investment when the new firm goes public. Many firms will never go public, with the **failure rate at about 70%,** even among the best VC bets. For secondary market funding, the VC will retire old debt if possible, to satisfy management and lenders alike.

How are Angels and VC people found? By professional and technical networking! People talking to people, not an ad in the Yellow Pages. Here we are talking about people who are knowledgeable about your business or work with you. In today's technical world, ideas are gold and electricity still moves at almost the speed of sound so everything connected to the computer is hot and fast. Today's ideas are not about how to melt iron ore faster; they are about computer applications and software or electronic shortcuts to synthesize the mechanical elements inside the "**Box**". Most of these ideas come to life in the Silicon Valley area (San Jose) above San Francisco where millionaires are created overnight and ideas abound like electrons. The number crunching MBAs of the business world do not work here; they are in New York or Boston creating or unscrambling the next Hedge Fund disaster (blame it on the computer model). The gold rush from Northern California to the NASDAQ is the product of the good technical schools that immerse these geniuses in the electronic synergy of the future. Venture Capitalists and visiting Angels provide the capital and management expertise matrix to make it happen.

PLANNING TIPS

Venture capitalists make their money on stock options and on stocks purchased when they initially invest in the company. There are risks and dangers to the ventures due to the following:

- may not take hold
- may be too late for the marketplace
- have inadequate management to grow to fruition

- may lack enough capital to successfully get public
- may not be feasible
- the stock market or economy may not ready when the firm is.

A bad plan could break over patent disputes or technical failure, collapse from bad strategy, failure from an inability to merge with necessary technical partners, and bad chemistry between managers or with the financial community. A good tip is probably to consult your crystal ball to make sure the stars are lining up right. Better yet is to look the people in the eyes to show you can trust them with their investment money and make them believe in the "idea" as much as you do.

TAXES

We are still working with equities so the capital gain or loss on stock purchases is recognized only when the stock is sold (or liquidated in a bankruptcy). Dates and timing are important for losses in tax returns. A stock option is different because the **option (purchase) is exercised** only at the time of sale. The money that changes hands is the profit from the difference in the option price and the market price (**strike price**). This is a **short-term gain** subject to ordinary income taxability. Many companies are now marking down the purchase (cost) price of options to reflect lower levels in the stock market, thus making sure management gets a profit even when they have the opportunity to unload in a lower market. So much about the added value concept of successful management remuneration! Value is not just sales or net earnings; it is the Concept of **Total Market Valuation**---the value of the number of shares outstanding at the current market price.

At year-end, equities could be sold to recognize losses, then purchased again to maintain a position in the stock. If the stock is repurchased within 30 days from the sale, a wash-sale tax problem arises due to a special tax ruling to disallow losses on reinvested repurchases. So, it is best to wait at least 30 days before reacquiring the securities or the loss will be disallowed. Year-end is always the best time to sell losers, to take a tax loss.

Corporations are allowed to deduct qualified charitable donations of up to 10% of taxable earnings. A qualified charity is a tax-exempt organization that is not run by your brother-in-law. This is a good way to get money out of the corporation for a good cause. Successful corps accumulate funds that are hard to get out without paying more wages, benefits or taxable dividends…all which have tax consequences to the recipient. Paying it directly to the charity is as easy as writing a deductible check for a legitimate expense. Why pay it out of income that has already been taxed at the individual level? What if you do not usually itemize?

A Corporation can carry net operating losses back three years and any remaining losses forward for five more. If a Corp has had successful tax-paying years when suddenly a disaster happens, the results can desperately refund taxes paid for corporate earnings in the good years. Your accountant will gladly file the forms for you, especially if he has had problems being paid lately. The refund and carryback of losses are completed when the current 1120 corporate tax returns are filed with final year-end data.

Capital gains from property not used in the course of business have no special tax rate, the same as inventory. But, a capital loss is subjected to limitations (can only offset other capital gains). This is a great reason to keep real estate out of the business and rent it to the corporation. That way the individual favorable tax rates will work for you. The basic rule is that real estate should also be out of the business because of taxable appreciation over the years. It can also be separated from corporate liabilities.

LEGAL COMPLIANCE

Buying shares of unlisted stocks are almost completely without protection. These stocks cannot be advertised to attract new buyers (owners). They may become completely illiquid if the company fails or if the founder will not buy them back. The best way to get a proper return on investment is through an IPO but that means that you are either the initial progenitor or the venture capitalist to be at the head of the line initially. Arriving at the winning end of a small-maybe-public-some-day business is like striking it rich, and that is why VCs call it **prospecting.**

SUCCESSFUL STRATEGIES

A young man from Boston always wanted to become a radio person. This was back in the 1950s when Big Radio was the alternate to movie media and CBS was the stock to own, not Disney, yet. He hung about radio stations in town making a nuisance of himself by getting in the way to run errands and help around the place. They liked his enthusiasm and did not mind his questions and observations while absorbing all the thousands of details that make up any technical business. He attended college nearby but quit when he was offered a full-time job at a local station. Somehow, he saved his money by living like a miser, once worked for an auto manufacturer got married and divorced without children, and moved to California. All of this in a few short years.

In California, he took on a financial partner and bought a low wattage radio station. This station operated out of a van while living in a motel that leased ground floor business space for the people who did not generate people traffic, such as retailers. The man operated the station, day and night living next door, while his partner found advertising clients in the City. In business, the inside man always wins because he has his hands on the controls, so it was a matter of time before the sales partner was bought out and the business moved to better quarters at the Mission Inn in Riverside, California.

This man was obsessed with the business and his new wife. He became a technical giant in the time of vacuum tubes and rectifiers. The business grew and he became an extension of it, sleeping and breathing the airwaves, living in the hotel a few rooms away from the business near the Rotunda. He had an opportunity, and they happen often for a person always doing the same dedicated job, totally immersed as they become in an industry, to purchase a higher wattage station and he did so. Now with a larger market reaching into Metropolitan Los Angeles, he outgrew his rented space and moved to another part of town where he built his own large office building with two complete sound studios. The record library room was as big as a small house and filled with records from that era. The man, who was truly an electronic genius, ran prepared music with a minimum of inside staff while he concentrated on programming and managing the sales force. Because the business was efficient, he purchased a fine house next door so he could always be close to his work. He was so dedicated to the business that he never left on vacation even though he owned new cars traded for radio advertising and could have gone to Hawaii free from a travel agency client.

This is a true example of how a person with a single purpose in life can accomplish his goals by using a financially active partner (Venture Capitalist) when necessary and evolving a business worth many millions of dollars. It is also worth noting that the only money he ever owed, after paying off his partner, was the mortgage on the large studio-office building. Investment Advisors consider interest expense as "consuming next year's seed crop money," a danger to future growth. His corporation thrived and absorbed three radio stations in all before the business ended.

HORROR STORY - THE RADIO STATION

Many things in life are balanced. There is a time for everything; such as good vs evil, a time to find, and to lose, etc. The above radio station entrepreneur is now in jail for murder (over a woman). All of the wealth has dissipated over legal fees. The radio station sale was suspended over the **FCC Second Thursday ruling**. This famous court case reinforced the government's position that the airwaves are public property and a felon cannot profit or benefit from their sale. State ABC statutes apply the same moral restrictions when issuing liquor licenses.

His ex-wife once claimed he could build a radio station from scraps of wire and make it work. Perhaps the call letters would now be Radio C-O-N. A very sad ending to the beautiful story of a truly successful entrepreneur, who could buy almost everything he wanted in life. Sometimes the seeds of success contain the DNA strand of failure as well. Afterward, I testified to the court and jury that he kept his business compliant with other business matters and his purchase of executive liability insurance paid off in a wrongful death suit.

SECOND HORROR STORY - ILLIQUID STOCKS CONTINUED

The client was an American Indian whose father was quite successful in his time before casino brought wealth to many. He inherited stocks in a Long Beach bank for a good deal of money and wanted a broker to cash them in. Unfortunately, his stocks were in a small bank which was capitalized by very few people. The certificates were not publicly traded. That means he could only sell them to people he personally knew, back to the bank for treasury stock redemption, or to the other shareholders. I couldn't trade an unlisted security and suggested that he contact the management people at the bank directly. He did and the response was that they weren't interested in the bank securities.

The client's father had bought **illiquid stocks** that may never be redeemed unless the bank merged, was sold or went out of business. It probably was part of the initial capitalization where several people decided to open their own bank. They put money and family assets into the bank and had very limited capital. To acquire more capital, they sold shares to others they knew but would have no management or true ownership interests in the operations. As the years went on the family or families operating the bank got good jobs and perks but the other shareholders were ignored and treated as bondholders, but with small or no dividends. That is the danger of closely held corporations. This business, as a FDIC Federally Deposit Insured Corporation would have annual certified audits but the shareholder interest was beyond the scope of the financial audits. The client will never be able to recover the investment until something changes.

PROS & CONS OF CLOSE CORPORATIONS AND VENTURE CAPITAL

- A close corporation is a separate legal entity tax-wise which acts as an extension of the incorporating founders. Thus, ownership is never separated from management control or remuneration. It is the best business form for successful small business because it takes the whole business out of the personal tax returns while providing better fringe benefits and family succession. This business cannot be sold by exchanging stock for cash and changing management without liquidation of assets.

- Stock in a close corporation can be sold without closing the doors, selling assets, changing names or closing the business itself because it is the sale of securities, not the business and the gains or losses go to the seller (owner) of the business' securities allowing uninterrupted continuity.

- A public corporation is subject to the scrutiny of the SEC and IPO scrutiny but is the logical source of public financing through the sale of securities.

- A business partner, unless providing a complementary function to the business (you handle sales, I'll take care of production) tends to become a source of legal contrition at later dates.

- A financial partner is a dangerous kind of bank loan who takes days off when needed, will make unreasonable demands on company resources and people, and can destroy the company on a wild weekend. They love opening the mail and doing the banking.

- Venture capitalists are the proper avenue for expansion by providing management guidance, proper business plans, and capital for growth. Their price is for a big piece of the action.

- Corporations can receive cash refunds from taxes paid in the past recent years, if the current year shows a net operating loss.

- Angels can be related family financial interests or small financiers, after the mortgage refinance runs out.

- Vertical integration, which are companies buying smaller companies (usually by exchanging securities) to aid in basic profit center functions, works in reverse with opportunities to sell out to larger firms. The big fish eating the little fish analogy. This is a viable option for an entrepreneur who may have lost his ambition or want to get away from his business.

- Business is a tough game with opportunities to go broke or make it big. The risks are so real that many business people commit fraud to make it work. There is always the moral issue of survival or success. Fortunately, not everybody needs to make that critical decision.

- A management consultant friend summed it up for me one day. The President of every company I have met is always the best salesperson. He will sell you the company as well as the product. Be a good salesperson to succeed and grow your business.
- Beware of corporate shells that are formed to attract investors but lack the business plan and substance to perform a truly viable investment function. They can be an illegal hollow sham arrangement.
- Corporations are a poor place to keep appreciable assets such as real estate, because there are no favorable capital gains taxes and capital losses are limited. Best to lease which creates individual passive income.

CHAPTER 9: APPLICATION EXERCISES

1. Venture capitalists make their money on stock options and on stocks purchased when they initially invest in the company.
    ___ True ___ False

2. Corporations are allowed to deduct qualified charitable donations of up to 15% of taxable earnings. ___ True ___ False

3. Corporations can receive cash refunds from taxes paid in the past recent years, if the current year shows a net operating loss.
    ___ True ___ False

4. Privately held corporations are a poor place to keep appreciable assets such as real estate, because there are no favorable capital gains taxes and capital losses are limited. ___ True ___ False

5. Total Market Valuation is the value of the number of shares outstanding at the current market price. ___ True ___ False

6. Restricted Stock Corporations:
    ___ a. Are very uncommon
    ___ b. Can be publicly traded if they get big enough
    ___ c. Are small businesses which are restricted to private non-public ownership
    ___ d. Can issue stock options for management

7. Initial Private Offerings (IPO) usually:
    ___ a. Need an Angel Venture Capitalist for seed financing and to be discovered
    ___ b. Don't survive the 70% new business failure rate
    ___ c. Retire old debt for a new IPO
    ___ d. Take a large equity interest and will expect to earn 3 to 20 times investment
    ___ e. All of the above
    ___ f. None of the above

8. Stock Options are:
    ___ a. Taxable as long-term gains
    ___ b. Automatically exercised if the stock values decline on the strike date
    ___ c. Taxable as short-term taxable income through payroll
    ___ d. Never exercised as a sale and purchase on the same day
    ___ e. All of the above
    ___ f. None of the above

9. The Horror Story involving a Radio Station murder is about:
   ___ a. The Second Thursday ruling, concerning corporate record keeping
   ___ b. An entrepreneur who built a radio station empire with inherited money
   ___ c. An entrepreneur whose wife left him for another man, who he murdered
   ___ d. A man whose business was his life and afterward started a radio con from jail
   ___ e. All of the above
   ___ f. None of the above

10. Which of the following is discussed in the Second Horror Story about a bank:
   ___ a. Banks, because their depositors are insured by the FDIC, are always publicly traded
   ___ b. Banks, before they go public, must redeem all their outstanding stock
   ___ c. A Long Beach, California bank issued $25,000 in stocks to a wealthy individual and years later refused to buy back the shares, which made the stock illiquid
   ___ d. Selling small business stocks is legal in California
   ___ e. All of the above
   ___ f. None of the above

CHAPTER TEN
REAL ESTATE INVESTMENT TRUSTS

There are so many kinds of REITs that to describe them is like asking a cat person what colors cats come in. REIT is a real estate corporation that acts as a trust. The origins of the first REITs date back to the 1880s when trusts were not taxed as corporations because the dividends flowed through to individuals. The REIT issues stock shares and can be a publicly-traded organization or privately traded (with a prospectus) corporation. The public Corp is found on the NY, AMEX, or NASDAQ listings where it can be tracked for performance and price. Most REITs are quite large, with about 1/3 billion dollars average capitalization. The other REIT is private, which means there is no public source of information, thus the big prospectus, and that only the corporation itself can sell or buy your shares back; it's almost like a limited partnership with limited exposure to investors.

Modern REITs were created when President-General Eisenhower signed the **Real Estate Trust Tax Law of 1960**. Basically, the provisions are that there must be over 100 shareholders and that most of the investments must be in real estate. This made an investment offering possible for the general public, instead of becoming one of the terrible Section 144 privately held (with restricted stock) small business corporations. A REIT is very special tax-wise though. The corporation pays no income taxes at all if 95% or more of the net income is regularly distributed to the shareholders. This eliminates the double taxation of corporations that pay corporate taxes (very high) and distribute the remainder as taxable dividends. Of course, the whole distribution becomes taxable to the recipient unless part of an IRA or pension.

All REITs are in the real estate business. Some of them simply manage mortgages and redistribute the cash income directly through the central organization, acting as a mortgage holder or bank (**financial REIT**) for the shareholders. Other REITs, the more common ones, purchase and manage or operate the real estate (**equity REIT**). There are two keys to the REIT business; the first is management. How efficient and experienced are the principals at buying and managing the property? The second is financing. Privately traded REITs have an initial financing cost of about 10% including registration and start-up costs. Bank financing (leverage) has smaller initial costs mostly from organizing expenses but also has an ongoing interest cost. Thus, there are usually some of both in the deal because large purchases or new construction take-out money needs to be financed while new investor capital flows into the corporation. On an ongoing basis, if the property is efficiently managed, the return on capital from leases (**cap rate**) can exceed bank-financing costs, and a blend of some leverage to investor capital is usually optimized to maximize investor returns.

REITs tend to specialize by property types. One will offer office buildings while another could be strip shopping centers. In 1965, one REIT was a single building, called the Pinnacle Building, in Burbank, California. Later on, the principals would look the other way when asked how it went. Today, however, REITs own and manage over 8% of the commercial real estate market in this country.

REITs tend to grow into huge organizations owning many millions of square feet in property. They start out privately and go public when reaching proper critical mass. Then all the shareholders usually get a bump in share price over what they initially paid. Going public does not create internal profits; in fact, it would dilute earnings for new shareholders or if additional shares are authorized and sold because the share price is higher. Also, the internal value of the real estate holdings of the REIT may have appreciated so a higher public trading price could return equity to the shareholders. A public REIT offers an easier way for shareholders to sell their stocks on the open market without selling it back to the corporation or the secondary market. At this time there are hundreds of Public REITs and even Index funds of REITs. Today REITs are in most investor's portfolios and are offered in mutual funds and some variable annuity's investment spectrum of managed assets. REITs are a powerful economic deep pocket force that can acquire existing properties for cash or have new projects built for them.

Then how can some REITs lose money? The health of a REIT is simply cash flow. If the cash pulse is not beating, then the properties are badly managed or the purchase price was too high. Rents can fall in a recession or the neighborhood could go sour. The management (which could be a brokerage firm) may have bought bad properties just to have a REIT to sell; they might have tenant vacancy problems, maybe too much leverage with the rents going to the bank instead of shareholders, or very high administrative costs. Sometimes the organizers are financial people who wheel and deal with numbers and have lack skills needed to acquire and manage good properties. There is always a secondary market, highly discounted, to buy back REITs from shareholders with cash needs.

Economic factors can enter into the profitability of REITs. A REIT of shopping malls can be affected by changes in retailing (Internet), changes in population demographics, newer competitive malls, overbuilding in some areas, and an economic downturn. All of these factors can lead to lower rents and vacancies. This liquidity problem translates into a lack of capital for distributions or to buy back shares from shareholders. Illiquidity is also the danger of most close corporations.

PLANNING TIPS

The simplest method of determining the viability of a REIT is to look at the cash flow. If there is negative cash or no distributions, then feel lucky you are looking at other people's problems, not your own. If the cash flow is high, then these are good properties that are well managed. Private REITs will return better earnings than Public because the share prices are lower (not bid up over the market). A newly organized REIT, no matter how well managed, will have lower earnings than an established one because of organizational and growth costs.

1993 tax law changes allowed pensions to include REITs for the first time, which is a logical move since corporate shares are transferable (can be bought and sold) and they are a tangible viable equity and producer of dividends. The average dividend yield of a REIT is about 8%, which is six times that of the Russell 2,000 average dividend.

REITs have two goals. The first is to acquire good properties that will generate solid earnings, the other is to go public and create a bump in share price for additional capitalization or profit-taking. Thus, you need to buy private and look hard at the experience of the people putting it together if it is new. A private REIT will state in the prospectus if they intend to go public later (if they get big and good enough). REITs usually sell original shares at $10 until they cease and go public.

REIT earnings can be reinvested directly back into the corporation to buy more shares unless it is in a retirement plan. The reinvestment usually buys shares at a reduced cost because there is no selling commission and administration (like mutual fund reinvested earnings) expense. This is a good way to increase holdings at a reduced cost if there is no immediate need for taxable cash dividends.

TAXES

Earnings from a REIT are on a 1099 dividend form, the same as other passive investments. They are subject to ordinary income taxes. Because real estate and organizational costs are subjected to straight-line depreciation and financing costs are immediately deductible by the REIT, the distributions do not vary much from the actual earnings. The cash distributions received will be higher than the taxable income, however. The sale of REIT shares are capital gains or losses and subject to capital gains rules.

LEGAL COMPLIANCE

Private REIT sales are restricted about the same as limited partnership sales by most BD firms. There are restrictions on investor net worth and income, which vary by state. A prospectus must be delivered to the investor at the time of sale. Commissions and selling costs paid by the REIT are without reducing the customer investment, so they are not required to be disclosed. Most REITs will restrict the repurchase of investor shares for the first year and will charge the investor a fee afterward. This gives the REITs more liquidity than limited partnerships, resulting in REIT deals replacing older illiquid real estate partnership deals in broker-investor offerings. Repurchases and redemptions are highly restricted.

A publicly traded REIT is purchased through the stock exchanges, the same as any ordinary stock purchase. The purchase amount for additional authorized shares should be a more efficient source of corporate funds because the prior high expenses of sales commissions from private share sales will not be required.

SUCCESSFUL STRATEGIES

Integrity is easier to define, than to find. The object of this book is not to sell investments but to inform the reader about them. One REIT in the mid-west was born 30 years ago by school teaching people who fell in love with real estate through buying old houses and apartments and managing (another word for repair, remodel, renovate, and evict) them after work evenings and weekends. They sacrificed work for play and family time, a common characteristic of professional entrepreneurs. Decades of hands-on growth and experience led these schoolteachers to leave their teaching jobs to manage a very large portfolio. The portfolio grew and grew exponentially with a vast experience of difficulties in various deals.

Presently these very conservative people manage millions of square feet of property and the conservative principals of major REITs in the mid-West. The key to their success is hands-on experience and conservative management. There are no chauffeured limousines in their parking lot. Nothing fancy is noticed about the plain office building which houses dozens of lawyers and accountants monitoring the properties. Nothing fancy except the high earnings flowing monthly to investors.

HORROR STORY - CALIFORNIA REAL ESTATE

This chapter is really about real estate. The California economy in recent decades has been difficult to commercial real estate deals. Real estate values follow the terrible economic roller coaster busts and crashes, like ocean swells behind a storm, the effects of which are experienced long after the storm has departed. Real estate is by nature a large capital long-term investment subjected to fixed costs and financing but strongly influenced by short-term economics. The volatile California real estate market has spawned many real estate tragedies that hardly fit the best-made plans for investors. Most investor participation, from the brokerage point of view, has been limited partnerships. Their long-term maturity has led to many losses and cash flow problems for their investors. In Southern California at this time of writing, some commercial real estate property values are still less than the prevailing selling prices ten years ago.

For the above reasons, most successful REITs stay clear of the California market at this time. The Pinnacle building is probably still in Burbank but the REIT probably is not.

PROS & CONS ABOUT REAL ESTATE INVESTMENT TRUSTS

- A REIT is only as good as its management. Find good antecedents on these people before you think of investing.
- The geographical area of the REIT is very important because some areas are lucrative and others are dead as a doornail (what is a doornail?).
- The type of property is important. Some work much better than others. Rental REITS would do well in upscale areas where housing is scarce, shopping centers in others.
- REITS can be illiquid during inception, although buyback provisions are available in a highly discounted **secondary market**. It is always impossible to cash in your shares in the first year (the prospectus tells you so). Keep in mind that real estate is capital intensive and requires highly fixed commitments.
- A properly managed REIT will provide steady cash distributions of income, a great source of retirement benefits, without enduring the difficulties of the equity market. At this time with the market cap over 30X earnings, the REITs could provide better distributions than insurance fixed annuities.

- REITS also provide inherent equity build-up thus increasing the IRR over the actual distributions, because good properties usually increase in value with inflation. The rents are indexed to inflation and the value of the properties indexed to rents... see how easy it is!

- REITS should provide increased cash flow over the years as rents increase due to inflation. This would provide automatic inflation protection for the retired investor.

- REITS should be considered for portfolio balancing as an alternative to the excessive equity concentrations found with most investors today.

- Watch for performance consistency in REIT offers from brokerage firms. Did they make money on the last one? Is the new deal slammed together just to have a REIT to sell to their investors? Do you really feel good about the deal?

CHAPTER 10: APPLICATION EXERCISES

1. The Real Estate Trust Tax Law of 1960 states that there must be over 100 shareholders and that most of the investments must be in real estate. ____ True ____ False

2. Some REITs manage mortgages and redistribute the cash income directly through the central organization, acting as a mortgage holder or bank for the shareholders. ____ True ____ False

3. REIT earnings cannot be reinvested directly back into the corporation unless it is for a retirement plan. ____ True ____ False

4. A properly managed REIT will provide steady cash distributions of income, a great source of retirement benefits without enduring the difficulties of the equity market. ____ True ____ False

5. Publicly traded REITs are purchased through the stock exchanges, the same as any ordinary stock purchase. ____ True ____ False

6. Which statement is true:
    ____ a. REIT capitalization is not through banks, thus dividends are not fixed as mortgages would be
    ____ b. A REIT is a special real estate corporation
    ____ c. REITs begin as private investments with shareholder subscribers
    ____ d. REIT corporations not only own the properties but completely manage them
    ____ e. All of the above
    ____ f. None of the above

7. REITs:
    ____ a. Are Trusts and file fiduciary tax returns
    ____ b. Are privately financed by stock subscriptions until they are a gigantic business which go public
    ____ c. Must distribute 100% of the net income to shareholders
    ____ d. Cannot reinvest dividends in the private stage of ownership
    ____ e. All of the above

8. Which of the following is true regarding REIT restrictions:
   ___ a. Selling commissions are disclosed
   ___ b. Publicly traded REITs have higher corporate subscription costs than when private
   ___ c. Provide no liquidity for purchasers during the private stage of development
   ___ d. Sales are restricted by BD firms, same client qualifications as limited partnerships
   ___ e. All of the above

9. Which of the following are REIT tax considerations:
   ___ a. Dividends are not taxable because they are return of capital
   ___ b. Dividends are larger after the shares are redistributed as a public corporation
   ___ c. Economic downturns do not affect distributions because of leases
   ___ d. Dividends are reported on a 1099 form as passive income
   ___ e. All of the above

10. Which statement is false:
    ___ a. During bad economic times, REIT earnings can decline from broken or non-renewed leases
    ___ b. Over the years REITs should prosper (IRR) because of inflation and increased rents
    ___ c. Because of illiquidity during inception, discounted secondary market sales are possible
    ___ d. Antecedents and past performance of managers should not be a consideration when buying

PART TWO

BONDS

Bonds are interest-bearing certificates issued by any government, institution, or corporation. To a stockbroker, they are the most conservative long-term (money market would be short-term) investment available to diversify his client's portfolio. They represent the capitalization of both government and industry; thus, bonds will be diverse by nature and gigantic in monetary scope. It has been stated that the Rothschild banks financed the English war against Napoleon. If so, then it should come as no surprise that a minor change in the interest rates charged by the **Federal Reserve Board**, when the **Discount interbank rates** are altered, or when they inject money into the economy or subtract it from circulation by issuing or redeeming government securities, causes the bond market and whole economy to react instantly. The prime loan interest rates charged businesses change the next day, variable housing mortgage rates and payments change, margin rates securing security purchases change, and a hundred indexes move simultaneously. The seemingly secure bond market actually moves in waves with huge invisible underlying energy forces of economic change. As a result, the bond market to the average investor is an unknown sleeping giant of volatility.

CHAPTER ELEVEN

TAX-EXEMPT MUNICIPAL BONDS

Muni Bonds are a creation of Congress to fund state infrastructure projects. Many, many years ago, during the dawn of modern taxation, Congressmen found that they could turn their voters and supporters on by building pork barrel and some even useful projects with both federal and state tax-free interest-bearing financing. Better yet, the interest rates would be cheaper for the state government agencies, since they competed with low-interest federal government bonds which were taxable by the Internal Revenue Service, but not at the state level. Thus, the first **tax shelter** was born.

Financial institutions or the giant B/D firms purchase muni Bonds. They bid for blocks of the whole issue, which could be a toll road, sewer plant or local redevelopment movie house. They actually help determine the interest rate that the bond will pay. Remember that these bonds are secured by the above project. Try to imagine what happens when a toll road to nowhere folds or **Mello-Roos** development bonds have no payers. These are not secured financial instruments with repossessable assets! Then they mark them up and retail them directly to broker-dealers or institutional mutual fund customers. From this point on it will remain in a portfolio, which will collect the interest payments for the bondholders.

The interest rates are always slightly higher than US Government bonds, and much lower than corporate or almost any other financial instruments. They will always outweigh CD performance unless the investor is not a taxpayer. Munis are a **midpoint** between the **best risk quality for US Govt., medium for states**, and **lowest for corporate.** The **inverse interest rate yield** also follows: the lowest risk with the US Govt., medium for the state, and highest for corporate.

Some muni bonds are bundled and insured to compete with bank guaranteed deposits. This evades and competes with the $250,000 threshold for insured deposits at the banks and remaining savings and loans. The yield will be fractionally lower to offset the cost of the FDIC insurance. Elderly folks particularly like these investments because they always ask, "is the principal guaranteed?" Some elderly people have particularly long memories of the savings and loan fiasco that was created when the financial institutions were allowed equity participation in the projects they used to lend to (with strict lending guidelines). The results were a predictable speculative disaster and a completely new government agency, the **Resolution Trust Corporation**. It was created to bail them out (with taxpayer monetary assistance).

Only high-income people need muni bonds because the attraction is not just the interest rate, but the advantage of the tax-free interest. To put it simply, a six-percent muni bond could yield the same amount of cash as another nine or ten percent taxable bond. Of course, if a person is retired and in a low tax bracket with only a pension, some savings interest, and Social Security, then he would be better off with the higher-earning investments, providing that he is not risk-averse. The true **comparative yield** is simply cash remaining after taxes are paid.

Municipal bonds can be dangerous for the issuing agencies if they do not conform to the strict Federal tax guidelines. Riverside County, California recently lost a tax issue with the government because they failed some tests on a new development bond issue. Since the Federal Government couldn't go after all the taxpayers that ended up with the bonds, they simply fined the agency a huge amount for the taxes which will never be collected (the taxpayers covered again).

Some bond issues are important, such as for new schools, sewer projects, etc. Some are highly speculative and might compete directly with private enterprise, especially when they are redevelopment area bonds issued to develop slum areas or perceived economically deprived areas in town. Many hotels, entertainment projects, and other ventures have encountered disaster when built with the best wishes of City Hall and the wealth of bond indebtedness construction. Every town has a loser sports auditorium. All bonds need to be repaid, some easily from taxes collected in water bills or secured real property levies, but the redevelopment bonds might need to be repaid by the customers of the ritzy hotel in the wrong end of town, the grandiose dance hall featuring Lawrence Welk Big Bands, or giant movie theatres next door to loser movie theatres. The usual problem with redevelopment projects is that the people fled the old town for good reasons and new developments rarely bring them back. If those ventures fail to pay the bond notes then bankruptcy results and you know what that does to creditors. Unfortunately, the federal tax tests on issuer audits appear to concern how the bonds are issued, not necessarily what they are issued for.

PLANNING TIPS

Muni bonds are great for balancing a large portfolio. Sometimes the advantages of liquidity and low risk are ignored in the rush for speculative high equity returns. Individual purchases of munis can be speculative however, if they represent pork-barrel redevelopment projects, which could fail. The best bet would be mixed holdings in a large mutual fund, which could cushion or avoid adverse investments in their large portfolios. Their professional management could presumably exclude the dangerous projects, if conservation of principal is one of their goals. There are muni bond funds that have no state. That is, they have many different states bonds in their portfolio, thus qualifying for no single state tax exemption. Keep away from these funds, which would be federal tax-exempt but not state (unless you live in Texas or Nevada, which have no state taxes). I wonder what they call their infrastructure bonds. Puerto Rico bonds actually qualify as state tax-exempt although the place is not a state, but most likely to fail. All wealthy Americans have large positions of munis in their portfolio.

TAXES

Remember this: All interest earned is taxed by both Federal and state. Except: US Government bonds, which are only taxed by the same issuing government, and muni bonds which are taxed by neither the US Government nor state. Please note that under the Constitution, the states do not have the power to tax the Federal Government.

Muni bonds are only tax-free in the state-issued. If you live in NY and file New York tax returns and have bought a muni bond position in a mutual fund which does not specify that the bonds are all in your state, then the bonds are Federal tax-exempt only. Be sure the state name is in the mutual fund name (example: New York Municipal Bond Fund) or that the bonds you bought were from the state where you will file your tax returns. Each state's muni bonds are never taxable on the Federal returns, however.

Capital gains and losses can be realized by trading (buying or selling) bonds. Thus, there can be gains or losses on your tax return if you sell any individually owned muni bond shares or if your mutual fund does some trading during the year (they always do). All bonds when sold or traded mark to the current interest rate market. Thus, they will trade at a premium or discount of face value depending on the interest rate (**coupon**) of the original issue. If a 10-year bond at 5% sells five years later in a 6% market, then the bond will be discounted because it will earn 1% less than comparable new issues for each of the remaining five years.

LEGAL COMPLIANCE

Large brokerage firms have huge portfolios of financial products to sell. Their technical sales skills far outweigh the buyer's comprehension or knowledge (sometimes their technical selling skills outweigh the rep's own product knowledge). Some of the brokers have bonds available from everywhere and all kinds of issues. A real smorgasbord of selection and risk is available. When buying individual muni bonds for your portfolio be sure that the bonds are not a high-risk development project in the wrong end of town. Know the location and get some information about the bond issue before buying. Also, be sure it was issued by your state because there is no economic advantage to buy a bond from another state, which is not deductible all the way. Mutual fund munis are bundled by state issuer and are quite mixed from many agencies and periods. The funds do much trading, however, to increase yield and offset annual fund charges, which is a different game than buying and owning the actual bonds. They can actually lose money from trading, but you cannot lose money if you buy a good high rated bond and hang on to it, and it is not supporting the local redevelopment agency. Buy a bond fund that has the state name on the title such as **California Municipal Bond Fund**.

Buying the actual bonds is much cheaper than buying into a mutual fund with high commissions and possible trading losses (arbitrage). The commissions average about 3-4% for municipal funds, which also charges a percent each year to maintain the account. Muni bond commissions average only about 1% when bought directly through a broker. You need large amounts of cash to deal with in the bond market. If you can buy and hold the bonds, it is best to ignore the ups and downs of interest rate changes because they do not affect your investment which will generally pay steady dividends if held to **maturity**. Most bonds begin at $10,000 and up.

SUCCESSFUL STRATEGIES

The lady's portfolio was a patchwork quilt of dozens of individual stock picks and dozens of mutual funds. Most of the mutual funds were in **high yield bonds, which is high risk**. Some dividends were reinvested back into some of her funds, but none should have been because she was always selling her stocks to pay income taxes. Something was wrong with her broker who paid no attention to his client's needs. Why should she be cashing in stocks (with commission charges) to pay taxes on the bond portfolio? Why should she be in a dozen high yield bond funds (which were all losing money) instead of one, especially when they were all purchased at the same time? Most of all is the relationship between high risk and yield.

After a review of her portfolio, the high yields were sold to take advantage of the tax losses they had earned (high yield has taken on a new meaning with the advent of hedge fund and derivative investing in the 1990s). The name, should the contents of the portfolios be disclosed, should be changed to very high risk. This saved her some taxes in the current year because she had a fine portfolio of dividend-paying blue-chip stocks. Then the funds shifted to California tax-free funds without leaving the mutual fund family (avoiding front end commission fees because she held B shares) with the dividends paid to her cash account. Now, the next year, she should have no tax problems and the broker will not be selling her stocks for her cash needs. Share commissions are deducted off the purchase which reduces portfolio value the same day. B share commissions usually take five years to deduct and make clients feel much better.

HORROR STORY - QUESTIONABLE MUNI BONDS

The retail rag business was earning mucho bucks for the couple. They had started a small retail store selling clothing, while both were in medical school. The little business did so well that they quit school to do it full time. They were getting rich by not doing it the hard way...becoming medical doctors. After many years the business had evolved in a big way to shopping mall status and they were wheeling and dealing directly with the manufacturers. I remember seeing fashionable mink coats on the racks at one time. They were very secretive about business transactions but I knew that they would meet a principal of the clothing manufacturing company in Los Angeles, monthly. Then, in a darkened hallway, a briefcase full of cash would change hands. Several weeks later, a truckload of prepaid discounted apparel would arrive and the retailing couple would have a big parking lot sale, with the cash disappearing afterward. This was before credit cards replaced ALL the cash at the register. (Perhaps cash registers should be called credit sales accounting machines.).

The problem is what to do with all the hidden profits? Their solution was to buy muni bonds. The income disappeared from the tax returns from the investment that was paying risky high interest. The reason they paid high interest was that they were questionable performance muni bonds based on classy redevelopment projects that paid higher than usual muni-bond interest rates. The entrepreneurs went for it because they were not afraid of economic risk. They felt the tax advantages of hidden earnings from hidden income was worth it.

For years the interest on the bonds rolled in, uncounted on any tax returns, originally from unreported earned income. One day the principal on the unamortized bonds came due. No check appeared in the mail. Then, almost unnoticed, the pink bankruptcy forms started arriving showing them as creditors. Now the couple is reporting the capital losses on their tax returns and they will need to live many more years to use them up, at $3,000 each year after any gains. About a million dollars' worth.

PROS AND CONS OF MUNICIPAL BONDS

- If you don't have a tax problem, there are better bond investments.
- If you are not sure about safety, buy insured munis through a mutual fund.
- The bonds may be winners but you can lose money through mutual fund trading.
- Buy the actual bonds to be assured that you will receive the stated interest rate.
- Buying the actual bond is much cheaper than doing it through a mutual fund.
- If buying the actual bond be sure you understand what it is building or fixing.
- Muni bonds are highly liquid and can be sold for the same 1% fee, but will be subject to discount or premium based on the current market interest rates. Mutual funds, however, do not charge a fee to liquidate any portion of the portfolio (A shares).
- Make sure the bonds or bond mutual fund is in your state.
- Bond trading can create capital gains or losses for your tax returns.

CHAPTER 11: APPLICATION EXERCISES

1. Muni Bonds are a creation of Congress to fund state infrastructure projects. ____ True ____ False

2. High yield Muni bonds are typically high risk. ____ True ____ False

3. Buying the actual Muni Bond is more expensive than buying it through a mutual fund. ____ True ____ False

4. Bond trading does not create capital gains or losses for your tax returns. ____ True ____ False

5. Muni bonds are great for balancing a large portfolio. ____ True ____ False

6. Which of the following is true about Municipal bond qualifications:
    ____ a. Principal is always secured by income or guaranteed
    ____ b. Some bonds are convertible to other issues
    ____ c. Some bonds are callable and can be paid off early
    ____ d. Interest rates are higher than corporate issues
    ____ e. All of the above

7. Which statement is false:
    ____ a. Muni bonds fund State infrastructure projects
    ____ b. Interest is federal and state tax free for residents of the bond-issuing state
    ____ c. Interest is always cheaper than corporate rates unless the project is uneconomic
    ____ d. Muni bonds never default

8. Muni bonds are bulletproof because:
    ____ a. Sometimes they fund economic political redevelopments which fail
    ____ b. Sometimes the issuing agencies are poorly managed and not viable
    ____ c. Sometimes they can be called and paid off due to market interest rate changes
    ____ d. They are ideal for pensions because of their tax advantages
    ____ e. All of the above
    ____ f. None of the above

9. Which of the following is not a Muni bond advantage:
   ____ a. Five percent tax free interest would be equivalent to eight percent after tax income
   ____ b. Proven economic theory is that States can avoid bankruptcy by defaulting on Muni bonds
   ____ c. Muni bond interest rates are higher for badly rated issues
   ____ d. Wealthy people hold most of the bonds because of restrictions on tax-sheltered investments

10. Which of the following are pitfalls of Munis:
    ____ a. Riverside County lost a qualification for not conforming to Federal tax guidelines
    ____ b. They are not feasible for pensions because pensions are taxed when distributed
    ____ c. They are not for low-income individuals who have no need for tax sheltered income
    ____ d. Out of state bonds would only benefit people from tax-free states like Texas or Florida
    ____ e. All of the above
    ____ f. None of the above

CHAPTER TWELVE

GOVERNMENT ISSUES, ZERO COUPON BOND CONCEPTS, FEDERAL RESERVE BOARD DECISIONS

United States Government Bonds and Treasury notes are today's currency of the world. We are discussing a currency not backed by any precious metal, but is based on the **"good faith and resources of the US government"**. It is truly a consumer society currency because it is not convertible to anything tangible by the issuer, except an interest in the multi-trillion-dollar national debt. If you asked a bank teller to redeem your **$20** bill, she would ask you if you wanted two **$10**, four **$5**, or twenty **$1** bills. Gold and silver, which used to be shown on the bills, is gone. Perhaps, to properly explain currency exchange, a trade could be effected whereas a tank or fighter plane is bought directly from the issuer-government, and no money really changes hands.

All currencies have the same common source. Original world coinage was usually silver or gold, which was exchanged for goods or services. These portable currencies replaced primitive barter systems of direct trade. (Sometimes a King would get greedy and keep all the gold, and in the past, our government owned all of the US gold). During Colonial times and afterward all world coinage was similar, that is, the gold English Sovereign was about the same weight and value as the American **$5** gold coin, which was like the French Franc. Silver coins were large things, weighing about an ounce and called dollars or Tolars or Crowns. States, provinces, and countries all minted their own coinage because the value of the coin was the value of the metal itself. Milled edges appeared to discourage shaving the precious metal off to lighten coin weight (**an art still practiced by many jewelers on client's jewelry**), and the lumps of metal evolved to a beautifully engraved artform as well as a political statement (**rulers'**

faces have always been there) and economic unit. Then Gutenberg, a very clever German, invented the printing press.

People in high places soon discovered that more than Bibles could be printed and that paper could be substituted (**specie**) for the real heavy metal things and the resulting currency was called certificates which usually stated, **"Redeemable in Gold or Silver"**. And, for a while, it was true, that you could take your **$20** gold certificate to the bank or issuer and exchange it for a real **$20** one-ounce coin. Then, in the 20th Century, the exchange rate was changed to $35 for the gold ounce, which complicated making change. Meanwhile, a dollar certificate could be exchanged for the one-ounce silver **cartwheel** that required strong pockets or saddlebags to carry.

President Abraham Lincoln created the **National Bank Act of 1863** which regulated the banks by requiring the security of bank currencies with the Treasurer and a requirement of **25%** in gold coin to cover **banknotes** (**loans**) issued. Leverage of up to 4 to one was officially sanctioned, which shows how banks multiply deposits as loans.

In mid-1929, just before the stock market crashed, to prove that bigger was sometimes better, the size of the currency paper was reduced to the small undersized bills we now carry in our wallets with all the credit cards and cat pictures. On November 13, 1929, the value of the **Times Industrials** (stock market) was also bigger at 224. By July 28, 1932, it had deflated and closed at 58. The Treasury responded with the **Gold Reserve Act of May 1, 1933**, that required the surrender of all-gold certificates, coins and gold bullion for our current small-sized Federal Reserve Notes. Citizens were given until May 1 or go to jail for 10 years and pay a $10,000 fine. Gold redemption was discontinued. All of the beautiful gold coins that sell in coin stores for so much over bullion price were hidden from the government. Silver certificates would follow the recall in 1968 when converted into US Federal Reserve Notes as well.

One odd part of the coinage era remained for our financial dealers today. The use of thirty-seconds which would be a half-ounce silver coin, is used (**1/32 gold ounce**) in bid and **sales prices**. All bonds, as well as stocks, are sold in dollars and **3.125** cents. Rounding off is allowed to even dollars and cents in the stock listings of your local newspaper and the Wall Street Journal. Napoleon codified the metric system to simplify things for his military, but the rest of the world never caught on. As a result, we still have **36 inches to a yard**, which can never equal a **meter of 1,000 mm** or **100 cm**, water freezes at **32° f.** instead of **zero centigrade**, water boils at **312° f.** instead of **100° c.** There are also **28 grams** to our **avoirdupois imperial ounce** and **31** to the **Troy ounce** used for jewelry. I also weighed exactly **ten stones** when I was in England (150 pounds).

AT THIS POINT A SCHEDULE IS REQUIRED:

- Treasury Bills have a duration of less than one year. They can be one month, three months, and six months and are called short-term treasuries. Money market funds contain treasuries of less than one year.

- Intermediate-Term Notes range from one to five years in duration.

- Long-Term Bonds live longer than five years, ten years is the most common term; thirty-year bonds were also widely issued and may be reinstated to lock in low interest rates currently about 2%.

Most old bonds contained **coupons** that were clipped off and redeemed for cash every three months to six months. Today the computer has simplified the process, with the help of the U.S. Postal Service and electronic banking. The term **zero coupons** are used for bonds that do not pay periodic interest in cash, instead, they **accrue the interest** owed to the owner, payable on redemption.

Savings Bonds are the Series E savings bonds, actually, a zero-coupon bond, issued for small denominations from **$25** to **$10,000**. Payroll departments in large companies have always struggled to report the bond payroll deductions to the bank so the Treasury can issue and track these little things. Because they are issued for less than face value (**a $25 bond is sold for $12.50**) they are discounted and zero coupon (**interest is not received until cashed in or sold**). Individuals through Federal Banks (**I know of no state banks remaining**) readily trade these bonds. Very few people today buy them but many elderly people are now redeeming them. In the Army, they were a mandatory monthly deduction.

At one time the **U.S. Government** felt everybody should participate more directly in the national debt so they drafted all eligible males, then on the monthly payday, the captain (**man with .45 gun**) counted out your cash pittance and told you to give some back for savings bonds (**to the lieutenant EO who was the other guy with the .45**). Leadership always means the man with the gun and the money. Three months later they were always cashed in to pay the pawnshop back, reduce the bar bill, and for other routine necessities.

These **Series E savings bonds** pay from **4%** to **6 %** interest and have a **40**-year maturity if issued before **1965** and **30**-year maturity afterward. Unlike most savings accounts they stop paying interest after maturity. If you or your kin has any of these bonds look at the dates or just cash them in. The Bureau of Public Debt won't notify you when they mature because their records are shoddy.

Series H bonds are a **30**-year bond, series **HH** last **40** years and both pay interest by check and owners are notified of maturity because that is when the interest checks stop. All bonds issued over **40** years ago, and some over **30** years, cease paying or earning interest. Since millions of people own these things they can be located on the government computer by listing the purchase date and serial number and inquiring to the **Bureau of Public Debt at 1500 Pennsylvania Ave., N.W. Washington, D.C. 20220 or** https://www.publicdebt.treas.gov/. Any series bond can be cashed in at your local bank, which is an extension of the Federal Reserve System.

Owners of Government Savings bonds were not recorded until **1974**. Thus, the bonds act like **bearer bonds** and anybody possessing them can cash them in. Keep them in a safe place because they can be stolen and not traced when redeemed (the bank person will ask for a Social Security number, however, so you can be taxed on the interest).

The Treasury bonds or notes are not sold directly to the public, although the government is working hard on that at this time. The government holds auctions that determine true interest rates, which is what the market will pay, periodically. Financial institutions buy them in huge blocks to sell them to you through the smaller brokerage firms. Bonds are always sold in thousand-dollar units for small commissions. Short term notes pay interest every three months, ten-year treasury marks pay only every six months; these are the most common notes in use today. The extensive laundry list of bond closing prices from the prior day's trading is available in the Wall Street Journal. Exchange rates for foreign currencies are also shown there. The **US Dollar** is so dependable that all foreign currencies are pegged to it for value. It is a result of the 2008 financial fiasco and the huge increase in national debt, that the bond rating by **Standard & Poor's** dropped a notch from the top rating. Bonds are traded in the **New York Currency Exchange.** A bit of arbitrage is possible because sometimes a brokerage firm is buying the bonds for inventory and can sell it for different prices.

The true yield of the investment, as reflected in interest earnings, is the price paid and the interest rate earnings over the term divided by the years to maturity. In other words, if a thousand-dollar **6%** note with one year remaining to maturity was bought at **$1,010 ($1,000 face value at 1.01% cost which reflects the premium, plus $10 commission), then it would have yielded only 4% ($60 interest less $10 premium and $10 commission**). This is possible if the bonds in circulation were now paying 5½% and your bond was a winner. Thus, the value of the bond if not held to maturity, can vary according to prevailing interest rates. This interest rate market risk is especially true if the term of the bond is very long such as the older **30-year bonds** issued to cover the huge national debt. Lastly, the government issues new refunding bonds to refinance maturing bonds and other new issues for increasing debt.

The Federal Reserve Bank is the Comptroller of the US Treasury. It is responsible for issuing all bonds, notes, and currency through twelve major member banks. There is always speculation among brokers and economists about the Fed not issuing more or less long-term debt out of phase with the market when the prevailing interest rates are higher or lower. If they were tuned into the market when current rates are low, it would make more sense to issue more long-term debt and less short term. The opposite would be true if the rates were high.

In September 1998, the Treasury issued a new I bond. This is an inflation-indexed bond pegged to the consumer price index. The fixed-rate is 3.3% plus the inflation index change for the year. A 2% increase in the index would become a 5.3% bond interest rate. This is called a savings bond and acts as a zero-coupon bond that pays interest at maturity or when redeemed. Because it is a savings bond there is the added feature of interest not being taxed until it is cashed in, unlike other bonds. These new bonds come in denominations of $50 to $10,000 and because they are savings bonds, they should be available through your local bank. At the time of this publication, the interest cost of Treasury debt is a shade less than 2%. Interest not compounded reduces yield.

There are also **Treasury inflation-protected securities** (**TIPS**). These pay a return after inflation of about 4%. They pay a quarterly interest coupon, are sold directly at Treasury twice-annual auctions, and since the coupon is fixed the principal is adjusted to inflation. This yield is higher than average, although still below **CMO agency bonds**. They are generally bought by large funds, which will charge you management fees to count the coupons. Investors always factor inflation into earnings to calculate true yield/profit.

Through their member banks, the Fed can also control the volume or amount of cash in circulation by buying or absorbing cash to slow the economy down or increasing the amounts of cash currency **(literally printing money)** in circulation to expand the economy. In conjunction with the discount rate, which affects the bank prime rates, they exert a great influence on the economy. Paul Volker, past Chairman of the Fed for many years, was criticized for lagging behind the economy with the above actions, thus exaggerating the **1974** and **1982** economic slumps.

PLANNING TIPS

Bonds should be part of every portfolio. Because bond yields traditionally less than equities, a conservative portfolio would hold about **20%** to **25%**.

A sophisticated investor of considerable means should buy bonds directly through his/her broker. They are liquid but subject to interest rate risk, especially over the long-term. Very few investors should consider buying and selling especially through leveraged means to take advantage of interest rate arbitrage changes. A managed account by a Registered Investor Advisor (RIA) would hold some Treasuries and other bonds.

The average investor, however, buys bonds through mutual funds that are a more mixed bag of holdings of terms and yields. The fund would also conduct considerable trading to take advantage of interest rate changes to increase the yield. Successful bond trading involves considerable risk, which fund managers encompass through computer modeling and the movement of huge amounts of money on short notice. A bond portfolio in a mutual fund is not always as sedate and level, as an investor might believe.

Treasury strips are packaged by investment houses to provide quarterly maturity dates for investors requiring staggered cash flow during these periods. Bonds and their derivatives can be packaged for liquidity for various investment needs, subject only to the imagination of the broker/dealer.

TAXES

Government Treasury interest is not taxable by individual states, thus if you have interest income from mutual funds, the Treasury interest must be segregated from other interest earned. A chart or table is usually provided by the clearing house for this purpose. Holding state tax-exempt treasuries in a high tax state such as California can considerably increase an investor's after-tax yield. Sales of bonds and notes within a mutual fund or actual sales by individuals are taxed as capital gains and subject to the more favorable tax tables. The government will provide **1099** forms showing all interest earned so you may pay taxes on it as required. Redemption of Government Series E **(War Bonds)** creates taxable interest earned in the year redeemed. Hold back on cashing them in near year-end for tax purposes unless the money is dearly needed or they have quit paying interest. Interest earned on zero-coupon Treasury notes, unlike Series E bonds, is taxable as earned even though the interest is not paid until maturity or at the sale.

Government Treasury bonds have state tax-free interest, but **GNMA, FNMA, FHA, SALLIE MAE,** etc. are private agency bonds with interest are taxable by the states. Mutual funds tend to call some of their funds "Government Bond funds" which have mixed issues. Ask for a Government Treasury fund for tax purposes (they will earn less interest) if that is what you really want.

LEGAL COMPLIANCE

Elderly people, unless sophisticated investors or very wealthy, should have some bonds in their portfolio. Bonds, especially Treasuries, provide a safe haven base for investment. The United States Treasury debt financing (**the Dollar**) is still considered the most secure in the world, even against the new competing European Dollar currencies (**Eurodollars**). The yield is lower than many other securities but as long as the American Dollar is held above all others worldwide, the security is always there. Treasury yields have been trending down in the **1990s** and compete closely with bank guaranteed Certificates of Deposit. For investments exceeding **$100,000,** the bank's **FDIC** insurance is gone and nothing can match the Treasuries for security. A plus for Treasuries would be that the interest is paid quarterly, not at maturity as with **CDs.**

It is worth noting that there are also many other government agency issues, not to be confused with the Treasury issues covered in this chapter. Arbitrage is the science of trading currencies for coins.

SUCCESSFUL STRATEGIES

The most successful strategy is to buy bonds, or financial investments holding Treasuries, and hang on to them. Prior to the **1990** run-up in the stock market elderly investors held mostly Certificates of Deposit. They were reliable, predictable, and short-term. Every year the retired folks would shop the interest rates in the newspaper for the highest rate and move their funds at maturity.

Now the banks and institutions are all selling mutual funds or insurance products that charge large commissions (**load**). Elderly people are buying bond funds instead of bonds with the **CD** money. This is proving to be an expensive way to invest and has substituted mutual funds and confusing insurance annuities for simple investing. Government bonds, Treasuries to be specific, should be available to the public on a direct basis but are only truly available from fee-paid advisors and large brokerage firms. Elderly people are also throwing caution aside and joining the crowd for high equity yields. Since the Federal debt is so large, yet still acceptable as an interest-bearing investment, more Treasury notes and bonds should be made available directly to the public instead of the alternative risky and expensive commission generated investments. The old coupon War Bond should be revived as a modern financial instrument.

One last note. Have you noticed that the friendly bank financial rep (the one selling the costly mutual funds and insurance products) is now usually located just inside the bank door, like the Wal-Mart Greeter?

HORROR STORY - MEXICAN BOND

This elderly MD who had been educated after the WW2 GI Bill put unemployed veterans in school to change America, was then retired but working in a convalescent home. The doctor was not rich because he was a general practitioner, not a specialist. But, he lived very well with a large home and good investments. One of his investments was a **$10,000** bond issued by a Mexican Bank. This kind of bond pays unusually high-interest rates, (high interest is high risk) which is common for some foreign investments. The basic rule is that the higher the interest rates…the greater the risk. The good doctor held the investment ten years to maturity and presented it to the bank for payment. Then he waited and called; nothing happened for years. Finally, several years later he gave up and took the loss on his tax returns. Such is the risk of investing in third world countries, even seemingly secure bonds. The difference between a third world country and a fourth world place is that the third kind takes your money while the other, probably in darkest Africa, takes your life.

PROS & CONS OF BOND ISSUES

- **US Treasuries** are the safest in the world, but pay the lowest interest rates.

- Bond mutual funds hold a mixed bag of securities and do not pay steady interest rates because they are frequently traded by the fund advisors for arbitrage gains. They also pay dividends that may include principal instead of only interest and capital gains earnings or losses.

- Bonds are always liquid but commissions can be charged to buy and sell them on the market.

- Bonds will pay steady coupon interest rates but are subject to market gains or losses on the principal when sold or traded before maturity.

- Some Series E and H Savings bonds have matured and quit paying interest. The dates should be reviewed for maturity, and the bonds immediately redeemed and reinvested if the term has expired. Inflation devalues these securities, especially if they quit paying interest.

- Government Treasury-issued bonds should not be confused with Government housing agency bonds when risk is considered. The first is guaranteed; the other could be insured (By PMI).

- Investors in high tax states like California should factor tax savings into the yield calculations of government issues.

- The interest rate (coupon or stated interest rate when issued) is not the actual yield of a bond when purchased because the price is marked to the current interest rate market (**interest rate risk**). The broker will inform you of the actual yield at the time of purchase.

- Bonds are purchased and sold all day long in the market at various terms and interest rates (the yields tend to be very close, however) are available.

- If you have a large portfolio, you should be buying bonds through your advisor, not bond mutual funds. It will be much cheaper if you plan to hold them.

- Cashing in government savings bonds creates a taxable event; so timing should be considered. Bonds can be recalled (redeemed before the maturity date) at any time unless there is a no recall stipulation on issue.

CHAPTER 12: APPLICATION EXERCISES

1. The US Dollar is so dependable that all foreign currencies are pegged to it for value. ___ True ___ False

2. US Treasuries are the safest in the world, but pay the lowest interest rates. ___ True ___ False

3. Bonds will pay steady coupon interest rates but are subject to market gains or losses on the principal when sold or traded before maturity. ___ True ___ False

4. There are no tax liabilities when cashing in government savings bonds. ___ True ___ False

5. Series E savings bonds, a zero-coupon bond, are issued for small denominations from $25 to $10,000. ___ True ___ False

6. Government Treasuries are:
   ___ a. Taxable in the States that have income tax levies
   ___ b. Taxable for State income taxes
   ___ c. Convertible to bullion
   ___ d. Backed by the "Good Faith and Resources of the US Government"

7. Which of the following statements is false about modern currencies:
   ___ a. They lack the precious metal that represented the true value of legal tender coinage
   ___ b. They are based on paper which cannot be redeemed for anything except more paper
   ___ c. The term for gold coinage is Specie
   ___ d. The first paper money was certificates redeemable in gold or silver

8. Which of the following is true about Treasuries:
   ___ a. They are not highly rated
   ___ b. They are issued in only 30 year notes, same as mortgage loans
   ___ c. They are the top world class currency
   ___ d. They are unsecured

9. Which of the following statements is false about Zero coupon savings bonds:

____ a. They pay interest only when redeemed

____ b. They are issued by the US Treasury

____ c. The have a duration of one year, intermediate up to five years, and long term for ten or thirty years

____ d. They are also named savings bonds Schedule E in denominations of $25 to $10,000

10. Which of the following statements is false about other bond issues:

____ a. Tips are inflation protected Treasury securities which are inflation adjusted

____ b. Bearer bonds were not recorded until 1974, which means anybody could cash them

____ c. Local FDIC banks cannot cash Treasury bonds

____ d. Treasuries no longer have the highest rating with Standard & Poor's

CHAPTER THIRTEEN

HIGH YIELD BONDS, CORPORATE BONDS,
DEBENTURES, CONVERTIBLE-PREFERRED

Corporate bonds are first authorized by the company board of directors to finance expansion or operations. Then they take it to an **investment banker** or underwriter who will prepare the proposal required by the Securities Exchange Commission. This underwriter will sometimes buy the whole issue or guarantee the issue in order to have exclusive rights to the sale and huge fees generated by packaging and selling the deal. Then a **red herring public notice** (uniquely called a **tombstone** because a bunch of them look like a cemetery view in the financial newspaper) is posted (a large expensive display ad) in financial newspapers advising that the proposal is before the SEC and to think hard about buying it. No orders can be solicited until it is approved, however.

A sample of **red herring** would be:

$275,000,000

- XYZEBRA INDUSTRIES

- Senior Subordinated Notes

- Syndication & Administrative Agent

- Last National Bank of America

From that point on, after approval, the underlying bond issue is reviewed/analyzed and rated by **Moody's** or **Standard & Poor rating** bureaus, and sold through major brokerage firms. Like everything else, they are listed in the Wall Street Journal, first under **New Securities Issues**, next under the **Bond Exchange listings** that show the stated fixed interest rate, year of maturity, actual yield and selling price. Investors should subscribe to the rating services for further data that is required on the particulars on the company, the bond issue itself, and the rating. Remember that the yield to maturity is a function of the selling price, coupon, and term. A discounted price equals a higher yield. Very few bonds, except a few utilities, sell for 100% of the principal. A commission is charged by the brokerage firm to do the trade for you. Commissions are called basis points, with 100 points equal to one percent of the note or bond sold. A 1% commission is usually charged for bond sales although some bonds can demand a higher or lower commission.

Bonds have a language of their own:

Subordinated means that the other financial instruments take precedence during a **default, convertible**; that is, if the value of the stock should rise, the bonds could be exchanged for stocks; **zero-coupon** pays no interest until maturity; **sinking funds** accumulate restricted money inside the corporation to retire the bonds; **income bonds** accrue and pay interest only when the corporation earns a profit; **mortgage bonds** assure real estate collateral with grant deeds, while **equipment bonds** lien equipment for security. There are **call features** that allow some issuers to **recall bonds** and pay them off early without penalties before maturity; **serial bonds** that are retired incrementally, **variable bonds** pegged to current interest rates, etc. **Corporate bonds** pay higher fixed interest rates than state or federal government issues because they tend to be less secure and are not tax-exempt. They the ones in play and available, and are listed in the news journals under Corporate Bonds. They are shown as **callable** and **non-callable**. Because bonds all have a commission or cost to buy, the longer-term or non-callable option the better deal for yield to maturity (or call).

Debentures are unsecured **general obligation bonds** if issued by American companies, **secured if foreign**. Some debentures, to give them a sense of security, are convertible to common stock if the price and timing are right. Before stockholders get anything, the bondholder as an unsecured debtor, during the default, can receive principal payment only after all secured debtors have been paid. NASDAQ lists **Convertible**

Debentures that are traded on a daily basis in the **daily financial journals.**

Convertible preferred stocks can be exchanged into common stocks by the shareholder if the strike price for the common stock coincides, but the corporation may also hold an offsetting option to convert the preferred stock to convertible debentures. The important thing to know is that the preferred issue acts more like a bond than a stock because the dividends have a preference over common stock. Some newer esoteric convertible issues have a floating conversion ratio and are a **toxic convertible** because of the dilutive effect on the common stock shareholder's values and depressed share prices.

Bonds are long-term notes extending over many years and therefore subject to inflation risk. A good conservative measure of non-speculative earnings would be the inflation index plus 3%. Because taxes are also paid on the earnings, the net after-tax yield should always be considered. Banks like to earn a minimum of three percentage points (not basis points) over the **Federal Reserve Bank Discount Rate** to determine their **prime lending rate.** Uniquely, at this time of writing, the Discount Rate was 3% over the inflation index. The magic number three is everywhere, even in Japan where their Discount Rate is 0% and the economy is negative 3%. The bank cost for credit card money, however, is 7%, which explains why the banks are all in the credit card business these days.

The availability of cash can also affect bond interest rates. A **flight to security,** as experienced by the cash (**flight to safety**) flowing back to the US during the Asian meltdown in 1998, lowered bond interest rates to all-time lows. Again, this is a function of lower risk providing lower but safer interest rates. When the Asian economies recover, the reverse liquidity will occur as the money flows away from this safe haven and interest rates here will rise again (along with inflation, the offsetting index).

High-yield bonds own their own section on the bond listings in the financial journals. Rated as **fixed-income BBB or lower,** investing in them is comparable to buying stocks on the NASDAQ, which are highly volatile. Like all financial instruments, the higher risk equals higher interest rates…if you can get them.

High-yield bonds used as credit for corporate take-overs, bridge loans for buyout financing and for companies in trouble. None of the above are for expansion or corporate self-improvement. Sometimes the funds are used as **poison pills** to kill corporate takeovers by making companies more undesirable for acquisition. In most cases, the users are divesting assets by closing branches or plants and selling off non-performing assets to recover and pay off this high-interest corporate credit card debt. In the Wall Street movie, a pension plan (which held more in appreciated assets than it was legally obligated to pay out for employee pensions) was a horrible economic event. High yield means higher risk, always. Because of the risk involved, the junk bond listing includes bonds noted in default and companies in bankruptcy. A banker would call them **non-performing**. There are also special bonds for companies in bankruptcy to pay legal expenses and clean things up. Naturally, they get first dibs on remaining cash from asset sales.

PLANNING TIPS

Bonds should be part of every investor's portfolio. Corporate bonds are certainly riskier than government issues. High-yield bonds are very high risk. There are two ways to acquire bonds for your portfolio: The first being through mutual funds that offer professional management. The second is to buy them directly through your stockbroker or financial advisor. This approach requires some research and awareness of the risks. Individual investors think in terms of coupon rates and terms, which are long-term assumptions. Speculators deal in a current framework of inflation, short-term yield, and trading the bonds for changes in market interest rates. Unless you are buying mutual funds, and this chapter is not about that, investigate and familiarize yourself with the facts behind the issue and the corporate bond issuer. Better yet, positively learn to like and feel good about the company, product or service, and deal, before committing your money for the long-term. Otherwise, just tell your advisor, who you must trust, to be sure some bonds are in the portfolio, and let him/her do the job.

TAXES

Corporate bond interest is taxable with no exception. The 1099 amount is added to the top of your tax return from schedule B income, and taxed at the ordinary income tax rate applicable to your return. Offsets include capital losses (with limitations), business losses, net operating losses carried forward, and itemized deductions. It can cause Social Security distributions to become taxable, truly a double taxation effect, by pushing over the $25,000 single or $34,000 married thresholds. That is why yield after taxes is so important. You really need to review the whole tax return to get the complete picture.

LEGAL COMPLIANCE

Everybody is supposed to get rich because we are Americans and the Great Depression has been forgotten. This leads to the investor conundrum about how to catch up with their friends, who are making it in the stock market, without the risk associated with equities. Unfortunately, conservatism leads people into bonds, and since their yields are lower traditionally than the equity market, they can end up in high-yields. This is a trap, which elderly people talk themselves into by demanding better yields, which are not available with bonds, especially in times of low inflation and lower interest rates.

Stockbrokers can buy bonds for your portfolio, but the commissions are very low and bonds are generally large sophisticated ticket items. The individual investor will find himself/herself led to mutual funds. This is an OK place to be, especially if you are unsophisticated or elderly. Beware of high-yield bonds unless aware that they can be very risky, even in a professionally managed mutual fund.

A note about banking: US businesses are required to report cash transactions (**Patriot Act after 911**) of $10,000 or more. Banks are required to report $3,000 or more. Cash is the currency of the street. The government is anxious to keep track of the money in your pocket, under the "drug money" pretext. This invasion of privacy leads many people to consider offshore banking, which is free and liberal, with non-existent taxes and reporting standards. Many investment frauds are also conducted or centered on offshore banks. These banks are in the Cayman Islands or the Bahamas, which are handy tax-free places where people can get a wonderful suntan while they count their (or your) money. The US Government doesn't like money flowing there legitimately, or not, and can attack foreign bank accounts including the venerable Swiss banks if they also have branches in the US. If your advisor mentions the offshore banks in relation to your deal or spends his weekends there, check both him and the deal out very closely. After all, the pirates were there first.

Wire transfers successfully launder money. This professional handling is good for billions without much oversight.

SUCCESSFUL STRATEGIES

Bonds are usually considered a safe haven. A quality bond provides steady interest earnings for the patient investor. During uncertain times in the equity stock markets, a flight for safety ensues with investor money leaving the market for the safety of bonds. This infusion of liquidity can lower the bond yields that will fall if the rates go down due to unusual demand. With this in mind, it is best to keep a quarter or fifth of the portfolio in bonds, even if it is a contrarian position because the equities market may be running away and making everybody else millionaires. Even every military general worries about overextended positions when on the offense, always rethinking length of lines for supply & resupply, troop/supply reserves, and defensive fallback static positions. This is what bonds do for the investor; even when the yields are lousy...provide a defensive position for an offensive strategy. An example of a naked strategy was the Chosin Reservoir retreat in the Korean War where survivors named themselves, "the chosen few".

Inflation has averaged 3% over the past 75 years (except for annual Social Security increases which are always at least 1% less than all other benchmarks). If you can increase your investment yield above this amount, you are not losing money in real terms. Anything above this is gain. Treasury bills have yielded only 2% over this same period, while State bonds are almost 4%, and local municipal bonds just over 4%. The equities market has earned on the average, almost 9%, which will certainly be adjusted downward in the future.

HORROR STORY - HIGH-YIELD MUTUAL FUNDS

This horror story is about hidden risks. High-yield mutual funds are loosely referred to as mostly corporate (junk) bonds. The investors are dutifully informed by their BD VP salesperson that there is more risk than governments, which is why the yield had been much higher for several years. Historic yields have truly been higher than government bond mutual funds because there is some safety in the fact that the investment risk is spread about many different businesses and entities, which pay credit card interest rates for their funds. However, there was a demon hidden in most of the mutual funds during 1998. The demon was unleashed during midyear when the Russian financial markets (and the underlying government) collapsed. The connection was a little line in the mutual fund prospectus (which appears used by most funds with different advisors and numbers) mentioning that corporate BBB rated bonds are allowing "other foreign investments". Those other investments turned out to be insolvent Russian bonds, which defaulted and rolled over dead along with a currency devaluation. Unfortunately, the investors in these mutual funds, which most investors participated in the search for higher yield, never knew that much of their investments were stuck in kopecks or rubles instead of American dollars. Very sharp substantial losses followed, (30% of the HY portfolio) something that happens when professional fund advisors unsuccessfully compete with each other for yield with too many dollars. They also follow each other closely on the lemming's search for higher risk. A bit of high leverage here also enlarged the prior operating results. Discounted bonds increase the yield until they result in absolute losses.

BOND RATINGS

MOODY'S BOND RATINGS:

Aaa	Bonds of the highest quality
Aa	Bonds of high quality
A	Bonds whose security of principal and interest is considered adequate by may be impaired in the future
Baa	Bonds of a medium grade that are neither highly protected nor poorly secured
Ba	Bonds of speculative quality whose future cannot be considered well secured
B	Bonds that lack characteristics of a desirable investment
Caa	Bonds in poor standing that may be defaulted
Ca	Speculative bonds that are often in default
C	Bonds with little probability of any investment value (lowest rating)

STANDARD & POOR'S BOND RATINGS

AAA	Bonds of the highest quality
AA	High-quality debt obligation
A	Bonds that have a strong capacity to pay interest and principal but may be susceptible to adverse effects
BBB	Bonds that have an adequate capacity to pay interest and principal but are more vulnerable to adverse economic conditions or changing circumstances
BB	Bonds of lower medium grade with few desirable investment characteristics
B/CCC	Primarily speculative bonds with great uncertainties and major risk if exposed to adverse conditions
C	Income bonds on which no interest is being paid
D	Bonds in default

PROS & CONS OF BONDS AND INTEREST-BEARING INSTRUMENTS

- Bonds produce much less income over the long term than equities. That is about twice the historic long-term yield of 4% vs 9%.

- Bonds provide level cash income, if held to maturity. The cash flow (**coupon**) is based on the interest rates, although the investor's actual yield must include the commission costs and discount or premium to market rates.

- Corporate bonds must be graded for safety. This means that the lower the rating the higher the risk.

- The bond risk is proportional to interest rates; thus, the safest corporate issues offer interest rates less than 1% higher than government agency issues (usually housing agencies) and municipal bonds.

- High-yield bonds are very risky although they offer high-interest rates, commonly two or three times as high as highly rated bonds.

- Best to buy actual bonds than buying bond mutual funds. The cost is lower and the yield consistent without market risk of trading by advisors who market (sell and buy trading) to the market to increase yield.

- Corporate assets secure most bonds. Failing companies must liquidate to satisfy bondholders while shareholders can lose everything.

- Bonds are less subject to economic risk from economic ups and downs than equity investments.

- Bonds are a necessary ingredient for a diversified retirement portfolio because of steady cash flow and security.

- Puerto Rican bonds are considered muni bonds by an act of Congress, and accordingly, their bad news is not included here.

- Bonds are highly liquid and can be sold on the market with the usual 1% commission.

- Junk Bonds are traded at less than par value which leads to marketing manipulation by brokers and traders.

CHAPTER 13: APPLICATION EXERCISES

1. Which of the following are types of bonds (check all that apply)?
    ____ a. Income
    ____ b. Mortgage
    ____ c. Recall
    ____ d. Corporate
    ____ e. Variable
    ____ f. All of the above

2. Bonds are long-term notes extending over many years and therefore subject to inflation risk. ____ True ____ False

3. Corporate bond interest is not taxable. ____ True ____ False

4. The Patriot Act states US businesses are required to report cash transactions of $10,000 or more and Banks are required to report transactions of $3,000 or more. ____ True ____ False

5. Corporate bonds must be graded for safety; the lower the rating the higher the risk. ____ True ____ False

6. Which statement is false about High Yield bonds:
    ____ a. They are low risk investments for retired folk
    ____ b. They are higher risk bonds
    ____ c. They pay higher interest rates than typical corporate issues and government agency bonds
    ____ d. They sometimes include foreign currencies

7. Bonds have their own language. Which statement is false:
    ____ a. Mortgage bonds are for mortgages
    ____ b. Subordinated bonds are second to other bonds in default
    ____ c. Callable bonds offer higher yield to maturity than non-callable
    ____ d. Serial bonds are retired incrementally (laddered)

8. Which statement is false about High Yield bonds:
    ____ a. They are high risk
    ____ b. They are rated AAA by Moody's
    ____ c. They are used as poison pills to kill corporate takeovers
    ____ d. They offer higher yield with discounts to face value

9. In the Horror Story about High Yield mutual funds, which statement is false:
   ____ a. Bond risk increases with higher rated bonds
   ____ b. High yield in portfolio was presented as higher risk and earnings than Governments
   ____ c. Unknowingly the mutual fund accounts had a lot of Russian bonds which rolled over
   ____ d. The client lost 30% of mutual fund bond portfolio from one day to the next

10. Which statement is false:
   ____ a. Convertible preferred bonds can be exchanged to common stocks (like preferred stocks)
   ____ b. Debentures are unsecured general obligation bonds
   ____ c. Whole issues can be bought or guaranteed by an underwriter
   ____ d. A tombstone is a place where bad bond issues are buried

CHAPTER FOURTEEN

COLLATERALIZED MORTGAGE OBLIGATIONS, INSURED GOVERNMENT AGENCY HOUSING ISSUES

Mortgage-backed securities are referred to as **government income securities**. They are located in most mutual bond funds, and advisor's portfolios. Mortgage bonds are really agency bonds, that is, they are issued by the Federal government housing agencies, which are separate corporate entities that control vast amounts (billions of dollars) of housing mortgages.

These agencies are Government National Mortgage Association (**GNMA or Ginnie Mae**), Federal Home Loan Mortgage Corporation (**FHMA or Freddie Mac**) and Federal National Mortgage Association (**FNMA or Fannie Mae**). All require mortgage insurance or substantial equity by the homeowner borrower. The debt securities of these agencies are used to acquire Federal Housing Authority (**FHA**) and to secure Veteran's Administration (**VA**) mortgages. The alphabet soup is all under the prevue of direct federal government control.

The audit trail is as follows: First, a new homeowner goes to his bank or to one of the few remaining savings & loans, and makes out the standard FHA application. This application process and qualifications for income to debt ratios, credit points, adherence to structural code standards, down payments, etc. have become the standard used for almost all residential loans, and even private funding. In almost all cases, unless the down payment exceeds 20% of the purchase price, the buyer will be charged about 1% of the mortgage amount annually for **Principal Mortgage Insurance (PMI)** in case of default or foreclosure losses. The bank then advances the mortgage proceeds to the seller, via the escrow company. After a month or two, the homeowner (hardly true ownership since he shares his house with the Mortgage Company) finds that the loan has been "bought" by another mortgage company who will now collect the payments. At this time the mortgage has been sold to a housing agency, and the new Mortgage Company is simply a firm to handle the loan service. Most housing agency loans are very long-term 30-year loans. Once upon a time, people believed their mortgage was held by the issuing bank, like in the "It's a Wonderful Life" movie, but it is just really floating out there somewhere in somebody's portfolio. Many years ago, the banks would issue certificates of deposit for rich people. The money was invested in business loans and mortgages. Now, when the remaining CDs come due the bank rep talks the client into mutual funds or insurance products. They take their commissions but have to go outside for the mortgage money instead of participating with bank funds. That is why banks no longer loan their own money out.

Meantime, the housing agency has sold bonds equal to your mortgage, along with hundreds or thousands more in a "pool" or large lot at auction. These securities, also called **Collateralized Mortgage Obligations** (**CMO's**), offer interest rates higher than government securities. The pool is sold through brokerage firms and institutional houses (mutual funds) that buy them directly in huge multi-million dollar lots. Later the aging pool is broken into blocks, (**tranches**), of securities all having the same term and interest rates, and resold to investors in **tranche units**. The commissions on CMO's are only about 1%, which is much less than for mutual fund sales, so most brokers will only offer large amounts of these to their richest clients. These are a great investment for retirement or pensions because of the long terms. The interest and principal are paid monthly as the mortgage payments are paid, thus flowing directly to the investor. The problem is that the underlying principal may be reduced before the term expires, because of mortgages paid off early or retired by refinancing due to interest rate or ownership changes. In the bond business, this is a **call feature**. The average mortgage only lasts seven years before a refinance of sale of the property. Jumbo mortgages are very large mortgages and are subjected to higher interest rates and qualifications than typical mortgages.

Mortgage bonds are guaranteed by the issuing agency, not the federal government. The guarantee is enforced by the **Principal Mortgage Insurance (PMI)** Fund which is paid by the mortgage holder. Like car insurance, if the thing gets wrecked, everybody gets paid.

Veterans Administration loans are different. A first-time homebuyer must pay 2.3% of the loan amount while a second-time borrower pays 3%. This prepaid fee or PMI is added to the mortgage amount and not usually disclosed by the mortgage brokers. The bank lender is assured that 90% of the loan will be repaid to them if the borrower (generally a veteran without a down payment) defaults. The fee is not disclosed to the borrower as a fee when the veteran signs the loan docs (because it is PMI). Lenders are unscrupulous about refinancing the loans, even with considerable equity, and including the frontloaded PMI again.

Residential mortgages are generally termed for 30 years to keep the payments affordable. Most mortgages reduce the principal from the monthly payments about $500 monthly with the rest of the payment going to interest, and tax-insurance impounds. The average mortgage lasts only five years with constant refinancing for interest rate changes or equity withdrawal. With that in mind, the mortgage interest rate is calculated on the US Treasury ten-year note interest rate plus 3-4 % points [300 basis points]. From there the lender will add points according to FICO credit scores [currently about 700 minimum to 760+ for best rates]. A fifteen-year mortgage will earn a haircut of a half point, which is the rate usually advertised. You are late on a missed payment but in default if two payments are missed. When purchasing a home, you will receive a statement showing the purchase price as the basis of the secured county property tax bill. Compare this figure with your escrow purchase price. If it is higher make the call to the tax collector. If they have arbitrarily increased it then appeal. You have one month to file the informal appeal in writing. It is an interesting experience and the last time I appealed it took a nine-month gestation period of bouncing from one person to another to get to the highest level before they reduced the $50,000, they had added to my home purchase price.

Recently I saw a new prospectus for an **Adjustable Government Bond Mutual Fund**. At first, I thought that the government had gotten smart and was issuing treasuries that paid interest according to the market, instead of a fixed-rate at inception. Upon reviewing the prospectus, it became apparent that the fund consisted mostly of **variable mortgages** that are insured by government agencies. Therefore, there are funds holding variable mortgages now, which shows how flexible the investment business has become. A variable mortgage is a mortgage that resets the interest rate to market after a period, usually five years. Generally, this discounted rate rewards the lender if interest rates are higher in the future with the automatic reset. The lower interest rate makes payments smaller and interest rates cheaper for first-time buyers enabling them to qualify for larger mortgage loans.

In recent years **no-equity mortgages** have appeared. These first trust deed mortgages are only partly collateralized with funds advanced equal to 125% of the home purchase price or equity value. These mortgage lenders charge much higher than standard interest rates, are aimed at low-income FHA unqualified buyers, and are funded by secondary market money (finance companies offering credit card interest rates). They are not part of the above government agency financing and bond investments. These mortgages are at high risk and not insured. Fortunately, they have no place in anybody's portfolio. They were part of the 2008 real estate collapse.

The Wall Street Journal has a **Collateralized Mortgage Obligation** (**CMO**) section that shows the current prices and interest rates on various government agency mortgages. The yield can vary with the interest rate, term, commission charges, and price that can be more or less than the face value. Current interest rates have a direct bearing on the price, with old higher mortgage rates demanding a premium in today's market. The danger of old higher rate mortgages in a lower interest rate market is that they tend to redeem early by refinancing. This reduces the yield because all expenses are factored into your yield to maturity calculations.

PLANNING TIPS

CMO's offer a worthwhile alternative to mutual funds holding a mixed bag of fixed-term investments. A CMO portfolio offers some interest rate risk if the current mortgage rates should increase above the rates held in the portfolio. This risk, however, would be less than the income mutual funds that tend to also buy and hold higher-risk securities such as foreign and corporate. The cost would also be less than paying a full commission for mutual fund management. Mortgages in mutual funds tend to be traded frequently in interest rate arbitrage that distorts the yield based on the coupon interest rates.

TAXES

Government agency mortgage bond interest is subject to state and federal income taxes, unlike government debt obligation (Federal Reserve issues) securities. If they are mixed, as they are in some mutual funds, the government portion must be separated from the rest of the taxable portfolio. Most mutual funds will provide a detailed listing at year-end for splitting the state taxable vs non-taxable portions.

Interest accrued on all bonds, but not paid, is taxed as earned, although no zero-coupon government housing agency bonds are issued at this time.

The sale of government agency bonds, exclusive of interest earned and paid, is a capital gain or loss event, and subject to capital gains income tax rates.

LEGAL COMPLIANCE

The major risk in purchasing CMO's is that the principal is reduced much more than the term indicates. If the tranche shows a pool of ten-year mortgages (all the terms remaining are ten years) then portions of the pool will be paid off early as mortgages are canceled. Thus, after five years the remaining principal may be only half of the original mortgage total. The principal is also repaid, although very little at first, as the mortgages mature, thus increasing the cash flow to the fund in excess of the actual interest rate.

CMO's and bonds, in general, require the tough General Securities License, which most mutual fund salespeople do not hold. Larger broker-dealers and people working for major securities firms offer the securities. Most firms hand out small booklets describing how they work so the investor has an idea what is involved, although most still do not offer them.

SUCCESSFUL STRATEGIES

A proper portfolio would hold bonds, equities, cash, and other higher-risk investments such as REITs, equipment leasing partnerships, commodities or natural resources, etc. If the yield is not more important than taxes, and safety is at the ultraconservative level, government agency mortgage bonds offer a reasonably high yield with the safety of equity and the underlying mortgage insurance. These CMO's offer much less risk if purchased directly or through an advisor, than through mutual funds which tend to reach way out to increase yield with riskier investments. Because they are insured, they also offer an opportunity to break through the $250,000 jumbo insured limit for a certificate of deposit bank FDIC account.

HORROR STORY - CALIFORNIA PONZI SCHEME

There are no horror stories for government agency bonds or CMO's. None at all. However, you might want to know about a California Inland Empire **Ponzi scheme** where the lady bought very high interest-bearing second trust deeds. The actual deeds were recorded and delivered to her, and for several years, she did not worry about them as she received the interest payments on time from the financial person doing the mortgages. One day, the money stopped. She called to find out that there were many problems and that there were no good excuses. Nevertheless, there were no more principal or interest payments, either. Then the mortgage broker disappeared, so she ran a small newspaper ad to see if there were others, perhaps with a better story. Many people responded but there were still no answers. She went to the Riverside County District Attorney who told her it was a civil matter, because they were too busy with other more pressing cases.

To make a long story shorter, she visited the Title Company and found out the **law of mortgage recordings**. This law dictates that a million mortgages can be recorded against a single property, but there is only one first and one-second mortgage and that is the second recording, by date, of all the other recordings. Her mortgage was the tenth recording, which meant that there were nine people ahead of her on the trust deed. There was further investigation and, consequently, a large class-action suit filed by at least a dozen mortgage holders with the lady doing the entire legal work attorney pro per (**Plaintiff in Propria Persona**). Naturally, there was no money to be collected upon judgment because, in a Ponzi scheme of this nature, the next victim pays the interest of the last victim and the profits of the organizer, until the number of new victims slows down and the deal collapses.

Only one truth holds here, if it appears too good to be real (12% mortgages), then it is simply too good to be true (uneconomical). In addition, if there were actually 12% mortgages then, the rules of rate and risk would indicate that the high rate would indicate a high default rate. This is sustainable only in a rosy economic environment when everybody has a job and the interest rates have pushed higher than normal. The no-equity 125% mortgage backers experienced a sharp rude awakening when the economy tipped over in 2007-2008.

PROS & CONS OF MORTGAGE BOND OBLIGATIONS

- CMO's are for people with substantial means; they are not offered to everybody because they require a General Securities License and pay only a small commission to the broker.
- Government agency bonds are very secure and liquid. Many mortgage holders are paying for the mortgage **reinsurance** in case of default or foreclosure.
- Buying bonds directly from the broker-dealer are much more costly and yield efficient than through mutual funds.
- Bonds belong in every portfolio as a hedge against equity market meltdowns.

- Housing agency bonds pay a steady and increasing cash stream with insured interest rates.

- The greatest danger of mortgage bonds is that they would be paid off faster if the market interest rates decline significantly below the coupon rate, with refinancing.

- Mortgage bonds make a perfect retirement income allocation for elderly individual portfolios, especially since most retired people have retired their mortgage and can now participate in the receiving end of things.

CHAPTER 14: APPLICATION EXERCISES

1. If a buyer puts down less than 20% of the purchase price of a FHA residential loan, the buyer will be charged about 1% of the mortgage amount annually for Principal Mortgage Insurance (PMI) in case of default or foreclosure losses. ____ True ____ False

2. Mortgage bonds are guaranteed by the issuing agency, not the federal government. ____ True ____ False

3. Government agency bonds are very secure and liquid.
____ True ____ False

4. Collateralized Mortgage Obligations offer interest rates lower than government securities. ____ True ____ False

5. The PMI on a Veterans Administration Loan is automatically added to the mortgage principal and is not usually disclosed by the mortgage brokers. ____ True ____ False

6. Which statement about CMO mortgage bonds is false:
   ____ a. They are found in all government security bond mutual fund portfolios
   ____ b. They are secured by the federal government
   ____ c. They offer higher interest rates than Treasuries
   ____ d. They are sold to broker firms as tranche units of like age and interest rates

7. Which statement is false:
   ____ a. Mortgage backed securities are called Government Income Securities
   ____ b. Mutual funds and advisors label CMOs as Government bond funds although they hold no Treasuries
   ____ c. Government agencies are not secured by the government but most people believe they are
   ____ d. CMOs pay better interest rates than High Yield bonds

8. Government agencies have an alphabet soup of names. Which one is false:

___ a. GNMA is for Ginnie Mae, Government National Mortgage Assn.

___ b. GHMA is for Freddie Mac, Federal Home Loan Mortgage Corp.

___ c. FNMA or Fannie Mae, for Federal National Mortgage Assn.

___ d. VA or VFW, for Veteran's Association is only for retired veterans of foreign wars

9. Which statement about No Equity Mortgages is false:

___ a. They offer high interest rates for qualified buyers

___ b. They fund up to 125% of the home purchase price by finance companies in secondary markets

___ c. They are ideal for everybody's portfolio

___ d. They offer no mortgage insurance even though they are only partly collateralized

10. Which statement is true about the Second Trust Deed Horror Story

___ a. It was located in the Inland Empire area of Riverside County, California

___ b. The client bought a high interest second trust deed and received a recorded Trust Deed

___ c. The law of mortgage recordings dictates that there is only the first and one second recorded mortgage, so her tenth recording on a Trust Deed had no collateral or value

___ d. This proved to be a Ponzi scheme when the payments stopped coming in the mail and there was no remaining equity or cash flow

___ e. All of the above

___ f. None of the above

CHAPTER FIFTEEN

MONEY MARKET, CERTIFICATES OF DEPOSIT, FOREIGN CURRENCY & INTEREST RATE, ARBITRAGE, BOND DERIVATIVES, SPECULATIVE HEDGE FUNDS

Speculation is to investors as sex is to politicians. The presence and temptations are always there; the call to danger and excitement is part of the landscape and the offer of riches or bankruptcy is always a sweet breath away. There is no need to sell our soul, because we are buyers who listen to the offers of unheard of profits for signatures on leveraged loan documents. Moreover, the old axiom still holds, that you should not speculate with more money than you can afford to lose.

The brokerage and banking business is **yield-driven**. Poor earnings send resumes flying, good earnings equal good bonuses and pay raises. Watch the "Wall Street" movie for the rewards of risk (and **insider trading**) as practiced for **corporate takeovers**. Everybody wants a taste of the action, the heft of gold and the lift of adrenaline in the bloody chase.

First, there are conservative **money market accounts**. This is where the cash is parked. A safe haven to accumulate dividends, to earn some interest, and to accumulate funds for trading. Most brokerage money market accounts are now FDIC insured by passing them through a banking institution, checks are issued on them as needed, and funds can be wired, mailed, deposited in and out of them. Best of all, trades can be made directly from them because there are no checks to clear, no deposits to account for, no five working day holds when a trade must be covered in three days. It is instant trading cash. Every brokerage account has a money market account.

Broker-dealer money market accounts usually pay more interest than the lowly bank offers for interest-bearing checking accounts. The broker firm or backup institution invests the money in short-term US treasury bonds, corporate bonds, and pools of overnight bank lending (known as **no risk**). Mutual funds have money market accounts in all their family of funds concept to facilitate trading and offer a cash place (liquid income account) for pension plan distribution, although they pay low rates due to their overhead charges. The money market funds are devoid of speculation. In other words, they are also for scared investors. There are offsetting charges of about 1% to administer the accounts that caused BD panics when interest rates dropped in recent years.

Certificates of Deposit (CD) have their place in a conservative investment portfolio, especially for fixed interest rates of longer-term than money market accounts. The **Federal Deposit Insurance Corporation** insures them, along with other bank deposits up to $250,000, which is a big selling point. Most of the savings and loan institutions were converted to banks after the bankruptcy of the Savings & Loan Deposit Insurance Corporation. Early withdrawals on a year CD have a penalty of three months interest. Broker-Dealers offer CDs with higher interest rates than usual from banks seeking deposits and willing to pay a small commission and higher rates to find it. They pay interest rates higher than the money market because of the longer fixed term, most CDs, except the longer-term Broker-Dealer offers, ranging from 3 months to ten years term with the interest paid on maturity for the short-term issues and annually for longer than one year. Minimum deposits are usually $100,000.

During the Great Depression, the banks were blamed for some of the problems of the stock market crash and speculation by participation in the markets themselves. The truth was that businesses collapsed along with the economy that resulted in the **"bank holidays"** when the banks shut down to catch their financial breath and hold on to some cash. Because of the perceived relationship, the **Glass-Steagall Act of 1933** separated the banks from the insurance and securities business.

These barriers were broken down with recent legislation under the Clinton Presidency, allowing the banks to admit that the person on the floor (usually at the desk inside the front door like the Wal-Mart Greeter) is really selling insurance and securities to the bank customers from a BD owned by the bank.

Every day, the Wall Street Journal and other financial newspapers publish **Foreign Currency Exchange Rates.** Arbitrage investors buy futures of currency based on exchange rates. Naturally, it would be **leveraged** to enhance the effect, and it would help that the exchange rate swing be much greater to offset the interest expense of the arbitrage. Currency futures contracts trade on the Chicago Mercantile Exchange and a few smaller exchanges. A **currency future** is an agreement to buy or sell currencies at a set time in the future at an agreed price. **Federal commodity laws** exempt most foreign currency transactions from regulation to expedite bank and institutional trading and transferring funds.

Next, we have **stock index arbitrage.** This is simply buying and selling on stock movements in either direction…up or down, based on algorithm computer models, especially on hedge funds. The models are factoring the advantage of buying or selling of holding versus futures trading. They use an index of the market in general as the standard. We are working with large blocks of stocks, and computer trading can greatly influence market direction by accelerating trends in the market. With this in mind, the New York Stock Exchange has a "**collar**" restriction on futures trading (which short-circuits this dangerous trading) when the Dow Industrial averages have moved at least 2% or about 175 points in a day. There are stock market indexes by country also listed in the financial newspapers.

A new bank financial instrument is now indexed to the S&P 500 price. The earnings of the new, FDIC insured to $250,000, investment is guaranteed to return the principal with the profits or earnings pegged to the S&P 500 stocks. The minimum investment is $10,000. If the market goes south, the investor will still receive his initial investment back. If the market continues upward, he will receive income accordingly. This financial instrument is sold as a **Certificate of Deposit with uncertain earnings**.

Last but not least, there is **interest rate arbitrage**. There are interest rates for US government bonds, and everybody else's bonds as well, published daily in the financial journals. An interest arbitrageur gambles on interest rate changes, in a big way with the usual computers and big money. The best way is to leverage the deal to get more bang on the buck and big banks are always willing participants, anxious to lend a hand at it.

Then there are the **hedge funds**. These funds require country club membership fees and dues. The SEC provided strict membership criteria of individual income of at least $200,000 annually for two most recent years, or $300,000 per couple, and net worth of $1,000,000. Many funds require a minimum of one million dollars invested for a period of at least a year to open an account, some are $5 million. They became so popular with the country club set that a man needed both a trophy wife and a hedge fund to be truly visibly successful. Of course, a bank or brokerage firm can do their own hedge fund trading and the Bank of America in 1998 became an active participant when they bought up the D. E. Shaw & Co. investment firm that was making tons of money doing hedge fund trading. The gold turned green when, after the due diligence and ink had dried on the deal, the computer model failed and huge losses of over $562 million resulted. The losses, from both unsecured loans and stocks, were so big that many Bank of America senior officers lost their jobs later that same year as Nations Bank absorbed them as the biggest fish in the merger deal game.

Hedge funds are a two-way bet. They use **short positions** or bets that stock prices will fall and they will buy the stocks or securities to cover in the future. Corporate take-overs and mergers also are big bets, and currencies can be held in arbitrage as well. Leverage is extensively applied to multiply gains (and losses). The significant issue for hedge funds is that they are high-risk and big money. They work both sides of the fence at the same time, with the help of computerized trading.

HORROR STORY – LONG TERM CAPITAL

The best example of how a hedge fund works is to study **Long-Term Capital**, a huge hedge fund that was so big various banks and brokerage firms were happily participating with their own money. Their back room was so esoteric that two of their computer people held **Nobel Prizes in economics**. The Long-Term firm was started in 1993 by bond traders from Solomon Investment Firm. This hedge fund became prominent in handling US Treasuries and had a foolproof system to save losses by computer models that backed up all interest arbitrage with alternate strategies to maximize gain. The complex computer models consisted of buying and selling **derivatives**, which were stripped versions of the treasuries that magnified the interest variations. These hybrid investments used lots of leverage to get the ante up. Naturally, they made tons of money. Because they were so successful, everybody wanted a piece of the action; so the money poured in until the fund reached $6,000,000,000 invested. Yes, six billion dollars. Then, the fund became leveraged as high as 50 to one for maximum leverage, and at one time held positions on $100,000,000,000 (a hundred billion dollars) of bonds and other financial instruments.

Then something failed, maybe the interest rate changed, which was improbable but happened despite the model plan. The big early 1998 downward shift in Treasuries interest rates caught the hedgers by surprise, and huge losses resulted. The losses were so big that the invested capital shrank to only $600,000,000 (from six bills to six hundred mill, equal to a 10% return OF capital, not ON capital). Suddenly the Federal Reserve Board went into action and coerced a coalition of banks to take the fund over in 1998 to avoid a bankruptcy that would affect the strength of the economy, the US dollar, and bankrupt some of the large banking participants. The result...bigger is not always better!

PLANNING TIPS

- Unless you can afford to lose a million dollars, put your money in a safe place. Even money market account earnings look good when they make a secure 4% and no inflation.
- Certificates of deposit are still good because of the FDIC. When the market goes south, they may be the best bet in town because they are liquid and guaranteed.

- Electronic banking is important, but you may still need the local bank to make deposits, cash checks, and create an auditable bank account. The US Postal service may deliver snail mail but, like the local bank, electronic means do not deliver or record everything in proper form.

- Hedge funds charge huge commissions on gains, on the account balances, and do not share in losses. One successful hedge **Renaissance fund** has a sister fund, **Medallion Fund** for employees that charges 5% annually for all assets and 44% of all gains. This is higher than other funds but an example of a very select fund. Thanks to Wall Street Journal reporting.

- Accordingly, hedge funds can make money and be well paid or it loses money and fades away quickly. For every winner there is a loser.

TAXES

Since speculation and losses go hand in hand, we are subject to the capital gains and losses rules. The limit of $3,000 of carryover losses, after reducing any capital gains, will last many years for most people.

There has been some manipulation to convert capital losses into ordinary losses by changing the nature of the investments, but the IRS is always questioning these tactics because they also like to audit high-income taxpayers.

SUCCESSFUL STRATEGIES

Highly speculative investments are far beyond the realm of most people. Keep away from speculation, even when all your friends are doing it. Speculation is infective and somehow the herd instinct applies. For example, in the 1980's the banking rules relaxed to allow savings and loan institutions to actually participate in construction projects instead of just lending money on them. The results were predictable and the whole savings and loan institution itself collapsed under the weight of the newfound fraud and mismanagement. President Reagan, whose deregulation of quasi-public institutions without controls gave them the financial freedom to commit suicide, paved the way for the creation of the **Resolution Trust** to bail out the S & L's and sell off the banking real estate remnants. President Billy Clinton and Hillary Clinton, both lawyers, were involved in litigating these problem institutions before Billy became president. The Investor's Insurance Fund collapsed trying to cover the losses and the public treasury was tapped to complete the terrible fiasco payoff of individual savings accounts.

There is always considerable Congressional lobbying by the banking industry to allow these institutions to participate in securities offers and trading. After the 1929 Crash and Depression, Congress separated the banks from the bad speculation with the **Seagate Act**. Now, there are attempts to get closer to the action. The Thrift and Savings & Loan example of the 1980s is an excellent example of what happens when the wolves are mixed with the banking institution.

HORROR STORY - BOB CITRON

There is probably no greater horror story than **Bob Citron** experienced as the Orange County Treasurer. Bob liked working with **derivatives,** which are esoteric contracts whose values are derived from US Treasury bonds, with much help from major brokerage firms, of course. He lacked computer nerds and their sophisticated models as he invested up to $13 billion, some of it leveraged, much of it from other municipal agencies, in longer-maturity derivative securities. Instead, he consulted his astrologer's planet and star charts from the 1980s to 1993 and traded when the stars lined up right. The strategy worked and he earned from 10% to 17% year after year. All the Orange County agencies fell in line with the good news and wanted him to handle their money, especially their pension funds, even though these funds should be managed conservatively. The rules for brokers are very strict for fiduciary responsibility when handling trust and public funds, but nobody cared. Finally, in 1993, the interest rates dipped and the stars failed to respond. Bob kept with his strategy, hoping the market would change. The rates kept falling and by 1994, the County had lost $1.64 billion and filed for bankruptcy. Bob retired before the next election, as Orange County Treasurer, an elective office.

The point: Speculative strategies appear to be successful at inception but the strategy for success becomes the same strategy for future failure when market conditions change. Note that Bob's stars may have successfully worked longer for him than the Nobel Prize mathematician computer models for the Long-Term Investment hedge fund.

SECOND HORROR STORY - NICHOLAS LEESON

There have been various players in this game these past few years. There was the enterprising manager of the Singapore branch of Barings PLC English Bank. This reputable bank was an old institution, as conservative and pedigreed as Lloyd's Insurance Company LLD. The young rogue trader had some new financial tricks and in a few short years had garnished great support and backing from the parent bank, because his new ideas of arbitrage were making tons of money. Nicholas Leeson was a certified financial whiz while he worked for Barings during 1995. Then one day, in 1996, the game plan failed to change when the interest rates went the wrong way and he was stuck with huge mega-million-dollar losses. After much controversy, the bank failed and the cell was bought by a Swiss bank that wanted the famous old name. The star manager went to jail in Singapore for illegal trading.

PROS AND CONS OF INVESTING IN THE ABOVE

- Some of your money should be in CD's because they are safe, liquid and will always earn initial interest rates in excess of inflation (don't get it for too long a term, especially if inflation rises).
- Speculative investing in derivatives, interest rate, and currency futures is a dangerous business except for the wealthy who should be able to suffer losses easier than most investors.
- Money market accounts with a broker-dealer are a safe haven for short-term liquid investments. Checks can be written on these accounts to transfer funds or for large transactions. There are no charges or commissions and balances can be increased or decreased without contract or commitment. Interest is credited monthly and statements are sent out monthly as well. They are

very short-term and mark to the market overnight, always paying better than bank short-term savings rates. Some of these accounts are through banks with the usual FDIC insurance.

- George Soros gambled big and cornered the British currency market once which made him a billionaire.

- Bunker Hunt failed to corner the silver market. On paper, he owned more silver than was in existence until someone noticed it. Speculation is best left to the people with the resources to play the game. A bank repossessed his Rolex.

- Electronic banking does not create a good audit trail for canceled checks that government auditing agencies like. Cash and check deposits must also be maintained there, so a local bank account is still a must.

- Snail mail, the US Postage service, is not about to be replaced by electronic means and "the check is in the mail" story may be with us for a while longer.

- It is now official that banks are selling insurance and securities on the floor WITHOUT THE FDIC guarantee because the Glass-Steagall Depression-era legislation was voided during 1999 with the help of much lobbying and soft money. Remember that the bank broker now has the same licenses as the financial planner who also works closely with you to a greater depth when he covers your investment tax problems and other fiscal matters.

- Most bonds and money market funds pay interest much more often, usually monthly or quarterly (bonds), than bank CDs, which act like zero-coupon bonds by paying at maturity. CDs also charge a three-month interest penalty for early withdrawal-cancellations.

CHAPTER 15: APPLICATION EXERCISES

1. The Glass-Steagall Act of 1933 separated the banks from the insurance and securities business. ____ True ____ False

2. Federal commodity laws exempt most foreign currency transactions from regulation to expedite bank and institutional trading and transferring funds. ____ True ____ False

3. Speculative investing in derivatives, interest rate and currency futures is a dangerous business except for the wealthy who should be able to suffer losses easier than most investors. ____ True ____ False

4. A currency future is an agreement to buy or sell currencies with dollars at a set time in the future at an agreed price (arbitrage). ____ True ____ False

5. Hedge funds are low-risk and affordable and therefore a good idea for the everyday investor. ____ True ____ False

6. Which of the following statements about Money Market funds is false:
   ____ a. They are all FDIC insured because they act like banks
   ____ b. They are a safe haven for brokerage accounts to trade or receive dividends
   ____ c. They are the bank account for all brokerage firms and all mutual funds
   ____ d. They only pay small interest rates because their earnings are from overnight funds

7. Which of the following is true about The Glass-Steagall Act of 1933:
   ____ a. It resulted in barriers between FDIC insured bank deposit funds and speculation by banks in securities
   ____ b. The Act was sidestepped during the Clinton Presidency to allow banks to resume brokerage activities in their places of business, but not to participate in the ownership of the securities
   ____ c. A bank holiday in the Depression was to close the doors to stop a run of cash withdrawals
   ____ d. All of the above

8. Hedge Funds:
   ___ a. Are not sold by brokerage firms because they are high risk investment brokerages
   ___ b. Require high income or millionaire net worth to participate in their investments
   ___ c. Are regulated by the SEC but very loosely
   ___ d. All of the above

9. In the Horror Story involving Long Term Capital, which statement is false and illogical:
   ___ a. It was a giant hedge fund run by two Nobel Prize people who did the trading
   ___ b. They traded in bond derivatives with arbitrage positions to profit if the market went up or down
   ___ c. It grew so big that at one time it held positions on $100,000,000,000 (which is a hundred billion)
   ___ d. It was the most successful hedge fund in America before the time of takeover

10. In the Horror story of Bob Citron in Orange County:
    ___ a. The County Treasurer invested up to $10 billion of tax receipts in derivatives in Treasuries
    ___ b. The investment model Bob used was not computer generated but astrological
    ___ c. Bob was so successful that other County agencies gave him their funds to invest
    ___ d. Long term capital lasted longer than The Treasury of Orange County under Bob Citron

CHAPTER SIXTEEN

UTILITIES

Utilities are about electrons. These little atomic elements move from one atom to another creating a current that moves along metal wires until it comes back to earth via the ground. These electrons generate heat, luminescence, and magnetism. These effects move our society; thus, are directly related to economic activity. Because the generation of electricity (which is created with electromagnets) requires the application of huge amounts of physical energy, the costs are related to energy supplies such as gas, oil, hydroelectric, nuclear, and minor sources such as solar, wind, hydrothermal, wood burning, etc. All of the above require massive plant, equipment, and regulation, a larger scheme of the original when Thomas Alva Edison installed the first of his Edison power companies in the big cities many decades ago. Before Tom Edison's application, most industrial power provided by waterwheels stuck in rivers, and wheels that turned huge leather belts on smaller wheels throughout factories, which were lighted through angled windows on the roofs. Burning kerosene, candles, whale oil, or coal gas (very poisonous) provided household illumination. National economic (GNP) activity is gaged according to the amount of electricity consumed during a period.

Utility companies have always been heavily bonded and, because of regulatory guarantees, been reliable dividend generators from stock subscriptions. Because of the guarantees that the power will not blackout (or brownout), they have been a part of the conservative portfolio for many decades. The stock shares for utilities, which act as bonds because of dividend expectations, are shown as a separate listing called the **Dow Jones 15 Utility Average**. This average reflects the conservative nature of utility companies that do not do anything in a hurry. Yet, when the Dow Jones Industrial Average goes up or down, utilities join the **Dow Jones Transportation 20 average** that creates the 65 share **Dow Jones**

Composite Average. As a result, all the boats go up and down together with the tide.

THE MOST RECENT DOW JONES UTILITY AVERAGE COMPANIES AS OF DECEMBER 31, 2019

- The AES Corporation (AES)
- American Electric Power Co., Inc. (AEP)
- American Water Works Company, Inc. (AWK)
- CenterPoint Energy, Inc. (CNP)
- Consolidated Edison, Inc. (ED)
- Dominion Energy, Inc. (D)
- Duke Energy Corp. (DUK)
- Edison International (EIX)
- Exelon Corp. (EXC)
- FirstEnergy Corp. (FE)
- NextEra Energy Inc. (NEE)
- NiSource, Inc. (NI)
- Public Service Enterprise Group, Inc. (PEG)
- Sempra Energy (SRE)
- Southern Company, Inc. (SO)

You may have noticed that some of the utility companies are really fuel/energy companies. That is not a coincidence, because the industry is fuel-dependent. Telephone companies are utilities but not for this listing.

Both Moody's and Standard & Poor's rate utility bonds like all other bonds. The higher the grade, the better-quality bonds. Bonds, like stocks, can be severely downgraded after unnatural disasters such as the Three Mile Island meltdown or the Paradise fires in California.

At this time, the Utilities Average is under pressure from deregulation. New niche players have not done well against the entrenched dug-in giants because, one way or another, the stranded costs of the expensive nuclear-fired plants will be passed on to all customers, even as they leave the grid to produce their own power (industrial plants) or outsource power from newer suppliers. Localized natural gas-fired mini-plants (peaker units) now provide excess power when needed. The residential consumer will probably not see any benefit because, as with telephone deregulation, long-distance costs went down and the local bells added new costs to bring their billing up again. Overhead from older regulated industries tends to linger on far into the future, as well.

The alternative energy sources, silicon solar panels on houses or in farms, solar sodium (not good) melting generators, geothermal, windmill forests, etc. have proven very expensive substitutes for conventional nuclear, natural gas, oil, and coal production sources. These newer investments have proven to be great for the broker-dealers, but bad for investors. The real competition for the utilities are industrial clients who will find it easier to power up their own plant in their backyard with newer, more efficient, and smaller generators. Huge power generators located in remote places where fuel sources are plentiful lose considerable energy from transmitting over the wires for long distances. These will be the losers in the race for efficiency which deregulation will induce. Perhaps the efficiency levels of alternate electrical generating sources will rise enough someday to viably compete with burning oil or coal fuels.

Utilities still hold a large place in the overall diversified stock portfolio and still have a firm place in an advisor portfolio for stability and steady earnings. People who manufacture power generation equipment and those who bring new smaller efficient power sources online, will offer the more active and progressive investments in this industry.

The daily financial newspapers publish the national wholesale utility prices by region and kilowatt-hour. As usual, California has the highest rates of all. To make matters worse, some California communities such as Riverside, have added a utility tax on top of the bill. Convinced that their people like paying taxes and fees to the general fund, they even proposed raising utility rates as part of a creative plan to deregulate their money-making city-owned utility billing unit which marks up power and services received from Southern California Edison. California now has the highest state income tax rates in the nation and the sales taxes are very close to the top. A policy of regulating for tax increases has numbed the ruling party.

PLANNING TIPS

Avoid speculative energy-related investments that always begin with huge assumed hypothetical increases in utility rates. Unless there is a world war or other energy shortage catastrophe, the economic balance of supply and demand between electricity users and producers will keep rates steady. This huge stable entrenched industry, although faced with deregulation, will not offer near-term realistic market entry for newcomers or true rate decreases for users because of fixed plant, equipment, and bloated bureaucracies. Bankruptcies of large energy producers will result in higher rates to keep the lights turned on.

TAXES

Utilities offer taxable dividends and taxable bond interest income. Both are taxed as ordinary income in an investor's tax return. The sale of these stocks or bonds would create taxable capital gains or losses. Recent Californian bankruptcies of large utility companies will certainly generate long term losses for some investors.

LEGAL COMPLIANCE

The compliance officer of any broker-dealer firm will always be happy to find utility stocks or bonds in an investor's portfolio, especially elderly folk who require steady income from low-risk investments. It is the best fit for low-risk investments.

SUCCESSFUL STRATEGIES

An investment strategy would be either conservative by buying stocks or bonds in the old Edison companies, or aggressive by pursuing the stocks of companies manufacturing generating equipment. Firms also active at installing new equipment for industrial clients would be a good bet. Large corporations competing for head-on with the entrenched utility giants have not had much success at wresting market share away because of their entrenched bureaucracies shared with regulators. The risky strategy would be investing in new faddish applications such as the solar water heaters that were sold on the presumption of cost per kilowatt tripling or quadrupling in the next few years. Tax credits can also make some novel energy sources more appealing, but only in the short term.

HORROR STORY - DAGGETT, CALIFORNIA

Daggett, California is a place in the middle of nowhere. It is located in the Southern California Mojave Desert, where it is hot as Hell because the sun shines almost all of the time. A solar collector plant built to generate electric power by collecting sunlight in a gigantic dish that was covered with mirrors. The mirrors reflected sunlight into a tall tank of metallic sodium that vaporized to turn electric generators. This novel concept was in response to the public awareness of a need for non-polluting sources of electric power to replace or supplement growing local power needs.

About fifteen years ago, the California legislature mandated new credits for alternative electric power sources. They also arranged for the utility companies to subsidize the absorption of new power into the grid by paying premium prices for the additional wattage. Most of the assumptions for investment were not sustaining, and sellers of novel or experimental electrical or energy-saving investments relied on dramatic future Arab Oil Crisis energy prices and one-time tax credits.

A major brokerage firm (Merrill Lynch) funded the huge Daggett project. It was packaged as a limited partnership. The tax credits hid the huge packaging and commission costs built into the deal. Aesthetically, the project was appealing, because everybody expected energy and electric power costs to rise in the near future. The thing was sold to high-income customers, who always had tax problems and welcomed the losses always produced by limited partnerships. This was prior to the **Tax Reform Act of 1996** when partnership losses flowed easier through tax returns. Five years later, after the credits had been applied and the depreciation and operating losses absorbed, the project failed to produce an operating profit. High maintenance and unforeseen technical problems ate the revenue even though the solar collector functioned better than expected and was truly a remarkable sight. Finally, it was shut down. The project was a technical success but a financial failure. The projected higher future energy costs never happened, and energy capacity was assured as new national conservation policies prevailed along with the new San Onofre nuclear plant coming online near San Diego. No dividends or distributions were ever received from the solar investment. Future large-scale solar sodium plans also failed financially.

The sturdy mirrored monument still stands in the desert, a great technical achievement, useful as a bright spot on the desert floor for the visiting spaceships to beam in on.

SECOND HORROR STORY - ENRON

California began deregulating electric markets with the new **Electric Utility Industry Restructuring Act in 1996**. This law fixed (capped) the user prices of electricity but deregulated the cost by selling most of the publicly-owned power generating units to private operators. These operators were subject to limited regulation but were not regulated whatsoever on imported electricity from other states. To make a long story short, thanks to data from Wikipedia, by 2000 Enron and some related out-of-State company energy traders (brokers) conspired to shut down local units they controlled to create shortages and import spot priced power through them from out of state. The prices were so cleverly contrived that over a few years they billed up to 20 times the usual rate. This resulted in blackouts and shortages throughout the State and finally the bankruptcy of Pacific Gas & Electric and almost Southern California Edison. Enron Corporation traders, under colorful pseudonyms as Fat Boy, Death Star, Ricochet, Ping Pong, Black Widow, Big Foot, Cong Catcher, and others skillfully megawatt laundered the price up to an 800% increase at one point by gaming the market. The interstate regulating agency, Federal Energy Regulatory Commission (FERC) investigated the energy shortage pogrom caused by Enron's manipulation of shortages but did nothing until 2013. They shut down many plants simultaneously to create shortages as they manipulated the spot rates.

Meanwhile, Enron and related conspirators developed a network of new international businesses which were equally corrupt. The corporate culture created a new **mark-to-market accounting method** which was accepted by their audit firm **Arthur Anderson**, and entered into **esoteric capitulation** of a new venture called the Raptors, and many other affiliations and mergers. The capitalization involved derivative contracts, swaps, along with notes and bonds, to complete a deliberately confusing picture of a company culture which was totally out of control with greed and deception.

When it was over, a new term for California was termed "financialization" of the energy market. **Enron Europe**, the holding company **filed bankruptcy** on December, 2001. It was the **largest bankruptcy in U.S. history** with $63 billion in assets. Arthur Anderson, one of the five largest accounting firms in the world shared the honor of having the largest audit failure which resulted in their demise a few years later. **Merrill Lynch Brokerage Firm** was also involved and shared some responsibility as some of their people went to jail with the Enron crowd. But they survived to be taken over by the Bank of America. There was only one witness suicide. Millions of people were affected before the next decade passed which allowed us to forget what was allowed to happen by **administrative fiat.**

THIRD HORROR STORY - ENRON BONDS

Why are we covering this event in this chapter? Because sometimes the most conservative investments can get out of control and in a big way. They can affect us as shareholders or bondholders and as citizens involved paying to turn the lights on.

I had a client who inherited a large sum of money when living in Riverside County. She moved to Newport Beach to live with the rich people. She found a new broker who unloaded a huge amount of bonds into her portfolio. They were Enron and turned up worthless several years later.

PROS & CONS OF INVESTING IN UTILITY STOCKS

- Electrical power will be used for many years in the future. Thus, long-term investment in utility stocks or bonds, which are capital intensive investments in our infrastructure, is an assured good thing.

- Telephone companies are considered utilities but are not included in the Dow Jones Utility Average because they are much smaller and diversified than the huge power companies. They are much more speculative because of competition, than electrical utilities or energy-related companies. Telephone lines and switchboards were replaced with Landsat satellites and computers, now by Satellites en-masse at 60 per lift by Space-X Rockets

- Utilities have earned less than the transportation and industrial components of the Dow Jones Composite Average, which indicates less volatility and price stability which is needed for retired investor's lower risk portfolio.

- Strong dividends and bond earnings are always available from the capital-intensive utility portfolio.

- Speculation and high long-term earnings cannot be had from the utility portfolio because utility stocks act more like bonds in the long run.

- Deregulation will create speculative opportunity, as alternate power sources that will be plugged into the grids at industrial plants, shopping malls, and large office buildings. The producers and manufacturers of these better and more efficient systems will be good buys.

- Alternative energy sources may be quite close efficiency-wise (cost effective electrical sources) at this time and may become viable investments for the future. Tax credits helped get solar started. Some of them will become great investments for the speculator who, after doing his homework, will take a chance for higher long-term earnings potential.

An unusually good move was made recently in California when the state-mandated solar power panels for every new home under construction. The costs are only one-third of the cost of the door-to-door salespeople selling the same. $8,000 per unit is truly a reasonable cost because this is the cheapest way to add solar. There was a time when air conditioning was an add-on appliance for new automobiles. A whole industry put them in place after you bought the car. Now it is more efficient and nicely built into the electronics and mechanical parts of every car or truck. Solar has finally come to accept as a required and reasonable alternative to long-distance electronic power sources.

CHAPTER 16: APPLICATION EXERCISES

1. Both Moody's and Standard & Poor's rate utility bonds like all other bonds. ____ True ____ False

2. It's wise to engage in speculative energy-related investments that begin with huge assumed hypothetical increases in utility rates. ____ True ____ False

3. Utility dividends and interest income are taxed as ordinary income in an investor's tax return.____ True ____ False

4. Telephone companies are considered utilities but are not included in the Dow Jones Utility Average because they are much smaller and diversified than the huge power companies. ____ True ____ False

5. Speculation and high long-term earnings can be a benefit of the utility portfolio. ____ True ____ False

6. Which statement is false:
   ____ a. Utilities are companies who manufacture or distribute electricity, water or gas
   ____ b. Gross National Product is measured by the consumption of electricity during a period
   ____ c. Nicholas Tesla, who started Westinghouse, pioneered altering electric power but Thomas Edison used it to power the Edison Electric Companies in every city
   ____ d. Electric companies are not regulated by the Public Utility Commission like nuclear plants

7. Which of the following statements are true about Utility regulations and policy:
   ____ a. The Dow Jones Utility listing is the Dow Jones 15 Utility Average
   ____ b. Moody's and Standard & Poor rate utility bonds because they are heavily leveraged
   ____ c. Utility companies can never declare bankruptcy
   ____ d. Utility companies are highly regulated because of the public needs of constant and reliable electricity

8. Which of the following statements is false regarding The Daggett California solar-sodium electric generator:
   ___ a. It was an experimental non-polluting project which converted solar energy into electric energy
   ___ b. It was immensely profitable because it was highly efficient
   ___ c. The project was packaged and sold as a limited partnership by Merrill Lynch 25 years ago
   ___ d. The project proved the experiment worked but was not economic

9. Which of the following statements is false regarding the Electric Utility Industry Restructuring Act of 1996:
   ___ a. The act made energy costs cheaper by deregulation
   ___ b. Abnormal costs from out of state suppliers were noticed by FERC but were ignored
   ___ c. An energy supplier named Enron took over the energy production of most of California
   ___ d. Enron successfully shut down plants in California to import their electric power at prices up to 20 times the normal rate, which bankrupted the Edison companies.

10. In the Enron Bond Horror Story, which of the following statements is false:
    ___ a. People outside the brokerage business are always aware of corrupt investments like Enron
    ___ b. Enron founded a new organization called the Raptors, with deceptive capitalization
    ___ c. A client who bought Enron bonds from a Newport Beach BD lost it all
    ___ d. Arthur Anderson, Enron's national audit firm, went out of business, Merrill Lynch brokerage was suddenly taken over by the Bank of America and the Enron bankruptcy of $63 billion was the largest in US history. Many went to jail while more lawyers got rich.

PART THREE
MUTUAL FUNDS

Mutual funds represent the primary investment vehicle for the average modern investor. Although they have been available since the Great Depression, it was not until the 1970s that they became popular. In the early 1990s, **401(K) pension plans** began to replace the large corporate money purchase profit-sharing plans. The old plans were company managed because they were company funded, thus they tended to purchase only company securities. 401(K) replacement plans are funded by employees, sometimes with employer matching contributions in profit-sharing savings plans.

Individual Retirement Plans (**IRAs**) have been the self-employed investor's plan of choice along with rollover plans that were corporate pensions before retirement. They are usually managed by employees with investment choices of remarkably popular mutual fund securities. This change, which was the result of tax code changes and a rethinking of corporate cost structure, resulted in a tidal wave of investments from expanded participation and a stable booming economy. All of these pension investments hold mutual funds as all or part of their portfolios.

CHAPTER SEVENTEEN

MUTUAL FUNDS, FAMILY OF FUNDS CONCEPT & TYPES OF INVESTMENT

Mutual funds are the mainstay of middle-class American investment today. From inception by an insurance company in the mid-1930s, they have become the first choice of investment for millions of Americans. At this time there are approximately (how do you count closed funds or mergers?) thirty thousand funds, most of them listed daily in the financial news and even the local newspapers. The amounts invested are trillions of dollars and change by billions daily with the wax and wane of the stock markets. The whole economy is in the stock market! Some of the giant funds contain over $100,000,000,000 (100 billion) in capital investment. Their trading, which is done in large blocks, is reflected greatly in stock market prices and averages and is a huge part of the volume of stocks traded, which can easily be over a billion shares daily. Today millions of citizens and their pension plans participate in the mutual funds of their choice to extend their ownership of the American Dream.

Most mutual funds have separate distinct funds under the umbrella of the parent fund and are the "**family of funds**". Within these separate funds, institutional financial advisors, who may also advise for other funds as well, make trading decisions. They subscribe to hundreds of periodicals, research services, and publications with dozens of professional employees who graph, compute and make investment decisions hourly. The types of funds are generally the same from one institutional fund to another with some exceptions, although they will hold different portfolios under different advisors. Many funds offer similar type investments under different names.

THE TYPES OF FUNDS ARE AS FOLLOWS:

EQUITY

- **Small-Cap**: NASDAQ new issues of small companies in an early volatile stage of development, which generally reinvest any earnings and do not pay dividends. Speculative high-risk issues.
- **Mid Cap**: Medium-sized companies that are growing and have established a strong market or financial position. The focus is on capital appreciation.
- **Growth & Income (also called sovereign income or blue chip)**: Large established companies, in different market sectors that pay consistent dividends. Not growth stocks except in an expanding growing stock market.
- **Special Sector**: A stock portfolio specializing in one part of the economy, such as banking and financial stocks, or companies paying strong dividends for corporate investors.
- **Index Funds**: Contain a cross-section of the Dow Jones Industrial Average stocks to match the index composed of the average. Minimizes risks by sharing the rise or fall of the market without undue exposure to specific stocks or industries.
- **Real Estate**: These have appeared lately for Real Estate Investment Trusts. For those who like real estate, here is the chance to participate, although some REITS are badly managed.
- **Global**: International equities have recently been very dangerous for your portfolio. These are broken into different continents such as **European**, or the **Asian Tigers** that became extinct in most portfolios after the "crash" of 1998 and 2008. They also provide growth opportunities as the Occidental world economies recover.

FIXED INCOME

- **Money Market**: Short-term cash investments of less than one year, a place to park funds between trades or a fall back, a safe harbor to hold funds. Highly secure, earns only interest income. Poor earnings because of mutual fund advisory charges. A security because of portfolio holdings, but really a cash account.

- **Government Income**: Usually US Treasuries, insured mortgage government agencies, and a smaller percentage of "other" which can be anything including unknown foreign governments. A typical Government fund is a mixed bag of bonds and interest-bearing investments that might include **US government debt**, but will vary because treasuries yield is the lowest. Some bond funds pay steady dividends that exceed income, which can be very misleading. A government bond fund would only include US Treasuries which would yield low and state-tax exempt.

- **Global or International Income**: These funds reach out across the world to invest in treasuries and other financial instruments of foreign countries. Russian bonds and volatile third world Venezuelan politics come to mind here.

- **Adjustable USG**: These funds are included in a pool of the new adjustable-rate government agency, mortgage securities. This is for those who want to eliminate interest rate risk with secure agency-insured investments.

- **Global Currency**: Another name for hedge funds, very volatile and high risks betting on foreign currency changes in relation to the US Dollar. These powerful traders held up the almighty Sovereign Pound currency, cornering the entire British monetary system many years ago.

- **Federal Tax-Free**: This fund can own only US Government bonds, which are state tax-free. Expect low earnings for this safest of all investments.

- **State Tax-Free**: These funds can hold only municipal bond securities in a particular state, which makes the interest income both federal and that particular state tax-free. Beware of municipal bond funds, which do not specify a state because they would only be federal tax-free in a state tax-free state such as Texas, Washington, Florida, or Nevada.

- **High-Yield Bond**: Lower-rated corporate bonds, junk bond funding for corporate buy-outs, can include foreign trash mixed in. They might also use leveraged positions to enlarge gain or risk. Definitely high risk for high-yield, usually produces steady very high earnings until you are off guard, suddenly creates sharp losses. Not for the fickle or elderly unless they demand those risky high earnings.

- **Utility**: These funds are equity funds that act like fixed income funds. That is, they invest in utility stocks that pay high dividends with large holdings in preferred high dividend-paying securities. These funds are distribution-income rich for the retired or trustee investor who desires steady income from a non-volatile source. Sometimes the cash distributions exceed actual earnings during downtimes, which goes unnoticed by many investors. Deregulation could increase risk or reduce dividends as the public utility regulations and rules change.

COMMODITY

- **Precious Metals**: These specialized funds, also called hard currency funds, deal in the stocks and futures of gold, platinum, & silver precious metals bullion. Silver is hardly precious these days at $20 per ounce, except at the jewelry store. Uniquely, jewelry stores in Mexico weigh your silver purchase and negotiate their price by the gram. Commodity trading is conducted inside the physical locations of these securities, with no actual inventory of precious metals. These stocks inherently represent future bullion values because of the ore inventory of the mining corporations. Sometimes used as a safe harbor along with cash when stocks are in decline. A dip in stock market values always produces a spike in precious metals.
- **Natural Resources**: Not renewable resources such as trees, but usually oil and gas which is highly volatile, with some other commodities mixed in. Commodity trades are also part of the portfolio along with the stocks of various commodity producers.

The list of mutual fund names and ingredients are endless and prospectuses are sometimes vague. Just remember that these fund professional advisor managers know more than the average investor because they have bigger computers and more degrees, and that they must try to outperform the DJIA to earn their keep after subtracting commissions and annual charges.

PLANNING TIPS

Some mutual funds can be purchased directly without going through a BD. The fund families that accept these trades are advertised in publications for elderly people and through other financial media. Do not buy these funds unless you understand how they work and are sophisticated enough to make your own investment decisions and can monitor the results. In addition, if a fund family normally charges a commission, which most of them do, buying directly from the fund instead of the broker-dealer sales rep, will still subject the purchase to commissions and you will not have a broker to keep an eye on the investment for you. No-load funds tend to have higher annual charges to offset advertising and distribution costs.

Leaving capital gains and dividends in your mutual funds by reinvesting them is good business because it will save the commission charges that you pay for direct purchases. Leaving the gains in also makes it easier to compute actual profits or losses over the long run because you can easily compare the balance with the original investment without the dividends being sidetracked to the cash money market account.

TAXES

Mutual funds created a special opportunity for the federal government to raise taxes without telling anybody about it. All the trading gains accomplished during the calendar year within a mutual fund are taxable as capital gains. Forget the trading losses, just the gains! What happened to the losses? You must sell the fund (cash it in or close it out) to take credit for the capital losses. Whether or not the gains are reinvested does not matter. That means whenever you sell a mutual fund position you will finally have the capital losses to report because the gains were taxed over the years. As you see, this creates some bookwork to keep track of the taxed gains, which reduce the tax basis at the time of sale. That is why they invented the computer. Moreover, that is why the government works so hard to keep the stock market going up and up and up. Moving from one fund to another, even in a family of funds, creates a taxable event.

LEGAL COMPLIANCE

A **prospectus** must be delivered to a buyer at the time of purchase. In some cases, when a client asks for a certain fund or an order is called in, the fund at the time the order is placed can mail the prospectus directly to the investor. Some investment firms require a client to sign a document stating he received the prospectus. The prospectus must never be marked up (by the broker) and must be current (not more than 15 months old). The funds reprint the things every year with new numbers, so the data can get stale-dated very easily in a changing market.

The prospectus is very important and not very hard to read and digest. It contains condensed financial information on the prior experience (profits and losses over the last and for five years). Unless it is new, objectives of the fund and information on commissions and annual charges are the same. It also updates monthly or quarterly earnings performance information which is available for most funds, and can be invaluable in the volatile marketplace. Major stock holdings and positions will also be available for investors from these updates.

It is illegal for a financial consultant to shift you from one mutual fund to another unless the new fund is entirely different and not offered by the first mutual fund family. This is to avoid commission overcharges by **churning** or **twisting** the client.

MUTUAL FUND RISK DISCLOSURE STATEMENT REQUIRED FOR ALL PROSPECTUSES

"Fund results indicate past performance only for periods shown and do not predict future returns. Share prices and investment returns fluctuate and an investment may be worth more or less than its original cost when redeemed. In addition, periodic investment plans do not ensure a profit, nor do they protect against loss in declining markets."

Most correspondence from brokers regarding any investment, when mentioning past or anticipated future returns must also reflect the above warning. "There are no guarantees in this business."

SUCCESSFUL STRATEGIES

A portfolio should be diversified, but it can be diversified within most mutual funds. Everything is there from cash in the money market, to equities, fixed income, commodities, etc. One mutual fund family can generally create all the diversification for a simple portfolio. The cost of professional management is a one-time commission time at the time of purchase, and an annual small charge **of 1%** to keep it working. The mutual fund equity charts show phenomenal growth, from $10,000 ten years ago to $100,000 in the past ten years. These figures are real and unless the market does an Olympic dive, most investors will keep the gains. It did dive 50% in 2008 and recovered completely for new highs by 2020.

HORROR STORIES - FUNDS

There are various horror stories, deep inside a booming market, without naming specific funds. A fund will be merrily riding the roller coaster up with everybody laughing and cheering it on until it takes a turn over the top such as when the Asian Tiger Global bond funds returned to earth in a hurry in 1977. Another killer year after the real estate bust was 2008. The speculative gains turn to speculative losses when the bubble bursts from greed and overkill. Speculation is a normal human phenomenon, like mold growing on old bread; it happens naturally but is not good for everybody.

Speculation and scratching the risk ceiling for yield also caused many High Yield Corporate Bond funds to dive for cover in mid-1998 when Russia defaulted on seriously large amounts of investment. This caused an investor scramble while asking their brokers why the third world bad stuff was stuck in THEIR corporate bond account. One-third of some affected account balances disappeared from one day to the next.

Some bank and financial institutional equity funds also fell off a cliff in 1998 when financial institutions holding hedge funds, which were making tons of money, discovered the other side of the high-risk coin.

All mutual funds, because they own different parts of the stock and bond markets, will be subject to speculative splurges and shocks, hopefully for the short-run. The best way to avoid the fall is to buy individual stocks or index funds which spread all over the market by following the whole market...actually averaging the whole market, up or down, and also by investing outside the market by diversifying.

THE LIPPER DAILY INDEXES FOR MUTUAL FUNDS

- Capital Appreciation
- Growth Fund
- Small Cap Fund
- Growth & Income
- Equity Income Fund
- Science & Technology Fund
- International Fund
- Gold Fund
- Balanced Fund
- Emerging Markets

BOND INDEXES

- Corp A-Rated Debt
- US Government
- GNMA
- High Current Yield
- Intermediate Investment Grade
- Short Investment Grade
- General Municipal Debt
- High Yield Municipal Debt
- Short Municipal
- Global Income
- International Income

FINRA requires a mutual fund to have at least 1,000 shareholders or assets of $25 million to be listed and included in the above indexes.

PROS & CONS OF BUYING MUTUAL FUNDS

- Unless you are a sophisticated investor, this is the best place to be.
- Moving from one fund to another in a mutual fund family creates a taxable event from the sale.
- Reinvesting gains and dividends into the fund saves commissions, but not taxes.
- Avoid the broker who tries to shift you from one mutual fund to another unless it is different, justifiable, and not offered by the first fund.
- If you are hooked on mutual funds, then do not forget to diversify within the family of funds.
- A sophisticated person can save money by buying index funds that have small or no commission charges.
- Prospectuses, although informative, quickly become outdated. They are easily read. Always ask for the current performance sheets on particular funds when investing.
- Do not buy any mutual fund without a current prospectus. They are credible because they are reviewed and approved by the SEC periodically.
- Mutual funds have annual overhead and administrative charges, usually about 1+% annually (more if it is a no-load). Owning a stock or bond directly avoids these costs.
- Pay attention to the information sent you monthly, quarterly, or annually. This information tells you how well the fund is doing, besides asking for more funds.
- Keep in touch with your broker at least annually. This is a chance to review your investment. (And an opportunity for him to sell you more).
- Ask your broker to provide the largest five investments in the fund. This will give you a better idea of how and where it is working.
- Mutual funds buy and sell huge blocks of stocks or securities all day long and pay minimal commissions to do this. This helps justify some of the cost of having them professionally manage the fund for you.

- Mutual funds charge you a commission only when you buy into it, no commission on the sale, unlike buying or selling stocks or bonds directly for your portfolio.
- Mutual fund investments are traded all day long, but mark the purchase or sale value to the portfolio at the end of the day when the closing bell has rung.
- Mutual funds may contain more risk than shareholders know about because their advisors are always striving to beat the DJIA and their competition for greater yield.
- Mutual funds always keep considerable amounts of uninvested cash (money market equivalents) available for redemptions; more so when the market is falling (which also has a bad effect by accelerating the downward shift in the market by creating a seller's market).

CHAPTER 17: APPLICATION EXERCISES

1. Moving from one fund to another in a mutual fund family does not create a taxable event from the sale. ____ True ____ False

2. Reinvesting gains and dividends into the fund saves commissions but not taxes. ____ True ____ False

3. A sophisticated person can save money by buying index funds that have small or no commission charges. ____ True ____ False

4. All of the trading gains accomplished during the calendar year within a mutual fund are taxable as capital gains. ____ True ____ False

5. Which of the following are types of funds (check all that apply):
    ____ a. Index
    ____ b. Global
    ____ c. Mid Cap
    ____ d. REITs
    ____ e. Small Cap
    ____ f. All of the above

6. Which statement about mutual funds is false:
    ____ a. Global funds are broken into European and Asian economic continents
    ____ b. Growth funds do not usually pay dividends
    ____ c. Small cap are high risk and do not pay dividends
    ____ d. Real estate include REITS which pay high dividends

7. Which statement about mutual funds is false:
    ____ a. Money market funds earn only interest for the holder
    ____ b. Federal Tax Free funds own only US Govt. bonds which are Federal tax free
    ____ c. State Tax Free funds hold bonds in one state which makes the interest income non-taxable for both Federal and State
    ____ d. Global or International Income funds invest in foreign Treasuries, such as Venezuela or Russia

8. Which statement about mutual funds is false:
   ___ a. Global Currency funds act as hedge funds for volatile high-risk foreign currency arbitrage
   ___ b. Adjustable USG funds hold only US Government adjustable-rate mortgage securities (strip)
   ___ c. High Yield Bond funds are really high risk and have a lower-rated corporate and junk portfolio
   ___ d. Utility funds hold rich dividend-paying securities with absolutely no risk from deregulation

9. Which statement about mutual funds is true:
   ___ a. A prospectus must be delivered to a buyer at the time of purchase
   ___ b. Moving from one fund to another creates a taxable event
   ___ c. Risk disclosure statements are required in all prospectuses
   ___ d. A prospectus must never be marked up by the BD and should not be over 15 months old
   ___ e. All of the above

10. Which attribute of mutual funds is false:
   ___ a. Mutual funds are insulated from market splurges and shocks
   ___ b. Diversification is a safety valve for some market speculation
   ___ c. Hedge funds, as part of a mutual fund portfolio, creates a dangerous speculation
   ___ d. Speculation is a normal human phenomenon, like bread mold

CHAPTER EIGHTEEN

MUTUAL FUND OPERATIONS, ABC & BREAKPOINT COMMISSION STRUCTURE, LIQUIDITY, BUY & HOLD STRATEGIES, TELEPHONE REDEMPTION, DOLLAR COST AVERAGING, BETA RISK PYRAMID, REINVESTING

Mutual funds are considered liquid investments, for financial planning purposes. Why are they equal to cash if they are invested in the stock or bond market? It is because they can be redeemed, cashed in, transferred, bought or sold by a simple phone call (**telephone redemption privilege**)! That call initiates a trade based on the **Net Average Value** (**NAV**) at the end of the day. This trade is initiated without the seller or buyer actually knowing the share price until the day's end (price posted in the financial journals under the NAV column) which is the closing value from the prior day. The beauty of the mutual fund family is that the fund can be sold, transferred to another fund, and redeemed with the same phone call. Some mutual funds have the telephone exchange privilege available 24 hours each day, so if you hear about somebody nuking another country on the evening news you can pick up the phone and move things right away before the retaliatory strike on the market. Then you can sleep peacefully without worrying about joining the crowd at the opening bell early the next morning.

The stock market now has a five-day week, down from the also-Saturday routine that was in place during the 1920's and 1930's, so any trade placed after closing Friday will not be reflected until the end of Monday when the prices are redetermined. There is speculation about 24-hour trading on the stock market through the internet but the brokerage machinery will probably not allow the trades to clear until the proper business time the next day to allow a competitive playing field. Besides, even brokers need some sleep at night. We know that computers never sleep, though. Neither the **day traders** do.

Class "A" shares are bought ex-commission. That is, commissions charged to reduce the invested amount. A $1,000 trade becomes a $950 investment if a 5% commission is charged. The problem with "A" shares is that on the day after the buy, the investor shows a 5% loss in his new account and reaches for the telephone to ask his broker what went wrong with his investment.

The solution is the newer **Class "B" shares**, or deferred commission pricing. This arrangement provides for the whole $1,000 to be invested, but a commission is charged only on the shares during any of the next five years. The deferred commission table is as follows: Any money redeemed from the **B funds** in the first year would be charged a 5% commission, the next year 4%, and so on until after the fifth year where there would be no commission charged from the fund. Uniquely, the annual administration charges by the advisor to the "B" funds is higher than the "A" share charges and miraculously tend to equalize after the 5-year window. Some "B" share accounts are automatically shifted into A-share accounts at that point. The NAV net asset value also tends to be almost the same when comparing the "A" & "B" shares at this time. Funds offering these shares are becoming scarce to find in the current investment atmosphere.

Unlike stock equity trading when commissions are charged for both buys and sells, mutual fund commissions are a one-time event at the time of purchase. Average up-front commissions charged equity trades tend to be 1-5% but were as high as 8½ % not many years ago, which is a favorable consumer trend. To compensate dealers for lost commissions, 12b-1 fees were instituted, which paid the dealers a fraction (usually .001%) one percent each year on the account balances. Funds can be moved about within the family of funds without further commissions charged unless funds are withdrawn. The commission charge reduces the yield on the investment after reducing the principal. Some blue-chip high-dividend paying funds charge very low commissions of 2-3% because they are sold in large purchases to corporate buyers for parking surplus cash and for tax purposes.

There is also a **Class "C"** shares-pricing schedule for rich people and financial advisors. This pricing formula asks that you leave your million-dollar-or-more buy with the fund at least one year and there will be no commission load, either front-end or back-end. Bigger is better here!

Commissions can be reduced on "A" shares as well. These charges can be accumulated during one year and the sales rep should advise his client that the breakpoint commission reductions are available. The commission structure from one mutual fund is as follows:

AMOUNT INVESTED	SALES CHARGE
LESS THAN $50,000	5.0%
$50,000 TO $99,000	4.5%
$100,000 TO $249,999	3.5%
$250,000 TO $499,999	2.5%
$500,000 TO $999,000	2.0%

All of the mutual fund commission charges do not flow to the sales rep via the broker-dealer firm. The fund extracts from ½ to 1% off the top with the remainder dealer reallowance to the broker-dealer firm. The broker-dealer firm takes their haircut from the residual and passes it to the Office of Supervision Manager who shaves it further. The final commission remnant is then paid to the sales rep who is in business for himself unless he works for a large firm (then the sales commission percentage shrinks again because there are payroll taxes and overhead costs).

Mutual fund earnings are always shown with the dividends and capital gains reinvested into more shares (bought without a commission charge). This increases the actual earnings as the invested principal grows over the years. **Dollar cost averaging** is also affected by this move, as well as making periodic or monthly contributions into a fund because this takes the hills and valleys out of the investment process compared to just placing large lumps of money in when the market might be high or low at the time. The dollar cost averaging method actually increases the yield by smoothing out the investment pattern. Systematic deposits into a fund from a bank account will also accomplish dollar cost averaging and provide effortless investing. To find the value of your portfolio simply look up the mutual fund family symbol in the local paper…take the NAV share price and multiply it times the number of shares shown on your last statement. Yes, you actually own shares of a fund that owns shares of stocks or actual bonds. There are no commissions paid for redemption so this is your true cash price should you want to cash in some shares (unless you hold "B" shares).

Most mutual funds will show the largest ten holdings in the prospectus, monthly or quarterly investment guide, which are more current. This is a great guide for the investor, although highly leveraged high-risk investments could be very misleading when the results are tallied. The cash account-money market investment percentage of a mutual fund in equities is the advisor's headache. He is under pressure to keep this amount as small as possible because it earns only a minimal amount as it holds funds received from investors, stock sales, and dividends or interest earned for investor redemptions.

Because of the pressure to increase earnings, the fund advisors tend to keep the money working in more risky investments than the investor sometimes desires. The conservative nature of some fund advisors has led to sudden unemployment because of excess cash during volatile market moods. Retired folks aged 72+ are required to extract an annual cash amount from pensions. This is called **Required Minimum Distribution (RMD) Redemptions**. Of course this require cash, but not enough to keep large amounts of funds on hand because of the high liquidity of the market. The continuous infusion of cash, which used to go to the bank or insurance savings, has pressured the market by bidding up prices to the current highs, truly unhealthy speculation.

Meanwhile, Treasury bond interest rates are unusually low because of the non-inflationary (deflationary) economy and huge infusions of foreign cash which has freed even more cash into the equities market, thus pressuring stock prices higher, etc. Since nothing is forever, it will be interesting to see what correction beholds the market when the cash-price speculation subsides. The DJA is now at $29,000 in January 2020.

Most mutual funds proudly show the last year's earnings, last five years' earnings and the last ten years' earnings. A newer fund will merely show earnings from inception.

PLANNING TIPS

Risk avoidance is a term used to describe unsophisticated or elderly investors. Certain mutual funds can be very high risk and should be part of a portfolio only if the strategy fits the investor's desire. Every sector of a family of funds has some risk, including government bonds (due to interest or earnings risk rate changes in the market), not from systematic risk from outside sources, but in high-yield bonds that may have foreign securities or speculative growth funds and too many Internet stocks. Just because the fund belongs to an old name conservative family of funds, does not eliminate the inherent high risk of some investments. Risk and conservative investments are contrary terms that must be understood by the prudent investor. A bit of contrarian advice here: If the market turns down sharply, a quick telephone call to the fund will park your money in their money market account until you feel comfortable enough to move it back. There is no charge for this. This is the perfect insurance policy of mutual funds.

TAXES

Taxes are owed on capital gains whether paid out or not. At year-end, the mutual fund advisor's computers will break it all down for you on a 1099 statement showing your sales, different kinds of capital gains or losses, interest, and dividends for your account. The other end of these forms, via computer electronic transmission, goes to the big IRS computer that will match it with your tax returns later on. Differences can lead to an audit-by-mail **SC2000 notice**.

LEGAL COMPLIANCE

Distributions can be different from earnings. When purchasing a mutual fund there is an option to reinvest capital gains or dividends. The conservative investor without cash-flow needs usually opts to leave them in, thus reflecting a true yield later on when the fund totals are matched against investment. The retired investor with cash needs will usually opt to receive the earnings a check in the mail or wired to another account. With fixed-income investments, the retired investor will usually elect a fixed amount of distribution and loses track of the real earnings later on because the fund obligingly sends the same amount automatically. Some mutual funds elect, on their own accord, to issue cash distributions that will have nothing to do with earnings. The investor will be receiving the amount authorized by the fixed-income bond fund that may have been realistic in better times, while the fund might be currently losing money and **returning invested capital**. During the bad times, the fund reps and stockbrokers tend to refer to distributions while forgetting about real earnings.

Commission breakpoints are now tracked by some of the major mutual funds. You may pay a top commission for a large equity investment. Then six months later decide to add another large amount to it, but the sales rep didn't tell you (or didn't know you would send that direct deposit in) that the commission on the whole amount can be reduced (his/her year-end audit may point it out to him/her later) because you have crossed into a cheaper level. The mutual fund computer may then send you a letter advising you, and the broker, that you now have earned a reduced commission charge. The sales rep has also earned a reduced commission charge. Breakpoints are an important item if additional contributions are made, and your sales rep is supposed to keep you informed. This is one of the items in the prospectus that you are supposed to read diligently.

Breakpoints are also an issue if you are buying A-shares and the broker or sales rep divides the investment amount into different mutual fund families. This splitting can lead you to pay higher commissions than if it were all invested in the same fund of the family of funds. Sales reps are audited on this feature and there are internal broker-dealer software programs that track multiple mutual fund investments to assure that the customer is not being shifted around to avoid cutting commissions.

Be aware of a broker cashing in one mutual fund to buy into another. This is frowned on by both the SEC and the broker-dealer firm, because it can be an attempt to create commissions (**churning or twisting**) for the sales rep. Most mutual fund families have funds in the same investment areas, with few exceptions, and unless you have a changed strategy to indicate that you really want something different (there is a form you can sign to get the broker off the hook), then there is usually no need to change and pay more commissions for the privilege.

SUCCESSFUL STRATEGIES

The most successful strategy with mutual funds is to buy and hold within the same fund family. This reduces commission charges resulting from surfing from one fund to another for funds that always have different names but do mostly the same thing. Sometimes it is necessary to shift within a family of funds to reallocate a portfolio or move from one part that is not performing as expected. It is worth noting that shifting from one fund in the family to another constitutes a sale that will flow through to your tax returns at year-end. It also pays to watch your investment and compare it to other investments in the same family of funds. A phone call will move you wherever you want to go.

If a person wants to avoid personal supervision or pay much attention to the invested funds, then an index fund would be the best option because it should follow the market wherever it goes.

HORROR STORY - MUTUAL FUNDS

The horror story for mutual funds has not been written recently. There have been historic downturns and terrible October months (most downturns happen in October, probably because it is Halloween month) it may be a product of the next recession or some other future event. Since nothing is forever, allocating some funds to conservative bonds and cash accounts is always advised. The sweet siren call of new market highs has caused most investors to allocate too much of their portfolio to equities and other speculations which could have catastrophic consequences from having too many eggs in a basket.

MORNINGSTAR EQUITY STYLE BOX FOR MUTUAL FUNDS

	VALUE	BLEND	GROWTH
LARGE:	FUND I	FUND II	FUND III
MEDIUM:	FUND IV	FUND V	FUND VI
SMALL:	FUND VII	FUND VIII	FUND IX

MORNINGSTAR FIXED-INCOME STYLE MUTUAL FUND BOX

	SHORT	INTERMEDIATE	LONG
HIGH:	FUND I	FUND II	FUND III
MED:	FUND IV	FUND V	FUND VI
LOW:	FUND VII	FUND VIII	FUND IX

PROS & CONS ABOUT MUTUAL FUNDS

- A smart investor needn't buy no-loads to save on commissions. Understanding commission breakpoints and how to reinvest will still keep you in the good graces of a brokerage firm that will assist you with your portfolio in other areas as well.

- Avoid surfing from one mutual fund to another or other investments. Buy and hold unless something in the economy or the portfolio is moving the wrong way.

- Remember to use the telephone either for 911 emergencies or to cash out your stocks or bonds to the money market account if... The same telephone number will move your money back or elsewhere after the panic level subsides.

- The risk strata of a mutual fund pyramid dictates that the firmest base is government bonds, and the highest & riskiest part is shared by high-yield bonds and NASDAQ small-cap funds.

- Dollar-cost averaging, outside of one-time purchases, tends to increase yield because it averages the highs and lows of a normal market. This can be accomplished by reinvesting dividends and capital gains, and by making steady contributions as part of a savings plan.

- The best investment strategy is to buy and hold but not forget about it.

- Mutual funds provide ample statistical and performance data and their operations (back office) are client-oriented. They will make your investment experience a dream compared to the way the banks and government agencies operate.

- No-load fund performance is generally close to the loaded commissioned funds because annual expenses are larger to offset extensive advertising and overhead costs.
  Inform your broker sales rep of your risk tolerance so he will match your perceptions to the proper fund.

CHAPTER 18: APPLICATION EXERCISES

1. Mutual funds are considered liquid investments because they can be redeemed, cashed in, transferred, bought or sold by a simple phone call. ____ True ____ False

2. When Class "A" type shares are bought, commission is deferred and charged only on the shares redeemed during any of the next five years. ____ True ____ False

3. The best investment strategy is to buy and hold but not forget about it. ____ True ____ False

4. No-load fund performance is generally close to the loaded commissioned funds because annual expenses are larger to offset extensive advertising and overhead costs. ____ True ____ False

5. If a person wants to avoid personal supervision or pay attention to his/her invested funds, then an index fund would be the best option because it should follow the market wherever it goes. ____ True ____ False

6. Which statement about mutual funds is false:
    - ____ a. Telephone trades from an investor to the BD reflects the NAV the minute the trade is made
    - ____ b. Trades made after Friday closing will not be reflected until the NAV on the Monday closing
    - ____ c. Computers and day traders never sleep
    - ____ d Stock trades charge commissions for both buys and sales, mutual funds only for purchases.

7. Which statement about mutual funds is false:
    - ____ a. Dollar cost averaging is accomplished by reinvesting dividends and capital gains
    - ____ b. Mutual funds prospectuses will show the largest ten holdings in their investment guide
    - ____ c. Mutual Fund Money market accounts must provide cash for RMD senior citizen withdrawals
    - ____ d. The age requirement for Required Minimum Distribution Redemptions is 75

8. Which statement about Commissions on Mutual Funds is false:
   ___ a. Telephone redemption for purchases is a quick method for investors to move funds instantly
   ___ b. Index funds are a great way to bracket the entire market with a single fund
   ___ c. Index funds have high commission loads or haircuts because they trade so frequently
   ___ d. No load commissioned funds have higher administrative charges which equal earnings with loaded funds over five years.

9. Which statement about Mutual fund attributes is false:
   ___ a. Morningstar rates and classifies mutual funds
   ___ b. All commission charges go directly to the registered rep for mutual fund investment sales
   ___ c. Illegal Twisting-churning can be used by a BD to move clients between different fund families
   ___ d. Commission breakpoints are from 5% for sales less than $50,000 to 2% over $500,000

10. Which Mutual fund fact is false:
   ___ a. Investor Risk tolerance is always an important factor in choosing mutual funds
   ___ b. Younger investors have higher risk tolerances than middle-aged or retired people
   ___ c. Dollar cost averaging tends to increase yield by averaging highs and lows of the market
   ___ d. September is historically a bad downturn month for equity markets

PART FOUR

OTHER INVESTMENTS

Not all investments promise to return principal or pay interest; maybe they just pay off with tax credits greater than the original amount invested. Other investments blend bonds and **narrow sector equities**, thus returning (**guaranteeing**) the principal through the bond portion if held to **maturity**, even if the **underlying equities** all were to somehow dry up and blow away. For those brave enough to speculate, commodities have always been a quick way to multiply the profits...or losses.

Insurance products promise deferred **tax breaks** for long-term investments and the brokerage firm will now manage your account for you, the way the banks and investment houses did for the wealthy in the **Good Old Days, GOD. Packaged sector stocks** such as **unit investment trusts** are available for individuals interested in a particular industry while limited partnerships in equipment leasing will limit your participation as you wait many years for the results. **Bitcoin** and other **virtual currencies** are available for the computer-oriented investor. Finally, the brokerage firm will offer the meek a **certificate of deposit** (CD) shopping list dutifully insured by the **Federal Deposit Insurance Corporation, FDIC.** This is truly the last item the sales rep will offer because of the small commissions and constraints on investment choices.

Some esoteric investments have evolved in form but not objectives, such as **limited partnerships** in real estate, which have been replaced by **Real Estate Investment Trusts (REIT**s). **Investment Annuities** that participate indirectly in the stock market have replaced the old whole life insurance policies with savings features. Commodities are bought by the fearless investor directly through special brokers trading in the Chicago Commodities Exchange that offers highly leveraged gains or equally leveraged losses.

CHAPTER NINETEEN

LIFE INSURANCE, FIXED ANNUITIES,
FIXED INDEXED ANNUITIES

First, let us take a look back at the life insurance business when movies were mostly black and white and the candy bar or popcorn was only a nickel. Many years ago, during the predawn of financial institutions, the insurance companies sold whole life insurance as an investment and security vehicle. The young salesman in his power-dark suit and tie would make his weekly house calls over his debit route, collecting small amounts of money for insurance policies on everybody in the household with the pitch that the $500 face value policy cost only as little as "the daily price of a package of cigarettes". Every time he visited, he would attempt to sell more insurance. In those times, everybody made house calls because the mother-housewife did not work outside the house, that is. The milkman delivered to the front doorstep early in the morning, the coal (later oil) truck delivered during the winter, the ice truck would visit before refrigerators, the mailman and doctors visited, and the local grocery store had a two-wheeled pushcart which delivered locally after school let out, etc.

Most insurance policies today include a **RIDER** feature, at extra cost, to allow the policyholder to withdraw some or most of the policy death benefits for terminal illness or even convalescent end of life expenses. These keep the insured's policy intact without borrowing the savings account values. Be sure to go over these features to determine your options when the end of the road is apparent. Another end game is to sell the policy as a **VIATICAL SETTLEMENT**. If there are large values in the policy and the face values are over $100,000, it is possible to sell it to parties who will hold it as beneficiary. You are still the insured at all times but no longer the owner. This was a big deal some years back when people began dying prematurely due to HIV disease which lowered the person's immunity and, like today's super viruses, invited death from other causes. Many of these people sold their life policies to investors who planned on short-term results. New AIDS medical treatments reversed course and extended the lifespan of these people leaving the investors with huge losses.

It was a world of cash where people were paid weekly with cash and change in a little manila dollar-sized envelope and never visited the bank except to save money in a little **Christmas club savings account**. Checking accounts were a business device and not used by the common folk. Therefore, the only way a person could save money was to give some of it to the insurance person who sold his little policies, which had cash value built into them. Term policies were unheard of because they had no savings value. They later became a staple of the large businesses as a low-cost burial policy fringe benefit. A person could always borrow against the cash value in the future if he needed to, at only 3% interest. Moreover, there was a mortality feature that paid for the funeral, when needed, because people did not live as long then, either. A proper burial was an unthinkable expense during a time when most people had no savings or credit cards and cheaper cremation was unheard of. Sometimes everybody in the household, even the little children had insurance policies.

A modern variation of the whole life insurance policy (now renamed **universal life (UL) policy** is a policy where a person can contribute different amounts to the plan, with the excess going to an investment account. This policy sold as an investment plan with the insurance becoming secondary to the investment features.

All UL policies, excluding term insurance, after calculating the **mortality** and **overhead expense**, pay an annual dividend. This dividend is always reinvested and must be borrowed from the policy or the policy cashed in to receive the available cash accrued under the **Cash Values** section. Most insurance policies are cashed in before maturity, thus increasing the actual non-paid mortality earnings for the insurance companies. Policies generally offer a paid-up value of life insurance in lieu of cash values if a person desired to quit making payments and keep the insurance value instead of taking the cash out. This feature is popular for elderly people with reduced retirement income.

Because mortality charges increase as we get older, all insurance policies have costs based on the age of the applicant. Universal life insurance policies actually have a term that extends to either 95 or 100 years of age for the policyholder. When this age arrives, the face amount of the policy is automatically paid, less outstanding loans and the policy retired. This will give you something to look forward to if your genes and lifestyle are favorable. With the mortality tables changing due to better medical care, the centurion pay-off clause has caused some deep thought by insurance actuaries for the future.

Insurance companies are either **mutual companies** (owned by policyholders) or **stock companies** (owned by shareholders). Mutual companies pay profit dividends back to policyholders, which reduce their cost of insurance. The investor-capitalized stock companies pay dividends, after corporate taxes, to the shareholders that are not necessarily customers. Since the mutual companies act as a cooperative, thus not paying corporate taxes, the client should benefit directly by paying less net premiums. An example of a stock company would be Farmers Insurance Company stock company versus the State Farm Insurance Company that is a mutual company. Some mutual insurance companies have recently attempted to go public, which creates a bit of wealth for management later by exercising newly created stock options.

Fringe benefits at work were new, actually created during WWII to retain scarce workers, and usually with blue-collar unionized folks. For the lucky few with any benefits, there were cheap $2,000 group (**industrial policies**) **term life burial** policies. These were more of a benefit for the company than the employee because it avoided the family from passing the hat for donations at work after the bad day. It was also before **Workmen's Compensation** was in force, when many people were killed or injured on the job with no benefits, whatsoever. These policies, sold without physicals, were very cheap because of the low administrative expenses and the younger age of most employees.

The **master group policy,** which based the premium on average employee ages, insured the employee through the company and the employee existed only as a line in the monthly premium statement. The employee insurance policy document was an advisory paragraph in the new employee pamphlet. The term insurance policy naturally ceased when wars were excluded, and that works for all policies when the employee quits or retires (he would simply be omitted from the next monthly premium statement). These policies have a tax exclusion of premiums on $50,000 but if the insurance face value is higher the additional cost is taxed to the employee.

Corporations have special plans for business founders, key employees or executives, called **key-man insurance**. These are large policies equal to many times the insured's annual earnings. The company pays the premiums and owns the policy. Upon the key man's demise, the business receives the money to compensate for the financial loss from the missing employee and help pay to find his replacement. They are the insurance salesperson's dream because the business is paying the bill, all the management is covered, and the amounts are big (with fat commissions). Because the business owns the policy, there are no tax attributes to the insured as with the burial policies. It is barely worth noting that the social security fund used to pay a $155 stipend for funerals but that was recently eliminated.

The big benefit of term insurance is low morbidity, overhead costs, and no savings features, as in the whole life policies. Outside of the work industrial life insurance plans, most term policies are **burial policies** and the annual premium stays fixed for five-year intervals then increases for the next five-year level, etc. An alternative is **mortgage term life** insurance to pay off the widow's mortgage, which has a level premium but declining face amount of coverage, supposedly as the mortgage is paid down. Insurance mortality costs increase with age that is a declining statistic for people, as the older you become the fewer years you have to live. Since women outlive men, this is reflected by their cheaper insurance premiums. Most mortgages these days only last an average of seven years before refi or sale so that contributed to the demise of this specialized policy. Yes, we buy a thirty-year mortgage that statistically lasts only seven of those years.

Insurance was once the major investment for people, who later, in the monopoly rich industrial unionized labor post-WW2 years, began to also save money at company credit unions and banks that offered insured CD's. Now insurance is part of every business and employee benefits package and rarely an individual financial cost. Employers, however, have increased the amount of insurance to a multiple of annual wages, far exceeding the burial plans of the past.

In some states, especially Massachusetts, banks sold and issued insurance policies to individuals. The selling costs on the universal life policies were less than the usual house-call policy and the cash benefits were much higher. They were simply more efficient than the competition. The unique features were the small face amounts of the policy and the ease of payments made where you visited your little savings account. The ulterior motive for government involvement was to avoid poorer citizens becoming a **ward of the state** and for the state to pay for the pauper funeral.

Commissions paid to salespeople and their bosses are larger than most people are aware of. One year's premium for a new policy is usually paid upfront to these people for writing and insuring an individual. This is in addition to the cost of the physical exam, which is highly portable and personal…one of the few examples of house calls remaining today. The commission rewards are great but few between. There was a time when insurance companies would advertise for new people by promising great sales commission income. The new salespeople then would refer all their friends and relatives for the evening visit by them and the experienced sales manager, who would close the deals and share the commissions. After the referrals burned out, which usually took two or three months because of a lack of new unrelated clients, the new salesperson often filed bankruptcy.

Individuals can also defraud insurance companies by misstating age, hiding life-threatening illnesses, and committing suicide. Clauses and state laws limit the above with premium adjustments for age differences, **two-year contestable** features for material misstatement of information, and a one or two-year suicide exclusion. Medical records are usually requested by the insurance company for a closer look. A person must have an **insurable interest, meaning** that he should be related, or connected to the insured by business interests. This sometimes, but not always, keeps people from insuring strangers and doing them in shortly afterward. There is a double indemnity clause for additional accidental death benefits with additional premiums, and war exclusions for unnatural social disasters. The stuff for many movie thrillers abounds in insurance policies. Alfred Hitchcock was probably an insurance salesperson at one time.

Many insurance policies have a **paid-up feature**. That is, you would pay in a fixed amount for 20 years and then the payments would cease with the face amount of the policy in force until you die. The earnings assumptions have proven wrong over the past years as the prevailing interest rates and inflation have trended downward which resulted in the policies not being paid-up in the stated period and the policyholders still being billed for low fixed premiums. This has resulted in unexpected class action lawsuits that the insurance companies lost. Newer policies are more flexible.

Split-dollar plans allow an employer to share insurance costs with employees. The employer pays the premium amount equal to the annual increase in cash value, with the employee paying the difference. Upon demise, the employer gets the cash value amount back and the employee's estate or beneficiaries receive the difference from the face value of the policy.

Insurance companies sometimes pay money out for other insurance companies in a risk-sharing process called **reinsurance**. This is done on large multi-million-dollar policies when the selling insurance company's retention limit is reached; the rest of the policy is spun off, subject to acceptance by the other insurance company. Insurance at the policyholder level is simply sharing or distributing risk statistically over large numbers of people, so it is only natural for the insurance company to spread the investment risk at the other end. Natural or unnaturally-managed disasters such as California forest fires test the reserves of many casualty insurers and the reinsurance companies are called to the rescue.

Insurance companies also participate in employee company pension plans, the ones not funding corporate purchases of their own stock. These plans suit smaller companies or retailers, and are relatively cheap which results in poor benefits. 401-K plans have replaced most of these, which results in employee participation, matching benefits, and portability.

A different angle is when insurance companies sell package investment products called **Guaranteed Investment Contracts**, which offer a predictable rate of return. These are backed by investment-grade securities and by the bank or insurance company that issues them. They are not sold as an insurance product for retirement plans, but as an investment product to replace funds in a plan or create a certain cash benefit for an existing plan. Naturally, the insurance companies must earn money internally on their investments to cover all aspects of their operation. Real estate was once a big insurance company investment because they could buy huge buildings with their cash, but that has caused problems from time to time with real estate falling out of favor from economic circumstances.

Fixed annuities are different. An annuity guarantees an individual a certain amount of income monthly upon retirement. There are two different ways to buy these policies. The first and best is to pay a large sum of money up front and let it work for you. Pensions from people changing jobs are also a great investment challenge for these plans. The other way is to pay on it for many years. The single-pay annuity usually offers a teaser rate of higher earnings for the first year that somehow falls off a cliff afterward to a more realistic variable rate. Each year the earnings rate is changed and the client is notified with his annual statement that shows his investment values. Annuities are more investments than insurance. Sometimes instead of offering fixed investment options, they offer a minimum investment rate. There are declining deferred charges favoring stability on most policies, with terms stretching out for up to ten years because they need to hold your money long-term for it to work best. If the earnings, which are stated annually, decline below an initially stated percentage (the floor is usually about 2%) then the newer policies can be cashed without penalty. Commissions to the sales force are much less than for life insurance. The insurance companies make up some of the up-front commission costs with offsets from penalties charged for a policyholder's early investment withdrawal. After the first year, most single-pay annuities will allow a 10% annual withdrawal without penalty, which allows for hardship or retirement needs. If an annuity owner dies in the first year it was issued, his estate is refunded the policy investment without earnings and the salesperson also refunds his unearned commissions. Upon maturity at retirement age, a person is offered his payments of a guaranteed amount (**annuitization**) over his remaining life, or a ten-year guaranteed amount with a higher payment amount, an option usually taken by people in poor health.

An **immediate annuity** is for people who make a large payment to an insurance company so they can start receiving a steady stream of income beginning with the next month. Unless it is for a lawsuit settlement, the people opting for this method are usually elderly or retired. Unfortunately, because of the commission costs and overhead expenses, some of these deals are so poor that a person might not even get his/her original investment back. Elderly people may not be able to leave their money in the investment very long before it would be all drawn out. Sometimes leaving the funds in a bank savings account or various staggered-term (**ladder**) CD's while drawing a fixed amount out monthly or quarterly would be a better financial solution.

An insurance salesperson will always attempt to sell as much insurance as the customer can afford. Buy only what you need or perceive your needs to be, although inflation should always be a part of the plan. There must be a justifiable limit to the policy and the underwriters will inform the salesman if he has tried too hard to sell unwarranted insurance for the situation.

PLANNING TIPS

Insurance, in one form or another, is an important part of an investment portfolio. It has been neglected in the present years because of the runaway values of the stock market. An understanding of insurance as mortality, not an investment because of the large costs involved, is required to fit a proper financial plan together. There are important estate planning needs that can only be satisfied by life insurance. One day, when the stock market has leveled off, the insurance industry will still be providing cost-effective investments with special tax considerations and the safety of the principal. The insurance companies now offer investment options based on the S&P 500 indexes. This gives a boost to their earnings. Investors have no voice in the actual investment type in the indexed insurance company investment. That is the insurance company folio and you own a part of it.

All **fixed annuities** have a minimum guaranteed earning figure. For practical purposes, it is quite low in the 1% to 2% range. This is the bailout figure and if the actual earnings (every year they will send you a statement of earnings) should decline below this figure, the funds can be transferred or cashed in without penalty because the insurance company is unable to adhere to the original policy contract. Of course, this bailout figure is a hypothetical figure that the insurance companies will be watching very closely in this period of low-interest rates and deflation. The earnings, pegged to current interest rates that are an index of the insurance company's earnings and the competitive rates must be paid to you.

TAXES

Many years ago, the giant insurance companies made a deal with the government wherein the earnings or cash values accrued in life insurance policies should be taxed as income only when the values exceed premiums paid in. As a rule, then, taxable income is found on insurance policies on very old policies, have been in force for decades. The result of this policy is that the proceeds or distributions of any life insurance policy remain tax-free when paid, redeemed, or canceled. This tax savings feature is a major sales feature for insurance and cherished by the industry even today.

Section 79 of the IRS Code allows companies as an employee group fringe benefit, to buy up to $50,000 of term insurance costs as a deductible expense. The amount the IRS tables allow is liberal and can be applied to larger policies including whole life universal insurance. Any cost above the statutory figure is taxable to the insured employee.

Annuities also have special tax provisions that allow the earnings to remain untaxed until the principal and earnings are withdrawn. The government can also extract a 10% tax penalty on the earnings if the annuitant is not yet 59 ½ years old. Section 1035 of the IRS Code allows a tax-free exchange to another insurance product without paying taxes on accumulated earnings in the policy. It also allows people to move their annuities from one to another to take advantage of the higher-earnings teaser rate for new policyholders. Of course, this strategy only works well after the penalty holding period has expired.

Taxable earnings from investment insurance products are taxed as dividends or interest that is ordinary income on the individual tax returns. The tax is due only after the principal has been earned in cash or residual values; thus, insurance has great savings by sheltering or deferring taxable income into the future, especially annuities that have low mortality charges. The insurance salesperson will remind you of this and the time-value of keeping the tax dollars invested with gross, not net investment earnings.

Paid-up Life Insurance as part of an estate plan is important because the proceeds and cost transfer away from an estate after the three-year look-back period. This is an excellent way to reduce estate taxes on estates over five million dollars.

LEGAL COMPLIANCE

Beware of **churning**. This is the process of selling an insurance policy in the first year, then cancelling the policy to resell the same policy with another insurance company in another year. This is illegal because the premiums are subtracted from the policy cash value if it cancels in the first few years. Remember, that all of the first-year premiums are expensed, with most of it going to the selling salespersons. A salesperson once did this to my client with the story that he had found a better insurance company. She believed him and cancelled her policy without realizing that it was illegal or that she had lost the premiums paid. Later on, she declined to report him and take his license away, (my idea) "because he was a nice man," she said, not realizing that he would go on to do it to the next person, which he did. For the above reasons, the insurance salesperson is legally required to indicate on the application form that he is not "replacing a policy".

Fixed annuities have a surrender charge (deferred commission) that declines gradually over five to ten years. Each insurance company has different charges and terms. You should understand the charges in case the policy becomes cancelled or cash withdrawn during this period. A look-back period from one-week to one-month for all insurance policies allows the insured to return the policy for a full refund. This period is based on issuing State rules, owner's age, and the date they receive the policy (not when written). This is the **"buyer's remorse period"**. In some States elderly folks, over 60 years old may be allowed up to a month to digest the fine print on their policies before painless cancellation. Some people, after the period has lapsed, will still attempt to get the penalties refunded under the guise of many excuses, sometimes prompted by another agent trying too hard to churn the client's money at the expense of the prior insurance company and agent. A contract is a financial contract to which all parties must adhere. Fortunately, the law works both ways.

All insurance agents are state-licensed and required to take annual state-mandated continuing education courses. For some unknown reason, it appears easier for a person to pass the insurance exams than auto-driving exams.

SUCCESSFUL STRATEGIES

Insurance is a conservative part of any portfolio but the portfolio still needs diversification. An example of over-concentration is an elderly woman who used to shop the CD rates every year when her savings came due. Over the years, her savings and loan institutions began placing insurance agents on the lobby to snag extra commissions from diverting CD monies. Gradually her savings became converted to fixed annuities. Meanwhile, her friends began telling her about the millions they were making on the stock market during the mid-1990.

Finally, she began moving her penalty-free annuities over to stock market investments which underwent the roller coaster ride of the late 1990s, notably 1997 and 1998. As a result, she was buying high into the top of the peaked market and had trouble making money as her friends had during the decade. She still talks about her friends becoming millionaires in the stock market, which she missed. Fortunately, she has diversified enough now that she will be well ahead, even though she fell behind most of the market curve. There always seems to be a new curve to replace the old (about every ten years).

HORROR STORY - IMMEDIATE ANNUITY

An elderly couple used to visit my office every year. They would always recite the story about the husband having been in the Navy at Pearl Harbor on December 7, 1941, when the Japanese bombed it by surprise. Every few years he would fly to Pearl to reunite with a survivor's group on that infamous dastardly date. Finally, as the numbers of the group declined, he gave it up and settled in at his mobile home. The couple then sold a rental house and made a large purchase in a mutual bond fund. The fund did well for five years until one day I received a call from him. He wanted to liquidate the mutual fund but would not tell me why. I closed the account as he asked and forgot about it.

The next year a family member approached to inform me about their investment decision. They had bought an immediate annuity from an insurance salesperson. The man had been so aggressive and persistent that they invested the household money and some small savings as well as all the money from the mutual fund. The following week this relative received a desperate telephone request from them for groceries, as they had no cash left until the first check would arrive the following month, after the Social Security deposit. To make matters worse, after analyzing the deal with the insurance company, I found out that they would actually be receiving less money back than they had invested! They could have received monthly distributions from their old bond fund with a phone call if they had told me that that was what they really wanted.

ORDINARY LIFE EXPECTANCY (INTERNAL REVENUE SERVICE TABLES)

AGES		YEARS TO DEATH	AGES		YEARS TO DEATH
M	F		M	F	
6	11	65.0	7	12	64.1
8	12	64.1	9	14	62.3
10	15	61.4	11	16	60.4
12	17	59.5	13	18	58.6
14	19	57.7	15	20	56.7
16	21	55.8	17	22	54.9
18	23	53.9	19	24	53.0
20	25	52.1	21	26	51.1
22	27	50.2	23	28	49.3
24	29	48.3	25	30	47.4
26	31	46.5	27	32	45.6
28	33	44.6	29	34	43.7
30	35	42.8	31	36	41.9
32	37	41.0	33	38	40.0
34	39	39.1	35	40	38.2
36	41	37.3	37	42	36.5
38	43	35.6	39	44	34.7
40	45	33.8	41	46	33.0
42	47	32.1	43	48	31.2
44	49	30.4	45	50	29.6
46	51	28.7	47	52	27.9
48	53	27.1	49	54	26.3
50	55	25.5	51	56	24.7
52	57	24.0	53	58	23.2
54	59	22.4	55	60	21.7
56	61	21.0	57	62	20.3
58	63	19.6	59	64	18.9
60	65	18.2	61	66	17.5
62	67	16.9	63	68	16.2
64	69	15.6	65	70	15.0
66	71	14.4	67	72	13.8

68	73	13.2	**69**	74	12.6
70	75	12.1	**71**	76	11.6
72	77	11.0	**73**	78	10.5
74	79	10.1	**75**	80	9.6
76	81	9.1	**77**	82	8.7
78	83	8.3	**79**	84	7.8
80	85	7.5	**81**	86	7.1
82	87	6.7	**84**	89	6.0
85	90	5.7	**86**	91	5.4
87	92	5.1	**88**	93	4.8
89	94	4.5	**90**	95	4.2
91	96	4.0	**92**	97	3.7
93	98	3.5	**94**	99	3.3
93	98	3.5	**95**	100	3.1
96	101	2.9	**97**	102	2.7
98	103	2.5	**99**	104	2.3
100	105	2.1	**101**	106	1.9
102	107	1.7	**103**	108	1.5
104	109	1.3	**105**	110	1.2
106	111	1.0	**107**	112	.8
108	113	.7	**109**	114	.6
110	115	.5	**111**	116	0

Note that females outnumber the men's lives by five years at the start, which must be due to a lack of "aggressive genes". The way to interpret this thing is to read across that if a male is 6 years old, and a female 11, they will both live 65 more years longer. He will statistically die at 71 and her at 76. All of this without a nuclear war, of course.

PROS & CONS OF LIFE INSURANCE AND ANNUITIES

- Individuals with high taxes should consider the tax advantages of the tax deferred insurance annuity for their portfolios.
- Term insurance is mortality insurance with increasing premiums as an individual gets older, or the policy face amount will reduce annually if the annual payment is fixed. Most term life policies need to be renewed every 10 years (without physical exams).

- Buy life insurance as an investment against mortality, cash, or family planning needs while reserving worthwhile residual cash values for living.

- Caution against overzealous salespeople who may sell more insurance than needed or rollover policies needlessly. Ask neighbors how things work, if you do not really understand what is happening.

- An annuity, especially the prepaid one-payment investment, might have a higher **teaser** bonus earning rate for the first year. It might pay to consider (for older folks) **annuitizing** the policy after the 5-10 declining penalty period has passed. Some even credit a small percentage bonus for signing up.

- Do not cash prepaid annuities in, or take large withdrawals during the first five years or penalty term, (whatever the policy spells out) unless you are prepared to take a loss of premium for withdrawal penalties.

- Annuities provide a fixed or level amount of income pegged more to interest rates than the stock market. They provide excellent diversification as part of your portfolio. They are also a **safe haven** from a heavy stock equities portfolio.

- Fixed annuities and whole life insurance policies usually have provisions for owners to withdraw some cash in times of liquidity needs, or (Mandatory Required Distribution MRD beginning at age 72) without early withdrawal penalties.

- Insurance companies are generally very highly capitalized and highly regulated by the states where they sell policies. Beware of sales techniques, not the regulated company. The last insurance company, many years ago, closed down in California was Executive Life. Their reserves had fallen below the required limit. Everybody got all of their money back from the company when it closed.

- All policies have a look-back cooling-off period of one week to one month when a policy returns for a full refund. The period begins on the day a signed receipt for the policy when delivered, to the date the returned policy is received by the insurance company.

- Fixed Indexed (Standard and Poor 500) allows a passive exposure to equities from an insurance policy. The exposure earnings are capped at a reasonable 5-6% rate and if the S/P index loses money in the year, the policyholder suffers no losses against prior or future accumulated values. A true stop-loss feature.

CHAPTER 19: APPLICATION EXERCISES

1. Insurance companies are either mutual companies (owned by policyholders) or stock companies (owned by shareholders). ___ True ___ False

2. Individuals with high taxes should consider Insurance annuity deferred tax advantages for their portfolios. ___ True ___ False

3. Insurance companies are generally very highly capitalized and highly regulated by the states where they sell policies. ___ True ___ False

4. Term insurance is mortality insurance with increasing premiums as an individual gets older, or the policy face value will decrease annually if the annual payment is fixed. ___ True ___ False

5. Annuities provide a fixed or level amount of income pegged more to interest rates than the stock market. ___ True ___ False

6. Insurance companies have been important in everyday lives for mortality and savings. Which of the following statements is true:
   ___ a. At one time the insurance salesman had a debit route for collecting premiums and selling small policies for every member of the family
   ___ b. Pensions were only found with major unionized companies and government jobs
   ___ c. The savings element of a whole life policy became the only savings for many people, and life insurance of the working spouse was critical for family existence
   ___ d. All of the above

7. Which statement is false about other savings devices and challenges:
   ___ a. Banks could sell insurance if state regulated
   ___ b. Banks encouraged Christmas savings accounts for family members
   ___ c. IRA and 401-K pensions were not in existence until the 1990s
   ___ d. Bank CD savings accounts have been diverted to equities because of low yields

8. Which statement about modern insurance policies is false:
    ___ a. Have riders for extra benefits, such as terminal illness expenses, at no cost
    ___ b. Without end of life withdrawals for death benefits, a viatical settlement can be effected
    ___ c. Investors buying viatical policies for their death benefits lost money on AIDS patients
    ___ c. Policy holders of UL policies can borrow and repay with interest, cash values if needed

9. Which of the following statements is false about Universal life policies:
    ___ a. After deducting mortality and overhead expenses, pay an annual reinvested dividend
    ___ b. One way to cash in your policy for the face value, before death, is to reach 95-100 years old
    ___ c. Insurance companies are mutual, owned by policyholders, or stock owned by shareholders
    ___ d. Industrial term policies have replaced Workmen's Compensation policies in the workplace

10. Which of the following statements about Term life insurance is false:
    ___ a. Term policies accumulate cash balances the same as Universal Life
    ___ b. Term life policies are also called burial policies
    ___ c. A person without means or insurance could become a ward of the state for burial purposes
    ___ d. Common tactics to defraud insurance companies would be to misstate age, hide life-threatening illnesses or commit suicide

CHAPTER TWENTY

INDEXED-INVESTMENT ANNUITIES

One day the insurance companies made a deal with the Securities Exchange Commission and the Internal Revenue Service. They asked the SEC if they could include securities in their insurance portfolios, not as a passive investment vehicle, but indirectly with customer participation. Then they asked the IRS if they could treat the securities gains the same as an insurance product, meaning, with deferred gain instead of immediate taxation, so their investor is taxed when he took his gains out…many years later. The lobbyists showed up for work, making everybody happy and the marriage between the insurance companies, the SEC and IRS were consummated. Thus, the investment annuity insurance-security product was born and a lagging life insurance industry resurrected.

The securities broker-dealers would handle variable insurance products while giving investors direct participation in the market. The insurance companies would buy securities for an investment portfolio but exclude direct policyholder participation by allowing them to share in the changes of value-based on the S/P 500 index.

The caveat agreed to was that life insurance needed to be included in the annuity package. This works best, of course, when a large amount is invested, and the amount of insurance is bought equal to the original investment value. The mortality charge for the term insurance is an annual expense, along with an administrative charge for handling the security accounts. A **Verboten** word is now included in the sales package and prospectus, the word **Guarantee**, which is never allowed in conjunction with securities and promises, is now used. The insurance companies, however, are guaranteeing that the principal is insured if you die, not the cash balances, if you lose money. It is amazing how many different ways this magic word is used to sell annuities. The invested amount of your portfolio is generally limited to a percentage of the gain marked against the SP 500 index. Losses for the year are limited, resulting in no gain but no loss carried backward or forward against the cash balances.

An investment insurance annuity gives the investor a bit of term insurance and a taste of the stock market. The investor can allocate a percentage of his portfolio annually between fixed interest-bearing investments and insurance company investment portfolios, a process called reallocation. It is quite possible, however, not to lose money any year with the principal interest and market gain going to_the beneficiary. Any cash amounts withdrawn would also reduce the insurance benefit. The investment portfolio is managed by an alliance with outside investment advisers who also manage funds for other people, usually mutual funds. This way the insurance company administrator can remain in the insurance business, which is what they really like to do. Like with a fixed insurance annuity, there are declining surrender charges if a customer bails out within the usual seven-ten-year term. Sales commissions do not reduce the principal, hence the deferred charges for early bailing out helps offset the upfront selling expenses for the insurance company.

Index annuities have been a highly successful securities investment. This is a natural product for the insurance companies which have always been investing their own reserve funds. The downside is that, like all investments outside of cash savings or deposits, there is an initial charge, albeit deferred annual maintenance load and commission fees. These fees are close to the mutual funds because insurance companies also have overhead which reduces the yield. This compares to **broker-dealer mutual funds** that allow investors to allocate their investments within different specific product categories. The insurance company name is very important here. The commissions are about 5% with no breakpoints, but does not reduce the investment BD Security.

The following is an example of the choices within one variable annuity policy:

MANAGERS	PORTFOLIO FUND CATEGORIES
Xxxxxx International Investment, Ltd.	Global Fixed Income
Xxxxxx Inc.	Capital Appreciation
Xxxxxx Asset Management, Inc.	Value Equity
Xxxxxx Realty Securities, Inc.	Real Estate
Xxxxxx Management, Inc.	Small-Cap
Xxxxxx Investment Management, LLC	Limited Maturity Bond
	Liquid Asset
Xxxxxx Investment Management, LLC	Rising Dividends
Xxxxxx Financial Services Company	Research
	Mid-Cap Growth
	Total Return
Xxxxxx Asset Management, Inc.	Developing World
	Global Opportunities
Xxxxxx Associates, Inc.	Asset Growth
Xxxxxx Investment Management Company	Stocks Plus
	High Yield
Xxxxxx Investment Management, Inc.	Managed Global
	Emerging Markets
Xxxxxx Company Investment Management, LP	Growth & Income
	Value + Growth
Xxxxxx Associates, Inc.	Fully Managed
Xxxxxx Associates Corp.	Hard Assets
Xxxxxx Asset Management, Inc.	International Equity
Xxxxxx Advisors Inc.	Strategic Equity
	Multiple Allocation

All of the above, from this huge laundry list of portfolio choices, is available in the same investment policy. Some of the investment categories are redundant because the investor is allowed to cherry-pick the investment advisor's resumes to find the ones they like best. Because 17 of the above 25 fund categories showed losses during three months of the recent bull market period, the names are deleted. It's not all the advisor's fault; it's because there are always overhead expenses.

Variable annuities provide complete approved prototype pension plans for small companies, avoiding setting up a formal pension plan with outside advisors. A formal pension also requires the filing of a series 5500 tax returns each year and a plan administrator. Avoiding this formality saves thousands of dollars in fees for small businesses, which is very important because small businesses cannot become a bigger business or even survive without watching costs and taking care of their people properly.

PLANNING TIPS

Investment indexed life insurance products are good stock market limited exposure for the elderly individual who wants or perceives the need for the big insurance company umbrella and the salesperson in the black pinstriped suit. The sales pitch always includes the life history of the insurance company and the guarantee of insured values. No prospectus is available for the presentation, but a computerized proposal is generated for the client based on his proposal investment and historic earnings. This is a good investment for a person who desires to place all of his investments in one place, but wants a very conservative taste of the market. The ideal investor would be a person familiar with insurance or insurance company annuities and who usually has cash in bank certificates of deposit. It is also good for an IRA or pension rollover because it offers diversity to fit the investor's needs and the ease of having the investment in one place.

Variable annuities offer a good alternative to mutual funds within a 401-K plan at work (for small plans), although investment choices would be limited to keep it simple and easier to administer. The tax advantages would be moot here, but that still remains the biggest selling point outside of pension plans.

You are not directly buying the stocks within the investment index annuity but are buying units based on your purchase date. It takes a computer to compute your actual earnings within the annuity because of the blend of shares within the different advisor's selections inside the annuity itself.

Variable annuities offer automatic reallocation, which allows consistent percentages of your portfolio to realign periodically. An example of this would be 10% cash, 30% global, 20% bonds and 40% equities. If after one year because of earnings or loss changes to the mix, the portfolio was now 10%, 25%, 25%, and 40%, the computer would change the investment matrix to reflect the original percentages.

TAXES

The **insurance investment pension annuity** has unique tax properties. There are no taxes on non-pension investment gains until they are withdrawn or cashed in. As part of a pension plan or IRA, which is where most annuities reside, whatever cash distributions are drawn out are taxed as ordinary income. Thus, capital gains are converted into ordinary income. The pension annuity would also be subjected to 10% tax penalties if retirement age (59 ½) has not been achieved when funds are withdrawn. Being deferred also hides the declining surrender charges, so plan on keeping the investment in the long run after you purchase it. If the earnings disappoint the investor because of the overhead and mortality charges, try mutual funds instead. Variable annuities, broker-dealer plans, and insurance plan annuities have the same tax attributes when they are pension purchases or exchanges.

Because it is an insurance product, the tax code section #135 allows a tax-free transfer to another insurance investment. Beware of the deferred charges if the five-ten-year charge-back period has not termed out.

Unlike a fixed insurance annuity, a broker-dealer variable annuity has no guaranteed earnings or first-year teaser interest rates. It is strictly a securities investment through an insurance administrator.

LEGAL COMPLIANCE

A variable annuity is a security product and the insurance salesperson must be a stockbroker, although the brokerage licenses can be limited in scope. Because the annuity is a security, the investor must receive a current prospectus, showing earnings not more than a year old, giving advice about the fund and past five-year performance. Because of the time lag between publication and distribution to the investor, it is best to ask for the latest three-month earnings or performance record for the annuity. These are published monthly or quarterly and will help you make a meaningful decision. The performance history is always broken down into a year or longer, usually 5 years. There is no policy with the variable annuity but you will receive monthly or quarterly statements.

For insurance annuities, a free-look period of one week to one month may also apply from the date you receive the policy. The advisor will usually ask you to sign a delivery form at that time. If you return the policy (decline) it must be received by the insurance company within the cancellation deadline.

As with all investments of any kind, never, ever make out a check to the salesperson or give them cash. If he asks for it that way, call his company or broker-dealer immediately! All investments should be made out directly to the fund, the company, or the advisor firm. Never the sales rep. He can lose his license for handling funds or for misappropriating client monies. It is certainly a great temptation and some reps cannot survive the test.

Insurance companies like to give out illustrations and proposals for future income and portfolio values. The FINRA prohibits illustrations that assume gross returns greater than 12% on securities. If the stock market should be tearing along at a 35% annual gain, it is still illegal for an illustration to show more than the 12%. These are for variable annuities.

The word guarantee is used cautiously in insurance contracts. In almost all contracts the policy is **guaranteeing** that a certain amount is paid to the beneficiaries upon the owner's demise. In the case of an investment annuity, this means the initial investment is guaranteed. Thus, if you invested $1,000 and the underlying investment gained $100 in the first year and lost $200 in the next year, the insurance company would pay your heirs $1,100 if you died. This term insurance death benefit can be misunderstood by parties to the contract. The above policyholder has purchased a policy on the basis that if he loses money on the investment the loss will not exceed the current year's earnings. The cost of the term policy portion of the investment is minuscule if it is understood that a $100,000 term policy for an age 45 female person (non-smoker and healthy), is only $106 per year. That will offset a lot of losses in the stock market.

SUCCESSFUL STRATEGIES

Buy and hold is the strategy for an investment indexed annuity. It is truly an investment for elderly people and retirement plans where individuals are not intent on playing the stock market. Very few investment indexed annuity owners study their plan results and they expect their financial advisor to do it for them, if he is still around. Keep in mind that it contains insurance costs and higher overhead than mutual funds, thus the performance will be dull by comparison with mutual funds.

A variable annuity is a Mexican zebra. It has no insurance yet is sold by an Insurance Company administrator through a stockbroker. On Revolution Blvd. in Tijuana, there are photo opportunities by the curbside with mules or donkeys painted with stripes to look like zebras. These things don't look like either zebras (striped horses) or mules, but in some ways, they are both.

HORROR STORY - PENSION PLAN?

An insurance salesperson convinced a corporate business client that he had set up a pension plan for the company to include each employee. The plan would be a business expense paid by the employer and everybody would benefit. The employer was a good person who wanted to share a good business with the help, which was mostly family. After it had been in force a few years, the client asked me to review it.

The salesperson had taken advantage of the client and had packaged various individual annuity and insurance products on each employee for the corporation to pay. There was no formal pension plan; each employee simply had an insurance product paid by the employer. The plan, therefore, even though the company was paying the collective premium, was not tax-deductible. The client was advised about the problem and ended paying taxes on the premiums, which were supposed to be tax-deductible. An IRS audit confirmed the problem later on. After the audit, which was years after the bad advice was given, the client converted the premium to a wage bonus and gave the employees the choice of maintaining the policies themselves or cashing them in. Most elected to cash them in because the deal left a bad taste behind.

PROS & CONS OF VARIABLE AND INVESTMENT ANNUITIES

- Variable annuities are usually insurance company plans sold through stockbrokers that provide professional management in the stock market for the conservative investor who is interested in some of their advisory portfolio options.
- VA's are good for small pension plans because the insurance company can handle the administration inexpensively without creating a formal plan requiring an advisor.
- The term insurance included in the investment indexed annuity provides an investment floor for elderly people who plan on holding the annuity for retirement planning. If it gains money they are ahead, if it loses then the insurance guarantees the principal for the beneficiary.
- Broker-Dealers collect investment commissions up front while insurance companies waive them if the policy principal is not redeemed or cash withdrawn over the surrender period.

- Any insurance annuity can be transferred to another without taxes paid on the gains, although the penalty charges can only be avoided if held long enough. Pension VA's can be transferred from a broker firm.

- If an investment indexed annuity has not made money internally (the annual statements will tell), then there are no tax consequences of reallocating it in fixed income in the policy.

- Variable Annuities offer a blend of an insurance company, stock market, and professional management…a unique investment product, like a multiple vitamin covers all your health needs.

- All insurance products are subject to state and federal regulations. The VA products, because they are securities, are also subjected to review by the SEC. This reduces the opportunity of fraud and increases the odds that the offering insurance company is huge and secure. VA investments have no insurance attributes.

- VA's are a good investment for the unsophisticated investor but could lose money in a bad investment environment (declining stock or bond market).

- Only the mortality aspect of an investment annuity policy is guaranteed, a fact sometimes obscured by sales reps.

- There is no up-front sales charge for investment indexed annuities. Costs are covered by the insurance company, which is reflected in bailout penalties and annual overhead charges. There is no free lunch anywhere on this planet.

- The value of the term insurance portion of the policy provides psychic and positive satisfaction to the elderly or cautious investor.

CHAPTER 20: APPLICATION EXERCISES

1. There are no taxes paid on the investment gains of insurance investment pension annuities until they are cashed in.
    ___ True ___ False

2. Annuities are good for small pension plans or IRAs because the insurance company can handle the administration inexpensively without creating a formal plan requiring an advisor.
    ___ True ___ False

3. Insurance brokers collect no commissions if the policy principal is redeemed or cash withdrawn over the look-back cooling off period.
    ___ True ___ False

4. All annuities offer a blend of an insurance company, investments and professional management. ___ True ___ False

5. Buy and hold is the best conservative strategy for an insurance company managed investment indexed annuity. ___ True ___ False

6. Which of the following statements about Indexed investment annuities is false:
    ___ a. Indirect investments made by the insurance companies for the benefit of the policyholders
    ___ b. The units of investment are indexed to the Standard & Poor 500 Index
    ___ c. Policyholders are allowed to allocate part of their premiums or initial investment to this fund
    ___ d. Insurance agents need to pass securities exams to sell these indexed policies

7. Which of the following statements about Indexed Insurance annuities is false:
    ___ a. They are a successful investment product which limits S&P losses to the current year without offsetting prior year earnings
    ___ b. They indirectly blend insurance and investment with the equities market
    ___ c. They farm out the diversified equity investments with mutual funds or Investment Advisors
    ___ d. All of the above

8. Which of the following statements is false:
   ___ a. Insurance annuities have unique tax properties allowing no taxes on earnings until withdrawn
   ___ b. Pension investments are subjected to standard 10% for withdraws short of age 59 ½.
   ___ c. Insurance salespeople can take cash for initial investments, same as BD
   ___ d. Insurance clients don't receive a prospectus but initially receive a detailed proposal of future and past values

9. Which of the following statements about Variable Broker Dealer annuities is false:
   ___ a. They offer direct investments in bonds and stocks
   ___ b. They do not involve life insurance, just manage money as insurance firms
   ___ c. They guarantee earnings
   ___ d. They present a prospectus to clients instead of a detailed proposal

10. Which of the following statements about Variable Broker Dealer annuities is also false:
    ___ a. They reduce the investment by the commission charged
    ___ b. They are licensed by FINRA and the SEC
    ___ c. They are taxed on annual capital gains, interest, and dividends earned unless an IRA or pension
    ___ d. They have declining chargebacks for 5-10 years like an insurance annuity

CHAPTER TWENTY-ONE
MANAGED ACCOUNTS

There is an important variation to the financial sales and advisory business, which is the **Registered Investment Advisor (RIA)**. This is the person who can manage accounts for individuals and others, usually a person with the top business, educational and financial licenses. Firsthand, are the state licenses for insurance, then the demanding **National Association of Securities Dealers (NASD)** and **FINRA** licenses to sell general securities, the **Securities Exchange Commission Uniform Investment Advisory Law,** and the tougher one for principal-supervisor, the **Office of Supervisory Jurisdiction**, of which I was once a principal. Then, there is a separate SEC application process, duplicated by all states, to authorize a **Registered Investment Advisor-RIA** to manage people's money. This application reviews the above exams and licenses, education and work experience, and finally the customer or broker-dealer complaint file. The paperwork is massive, time-consuming, and absorbs many fees. If he/she survives, he may advise clients for a fee, manage their funds for a percentage, and talk to the crowd on the television LED screen.

A person must be a registered advisor to do all of the above, yet they are everywhere. They are managing the mutual funds, prudently investing pensions, hidden away in various institutions, putting their signature on financial newsletters, and submitting to annual audits for fiduciary responsibility and correctness. Some of these people operate under the **Registered Investment Advisor, Series 63 license,** an umbrella of their broker-dealer firm.

Some financial advisors offer a specialized function called **market timing**. What they do is take your mutual funds and mark them to the market by moving them in and out of a cash position as the stock or bond market changes course. They charge an annual fee for the privilege of applying their software and research. My experience was that they mostly failed to earn their fees.

One thing is clear. That is the scope of financial responsibility. An advisor who manages assets will provide a **Certified Financial Audit** of his business every year which must show he is managing his business correctly (no guarantees here on fund performance) and for the clients benefit. The SEC will also audit his business and the state will conduct its own audits. The only problem with advisors is that they want autonomy to handle your investments (a form of discretionary trading). Some advisory programs are scaled down for small investors but somehow that doesn't fit the sophistication needed to create a properly balanced portfolio. And for that, the advisors will charge a fee based on the amount managed. Bigger is better here, according to the following sliding scale of annual fees.

ADVISORY FEES	First $250,000	2%
SAMPLE FEE STRUCTURE:	$250,000 to $500,000	1%
	$500,000 to $1,000,000	.8%
	$1,000,000 to $2,000,000	.6%
	$2,000,000 +	.4%

An hourly fee can be charged for preparing a one-time financial plan. The fee usually ranges from $100 per hour depending on the adviser. There is a $500 annual limit for small plans that can be simple things but a large comprehensive plan would be complex with much time and require expensive software. The plan gathers up your financial affairs and places them before you and the advisor so that a financial plan can be formulated.

Advisers continually update their client portfolio and mark-to-the-market for stock and fund values with modern online software. All advisers will present monthly or quarterly financial statements to clients, which will usually show prior period and current total values so the client can see how well he is doing.

A good adviser would be awfully cheap because, in addition to doing the right things for you, he can make stock picks for minimal trading fees, buy no-load mutual funds (C Class) without paying commissions, manage index funds, and do all kinds of things to save you money so he can earn those fees and make you some money as well. This process avoids the commission structure that most brokers and sales reps rely on to make a living. This takes the pressure off trading for fees. It is a sophisticated and demanding business that some brokers evolve to when they achieve the proper client list and licenses. It is for the well-heeled and sophisticated investor who is tired of the phone calls from everybody's sales rep.

Each adviser has his own program for investment. Like children, they are different, yet somehow seem familiar. One of them advertises that they utilize the 1990 Nobel Prize-winning **Modern Portfolio Theory** to effectively risk-adjusted diversified global portfolios. I believe it was several mathematician Nobel Prize winners, who brought down the **Long-Term Capital** hedge fund. Others are more conservative offering **Tactical asset allocation programs** or **Valuation models**, "Classic" **five-step investment management process** or other **balanced** or **diversified portfolio models**. Today, I see many portfolios with computer-generated unknown shares of stock coming and going almost randomly in the portfolios. Even the advisor/brokers would not be able to describe what they were doing or anything about the new securities. The computer is now earning their salary. Naturally, the clients have no idea at all and just look at the bottom lines on the pages of activity on the monthly statements. Those are the sophisticated clients who look at the statements.

Attorneys have some authority to manage client funds for fees. Banks have traditionally had attorney managed trust departments managing accounts for clients. Uniquely, their fees are based on funds that included savings and certificates of deposit accounts in their own bank.

Recently the term **Fiduciary Responsibility** was tossed around Washington to further regulate performance vs fees in portfolios. The rules were to separate responsibility from broker earnings but failed to pass. How unfortunate because when I was in the brokerage business the client always came first for fiduciary responsibilities by the broker. That rule usually works best for all businesses as well.

Registered Financial Advisors all have one thing in common, maximizing revenue for the clients within the steel-walled framework of the **SEC supervision** and **FINRA** licenses.

In an earlier chapter, I outlined a successful RIA who put his clients first and was able to evolve his practice into the complete management of client financial affairs, including taxes and insurance. He was a gifted person, but a rare one that is not to be expected or found for your financial affairs. Most RIAs are not that personal and close. They handle your funds the best they can, with efficiency and professionalism, for demanding clients.

PLANNING TIPS

If you are tired of handling your portfolio in the usual piecemeal investor-sales rep method and have enough funds for professional management, then look around for an advisor. The advisor should match your style with his/her, if possible. If you wear cowboy boots, a large hat, and have tons of money from the ranch, you may not be happy with the stuffed-shirt banker type individual. On the other hand, you don't want a guy who looks like he just hopped off the tailgate of the pickup truck behind you. The best method to find a good anything is word of mouth. A referral is worth a hundred pictures and ads. Unfortunately, it is also the best way to find an unregistered **Ponzi scheme.**

TAXES

All capital gains, dividends, and interest earnings will flow through to you and your tax returns by form or schedule from the adviser or directly from the funds. There is nothing new here except the way your money is invested.

LEGAL COMPLIANCE

A Registered Investment Advisor should give his/her serious new investor two things. The first is the **SEC ADV form**. This is really a package of forms outlining the advisory investment objectives, the commission or fee structure, and the background of the advisor and his professional staff. This statement will also disclose any fee arrangements he may have with his clearing broker-dealer firm and how he will handle commissions on investment products. A second thing is a contract that will outline the fee arrangement. If you agree, then you will give him a check and sign the forms. The advisory fees are paid quarterly. Now you are in business. Next, he will gather information, complete a plan for you, and move your assets into the advisory so he can manage them.

The **Financial Industry Regulatory Authority** is a privately owned **Self-Regulatory Organization (SRO)** that maintains a Website at www.finra.org where everybody can look up an individual or firm to see their history of recent complaints. A complete work history and licenses held file is also available. All you need is a name to begin the process. It really works, I found myself there.

Some financial planners will create a mini-brief plan for no fees. This is fine for the small investor because all financial information brought to the desk will help you review your situation. An RIA can charge for the plan. There are good plans and some others would fill a garbage truck. If you like the planner, then he or she will have performed a good service for you and you could reward him by becoming his customer. He or she will then earn their fees by commissions on sales, never an annual fee.

Any individual investing money for you, if not as a licensed broker-dealer rep, can be acting as an **unlicensed Investor Advisor**. This can even be a friend offering to help you invest or doing some trading for you in his name, which is far beyond giving free personal investment advice. This is an **illegal activity** because there are no controls for an unlicensed person trading for another.

The following advisor expenses should be monitored and controlled by the investor: trading costs, custodian costs, and management fees. Always keep in mind that to make a profit you must deduct advisory fees and commissions, inflations, and taxes. This gives you the true net yield of your portfolio.

PROHIBITED TRANSACTIONS BY AN ADVISOR

- Sale, lease or exchange of property between the plan and party-in-interest.
- The lending of money between plan and party-in-interest.
- Transferring any of the plan assets to or use of plan assets by party-in-interest.
- Acquiring employer assets in excess of 10% of plan assets.
- Self-dealing by a fiduciary.
- Compensation paid to fiduciary by a party involved in a transaction with plan assets.

SUCCESSFUL STRATEGIES

The most successful strategy for working with a Registered Investment Advisor is to realize that he and his plan are still your responsibility. You can never delegate everything. His statements must be reviewed periodically by you or a trusted party. Losses must be justified, the risky strategy identified. Although your advisor is the professional, you must make sure you are not risk-averse to his philosophy or strategy. Everybody in today's financial business layers their clients and the public with tons of charts, graphs, statistical data, and worldwide economic datum. Even Elvis is alive somewhere in that stuff, and Hitler never died. You must exercise judgment and common sense. Never completely trust anybody with your money. All the laws in the world will not prevent somebody from stealing from you if it is made easy enough. It is your duty not to make it too easy.

Changes in lifestyle, divorces, deaths in the family, wills, living trusts, retirement plan changes, all aspects of your economic existence must be blended into the plan that the RIA has worked for you. Think of it as a lifestyle plan, not an investment plan. He/she is not allowed to practice law and should refer you to people with the proper licenses for wills, trusts, and legal matters. I am not a lawyer but from practicing taxes for estates, wills, and trusts I can vouch that most of the documents I work with have problems from not being created or administered properly. They all lead to headaches and misunderstanding by the parties benefited.

Performance monitoring should be conducted on a consistent basis, compared to an appropriate benchmark, evaluated for the manager's performance on a five-year basis, and verified that the investments are allowed in the investment policy or contract. Read the statements provided by the advisor and review them with him periodically.

A PLAN SHOULD ALSO BE EVALUATED TO DETERMINE THAT THE PLAN IS PROPERLY DIVERSIFIED:

- Amount of plan assets.
- Types of investments (stocks, bonds, real estate, insurance annuities, etc.)
- Projected portfolio returns vs funding objectives.
- The volatility of the investment returns (risk factor).
- Liquidity and future cash flows.
- Maturity dates and retiree distributions.
- Economic conditions affecting the company and plan investments.
- Company and industry conditions.
- Geographic distribution of assets.

THE INVESTMENT POLICY SHOULD BE COVERED BY THE FOLLOWING WRITTEN ITEMS:

- Normal return benchmarks.
- Definition of risk.
- Risk tolerance.
- The time period for review and evaluation.
- Allowable investments and quality standards.
- Liquidity requirements.

- Policy asset allocation.
- Procedures for selecting and dismissing money managers.
- The cash flow of the plan.
- Company finances, etc.

HORROR STORY - BERNIE MADOFF

Bernie Madoff was a very bright and charming man. He came from a Jewish family who had very good financial connections and in these situations, the people are very closely tied to each other by blood or nationality (Wikipedia). He began trading with penny stocks at a young age and was successful enough to create trading quotation and clearing software.

Bernie Madoff was very personable and well-liked which resulted in his governance and formation of the NASD. Afterwards, he separated his market-making clearing operation of Madoff Securities a.k.a. Bernard L. Madoff Investment Securities to form a separate brokerage division which later operated as a hedge fund for affluent boutique investors. He managed the investment fund while his sons operated the old and separate trading business. He played complex trading techniques which nobody understood, to attract new clients with better than average trading profits. Other brokerage firms were clearing their trades through his original firm which actually competed with the NASDAQ for a large portion of the trading and exchange business for small trades (pink sheet). He was personable, connected, admired and brilliant.

At one time he converted his firm from a sole proprietorship to his sole limited liability company. The hedge fund produced high consistent annual returns for the exclusive clientele of his fund. His clients now consisted of country club affluent families and executives who all were connected socially. He particularly attracted funds of non-profit foundations and corporations that maintained large capital reserves. He was also able to pay feeder fund managers large referral fees for wealthy clients and the business grew bigger and bigger. He had graduated, according to statements he published, from market-making penny stocks to puts, calls, and trading options with blue chips. Even in recessions, his returns were broadcast as outstanding as and always better than the market in general. His customers loved him and he was socially active among the rich and famous.

Bernie Madoff was brilliant, not only in his marketing and management, but in keeping investigators away because he never earned the huge returns he promised. Time and time again other brokers complained that his purported earnings were impossible to amass over the years as he projected. The SEC investigated and did nothing about the business which operated as an unregistered hedge fund. His back room continued to crank out phony earnings reports and the phony Ponzi scheme kept bringing in more money to cover the redemptions and operations of the business which lowered the investment-banking balances. So, what went wrong?

In 2008 the stock market and underlying economy crashed. Redemptions, for the first time in this over the four-decade-old business, suddenly exceeded new investments and the bank and investment accounts emptied. Bernie began moving money around even from his personal accounts but he could not recover from the wave of withdrawals. Billions were paid out and by year-end, Bernie confessed to his sons, who managed the legitimate trading arm that they were out of business, that the investment hedge fund was a big lie. One of them called their lawyers who immediately called the SEC.

Many charities went out of business afterward and the repercussions were immense. Bernie was sentenced to 150 years in prison with a restitution of $170 Billion. Clawbacks were instituted for the people who had received money back from those who lost their investments. Many of the losers were lifetime friends and family of Bernie Madoff. Prosecutors estimated the size of the fraud to be $65 billion but the data was always disputed because of the depth of the fraud over the years. The IRS amended the tax code to allow for some loss carrybacks. It was a monumental national tragedy.

SECOND HORROR STORY - SECURITIES FRAUD

A very smart fellow from Texas set up shop in a California Savings & Loan chain during the mid-1980. He was the first drop of water from a wave of financial people put on the floors of banks and S&L's to extract insurance and brokerage fees from clients who were cash-rich from the times when cash was certificates of deposit, not equity accounts in the stock market. This fellow did all the right things by rewarding the tellers for informing him when large client deposits were made, and ultimately reviewing the savings balances of every bank customer. His desk was near the front door and, as an attorney stated later, "you would walk by his desk where he would greet you with his charming smile; you would, therefore, empty your pockets, and go on to the teller line".

This fellow was very likable and sophisticated. After several years of investing with the bank clients, he had an argument with a client that led to his sudden disappearance completely out of the country. What he had done was copy the Templeton Fund Money Market prospectus, changing the name and created his own mutual fund. This new fund mailed client statements from a two-person office back in Texas where his partner and a model-secretary maintained the headquarters. Eventually, the deal was found out, after $9,000,000 was invested. Nothing was recovered.

The lawyers got busier than usual suing everybody and eventually the Savings & Loan sued their insurance company for more payments for customer claims. The phony advisor, after spending time in the Grand Cayman Islands, served several years in jail for securities fraud. He continued being socially competent enough to send designer Christmas cards to his trial judge each year. The investigations, which sent him packing, were initiated by the SEC notifying him he was acting as an unregistered investment adviser, then the FBI became involved, and finally the usual cops in blue suits and with detectives in better suits. The last time I saw him he was renting and leasing luxury cars somewhere in Texas.

THIS LETTER WAS SENT TO HIM BY THE SECURITIES EXCHANGE COMMISSION:

"Gentlemen:

Information has come to the attention of this office that indicates that representatives may be engaged in the offer and sale of securities, as that term is defined in Section 2 (1) of the Securities Act of 1933, issued by XXXXX Money Market Fund, Inc.

Unless exempt from registration, Section 5 of the Securities Act of 1933, as amended, makes it unlawful for any person to make use of the mails or other federal jurisdictional means to offer securities for sale unless a registration statement relating to that security has been filed with the Commission. Furthermore, that section makes it unlawful for any person to make use of the above means to sell or deliver a security unless a registration statement relating to that security is in effect. The Commission's records show no registration statements having been filed with regard to any securities issued by XXXXX Money Market Fund, Inc.

Furthermore, it appears that XXXXX Money Market Fund, Inc., may be operating as an unregistered investment adviser. The Investment Advisers Act of 1940 defines, among other activities, the term "investment Adviser" to include any person who, for compensation, engages in the business of advising others either directly or through publications or writings, as to the advisability of investing in, purchasing or selling securities. Section 203 (a) of the Investment Advisers Act makes it unlawful for any investment adviser to use the mails or means of interstate commerce in connection with such business without registration in accordance with that act, unless it has complied with the terms and conditions of an applicable exemption provided by Section 203 (b).

In addition, it appears that the XXXXX Money Market Fund, Inc. may be operating as an investment company, as that term is defined in Section 3 (a) of the Investment Company Act of 1940. Section 7 of the Investment Company Act prohibits an investment company from directly or indirectly offering or selling its securities by use of the mails or facilities of interstate commerce or engaging in any business in interstate commerce unless it is registered under Section 8 of the Investment Company Act. Our records reveal no registration statement having been filed by XXXXX Money Market Fund, Inc., under the Investment Company Act.

Finally, the possibility must also be considered that the XXXXX Money Market Fund, Inc., may be required to register as broker-dealers under the Securities Exchange

Act of 1934. Briefly stated, a broker is any person who is engaged in the business of effecting transactions in securities for the account of others; a dealer is one who is engaged in the business of buying and selling securities for his own account, through a broker or otherwise.

In light of the foregoing, it is requested that you contact the undersigned as soon as possible for an early appointment to discuss this matter.

Very truly yours,

Xxxxxxxxxxxxxx

Regional Administrator

Branch of Investment Adviser/Investment Company Examinations

An enclosure of the privacy act is attached."

Sadly, a branch cashier reported the huge drain on the bank deposits. She was ignored by management. These days, with securities and insurance reps on the branch floor moving cash deposits outside their banks to highly commissioned investment products, it is worth noting that banks rarely have lendable funds for real estate or commercial loans. They have become brokers of these services themselves.

PROS & CONS OF MANAGED ACCOUNTS

- Everybody today is some kind of financial advisor. This chapter is about the professional Registered Investment Advisor.

- Be sure the RIA gives you a copy of his official ADV statement. Read it.

- A good RIA will review all your personal financial documents, beyond handling your funds. He should look for proper beneficiaries on insurance policies, titling of assets, review your will, trusts or estate planning, and all aspects of your financial life.

- A RIA should review the tax aspects of your portfolio and compare them to your tax returns to be sure you are taking advantage of tax planning.

- Education and licenses are not everything. Monitor the results of your RIA portfolio to be sure he/she has the right investment philosophy for your needs. Do not let him/her lose money for you. He is supposed to be ethical but only you will prove that right or wrong.

- The fees invested in a competent RIA would normally be a bargain compared to piecemeal investing and high commission charges of most investor portfolios.

- There are no guarantees that any RIA would always make you money but a good one would diversify your portfolio to reduce risk.

- Not everybody has a net worth large enough or enough investment liquidity for an RIA. Your money could all be stuck in real estate or a company pension.

- A RIA is the top professional of the securities business.

CHAPTER 21: APPLICATION EXERCISES

1. A Registered Investment Advisor manages accounts for individuals and others and is usually a person with the top business, educational and financial licenses. ____ True ____ False

2. Any individual investing money for you, if not as a licensed broker-dealer rep, can be acting as an unlicensed Investor Advisor. ____ True ____ False

3. A RIA should provide you with the SEC ADV form which outlines the advisory investment objectives, the commission or fee structure and the background of the advisor and his professional staff. ____ True ____ False

4. The following advisor expenses should be monitored and controlled by the investor: trading costs, custodian costs and management fees. ____ True ____ False

5. In addition to reviewing all aspects of your financial life, a good RIA will also do the following (check all that apply):
    ____ a. Check for proper beneficiaries on insurance policies
    ____ b. Check the titling of all of your assets
    ____ c. Review your will, trusts & estate planning
    ____ d. All of the above

6. Which of the following statements about Managed accounts is false:
    ____ a. They are found with Registered Investment Advisors and licensed only by their resident state
    ____ b. They are under strict jurisdiction of the licensing agencies of NASD, FINRA, & SEC
    ____ c. They charge quarterly administrative fees based on client portfolio balances
    ____ d. They work directly under principal supervision in BD firms

7. Which of the following statements about Registered Investment Advisors is false:
    ____ a. They are allowed to charge trading commissions if they are compensated by advisement fees
    ____ b. Their advisory fees start on a sliding scale from 2% annually or less depending on the size of the account
    ____ c. Small brokerage firms turn advisory management accounts over to Mutual Fund advisories
    ____ d. Large brokerage firms manage their own accounts with great software and diversification

8. Which of the following statements about Fiduciary responsibility is false:
    ____ a. They are responsible with the client's money
    ____ b. The advisor is held responsible for abusing or stealing from clients
    ____ c. They can steal fees from clients by obscuring bad performance
    ____ d. They merge investment products into financial statements with computer trading which make them difficult to read

9. Which of the following statements about Advisory Compliance is false:
    ____ a. An advisor should present his clients with the SEC ADV form which shows his investment objectives, the commission structure, and the advisor's background and professional staff
    ____ b. An advisor must present a contract that will outline the fee arrangement, for client signature
    ____ c. An advisor can use portfolio money for his personal use if he signs authorizing documents
    ____ d. Self-dealing with a fiduciary is illegal

10. Which of the following is true about the Bernie Madoff Horror Story:
    ____ a. Bernie was a very bright and charming person who created computerized clearing data and trading quotations
    ____ b. Bernie was involved in the governance of the NASD
    ____ c. Bernie reportedly produced phenomenal steady profits and acquired many friends, paying other brokers to send him large client investors for his funds in his personal brokerage account
    ____ d. Bernie had a Ponzi scheme going until the 2008 crash caused more outflows than he had accumulated over the years without trading any real funds at all.
    ____ e. All of the above

CHAPTER TWENTY-TWO

UNIT TRUSTS

The favorite question for investors will always be, "is it guaranteed?" and from that point on the sales rep tries to find 234 ways to tell the client how great and safe the investment is without using the word guarantee. Well, an investment that works actually uses the word "guarantee". The investment is unit trusts that include government bonds.

A unit trust is a focused group or basket of investments in a specific industry, place, and time. Unlike a mutual fund that expands or contracts by buying and selling shares without limit, the unit trust is a **closed-end investment**. The trust sells a fixed number of shares then shuts off all sales and repurchase activity leaving the investor to forage on the stock exchange at **Net Average Value** for redemptions and purchases. The packager investment firm will gather from ten to fifteen blue-chip stocks in telephones, or health care, or utilities, food manufacturers & processors, or other more conservative companies. Then they will buy ten-year **zero-coupon Treasury notes**. The notes and stocks then are married to a unit investment sold through brokerage firms. The commission is high…about 5%, which reduces the number of shares, purchased or is added to an even amount (rounding up to even thousands is fun) of shares. What the packager has created is an investment that will never decline in value. Even if none of the stocks pay dividends and all become insolvent, you will still get your initial investment back. In other words, the investment is guaranteed.

The group of stocks acts as an index for that particular industry (one was in major California businesses) and will go up or down following the market trend for ten years. During that time dividends will be paid quarterly and credited to the client's cash account at the broker-dealer, and after ten years the zero-coupon Treasury note matures and pays the owner the initial cost of the investment (not including commissions) as long as the Treasury is earning 7% or greater. Seven percent compounded will double and equal the principal in ten years. The unit trust will buy and sell securities within the trust during that period. It also charges a laundry list of trustee and administration fees.

AN EXAMPLE:

$10,000 invested in a unit trust plus 5% commission equals $10,500 cost.

$5,000 invested in 10 different California Golden Fleece Mining Company stocks (each mine is a separate corporation).

$5,000 invested in 7% zero-coupon Treasury notes.

Ten years later $650 was been received in cash dividends and interest on the cash dividends (after trust administration and trustee fees). $9,850 was received from the 7% matured Treasury note. Then it is discovered that all of the stock certificates were Ponzi schemed and bankrupted in the last year because the promoters used new security sales money to keep the deals going (it was later disclosed that the preliminary ore core samples from the new mines were salted with gold dust and old dental gold). Alas, the stocks are worthless! However, not all is lost because you got all your money back from dividends and the Treasury note ($10,500). Maybe it is really guaranteed or close to it.

At the time of publication treasury interest rates are at all-time low of 2%. Because unit trusts need 7% to double in ten years, it is unlikely there be any new issues until inflation drives rates higher.

Most of the unit trusts are very conservatively invested because investors who want to protect the downside of their investment with fixed-income securities buy them. As you can see, even in the worst case where the entire underlying stock portfolio is lost, the initial investment is still protected. Unit trusts like to buy low and sell high like most people. They tend to concentrate the portfolio in "dogs of the Dow" which are companies that have high earnings (yield to cost) compared to other stocks in the market. They calculate the portfolio will rise in value and have basic integrity because of good earnings.

AN EXAMPLE OF UNIT TRUSTS:

Cost of unit trust (including commissions paid)	$ 10,500
Investment in 7% zero-coupon Treasury note	$5,000
Investment in S/P 500 stocks	$5,000
Ten years later the Treasury note matures for	$9,850
The S&P indexed (18% annual increase) stocks are sold	$26,169
Dividends and interest earned	$481
Total return	$36,500
Less initial investment	-10,500
Net gain	$26,000

Of course, if the whole thing were invested in stocks, then the net return on our $10,000 investment would be over $40,000, which gives us the cost of being conservative in a bull market! The administrative and trustee costs are not included in the above example.

Unit trusts trade over the counter and are never listed in the Wall Street Journal or other financial publications. They are available only through brokerage firms, who trade with the trustee for shares or redemptions, if available. They initially sell for $10 per share by the institutions that package them, and go up afterwards, if there are any available for secondary sale. Units sold in the secondary market have accrued interest on the note as well as (hopefully) increased stock prices over the years, so they always sell for more than the original $10 offering price. They are truly unique and represent a conservative part of the marketplace.

The biggest drawback to unit trusts is the commission and administration cost vs doing it yourself, and the lack of control over stock picks. For the unsophisticated investor, this is a useful and unique investment.

PLANNING TIPS

Unit trusts focus on specific sectors of the economy. Best to select a part of the economy that you feel good about, such as pharmaceuticals if you spend a lot of time at the drug store, or energy if you worry about rising gas prices, and buy the units ($1,000 for 100 shares when first issued) if available. With interest rates below 6% at this time, the ten-year notes would yield only about $800 per thousand (1/2 of the unit trust investment), but the concept still stands. The higher the stock market, the lower the bond rates. They might be offset by higher stock prices on redemption. Naturally, as the unit trusts get older on the resale market the offering price would reflect higher stock prices by marking to the market (hopefully, over ten years) and accrued interest earned on the notes.

TAXES

Unit trusts create three kinds of taxable income. There is interest accrued on the Treasuries, payable as earned but only accrued. Then, cash dividends from the stocks are taxable, again as ordinary income. Dividends from stock splits are not taxable because they are only a splitting of equities, not cash or earnings. Finally, there are the capital gains (-losses?) when the units are sold. Trustees can redeem securities in the units during the term of the trust, which could account for some gains or losses.

LEGAL COMPLIANCE

Unit trusts are securities that need initial approval for the packager by the SEC for sale. Afterward, unlike mutual funds or many other securities, there is no prospectus to give the buyers. They are a closed-end security. After they are sold out, they are not administered like a mutual fund. There are only a fixed number of shares outstanding in the marketplace. Many unit trusts have an initial booklet showing the stock portfolio, including the company shares purchased, and objectives. The rest is up to the marketplace. The unit trust is unique and only available through broker firms; thus, it can only be sold by qualified stockbrokers. Because of the Treasuries, the unit trusts will deliver the original investment back to the buyer if held long enough (10 years at 7%) even if all of the securities disappear in a nuclear mushroom, so it is safe to say, "It is guaranteed." Not all unit trusts have Treasury bonds; however, any highly rated bond would do.

About guarantees. No stockbroker can guarantee any returns except a Treasury bond or note (Because the government guarantees it!). There is a possibility of default from any bond or note issued in the world except US Treasuries as far as American investors are concerned. That is the SEC opinion and all risk is judged from that starting point. Even then, there is a market interest rate bond risk whereas a sale before maturity in a higher interest marketplace can reduce the yield which would not happen in a unit trust. At any rate, a stockbroker cannot promise or pay off losses or personally guarantee an investment. That would destroy the securities industry based on investment risk.

SUCCESSFUL STRATEGIES

A wild speculative person would put all his/her money in the Internet, attach the portable television set next to the ceiling fan over the bed and quit sleeping nights. The conservative or diversified investor would share the bond and equity market and sleep peacefully with his unit trusts firmly in place. Best of all, his unit trust equities can be in an area he particularly likes, such as giant food companies because his grandmother used to talk about the potato famine in Ireland, or a Standard & Poor Indexed basket to cover the whole market. Therefore, he rests secure with the best of the market working for him, not fast like a jackrabbit, but more like a tough old raccoon.

HORROR STORY - UNIT TRUSTS

Every investment needs a downside. Remember that unit trusts can lose money if not held until the note matures. Some unit trusts, which held foreign stocks in telecommunications (simply the right idea in the wrong places), did fall in value when sold before maturity. Global securities, especially Asian, like the flu, have inherent investment culture risks. If the note/unit trust is held to maturity (and the note rate is at least 7%, remember that the older notes were higher than today) of ten years, at least the principal will be returned. To complete the horror story, close your eyes and imagine a focused portfolio on nuclear power plants including Three Mile Island, Chernobyl, and San Onofre and with the usual 50% offset in ten-year Russian bonds!

PROS & CONS ABOUT UNIT TRUST INVESTMENTS

- Unit trusts have a high cost compared to buying securities in decent quantities.

- Unit trusts are liquid and can be sold as easily as any security in the market.

- The Treasury bonds or strips will guarantee the return of principal even if most of the security portfolio is wasted.

- Buying Treasury bonds or notes is three to five times cheaper through a broker, than as half of a unit trust.

- Unit Trusts are a good investment for an individual who wants a taste of the market without being a good individual stock picker.

- Unit trusts focus on market sectors, unless they are an index trust, thus concentrating the investment in an area desired by some buyers.

- The principal disadvantage of a unit trust is cost, because costs are always cheaper for well-heeled large investors.

- Unit trusts selectively pick strong stocks with high yields, which is a conservative approach to the market, for that kind of investor.

- The bond portfolio in a guaranteed unit trust will not be traded constantly by being marked to the interest rate market as mutual funds do, because it is held to maturity.

- This is an advantage for an investor who thinks in terms of constant yield to maturity instead of hedging and speculating on interest rates.

- Last, low treasury interest rates have ruined this market and because Unit Trusts usually are ten-year issues, there probably are no more available in the current market.

CHAPTER 22: APPLICATION EXERCISES

1. Unit trusts are liquid and can be sold as easily, if available, as any security in the market. ____ True ____ False

2. Buying Treasury bonds or notes is three to five times more expensive through a broker than as half of a Unit Trust. ____ True ____ False

3. The Treasury bonds or strips will guarantee the return of principal even if the other half of the security portfolio is wasted.
____ True ____ False

4. A Unit Trust is a focused group or basket of investments in a specific industry, place and time. ____ True ____ False

5. Unit Trusts trade over the counter and are never listed in open market on the Wall Street Journal or other financial publications.
____ True ____ False

6. Unit trusts are a unique investment product. Which statement is false:
   ____ a. The principal of the investment is not guaranteed
   ____ b. A unit trust is a focused group or basket of investments in a specific industry, place, and time
   ____ c. The UT is a closed end investment which, when fully subscribed, closes sales and repurchases
   ____ d. The Trust is now allowed to be traded on the stock exchange for Net Average Value

7. Which of the following statements about trusts is false:
   ____ a. A ten-year zero-coupon Treasury note (costing $5,000) is matched with an equal amount of securities in a specific industry
   ____ b. In ten years, if the Treasuries earn 7 % (remember the good old days) it will mature at $10,000. This also creates interest income which has been reinvested and compounded for ten years. That was a guarantee of return of principal
   ____ c. The matching investment, usually in telephone or utility stocks, will hopefully earn that much or more in the time, which will be pure profit.
   ____ d. All of the above

8. Which of the following statements about Unit trusts is false:
   ___ a. Dividends received are reinvested during the ten years in addition to possible stock appreciation
   ___ b. Securities within the trust are traded during the ten years
   ___ c. Trustee and administration fees are also charged to the trust as incurred
   ___ d. The treasuries can earn less than 7% interest and still double in value over ten years

9. Which of the following statements about Unit trusts is false:
   ___ a. They trade over the counter and are never listed in the financial publications
   ___ b. They never trade successfully in the secondary market
   ___ c. They always sell for more than the $10 original offering price from the appreciated Treasuries
   ___ d. Accrued interest, dividends received, and capital gains on traded securities received by the Trust are all taxable

10. Which of the following statements about Unit trusts is also false:
   ___ a. All unit trusts have Treasuries for the zero coupon bonds
   ___ b. Only US Treasuries have a valid guarantee
   ___ c. Outside of owning Treasuries, this is probably the most conservative equities investment
   ___ d. They are a good investment for individuals not used to following individual stocks

CHAPTER TWENTY-THREE

LIMITED PARTNERSHIPS, OIL-GAS WELL DEALS, SOLAR–ELECTRIC CAR CREDITS, VIRTUAL CURRENCIES

Limited Partnerships are a legal entity involving an active **general partner**, who manages the business, and the **limited partners** who are investors. As long as the limited partners keep away from the business activities and remain passive partners, they are exempt from lawsuits and liability concerning the affairs of the business. Limited partnerships have successfully been around for hundreds of years involving the ancient trading companies of the British Empire and more recently Lloyds Insurance of Great Britain, the renowned insurance company. **General partnerships** are not handled through securities brokers and are not part of this chapter until the end.

The **Securities Exchange Commission (SEC) must approve limited partnerships** for sale to the public. Unapproved partnerships cannot be sold to strangers and must be on a business-personal basis, otherwise, they are illegal. Limited partnerships, the approved versions, tend to be riskier than ordinary investments because they are very large, involve huge amounts of money, and are long-term. Some of them pay cash dividends regularly; some have deferred distributions. In all cases, the true income results are not known until the term of the partnership has ended and the books are closed. There is an old saw about L/P's that goes, "in the beginning, the investor has the money and the general partner the knowledge, at the end the investor has the knowledge and the general partner has the money."

Partnerships, because they are long-term, are generally hard to sell before conclusion or term except through a secondary market of brokers who handle them as a specialty. They are usually heavily discounted (up to 50%

of book value) if sold prior to maturity. Because of the liquidity and exit considerations, there are special State and SEC qualifications for buyers. They are not for everybody except the people who can afford to have their money tied up for a long time and can diversify.

THERE ARE MANY KINDS OF PARTNERSHIPS, A FEW OF WHICH WE CAN COVER HERE:

- **Venture capital programs** which buy stocks or controlling interests in high-tech new firms, especially drug or software. Most of these have not succeeded very well because of the hands-on management aspect of being involved in small firms. They were superseded, for the most part, by small private partnerships of well-heeled venture capitalists.

- **Solar energy** and other government tax credit programs. These programs come and go with the political winds of time. They tend to reflect highly inflationary assumptions for future energy costs, can be economically unviable as an investment, and can reflect special state subsidy programs, not federal mandates. Sometimes broker-dealer firms, to generate commissions internally, help create or promote them if the scale is large enough.

- At this time there are federal (and some State) credits for purchase and leasing of Solar panels on commercial and residential properties. There are also federal credits on the plug-in electric automobiles, but not hybrid plug-in cars, and for lithium battery units connected with solar energy generation. These are investments, but not of the scope covered by this book. The tax codes surrounding these items are complex and constantly changing. I have doctor clients who buy Tesla cars every year for the tax credits to offset their generous income. That will change now but it is a moving target for the middle and upper-class citizens who can afford it.

- **Oil**. The old Midland Oil drilling LP programs are in two categories. The first is to buy stripper well reserves. The second is drilling and exploration. This is where I learned about slant drilling and other methods of tapping reworked oil fields in Midland,

Texas, and other old oilfields. Small uneconomic oil deposits are consolidated into larger uneconomic entities through these programs which probably only make money during the best of times when petroleum prices are high. Again, the uneconomic pricing of wholesale and retail energy prices sometimes dominate the sales pitch.

- **Natural Gas General Partnership.** A very special deal. An oil or gas well drilling operation is allowed to write off all their costs at completion. This is because it is not known to be a productive well or not until it is finished. Accordingly, a general partnership is formed to drill half a dozen wells in a specific area. The partners, who must be very high-income individuals, will share in the combined venture all as general partners. That allows them to write off all of the drilling costs against other income as active losses. The large losses are deductible against ordinary income. After one or more wells are productive, the partnership reorganizes as a limited partnership and the partners are now inactive passive investors. They took the losses, and the wells produced the highest pressured gas in the beginning, and trailed after a few years. It seemed like the entire high plateau of Colorado was marked for drilling. This was before fracking, which is an entirely new game. I never found out if my client got his investment back because the wells produce for many years with the profit predictably at the end.

- **Real Estate.** This was the basis of most limited partnerships until the tax rules changed in 1986. The properties would be allowed quicker depreciation than economic life, thus would produce tax losses to offset investor's wages or other income. Most of the deals were leveraged with bank money and not well managed. Today most of the real estate deals are Real Estate Investment Trusts and some of the same problems prevail.

- **Equipment Leasing.** This is the oldest and best form of limited partnerships because they produce a steady income flow paid to investment partners. Early programs involved mainframe computers. Computers represent a huge investment for national companies because they involve proprietary software and the management of huge databases. IBM Corporation used to lease more equipment than they sold, in the good old days before chained microcomputers. Computer leasing partnerships made sense and as in all equipment leasing partnerships, the partnership deal would attempt to recover their equipment cost from the first customer (a full payout lease). Then, they could re-lease the equipment back to the user who was married to it, with his own software, people, and systems, or it would be sold like an automobile to another user.

One day microcomputers and minicomputers showed up. Some newer entrants to business computers such as Monroe and Burroughs blew out all their smaller clients who bought and managed their minicomputers. The mini's that came from nowhere (Radio Shack's Tandy first generation was a new big seller), did not go away, and Mike Dell changed the world. The mainframe computer business was now threatened and the computer leasing deals faded away with mainframe sales. The leasing industry still refers to computer leasing deals as high-tech and brokers are gun-shy because of problems with fast obsolescence.

Transportation equipment partnerships are still viable. They buy equipment such as airplanes, cargo containers, locomotives, rolling stock, and other types of low-tech equipment.

The problem is that they are competing with major banks for the same deal and they are using investors as the banks use depositors. The difference is credit rating because the better rated the leasing client is the cheaper the rate a bank will offer for leasing or financing (**even below prime rate**). **Leasing is another word for renting** because the owner (bank or partnership) has the title to the property until it is purchased as a separate transaction (preferably, after the lease has concluded). The leasing company has a **collateral title** to the property. They will file **Uniform Commercial Code (UCC-1)** documents with the State to secure the lien until the lease has expired. Manufacturers also offer leasing programs for their equipment, but mostly use an outside source of capital to help them sell their equipment. At any rate, at the end of the lease, the equipment goes back to the partnership owner for disposal. The disposal residual value after the initial lease expires is where the true profit of the partnership resides.

Since the equipment has been subjected to depreciation wear and tear, the general partner's monthly check in the mail to the investor usually represents some return of capital. The true profit is not realized until the equipment has been disposed of and that can take up to ten years or more, which is usually twice the original lease term. The cash distributions might be 5% to 15% annually to the clients and the deal might be earning -0- to 20% but there is absolutely no way of knowing the real profit or loss until the deal is concluded and all the equipment is sold or disposed of. Of course, there are also high organizational expenses, broker commissions, audited financials, and management fees to contend with for the life of the partnership. Most leasing deals are written inside the continental United States, thus the recent slowdown in exports from here resulted in excess container shipping capacity because the Asian shippers own their own containers and their business was up.

Secondary leasing limited partnerships have been around for some time. These LP's buy up the property from banks and large companies when the lease term has expired or when the institution has recovered their cost. The seller realizes an immediate profit because his costs are now recovered. This is an opportunity for the L/P with big bucks to wheel and deal in the part of the market where there is more money to be made. The difference is no different from dealing with autos. New cars have a slim margin but used cars are marked up to 100% of cost or more. This equipment is leased out again, if possible, or sold outright. Generally, as with new-equipment leases, there is little if any principal risk, but there is always a yield risk. The secondary L/P dealer is working in a secondary niche market or looking for specialized big deals.

Again, like all L/P's, the general partner receives a good share of the profits when the equipment is ultimately disposed of. The internal rate of return is probably higher for secondary wheeler-dealers than original equipment leasing deals because they are not competing with bank money rates to get the equipment to the clients. They also tend to have shorter terms than new equipment leasing deals. It is possible for the secondary market buyer to participate in purchase and leaseback functions with large companies who need the cash. Cash is always king.

VIRTUAL CURRENCIES (Cryptocurrency) are not legal tender and are considered property by the Internal Revenue Service. **Bitcoin, Ethereum, Litecoin, and Ripple** are now in the dictionary as investments and are noteworthy. These currencies can be digitally traded between users and can be purchased or exchanged into US Dollars, euros and other real or virtual currencies. Accordingly, they are real if not "hard" currency and available only online through exchanges. They are not legal tender and not backed by any institution or national bank. It is truly a computerized medium of exchange that clears through a **blockchain** security ledger system. **Facebook** considered their **Libra Bit** but put it on hold, Sweden's **Riksbank** has an **e-krona** program, **Uruguay e-pesos** in a crypto wallet, central banks at **Caribbean** and **Bahamas** are also working on it, per the Wall Street Journal. The values of these virtual currencies are, as well, esoteric.

Cryptocurrencies are a big issue with the Internal Revenue Service these days. They demanded and received lists of people holding the pseudo coin from major issuers and controllers of the currencies such as Bitcoin so they can tax activities as a capital investment, not a currency. There have been many new scams involving these invisible currencies such as Plus Token, which established holder wallets for their own benefit. The Securities Exchange Commission has been pursuing many fake scams as the original currencies have taken traction. They label Virtual Currencies as Securities. IRS labels them as property. Nobody calls them currency except the holders of the things. The Wall Street Journal has published many articles about these activities and overall, they present tax nightmares and investment speculation of a new genre. These things come with their own language; Airdrop is the distribution to a ledger which also results in taxable income, Bitcoin is the surviving creator of this computer-generated currency, Cryptocurrency, Hard Fork is the creation of new currency split off from existing currency, virtual currency. Although there are legitimate currencies out there remember the axiom, out of sight, out of mind.

PLANNING TIPS

Limited partnerships have a place in a large portfolio or a small well-diversified portfolio. They can provide reliable cash flow for many years. To participate you need to know that there has been a favorable track record for the company managing the deal. A limited partnership is very large and complex, which means that a large experienced hands-on management company should be behind the deal. Their references are the key to the deal. Because partnerships live so long, there may be a lack of completed deals to reference. Most successful limited partnerships today are in equipment leasing and there are more kinds of deals than there are kinds of equipment to be leased. The term is so long...up to ten years or more, and because of the risk of obsolescence and market, these investments are not for the average citizen.

The prospectus of every partnership must show the prior performance of all other deals, even the ones not closed yet. If it is equipment leasing, there will be schedules showing asset sales by type. Look for profitable sales; after all, this is where the real profit is. A limited partnership packager who cannot earn money on the back end is dooming his investors to losses. There is also a schedule for each deal, closed or open, which shows distributions returned to the partners. They will tell how much of the capital has been remitted to the investors and give an indication of any profits returned as well.

Solar energy for residential housing has been grossly overpriced to sales expenses and overhead. Installation on new housing construction is averaging only 25-30% of the unit costs of the people in the retail establishments and door-to-door salespeople. They have not, like electric cars, held their value (based on purchase price) in the resale market after the income tax credits are gone. There is no indication that the real cost of the large solar residential purchases will sustain after the credits go away. Plug-in cars will be priced and sell well without credits due to mass production cost reductions as experienced by Tesla.

TAXES

Limited partnerships produce K-1 forms at year-end. The investor schedules are for passive income or losses. These amounts flow through to the Schedule E that is also used for rental income and expenses. Self-employment tax is avoided on these earnings because of the lack of active investor involvement. The K-1 form (capital section) shows the cash disbursed during the year as a reduction of capital and sometimes passive losses as well. This is because there is no true taxable income or loss known until the capital has been returned to the investor. This is the fundamental difference between cash distributions and income. Some K-1 forms show passive losses (mostly because of depreciation expense) but since the new tax rules effected in 1986, these losses cannot offset ordinary income until the partnership files a "final" K-1 form. The losses can offset other passive income, however. In practice, the passive losses are accumulated until the partnership has shown taxable income or closed out, in which case other income can be offset (and the losses all used up in that year).

When included in **pensions, limited partnerships** can create **Unrelated Business Investment Income (UBIT)** that is limited for this application because a pension is a trust. These complex passive income-loss rules took several years to get used to. An IRS auditor once told me that when they first audited the 1986 returns, it took them several years later before they finally knew what they were doing. People who didn't know what they were doing at the time because the rules were so complex and confusing, ended up preparing tax returns being audited. This was very true and gave the IRS plenty of changes. The new tax code takes time to change, especially the last one of 2018 with the new complex business credits.

Tax credits for solar residential units and electric qualified automobiles are sometimes retained from the purchaser in leasing programs. When buying or leasing these large purchases, buyers must be adamant that the credit is part of the purchase price and should flow to you, not the financing agency. The cost of the units without the credits can be marginal for utility energy billing savings, especially solar when compared to realistic usage. Auto savings must compare to gasoline mileage costs but are only now becoming feasible with lower prices for improved vehicles. California electric utility costs will dramatically exponentially increase from the costs of the PG&E bankruptcy, partly due to the poor forest management by the State. All of these factors create a mobile investment situation. Buyers beware.

There has been so much fraud in the tax credit programs that the IRS currently verifies the qualified auto VIN numbers on the tax returns claiming auto energy credits before they release the tax return. In other words, they hold the return up and delete the credit, if not verified.

Virtual currencies are considered taxable transactions and there is a question on the 2019 tax returns asking, "At any time during 2019, did you receive, sell, send, exchange, or otherwise acquire any financial interest in any virtual currency?"

IRS Notice 2014-21 states that crypto currency is property for tax purposes based on fair market price when bought. Subject to sales price fair market value when sold or exchanged.

The IRS will compare the cost of the virtual currency with the value of the purchased or traded product to find a taxable gain therein. This generates a huge argument over the fair market value of items purchased or traded. They are also concerned about buying and hold investors in the currency itself who will have a taxable gain on use or exchange.

The IRS obtained lists of 10,000 crypto tax payers' user transactions directly from Bitcoin and will engage in letters of tax advice to owners resulting from their information. Beware, the taxman cometh.

LEGAL COMPLIANCE

Both the SEC and the broker-dealer firm must approve limited partnerships. They are unwieldy deals with large complex prospectuses. A prospectus must be given to the client at the time of presentation or investing. Because the term is long and future uncertain, there are sometimes different state and SEC investor income and investment net worth requirements (not including home, furnishings, or autos). An investor is usually required to sign a form acknowledging that he has received the prospectus and understands the risk involved. A principal at the broker-dealer firm must review the investor qualifications and limited partnership investment before the investment purchase is approved. The investor must understand that the amount of cash distributed during the term of the partnership is not truly income but is shown as the return of capital until the deal is closed out, many years later. The investment is not considered a liquid investment because the money is held for long periods of time and a premature sale (usually at great cost) must be conducted in the secondary market, which can take months to conclude.

Owners frequently mistake that cash distributions are profits, not refunds of capital cash distributions when there is no big check in the mail on termination. For that reason, after ten years with my broker-dealer, I quit selling L/P deals.

In recent years, many legal firms have obtained client lists of people invested in various ongoing limited partnerships. Then, they send out mass mailings of nebulous letters to people suggesting that they may have a loss that the friendly law firm will gladly litigate. This is the introduction to a frivolous nuisance claim. The firm will be happy to file it with the expectation that the broker-dealer firm will be glad to pay only $10,000 to $15,000 to avoid even more in legal fees for a trial. Fortunately, these claims have subsided, as most investment clients must now agree to arbitration (no formal courtroom trial) to invest with the broker-dealer. There is no loss on any investment unless there is a loss of principal (initial investment capital). Loss of earnings is not a legal defense because there is always a risk in any investment. If a limited partnership has not closed out, then it is probably impossible to determine the loss.

If you, as a client, receive such a notice, please contact your stockbroker and have him/her take a close look at the investment for you. He/She should be able to give you information on the status of the deal so you will understand how well it is doing. If your clients file a legal claim, it will appear as a negative entry on your and the B/D record and may cost him/her a large amount against legal fees or malpractice insurance claims from him/her broker-dealer firm. The lawyers tend to go for misrepresentation and clients are not risk qualified for the deal. I quit selling LPs after the first of them termed out and the results were lousy. If you sold a lot of them, your relationship with the B/D may end. Smart stockbrokers try to discover and turn away litigious or crazy new clients. The broker-dealer firm's instructions to reps, are always to "know your client" and "keep out of trouble".

SUCCESSFUL STRATEGIES

The best strategy of the limited partnership is one that provides a steady income for a person who has a diverse portfolio. The use in pension portfolios is recommended only if there are considerable liquid assets available for employee terminations or distributions and if there are no immediate prospects of closing the pension down.

Sales to elderly people, who seem to have most of the available cash these days, is cautiously recommended. Once a woman who wanted a partnership deal for her mother approached me. The mother was 85 years old. "But she will live to be a hundred," she said, "all of our family live a long time." I sold it to her and the mother lived longer than the LP, to be one hundred years old.

A good strategy would be to avoid visiting Venezuela and being compelled to change dollars for their worthless cryptocurrency.

HORROR STORY - UNREGISTERED PARTNERSHIPS

Once upon a time, a company sold unregistered partnerships to wealthy people. The deals were before 1986, offering highly leveraged for a maximum write-off. They were in computer equipment and created accelerated depreciation losses of four times the investment, which required some bank leverage as well. There would be no cash flow back to the client until near the end of the deal, but the time-value of the losses (**internal rate of return**) and resulting invested tax refunds from highly taxed individual returns would create income in itself. The deal was sold, outside broker-dealer firms because it was a private offering, and the customers pocketed the big tax refunds.

Everything went well for some time. The losses showed up and the investors invested or spent their huge tax refunds. Then after five years, the losses disappeared, but there was no promise of cash flow yet because the computer equipment was not re-leased due to some technical problems. The investors waited for their cash back, but nothing happened. After the losses were applied, the leveraged excess losses, which were three times more than the investment, began showing up as income for the tax returns. The amounts overwhelmed the investors because it was now in the early 1990s and the investors, mostly executives, were taking pay cuts due to the recession.

One tax client who had invested $25,000 for one partnership unit suddenly had a K-1 taxable income of $75,000 while he was having a terrible time with his business. Although he had secured the benefit of the large tax refunds when the tax tables were much higher, he was totally unprepared for the tax bill. That was the good news. The bad news was that I remember the sales guys talking about somebody from Bakersfield with oil money who had bought ten big units at the time!

SECOND HORROR STORY - GENERAL PARTNERSHIP

These computer equipment promotion people came up with another deal after the tax rules changed in 1986. Since they could not write off passive losses against other income, they had a deal, which would make an investor an actual owner instead of a limited partner. What they proposed was to buy big-rig tractor-trailer trucks and the partnership, now a general partnership, would help operate them as a business for the investor. They would then borrow most of the cost from a bank, signed and secured by the investor. The deal would provide tax breaks at the beginning from depreciation and other expenses then provide a real operating profit for the investor. A trucking company client reviewed the deal and told me, "Nobody could run a truck that many hours to make the deal work." Sure enough, the deal went sour for some investors and hit the Los Angeles Times from all the legal activity generated from this and other bad deals. The worst part began when somebody parked the trucks in front of investors' houses and the bank visited later to collect the money owed them.

PROS & CONS ABOUT LIMITED PARTNERSHIP INVESTMENTS

- Limited partnerships provide reliable long-term cash flow for retirement or other needs.

- L/Ps sometimes return capital initially instead of earnings because the true return is not known until the deal is closed out. It is also possible that the partnership may never return a profit but it will not be known until it is over. There are no tax consequences until the distributions have exceeded the initial cost or the partnership has closed out.

- L/Ps are a long-term investment. You are locked in the deal for many years because the intent and plan is to buy assets that will last for many years, usually leased equipment.

- Never try to sell your L/P unless you are desperate because the secondary market for these things will take a huge discount from the book value.

- Most partnerships buy more new equipment with earnings during the first five years of operation, which is one reason the deal is so long-term.

- Never buy any L/P which is not subject to the FINRA/SEC review and rules, which allow them only to be sold through licensed broker-dealers. In other words, keep away from any private L/P.

- L/Ps are inherently riskier and relatively illiquid, so they are only for the investor who has a lot of faith and understanding of both the broker and the deal.

- The most promising aspect of the L/P is the steady cash flow, usually from lease payments received on partnership leased equipment.

- The most negative aspect of the L/P is that you will never know how much money, if any, you have earned until it is closed many years later.

- If an L/P is inherited, it is best for the heir to change the title on the investment rather than unload it for a big losing discount in the secondary market. The sale of the security could also delay closing the estate because the process takes months to find a buyer.

- If you or your accountant are smart enough, be sure to review the history of current and past deals in the prospectus to see if the general partners are making money when they sell off leased equipment and to see how much money is redistributed back to the limited partners. Only distributed amounts over 100% of initial investment (after return of capital) are profits for investors.

CHAPTER 23: APPLICATION EXERCISES

1. Limited partnerships are a legal entity involving an active general partner, who manages the business, and the limited partners who are investors. ___ True ___ False

2. Virtual currencies (cryptocurrency) are not legal tender and are considered property by the Internal Revenue Service. ___ True ___ False

3. Limited Partnerships provide reliable long-term cash flow for retirement or other needs. ___ True ___ False

4. The most negative aspect of the Limited Partnership is that you will never know how much money, if any, you have earned until it is closed many years later. ___ True ___ False

5. Most partnerships buy more new equipment with earnings during the first five years of operation, which is one reason the deal is so long-term. ___ True ___ False

6. Limited partnerships are large and complex. Which statement is false:
    ___ a. They are a legal entity
    ___ b. They create passive income for limited partners
    ___ c. They have no general partners
    ___ d. They are long-term, over ten years average, risky ventures

7. Which of the following statements about Limited Partnerships is false:
    ___ a. They require approval by the SEC which involves huge legal fees or huge deals
    ___ b. True income is shown as regular distributions
    ___ c. Most partnerships are financial arrangements such as leasing or renting
    ___ d. Some compete with banks for financing equipment or real estate

8. Which of the following statements about Limited Partnerships is also false:

____ a. They must have a general partner responsible for corporate matters

____ b. They have limited salability in secondary market with heavily discounted prices

____ c. They are restricted to clients with higher risk income and aptitude

____ d. They have the same tax attributes as active general partnerships

9. Which of the following statements about Oil and Natural Gas Drilling Partnerships is false:

____ a. There is a very high risk of dry wells so many are bundled into single partnerships

____ b. They have easy qualifications for investors

____ c. They begin as general partnerships for tax purposes, then reorganize as limited partnerships

____ d. They incur losses from drilling costs then recover income later when the oil/gas comes on line

10. Which of the following statements about Virtual-Crypto currencies is false:

____ a. They are a new computer exercise in financial speculation and exchanges

____ b. They are legal tender in some states

____ c. They are considered taxable property for exchanges and trading by the IRS

____ d. While some have appreciated in value, many have disappeared with speculation

CHAPTER TWENTY-FOUR
COMMODITIES

A business client had a slow period during December 1998. To keep his help busy, he cleaned up the shop and yard with a bout of annual housekeeping. Then, he sold a truckload of scrap fencing wire and posts to a local scrap yard on a railroad spur. "They only gave me $5 a ton," he unhappily told me. Then he added, "I don't remember how many years ago when the price was that low." This was his introduction to the **commodities market** of the year ending 1998.

The big scrap dealers nearby in Long Beach-Los Angeles harbor weren't paying much for his scrap light-iron steel (sheet metal, wire, posts) that would help fill a 40-foot Corban rust-resistant steel cargo container which had been sold for $2,235 in China to shipping companies earlier during the year, an all-time low price as well. The electric furnaces, which would melt the scrap someplace in Asia, were also having a capacity problem and were dumping their steel at cut-rate prices in the States to offset reduced local consumption in collapsed economies. Even the cargo container people were having a capacity glut problem from buying too many cheap containers and trying to keep them all leased for overseas and land duty. Their rental capacity percentage of 60% was also a new low with almost a hundred-thousand containers lining the Long Beach dockyards, emptied of expensive electronic goods and Christmas toys, now **deadheaded** without cargo for a return trip.

The shortage of capital in Asia from the financial speculation meltdown of 1997-8 also created world currencies to collapse, from Russia to South America, thus lending to currency exchange problems and scary trade-balance totals as most of the world powers preferred to be sellers of goods, not buyers. Why are we going over all of this? Because the world economy is part of our economy and the raw materials of this economy are commodities. Everything used in the economy is a commodity, from the scrap steel above to the paper this book is printed on. It influences everybody's life in many ways.

Commodities are traded on the **Chicago Board of Trade**, the **New York Mercantile Exchange,** the **Chicago Mercantile Exchange** and other exchanges the world over. A commodity can be anything from precious metals to wheat, literally any measurable thing that can be sold today or in the future. The **U.S. Crude Oil Futures** are traded by the 42-gallon barrel on The New York Mercantile Exchange. The **Brent crude** which represents the global gauge of oil prices is traded on the **Intercontinental Exchange**. The US prices for oil usually produced and consumed here, are usually about 10% lower than the Intercontinental because of shipping costs. The available commodities can be influenced by the weather, wars and political moves such as Brazil controlling coffee exports. Likewise, overproduction such as an oil glut in spite of **OPEC**'s influence misjudged California's long-term capacity considerations for electric power which caused shortages and huge price spikes and resulted in the demise of Enron. Even monopolistic hedging such as Bunker Hunt on silver, **Soros** cornering the **British Pound**, Governmental policies such as Australia's central banks **disgorging gold inventories,** etc. had their impact on these commodities. They are a gamble because they a present value purchase of an item hopefully delivering a profit in the future, as all investment goals are.

The commodities markets took a bath in 1998. Crude oil reached new twelve-year lows at $10.72 per barrel, gold settled down for new impossible lows of $271.60, platinum ranged from $440 to $364.50 per ounce, silver ranged from $7 to $5.62 per ounce, farming grain and animal prices went to the bottom, copper and coffee went down. The world seemed to be in an oversupply of commodities. Was it all due to the Asian, South American and Russian economic problems? Probably not. The basic problem is that the world is becoming more efficient at extracting, refining, recycling, and managing the basic stuff of nature. Recycling materials is a big factor affecting the quantity of raw materials required; manufacturing efficiency has its quantified position, hybrid seeds and modern irrigation help farmers overproduce, mining is more efficient…with equipment replacing cheap labor (once slave labor in South America and Russia), and so on. A psychological barrier of things always costing more was broken, but not forgotten.

The commodities market is broken down into currency and interest rate futures, grain and meat, and two types of metals. There are primary metals, such as copper, aluminum, iron, etc. Then there are the precious metals commodities such as gold, silver, platinum, now palladium, etc. The metals are traded on the same exchanges, primarily the **Chicago Board of Trade**, where food commodities are also traded. The **New York Commodities Exchange** handles currencies and interest rate futures. The **Philadelphia Stock Exchange**, the original home of Benjamin Franklin and the cradle of democracy, maintains a **gold and silver index**.

How do we buy commodities and how do they behave in the marketplace? One way is to open an account with a commodity broker (an ordinary stockbroker is not licensed to trade here) and buy **futures (puts)** of the commodity you are interested in. Perhaps you want to buy pork bellies (bacon) and make a killing, so you borrow money from your broker (who borrows it much cheaper from a bank) to leverage your purchases with a 50% **margin account**. You can buy now for delivery (on the market) in the future when the price may be up, or you can buy hedge (**call**) for future delivery when the price may be cheaper. The Wall Street Journal and financial newspapers carry the future prices of commodities every day. They are listed by categories such as grains and oilseeds, livestock and meat, food and fiber, metals and petroleum, and interest rates. Cash prices are also listed for the above in the **Cash price listing**. Many large companies secure future raw material needs and define their costs by buying both spot market and futures as a basic part of their business strategy. **Mercury** is still sold by the **76-pound Florence flask**, the same as over 200 years ago. Gorham Silverware Company buys silver futures to hedge their precious metals costs. Airlines hedge their fuel purchases because fuel is 50% of their flight operating costs.

OPTION CLASSIFICATIONS

	Call Option	Put Option
In-the-money:	Futures Price > Strike Price	Futures Price < Strike Price
At-the-money:	Futures Price = Strike Price	Futures Price = Strike Price
Out-Of-The-Money:	Futures Price < Strike Price	Futures Price > Strike Price

FUTURES POSITIONS AFTER OPTION EXERCISE

	Call Option	Put Option
Buyer Assumes:	Long Futures Position	Short Futures Position
Seller Assumes:	Short Futures Position	Long Futures Position

It is also possible to order precious metals bullion directly from dealers who are not connected with the Commodity Exchanges. A word of caution, however, because many coin dealers pretend to deal with bullion coins, but their business is not dealing with coins for melt value, but with items of numismatic value which is more like buying used cars, not precious metals. One true precious metals dealer charge from 1% to 2.9% commission plus shipping for bullion (gold, platinum or silver) purchases. They will also store it for you for a charge that includes insurance. The bullion coins sell for a 1% to 2% premium over the spot metal price with the smaller coins, especially tenth-ounces going for more, because of the conversion cost of minting the metals. Many coin dealers in shopping strip centers quote buy prices for gold or silver bullion and don't remember when you show up at the door. Be prepared to walk.

An example of how the independent bullion dealer works: You telephone their office to receive market quotes on the precious metal. If you agree with the spot market price to place the purchase, they respond with a contract confirmation number. The dealer buys or takes the bullion out of inventory and waits for your check. It must be postmarked within one day of the order to eliminate speculation. This is one instance where somebody will take your personal check without asking for your identification, because they will wait for the check to clear (an ample two weeks) before they ship the goods by registered-insured US Post Office. The reverse process works for them, except that the check is sent within one week upon receipt of the goods. This big dealer offers to finance without a credit check because they hold the goods as collateral. Their disclaimer reminds the client that they are not trading in **future contracts** (which would require securities licenses and supervision) because you control the holding period which otherwise would be fixed by contract.

An article in the **Scientific American** on dismantling nuclear weapons noted that atomic bombs are little precious metal gold mines because of exotic metals used in the fabrication of these devices. After all, the cost is not much of an issue in building these compact heavy deadly things. Gold is an excellent conductor that never tarnishes or rusts. Silver was used, when copper was scarce, to wire the centrifuges used to refine uranium for the first atomic weapons during WW 2.

It is worth noting that the US Government currently mints gold, silver, and platinum one-ounce **Eagle bullion** coins that are guaranteed to contain one ounce of pure metal and have a legal tender face value of $50 for the gold ounce, $25 for the half-ounce, and $5 for a tenth-ounce, $100 for the platinum ounce, $50 for the half-ounce, $10 for a tenth ounce, and $1 for the silver ounce. The coins are minted from **strategic reserve metals** that were reserved for the time of war. The original government cost was $20 from the depression years in 1933 when gold ownership was outlawed. The **International Monetary Fund** (**IMF**) gold reserves, which are second in quantity to the U.S., has only a $48 cost basis (for whatever that is worth knowing). There is a difference between the spot bullion price (which is set twice daily by the **London Exchange**) and the selling price for coins, with a premium on the smaller pieces. However, would you trade gold for paper at the bank for these rates?

PLANNING TIPS

The advertising for precious metals and commodities consistently states that the price is going up, so buy now while it is cheap. Well, if the price is always going up, then gold would be worth a million dollars per ounce and we would all be paid in 1923 German inflationary currency, which began with billion-mark bills. A word of caution about trading in commodities. Do your homework, and if the commodity has fallen in price and you feel it will move up, then buy some of it. Silver has been quantified in a short supply of production and inventory vs demand for over 50 years now. The commodity brokers on television have about a zillion ways to show you that you will always make money if you do what they say. Believe in them as you would believe in politicians.

TAXES

Some states charge sales tax on bullion coin purchases. The government pretends that you will melt it down and make jewelry out of it. Then they would tax it again at sales tax. Taxes of any kind create a prohibitively uneconomic cost for a true investment. Find out the rules; even buy out of state if you are accumulating bullion. Note that I said "bullion" not numismatic coins that are valued by historic scarcity or other factors. Numismatic bullion purchases over $1,000 are usually exempt from sales tax in many states.

Income taxes on ordinary income would apply to dealers' profit or losses. Commodities trading would be considered capital gains because they create a broker-originated paper trail of purchases and sales for the IRS computers. Purchases of gold coins or bullion for personal investment might not be taxable unless an individual reported it (especially losses). The terrible IRS audit word **"hobby"** comes to mind when losses show up on tax returns. Hobby losses are limited to net business income.

The government has made a concession about the tax treatment of collectibles, which are defined as works of art, rugs, antiques, metal or gems, stamps, coins, alcoholic beverages, or other tangible personal property. For many years the above nice things could not be held in an

IRA or pension plan but the rules recently changed. Except for platinum coins, the Tax Code now allows the pension to hold gold or silver coins issued by the United States Government. A pension administrator must hold the bullion, where usually you cannot hold or look at it. Note that the new platinum coin is not included. Uniquely, this change allowing bullion in pensions occurred at the same time the government began minting its surplus bullion into coins. The American coinage is currently minted from the Strategic Reserves of commodities saved for the next world war or security threatening shortage (which probably includes asbestos).

LEGAL COMPLIANCE

Commodity trading sales require a commodity securities license unless you are a farm bank lending against the next wheat crop. Ordinary stockbrokers cannot sell commodities and stockbroker principals cannot approve these trades without special qualification. The commodities business is a highly speculative leveraged business. People who indulge in trading must use personal judgment because there are no prospectuses or financial data as would be available for securities. There is also no due diligence and limited client- qualifying for risk tolerances.

HORROR STORIES - PRECIOUS METALS

The mutual fund securities client arrived at the small office to find the FBI agent sorting through piles of paper, blank letterhead, invoices, trash, evidently looking for evidence. The office was turned upside down as if somebody had left in a hurry before the housekeeper arrived. "What's happening?" the surprised client asked. Instead of answering, the FBI agent, dressed in a regulation proper white shirt with tie correctly knotted, dark suit with matching shoes, and perfunctory short hair, began interrogating the client, instead. An hour later, the client who was a retired person was released. The agent reminded him that he was now a witness in a securities fraud case and that his investment in a phony money market fund was gone forever.

As the client turned around to leave, he noticed a stack of brilliant gold Krugerrand one-ounce coins on a corner table, and stared at them for a moment. The agent noticed him glaring and grinned, "Let me show you something, sir" he told him. Then he went to the stack, picked one up and brought it over to the client. "Watch this," he said as he scratched the surface with his fingernail. The gold disappeared under his nail as a light gray scratch appeared below the surface. "Counterfeit! Lead money!" the agent exclaimed, as the client's mouth fell open.

End of a true story.

Another story is a client who had a small corporate business. Within the small business, he had a pension plan for himself. He was a wheeler-dealer of sorts who had incorporated his California business in Nevada to evade California taxes. Naturally, that did not work. Then he found someone who would let him show gold and silver bullion in his pension, even though it is in his garage safe. Now, he is trying to close the corporation to get rid of the pension but the problem is that he cannot find a legitimate pension plan to take the gold. The next problem will be taxes because the pension he has cannot sell the gold as it exists only on paper. He cannot close either the corporation because of the unfunded pension plan.

EC REGULATION 1.55 RISK DISCLOSURE STATEMENT

The risk of loss in trading commodity futures contracts can be substantial. You should, therefore, carefully consider whether such trading is suitable for you in light of your circumstances and financial resources. In considering whether to trade, you should be aware of the following points:

- You may sustain a total loss of the initial margin funds and any additional funds that you deposit with your broker to establish or maintain a position in the commodity futures market, and you may incur losses beyond these amounts. If the market moves against your position, you may be called upon by your broker to deposit a substantial amount of additional margin funds on short notice, in order to maintain your position. If you do not provide the required funds within the time required by your broker, your position may be liquidated at a loss, and you will be liable for any resulting deficit in your account.

- Under certain market conditions, you may find it difficult or impossible to liquidate a position. This can occur for example when the market reaches a **daily price fluctuation limit (limit move)**.

- Placing contingent orders, such as **stop-loss** or **stop-limit orders**, will not necessarily limit your losses to the intended amounts, since market conditions on the exchange where the order is placed may make it impossible to execute such orders.

- All futures positions involve risk, and a **spread position** may not be less risky than an outright **long or short position**.

- The high degree of **leverage (gearing)** that is often obtainable in futures trading because of the small margin requirements can work against you as well as for you. Leverage (gearing) can lead to large losses as well as gains.

- You should consult your broker concerning the nature of the protections available to safeguard funds or property deposited for your account.

All of the above points noted apply to all futures trading whether foreign or domestic. In addition, if you are contemplating trading foreign futures or options contracts you should be aware of the following additional risks:

- Foreign futures transactions involve executing and clearing trades on a foreign exchange. This is the case even if the foreign exchange is formally "linked" to a domestic exchange, whereby a trade executed on one exchange liquidates or establishes a position on the other exchange. No US domestic organization regulates the activities of a foreign exchange, including the execution, delivery, and clearing of transactions on such an exchange, and no domestic regulator has the power to compel enforcement of the rules of the foreign exchange or the laws of the foreign country. Moreover, such laws or regulations will vary depending on the foreign country in which the transaction occurs. For these reasons, customers who trade on foreign exchanges may not be afforded certain of the protections which apply to domestic transactions, including the right to use domestic alternative dispute resolution procedures. In particular, funds received from customers to margin foreign futures transactions may not be provided the same protections as funds received to margin futures transactions on domestic exchanges. Before you trade, you should familiarize yourself with the foreign rules which apply to your particular transaction.

- Finally, you should be aware that the price of any foreign futures or option contract and therefore, the potential profit and loss resulting therefrom, may be affected by any fluctuation in the foreign exchange rate between the time the order is placed and the foreign futures contract is liquidated or the foreign option contract is liquidated or exercised.

This brief statement cannot, of course, disclose all the risks and other aspects of the commodity markets.

PROS & CONS OF SPECULATING IN COMMODITIES

- Buying precious metals is best done with one-ounce bullion coins.
- Precious metals must be purchased without a sales tax load, and without excessive markup. The larger the purchase, the less % markup on the deal.
- Precious metals should be stored in a very secure place. Never trust the seller to store or warehouse your purchase; a third party or bank safe deposit box is best.
- Precious metals in a pension plan must be held by a fiduciary, best yet an insured one.
- Precious metals for speculation and possession are an assumption that the market price will increase in the future because you are buying in a long position.
- Precious metals can be traded as leveraged commodities through many brokerage and precious metals firms.

- Precious metals can be purchased through margin accounts with many dealers. They will hold the coins or bullion, as collateral for the money and you will not see the shiny stuff unless you close out your account.

- Other commodities from wheat to dollars can be purchased or sold as options on various commodity exchanges, usually with leveraged and borrowed funds.

- Commodity speculation is not for everybody and has a very high inherent risk along with the promise of very high gains.

- Limited commodity positions are purchased by manufacturers to assure level prices for production needs.

- It is common for commodity salespeople to pitch high gains through leveraged positions, but if you stay to the end of the show there is always the disclaimer that there could be large losses as well as gains.

- Never speculate in commodities trading with money that you can't afford to lose.

- Information is available which shows the actual cost of production by different mining corporations. This can determine profitability in a business dominated by varying commodity prices for their output, and help you pick your stocks accordingly.

- Buying "rare" coins and collectibles are like buying a used car. There is a great deal of markup between cost and selling price because it is hard to find a reliable reference, such as the published **spot price for bullion**. If you buy the precious and rare things, be sure to buy professionally graded and sealed uncirculated coins which can be held to a basic standard value for grading and sales (unless you enjoy haggling over prices).

CHAPTER 24: APPLICATION EXERCISES

1. Commodities are traded on the Chicago Board of Trade, the New York Mercantile Exchange and the Chicago Mercantile Exchange among other exchanges around the world. ___ True ___ False

2. Buying precious metals is best done with one-ounce bullion coins. ___ True ___ False

3. Small quantities of precious metals are purchased with a sales tax load and with excessive markup. ___ True ___ False

4. Commodity speculation is not for everybody and has a very high inherent risk along with the promise of very high gains. ___ True ___ False

5. Precious metals can be traded as leveraged commodities through many brokerage and precious metals firms. ___ True ___ False

6. Which of the following statements about Commodities is false:
   ___ a. All commodity values are based on worldwide supply and demand
   ___ b. Most commodities are traded as future purchases or sales on specialty exchanges
   ___ c. Precious metals are not commodities
   ___ d. Margin accounts are usually used to trade for commodities

7. Which of the following statements about Commodities is also false:
   ___ a. Almost everything is a commodity including interest rates
   ___ b. Silverware manufacturers hedge silver purchases to guarantee supply prices
   ___ c. Only specialized commodity brokers can trade on commodities
   ___ d. Silver or gold bullion coins must be bought through commodity brokers

8. Which of the following statements about commodity metals is false:
   ___ a. Platinum prices are in direct relation to catalytic converter demand, not jewelry
   ___ b. Gold prices are an inflation hedge for many investors or speculators
   ___ c. Metallic mercury is sold in 76 pound flasks
   ___ d. Bullion coins cost the same as the spot price per ounce of the precious metals

9. Which of the following statements about precious metals is also false:

    ___ a. The legal tender value of a U.S. Eagle bullion gold ounce coin is $100

    ___ b. False advertising centers on misleading statements of bullion shortages and higher prices

    ___ c. Less than a thousand dollar purchase of bullion coins, or any coins, is subjected to sales tax in California

    ___ d. The scarcer a metal becomes, the more money can be spent to mine

10. Which of the following statements about the precious metals Horror Story is false:

    ___ a. FBI Agents usually wear suits with white starched shirts and proper ties when on duty

    ___ b. A client visit to the address of his investment advisor turned him into a witness when meeting up with an FBI agent. The agent showed him gold plated lead Krugerrand ounces left behind by the fleeing unregistered broker

    ___ c. Gold and silver can be purchased and held by investor for his/her pension (in the garage safe)

    ___ d. Precious metals can be bought for pensions as long if held by a secured party administrator

CHAPTER TWENTY-FIVE
LOW-INCOME HOUSING CREDITS

Many years ago, Congress created an income tax credit to build low-income housing. This marriage of social/political objectives legislated tax laws that created investment opportunities. One of these objectives was to provide subsidized housing for low-income people who are people on welfare, single parents with children, and elderly people who subsist on minimum wage jobs or Social Security, or both. These housing programs were in addition to the **Housing & Urban Development (HUD)** programs to build apartments and welfare cities for low-income people. The **Section 42 IRS Code Tax Reform Act of 1986** provided tax benefits to investors (as a **tax subsidy**) to build or convert apartments for low-income tenants. This did not apply to **Section 8** low-income direct-subsidy housing administered by local authorities.

These apartment units are quite large to aid in administration management and tend to be in rural areas of a small population. They are certainly very long-term with a period certain of at least 15 years. The tax credits issued by the Tax Credit Investment, a limited partnership, are federal credits that can offset federal income taxes dollar-for-dollar over the ten-twelve years they are allowed. The credits can equal 110% of the original investment. At the end of the term, which is about 15 years, the properties can be sold and the proceeds remitted to the limited partners. Failure to manage the mortgaged properties properly can result in foreclosure and recapture of tax credits by investors, resulting in total loss of principal and tax benefit; a risk not afforded by ordinary investors.

Because the investments are for credits first and recover of principal last, these investments only work for high-income taxpayers or investors. The investments also work for corporations, but not pensions as there is no distributable cash flow because of reduced rents which offset mortgages and maintenance, and there are no tax considerations of this nature for pension plans.

The limited partnerships are also subject to income and net worth qualifications of the investor. There is also a limit on income tax offsets for the amounts of credits each year, with the unused balance carried forward to future years. These general tax credits are subject to alternative minimum taxes I call **Alternative Maximum Tax-AMT**.

The credits are useful for the properly qualified investor who wishes to trade taxes for investment during the long term of the commitment. Federal regulations concerning the tenant qualifications, administration of the units, and management of the limited partnership are very complex. Socially, these investments provide a great source for quality housing for the elderly on a large national scale. If the tax credit partnership holds together for the retired term, the investor will at least receive his principal back in the form of tax credits, even if the property falls over afterward. As with most limited partnerships, the gain is not determined until the deal is forever closed.

These entities are **Limited Partnerships** which have **passive income partners** (investor shares) who will have no active say or voice in the management of the deal.

PLANNING TIPS

Tax credits are an important part of the large portfolio. These credits do involve a large amount of risk however because of the onus of foreclosure due to mismanagement, tenant problems, or other unknown events over the long 15 year expected term of the project. There is also a lack of liquidity because the projects are usually highly leveraged with mortgages and can encounter cash-flow problems due to rental problems or unforeseen circumstances. Best that the investor is well-heeled ($5,000 minimum investment is required) and able to utilize the credits more than the capital until the end of the term. Because these are limited partnerships, disposal or sale in the secondary market would be very slow and expensive.

TAXES

This program is a creation of the federal social tax code and has complex tax implications. The first is related to a taxable limit offset of income taxes, which does not include self-employment and penalty taxes. Alternate taxes can be applied, though, to both individuals and corporations as a penalty to paying no taxes at all. Unused credits can be carried forward 20 years until used up, however. In practical terms, the maximum benefit per year of tax credits may be considerably less than the actual credits offered or earned. There are no provisions for credits on some state tax returns.

The AMT is a threshold tax amount inherent in both corporate and individual tax returns that restricts credits and losses, therefore, guaranteeing that the entity will pay a certain amount of taxes no matter what. Any credit reductions due to the AMT can be carried both forward (for many years) and backward (only one year) and be applied to other years.

Some passive operating losses will also be generated. These will flow through to the investor's tax returns to be offset against passive investment income or accumulated until the final disposal of the limited partnership.

TAXABLE INCOME RATE SCHEDULE:
COMPLIMENTS OF IRS: 2019 TAX YEAR

MARRIED FILING JOINT: TAXABLE INCOME:

$ -0-	to $19,050	X 10%	less	$ -0-	== tax
19,051	to 77,400	X 12%	less	381.00	== tax
77,401	to 165,000	X 22%	less	8121.00	== tax
165,001	to 315,000	X 24%	less	11,421.00	== tax
315,001	to 400,000	X 32%	less	36,621.00	== tax
400.000	to 600,000	X 35%	less	45,621.00	== tax
600,001	and over	X 37%	less	60,621.00	== tax

I have included this chart because nobody receives tax booklets in the mail from the IRS anymore where this boring schedule is found along with the more costly rates for single, head of household, or married filing separate.

CORPORATE TAX

The corporate rate is currently a flat 21% as of 2020. Previous tax rates varied based on income. Corporations do not enjoy capital gains rates.

LEGAL COMPLIANCE

Limited partnerships have SEC-mandated minimum suitability investor qualifications. Which are a minimum gross annual income of $35,000 and a net worth not including home, furnishings, or auto, of $75,000. The exception is a net worth of $75,000 if income qualifications are not met because a person might be retired or not working. The client must receive a prospectus at the time of investment. Most broker-dealer firms require a signed statement from the investor that states that he is aware of the long-term risks and that he has received a prospectus. His income and net worth data is part of the client application, subjected to an annual audit. These minimum qualifications may have been increased with inflation so always be informed by your broker, who must be informed.

Because of the very long-term commitment for the housing units, historic operating data on CLOSED and COMPLETED deals is generally unavailable or in the prospectus where it would be listed under experience. Thus, the actual operating results of these deals are generally unknown, which is another way of saying there is no guarantee you will ever see a gain or return of principal on these deals.

It is worth noting here that a stockbroker must be licensed in every state the client-investor lives. Therefore, if you move to a different state and invest further with your old rep., he should notify his broker-dealer firm that he needs a license for the new state. If not, they will find it out anyhow and remind him as they deduct another fee from his commission check.

SUCCESSFUL STRATEGIES

Some corporations, especially small close corps that shelter a natural shareholder-**entrepreneurial** aptitude of hating tax payments choose these tax-sheltered investments. The biggest investors of housing credits are corporations because they tend to make more money and owe more taxes, to need the credit, unlike most individuals.

Remember the old bulge in the tax rate percentages, which ensured that the successful small business pays a higher rate of taxes than larger corporations do? This is known as the **lobbying effect**. Corporate tax rates have leveled off now and some of these **tax shelters** may disappear except in Washington political debates.

Politics have a decisive influence on investments managed by government entities. Huge housing development in New York City recently generated a situation whereas a woman required a two-year wait before the six labor unions maintaining her building could repair a shower. She had to wait two years to take a shower in her apartment. No wonder they say that, "What happens in New York," stays in New York. Or was that, "O.J. Simpson was not leaving Las Vegas."

Tax credits have a place in the individual portfolio that has plentiful cash, tax problems, and time to wait for the final results. Most of the tax real estate credit programs appear well managed and have constructed appealing modern housing for mostly retired folk. There is no reason to believe, that under reasonable normal risk circumstances, there should not be a return of some capital upon termination. It can also be that the horse designed by a well-meaning committee created the camel.

HORROR STORIES - HOUSING PROJECTS

To date, some of the tax credit housing projects started after the **1986 Tax Reform Act** have completed their 15-year term. I expect that many of them have been given another breath of life from subsequent investments. There was no information available at this time but these investments should be for tax credits, not income or earnings. In other words, not with money you would miss otherwise. Thus, it is impossible to gauge the results of the investments in dollars returned on investment as well as total tax credits applied.

It would be a horror story for any investor to experience a default and foreclosure on any housing project that was badly managed or poorly conceptualized. The credits could be subjected to recapture rules and the investment money would be lost forever. This is the real risk, and investment results are only as good as the project social circumstances and location of the management controlling the project involving large collective investments usually exceeding a million dollars. For this reason, investigate the history of the project manager (included in the complicated prospectus) and invest only money you can afford to lose sight of, except in your tax returns.

PROS & CONS OF LOW-INCOME HOUSING CREDITS

- Only wealthy investors or highly profitable corporations should even think of investing in this deal.

- Because the credits are a trade-off of tax dollars, the true investment potential is obscured and can be delayed because of the usual 15+ year terms of these limited partnerships.

- The tax credit advantages could be lost if the future taxable income of the individual or corporation declines.

- A fifteen-year investment term in today's fast-moving world is unthinkable unless you are planning to use it to put your grandchild through college.

- The certainty of receiving a steady stream of credits, or the relevant tax laws not changing for the long-term, is a high investment risk.

- Will you or your corporate business be alive fifteen or more years from now?

CHAPTER 25: APPLICATION EXERCISES

1. Only wealthy investors or highly profitable corporations should consider investing in low income housing credits. ____ True ____ False

2. The certainty of receiving a steady stream of credits, or the relevant tax laws not changing for the long-term, is a high investment risk. ____ True ____ False

3. As of 2020, the corporate tax rate is currently a flat 15%. ____ True ____ False

4. Because the credits are a trade-off of tax dollars, the true investment potential is obscured and can be delayed because of the usual 15+ year terms of these limited partnerships. ____ True ____ False

5. A fifteen-year investment term in today's fast-moving world is unthinkable, unless you are planning to use it to put your grandchild through college. ____ True ____ False

6. Which is the following statements about low-income housing credits is false:
    ____ a. Section 8 is the low income housing subsidy for needy people
    ____ b. HUD programs to increase apartment housing resulted in IRS Sec 42 tax benefits for investors
    ____ c. These tax credit programs required 20 year ownership by investors
    ____ d. Credits were equal to Federal tax credits of 110% of housing costs

7. Which of the following statements about low-income housing credits is false:
    ____ a. Limited partnerships were created to manage deals and could profit from sale after termed
    ____ b. Problems with management would result in loss of principal and tax credits for foreclosure
    ____ c. Deals were high risk because of possible management losses and long terms of 15 years
    ____ d. These were for regular low risk investors because it was a tax shelter

8. Which of the following statements about tax and other low-income housing credit consequences is false:
   ____ a. Alternate Minimum Tax-AMT is a consideration for investors because it is a tax shelter
   ____ b. These are Limited Partnerships where passive investors help manage the properties
   ____ c. These limited partnerships have SEC mandated minimum suitability investor qualifications
   ____ d. Gain is not determined until the deal is forever closed

9. Which of the following statements about low-income housing credits is false:
   ____ a. Only wealthy investors or highly profitable corporations should be interested in investing
   ____ b. A fifteen-year risky investment term is unthinkable in today's fast-moving world
   ____ c. People with low taxable income are good candidates for this tax shelter
   ____ d. Tax shelters obscure the true economic investment potential over 15 years term

10. Which of the following statements about the 1986 Tax Reform Act is false:
    ____ a. By now the tax credits are used or forfeited from foreclosures or bad management
    ____ b. Many Senior Citizen housing projects have evolved to young people slum management
    ____ c. Most low-income projects are well managed by socially conscious entrepreneurs or slumlords
    ____ d. Tax shelters of any kind tend to focus on the tax returns, not the project management

SECTION II

LIFE PLANNING

PART FIVE
FINANCIAL PLANNING

Financial planning is the sum and future of your family's economic life. This is when you plan for a retirement lifestyle, your children's future, your parent's needs, and legacy, and organize your affairs with the help of your financial planner with his little Hewlett Packard 12C calculator. The plan begins with pensions and how they work. Employment, lifestyle, and savings are important daily considerations. Insurance factors into all plans, although not as much as in the past. It also includes business considerations because many of us are self-employed or wish to be so. Social Security will play a big part and personal investments such as residential real estate needs to be updated or considered. **Individual Retirement Accounts (IRA's)** and the newer tax code Devil, the **Roth IRA**, need serious consideration. The financial planning industry has everybody convinced that a financial plan is a compilation of your whole life into a number that you need to invest to survive economically until age 100 or more. That would be like driving from San Diego to Los Angeles and naming all the off-ramps afterward. It is a complex series of events, many not experienced yet, for the journey of our lives.

Corporate businesses should also plan for family succession, annual tax breaks with deductions, ownership perquisites, employee benefits, future goals, but we all know corporations do not usually retire unless they merge or go bankrupt. Trusts & foundations which are discussed at the water cooler are truly scarce and very complex. The first word in any foundation is charitable, which is good, and the lawyer who packaged grantor trusts for tax deductions, which are bad, served jail time under Horror Stories. This planning section begins to prove how hard we work for the harsh IRS tax code and its complex Congressional tax-driven social implications.

CHAPTER TWENTY-SIX

INDIVIDUAL RETIREMENT PLANS, SEP IRAS, ROTH IRA'S, SOCIAL SECURITY, EDUCATIONAL SAVINGS PLANS, TAX PENALTIES

It is hard to write about any kind of investments, especially pension or savings plans, without also writing about the tax effects. Dealing with investment planning is akin to building a house with the tax code as the building code. Somehow, the code becomes more important than the house because it affects every aspect of construction. The building code results in the house being strong and conforming to a community standard. The tax code is also the basis of all investment decisions used in the planning process. That is, you must plan to save money and you will plan to pay the least amount of taxes on it through legal tax-deferred or legal avoidance, in order to increase the benefits. Because planning implies lengthy periods, the amount saved on taxes is magnified by the time-value of investment earnings, especially when reinvested (**Internal Rate of Return or IRR**).

There are many kinds of **IRA**s at this time. The first is the **Roth IRA** that allows no tax reduction on the purchase, but allows the earnings to remain untaxed after age 59 ½ when it is withdrawn. The advantages of this plan are having the earnings taxed when earned, but the earnings also untaxed upon distribution. There is also a taxable **phaseout threshold** allowing participants to participate while earning from $196,000 to $206,000 for joint filers who do not have a pension plan.

The second kind of IRA is the old-fashioned **Traditional IRA** plan, which also allows contributions up to $6,000 to $7,000 per individual, subject to income qualifications, age, and pension disqualifiers, as a tax deduction. The traditional IRA is fully taxed when received and is subjected to 10% penalties if the individual has not reached 59 ½ years old (the official penalty breakpoint retirement age). The penalty is waived for qualified educational expenses. There is also an exclusion for first home purchase amounts of $10,000 for an individual and another $10,000 for the spouse. The principal amount would still be taxed as ordinary income.

To have a SEP IRA you must have self-employment income. Keep in mind that if you are an employer you should not reclassify employees, as 1099 self-employees. California law now fines employers $5,000-15,000 for each individual misclassification and another $10,000-$25,000 for each violation if found as pattern practice.

Self Employed IRAs allow 25% of net income (actually 20% after offsets) to invest in a plan up to a generous $55,000 per year. There is the **Simple IRA** an employee payroll contribution plan that features 3% matching benefits. All the traditional **IRA** contributions offer a dollar-for-dollar reduction of taxable income. An IRA investment must be funded by the tax return due date of 4/15.

The new **Education IRA** is a misnamed IRA. It is a plan to save up to $500 per child with tax-free earnings when spent on postsecondary education expenses of dependent room & board, tuition, books, etc. The misnamed IRA does act as an IRA when high-income taxpayer limits are imposed to limit contributions. Best to bother your banker with this tiny savings account, for ease of administration and funding. I do not believe this plan has been federally approved yet although some states are attempting to authorize it. The annual administrative fees proposed were only ten to twenty-five dollars. Remember, that the more money that goes into the stock market, the higher it goes, like water levels in a barrel. With the market always at new highs it is no surprise that there is so much pressure to overfund it.

The **Simplified Employee Pension (SEP)** is worth mentioning here because although it is a pension plan which requires employee participation, for most self-employed individuals it acts very much like a large IRA pension with a larger contribution limit. The maximum contribution is 15% with offsets that reduces it to 13% of income up to

$30,000 (maximum investment of $26,000). Like an IRA, it can be simply administered without formal pension reports, and invested in the same types of investments. Contributions must be made for each qualified employee; three-year cliff vesting is best because it is simpler to fund and eliminates short-term employees, in which case an IRA is bought in their names at year-end.

The SEP allows a tax deduction for the business employees, unlike the normal IRA that is a tax reduction only for the individual. Most small businesses have very few employees because tenure is tenuous there, so the SEP works very well for both the eligible employee as it is portable, and for the employer. A great advantage of the SEP plan is that it can be funded later in the year, on an extension date of 10/15 that allows the participant to shift the funding into the next year's cash flow. The SEP plan with employees does not allow a business deduction for the proprietor, but a deduction from his 1040 form adjusted gross income the same as a regular IRA. The above IRAs and SEP plans can be invested in most bank savings and brokerage accounts.

California has a new **CALSAVERS** Retirement Plan. This ROTH-type IRA is for private employers and mandates employee participation over June 2020-2022. For not enrolling employees, penalties of $250-500 per employee will be assessed to the employer.

Bullion pensions, including American eagle gold and silver coins, in all cases, must be held and administered by an outside fiduciary. An insured independent depository should hold the bullion coins. These come with fees for handling and storage costs.

Roth IRAs have a much higher income phase-out limit for individuals who also have pension plans at work. Thus, an individual could invest in a Roth when he might not qualify for an ordinary IRA. In any case, an investor can only have either a regular IRA or a Roth IRA each year, but not double up.

IRA AGI PHASEOUT THRESHOLDS FOR INDIVIDUALS WHO ALSO HAVE EMPLOYER PENSION PLANS:

Tax Year	Married Participants	Single Participants
2020	$ 104,000 to 124,000	$ 65,000 to 75,000
2019	103,000 to 123,000	64,000 to 74,000
2018	101,000 to 121,000	63,000 to 73,000

The phase-out rate is 20% per year of income over the left-hand columns, which makes the contribution nil when $10,000 is reached ($200 per year phase-out).

Social Security began as a retirement program in 1935 (when life expectancy was below 50 years, yet 65 was the social security requirement full benefit age). The first contribution percentage was 1% on very low wages. Today, in 2020, the payroll tax is split into two sections, the Social Security tax of $12.4% on wages or self-employment income up to $137,700 and Medicare of 2.9% on unlimited wages or net income. This is a lot of tax money, especially when it is taken from (the employee's half) after-tax wages and also on total self-employment income (with a tax deduction for ½ of the total). Survivor's benefits are available for disabled children and widows or widowers with surviving children, and disabled adults under certain circumstances.

10% penalties are imposed on IRAs and any pension withdrawn before age 59 ½. The exceptions are if disabled or received by a surviving spouse (who still pays taxes on it). There are also penalties if after age 72, an individual does not start withdrawing part of the IRAs based on his life expectancy (the same as for any pension). An IRA can be rolled over; that is transferred from one trustee to another, without a penalty if the transaction is completed within 60 days. The best way is to directly transfer it instead of taking the cash out because the trustee may withhold 20% if it goes directly to you first. Only one rollover per year is allowed

This is as good a place for **disability insurance**. A large percentage, about 20% will, unfortunately, be disabled before reaching the retirement age of 66. Supplemental income medical-disability insurance policies are available to bridge the gap. The idea is a good one if there is no employee benefit plan in place to fill this need. There is a problem, however, if the people electing coverage are usually close to retirement age or at least thinking about it. That means that they are middle-aged, must be in relatively good health, and must pay very high premiums for this bridge coverage. The other is that the policies are very restrictive as to types of disability. They have a long disability qualifying waiting periods before the policy makes any payments. Generally, in my opinion, they are uneconomic for the benefits expected. Medicare insurance is available at age 65, which is a year before receiving SS benefits. It is great insurance for the gap, (a must do) for reasonable fees if you have no other medical plan in place at work or pension.

Full retirement is at age 66. Early retirement is a 20% graduated permanent loss at age 62-66.

PLANNING TIPS

The one planning tip that never changes is to pay as little taxes as possible. It is entirely possible for a person to collect IRAs and Social Security tax-free if his taxable income is low enough. This implies a scenario where there is hardly any other income such as earnings from wages, pensions, or investments. The threshold for Social Security taxability for singles is $25,000 including the SS amount and $32,000 for joint returns. A very low threshold, indeed. The excess taxable SS would be calculated at 85% above the threshold.

Most individuals retiring today, because of their generous pensions and other income, are paying taxes on some or most of their retirement income. Medicare will pay for reasonable medical needs, but many elder individuals these days find enough money from personal savings to pay for cosmetic surgery, something unheard of a decade ago.

One Social Security decision everybody faces is the tradeoff of the 80% for lifetime benefits vs initiating benefits three years earlier (It takes 12 years to recoup the difference). This is also the period when Medicare does not apply (not before age 65 unless disabled). There is no easy solution to this equation, which is a factor of individual earnings ability, lifestyle, general health, and retirement activity focus. These decisions are easier with company-paid pensions that might include medical benefits to bridge the gap. There is a small monthly deduction from the Medicare check to help cover medical benefits. The good news is that many HMOs will still accept Medicare as full payment for inclusive medical services. Medicare, however, does not cover dental, glasses, hearing aids, psychiatric or institutionalized permanent care after one month and certain other medical procedures.

People today work in their later years, have pensions, and try to maintain normal standards of living in their senior years. Delayed retirement from Social Security has its benefits. The **Social Security Administration (SSA)** will increase your benefits automatically by up to 8% each year until you reach age 70 if you should decide to delay receiving benefits until then. If you have ample funds, this might be a good move, especially considering the actuarial table lifespan of healthy people with good medical care today. Medicare, because it is independent from Social Security structurally, can be applied for and received at age 65 even if Social Security benefits are delayed until future years. This is a tremendous benefit because many people are ineligible for medical insurance because of health or other reasons, even if they could afford it at that age because it gets more expensive as we age.

Supplemental Social Security benefits (Medical in California) are available in addition to Social Security for low-income individuals. These benefits, which are administered by the Social Security Administration, are funded from the government general fund. A person must have savings or the cash value of life insurance, but not including a home, of less than $2,000. Many states will take title to the home however, because they match some of the federal money through their welfare office (a reverse mortgage would work here). With nursing care or convalescent home expenses over

$40,000 per year, and many people living into their 90s… some with dementia, it is not unrealistic for people without large estates to end up with the government paying more of their support. There is a lookback period of several years on home sales to catch people trying to avoid paying for nursing homes. The lookback period is actually noted in living trusts for planning purposes.

TAXES

Social Security is now subject to income taxation. Social Security is withheld on an after-tax basis from wages or paid from net earnings from the self-employed. However, some years back, in an attempt to raise more taxes, the government (Bill Clinton) somehow determined that retired folks might be receiving more Social Security benefits back than they paid in, started taxing Social Security income. A magic formula was produced which taxed up to half of the benefits. Then the noose was tightened further so up to 50% at one income level (over $25,000 single, $32,000 jointly) and 85% at a higher level (called provisional income over $32,000 single, $44,000 jointly) is now taxed, based on the formula which adds half of the benefits received to adjusted gross income to arrive at the above threshold taxable income figures. Whether or not the excess benefits over 15-50% would constitute real income for the recipients is debatable, since the funds are used as a base for disability payments of a younger family who may not have paid anything into the program. An additional 1% Medicare tax is assessed on Earned Income over $250,000 joint. A danger of receiving reduced benefits before age 66 is if the senior citizen earned over $18,240 one dollar is deducted from your earnings for every $2 earned over the $18,240.

This causes tax shortages on tax returns for retired folks because there is no automatic withholding from the monthly benefit checks. This can be requested, though. Retired persons receiving benefits the first time and lower-income people who have sudden income from the sale of property usually are caught by surprise (tax shock) by the effect of the higher taxes on their Social Security benefits and Medicare increased charges. If the taxes are consistent, quarterly estimates are required to avoid underpayment penalties. There is also a problem with investment income or pensions, which cause double taxation by first being taxed as income and then causing the Social Security to be taxed as well.

LEGAL COMPLIANCE

Roth IRAs can create tax-free investment income during retirement. Ordinary IRAs can also be converted over to Roths without early withdrawal penalties, but become taxable on rollover. To alleviate the problem, a five-year tax period was established which allowed the individual to pay the taxes gradually. There is also a five-year holding period for Roths to qualify for the tax-free earnings status. This brings a problem to bear whereas there is a trade-off of reduced investment from the taxed IRA going into a plan that produces tax-free income. To be put simply, a $10,000 IRA, which has been reduced to $5,000 after taxes, certainly needs to earn a great deal to make up for the investment capital reduction just to break even. It is a great step further to generate enough additional income to justify the original tax savings. The older a person is, the harder it would be to make the investment change pay off. Many states have not conformed to the Roth tax provisions as well so a person could end up with a federal Roth IRA after conversion and no state IRA at all. Especially after paying taxes on the whole amount.

Many investment planners, anxious for commissions on new Roth IRA rollovers, have come up with optimistic projections of very high earnings to justify the tax savings advantages of leaving a perfectly safe IRA investment for another. The insurance companies and mutual funds have provided interesting sliding paper computers that factor age and investment expectations into rollover scenarios. The results can be quite interesting when the earnings rates are ratcheted up for a forever highly optimistic future. Recently, I saw a proposal made to a 70-year-old person, showing him how much money he would be ahead to roll his large IRAs over (and never use it). Realistic tax and economic earnings projections are in order for all rollovers. Be cautious of over-optimistic projections and assumptions. Most of us will not live forever.

A "Request for Earnings and Benefit Estimate Statement" form can be obtained directly from the Social Security Administration. This simple form will obtain a computer-generated statement that will show the amounts you have paid into Social Security each year for your whole lifetime. It will also show proposed benefits at retirement age. The Social Security toll-free number is 1-800-772-1213. Their Internet address is https://www.ssa.gov/myaccount/.

SUCCESSFUL STRATEGIES

Widows and widowers, whose sole income comes from relying on their deceased spouse's income, can encounter a blackout period of no benefits from Social Security when they are in their fifties and cannot collect retirement benefits until age 62 or older. This period comes as a shock when there are no dependent children at home and the surviving spouse has relied on their mate to provide substance.

Spouses can receive **survivor benefits** from age 60 (50 if they are disabled), at rates ranging from 71.5 percent to 100 percent of the late spouse's social security benefit, depending on the survivor's age. Widows and widowers can restrict their application to file for either their own benefit (if the surviving spouse worked) or the survivor benefit, and then later switch to the other amount. You might do this if your own benefit amount at age 70 would be larger than your widow benefit. You could claim the widow benefit for several years, and then at age 70 switch to your own benefit. A widow or widower at any age who is caring for the deceased's child who is under age 16 or disabled can receive benefits at any time.

In the case of a living or divorced spouse you may be eligible for up to 50 percent of their benefit if their benefits are bigger you're your individual benefits. In the case of divorced but living spouses you can file at any time but in the case of living and not divorced spouses, they must file for benefits first. The only way around the problem, for people without a large estate or much cash, is cheap term life insurance.

There is a trade-off between early retirement at age 62 with the reduced 80% Social Security benefits, and waiting for full retirement age at 65 or later. Because wages will reduce benefits until age 70, and because other earnings can cause Social Security to be taxed, this should be considered an option only if a person is not employed or has very limited income. If a person has a normal life expectancy at retirement age, which would be 80+ years for a healthy person, then the early retirement for three years might prove very costly when weighed against 80% benefits for the rest of his or her remaining life of perhaps 20 years (break-even is 12 years). For this reason, very few people elect early-reduced Social Security benefits.

If a person continues employment while receiving benefits before age 65 (and is not disabled), half of the earnings above $18,240 (2020 tax-year) will be deducted from the Social Security benefits until they disappear. A person older than 65 can earn up to $43,360 before his/her benefits will be reduced by one dollar for each additional three earned. At age 66, the earnings limits do not apply. If you delay your benefits until age 70, you receive 132% of your benefit. Your earnings and wage figures are verified by the Social Security Administration as their computer peruses the employer generated year-end W-2 payroll reports and individual 1040 SE schedules from tax returns. This results in a computer letter later the next year advising why your benefits have been reduced or shut off if you failed to advise them of the earnings in time.

Economic theories abound on the tax effect of forcing elderly people off active employment because of the reduction and/or taxation of Social Security benefits. It is something thought out by most people sooner or later.

A Social Security recipient will not receive benefits for the month in which they became deceased, they must live the entire month to qualify for benefits. Social Security does not prorate the month of death and if a representative payee receives payment for that month it will have to be returned. There are death benefits of $255 but they don't automatically go out to the deceased's beneficiary. The SS Administration must be contacted by the administrator or the next of kin if there is none. After proper verification by mail or phone, they will mail the check or e-deposit to the next of kin for funeral expenses. When the author's mother passed in a nursing home on the last day of her month, her Social Security payment had been wired to her nursing home account the same day. The next day it was wired back [reversed] from her account. This is a true example.

HORROR STORY - INSURANCE

A proper horror story for this chapter would be the family who failed to provide for the working spouse by buying insurance, even term insurance in the form of an inexpensive mortgage policy or otherwise. Large companies tend to properly insure their employees with cheap company-paid term blanket policies, and there are pensions, but the self-employed people and many individuals working for low wages without benefits leave the family economically naked should a tragic accident or illness remove the prime wage earner. Two working people, that is the basis for economic life today in America, provide a living standard that is impossible to maintain for a single surviving spouse.

Social Security is designed to provide for disabled individuals and surviving spouses with dependent children, but provides nothing else for a person short of retirement at retirement age. It is prudent for individuals to look beyond lifestyle and credit cards to provide for the lack of earned income.

TABLES FROM THE SOCIAL SECURITY ADMINISTRATION

AGE TO RECEIVE FULL SOCIAL SECURITY BENEFITS: (FRA)

Year of Birth	Full Retirement Age
1937 or earlier	65
1938	65 and 2 months
1939	65 and 4 months
1940	65 and 6 months
1941	65 and 8 months
1942	65 and 10 months
1943-1954	66

1955	66 and two months
1956	66 and four months
1957	66 and six months
1958	66 and eight months
1959	66 and ten months
1960 and later	67

A TABLE SHOWING INCREASES FOR DELAYED RETIREMENT

Year of Birth	Annual Rate of Increase
1917-1924	3.0%
1925-1926	3.5
1927-1928	4.0
1929-1930	4.5
1932-1932	5.0
1933-1934	5.5
1935-1936	6.0
1937-1938	6.5
1939-1940	7.0
1941-1942	7.5
1943 or later	8.0

PROS & CONS OF IRA AND SOCIAL SECURITY BENEFITS

- Many people believe that the Social Security fund will dry up and blow away before they retire. Unless a person is a teenager (and they worry about other things anyway), this should not concern their retirement planning.

- The Social Security rules are complex so be sure to write or call for the official publications at least a year or two before planning to retire. Then study it carefully. If still in doubt about how it works, ask elderly neighbors or your friendly tax advisor who has to live with the stuff every spring.

- IRAs are only deductible if you have taxable earned income, and if you don't make too much income. All income reserved and deferred from current taxation, whether it is a Roth IRA, regular IRA or SEP IRA, are worthwhile.

- One confusing issue for some people is that they think an IRA is a specific investment. It is really only the tax name for any investment in a qualified plan.

- Conversions to ROTH IRAs are not practical for elderly people because they must first pay taxes on the rollover amount, and second because they may be drawing the principal down afterward before it has time to earn back the tax advantage.

- Be conservative with your IRA investments. Retirement should be conservative and secure, save the speculation for other monies.

- ROTH IRA conversions are sometimes based on exaggerated earnings offsetting the tax costs of turning the old IRA in. You should really question whether the stock market could earn 18 to 25% EVERY year to make it up.

- People are shocked when they see the tax bill for Social Security when it is added to wages in the tax return for the first time. The only thing that could take it away would be the people in Washington who put it there in the first place.

- IRAs and pensions are taxable to your heirs, should you retire from this earth suddenly before they are spent.

- Some (most) state municipal pensions anticipate huge earnings to support huge pensions.

- IRAs and pension can be redeemed and taxed at death-an option based on the stock market earning 25% annually for the next 50 years. Fortune magazine states that if the market only earns 10% annually, and spending doesn't change, there could be deficits. Don't be foolish by not planning your affairs a little better than that.

CHAPTER 26: APPLICATION EXERCISES

1. A Roth IRA allows no tax reduction on the purchase, but allows the earnings to remain untaxed after age 59 ½ when it is withdrawn. ____ True ____ False

2. A traditional IRA is tax exempted when funded and is subjected to 10% penalties if the individual has not reached 59 ½ years old (the official penalty breakpoint retirement age) when it is withdrawn. ____ True ____ False

3. Social Security is not subject to income taxation. ____ True ____ False

4. IRAs and pensions are taxable to the estate if cashed or to your heirs, should you retire from this earth suddenly before they are spent. ____ True ____ False

5. IRAs are only deductible if you have taxable earned income, and if you don't make too much income (phase-out threshold). ____ True ____ False

6. It is unnecessary to consider the tax code when planning for your future. ____ True ____ False

7. To have a SEP IRA you must have self-employment income. ____ True ____ False

8. An Education IRA is a plan to save up to $500 per child with tax-free earnings when spent on postsecondary education expenses of a dependent's tuition, room & board, books, etc. ____ True ____ False

9. In all pension-IRA plans, bullion pensions, including American eagle gold and silver coins, must be held and administered by an outside fiduciary. ____ True ____ False

10. If you decide to delay receiving full Social Security benefits, the SSA will increase your benefits automatically by up to 8% each year until you reach age 70. ____ True ____ False

CHAPTER TWENTY-SEVEN

PENSION PLANS: 401 (k), MONEY PURCHASE, EMPLOYEE STOCK OPTIONS, DEFERRED COMPENSATION, SAVINGS MATCHING

Conservative and far-reaching social legislation during this late century dramatically changed the pension and savings attitudes of the country. Before Congress got into the act, personal savings consisted mostly of **Federal Deposit Insurance Corporation (FDIC)** for federally chartered banks insured certificates of deposit. There was little incentive for people to save for retirement outside of the limited corporate money purchase pension plans because they were always top heavily funded for management. Because the corporations paid for the plans, which were always invested in the corporate stocks or inexpensive insurance company annuities, long-term vesting of ten years or more kept more in the pot for only long-tenured employees or managers. Unions and the government took care of their own people and a huge part of the population had only Social Security to look forward to on retirement. After all, the country had been through a highly prosperous period since the end of the Second World War when most pension plans got started. The government was aware that when people retire with no money, they could end up needing social assistance, which would fall back on the government itself. We are dealing with "the human depreciation concept" whereas industry owed a debt to the working individual and society for the use and wearing out, like machinery or equipment, of people who retired afterward.

Some of the earlier plans pitifully rewarded ownership (management) richly while hourly employees retired with only a few dollars monthly, if anything at all. I actually know of an old medium-sized business where the owners lived in luxury like Lords. One day, one of the long-term employees retired to find out that his company pension plan (a lowly insurance plan at that) was good for only $11 per month. The Great

Depression was not that far away for some of the older folks. There also was no Workmen's Compensation and people would die at work or in the mines with no burial money or anything for a widow or children to live on.

The federal government decided to liberalize the retirement laws in favor of employees by penalizing and restricting corporate management-oriented plans. There were two approaches. One was to loosen up corporate pensions by disallowing some self-serving corporate pension deductions with discrimination tests (discrimination against ordinary employees, naturally). The other was to allow individuals and the self-employed to save more, especially with tax incentives. The **1974 Employee Retirement Income Security Act (ERISA)** was passed allowing Individual Retirement Arrangements (IRA's). The first IRA allowed the working spouse to deduct up to $2,000 from taxable income and $250 more for a non-working spouse. This worked fine until the **Tax Reform Act of 1986 (TRA'86)**, which limited the deductions for people already covered by other pension plans. Now a non-employed spouse can also buy a whole $6,000 IRA.

Legislation passed allowing self-employed people to set up simplified **Self-Employed Pension plans (SEP IRA)** in 1978.. Prior to this all, pension plans were huge complicated things that had to be packaged and approved individually by the Internal Revenue Service. Uniquely, the IRS in Atlanta still processes all estate and pension plan returns. **A trustee or fiduciary** would be responsible for filing the 5500 series tax returns at year-end, as well as monitoring the investments. This was a very expensive but necessary requirement which fits the pocketbooks of large firms best of all. The SEP-IRA legislation changed all of that by allowing individuals to deduct 15% of their net profits up to $7,500. The 1981 **Economic Recovery Tax Act (ERTA)** raised the bar to $15,000. The 1982 **Tax Equity and Fiscal Responsibility Act (TEFRA)** increased the max deduction to $30,000 and further legislation has raised it to $56,000 max where it stands today. The 15 % has been modified to become 13.0435 % of net income, which is based on subtracting 15% from the beginning net income. Thus, a $30,000 deduction becomes $24,000. Confused? Well, that is how Congressional lawyers work. First, they give you a break, and then they take some of it away afterward or defer it until after the next election. The prime qualification of the SEP is that it must include all employees, which means it works best if there are none. Ask your dentist how many wage employees he has the next time you visit, and you will find out how pensions really work. There is also a small business SEP for employees. All IRA's require a trustee, which is a simple process of signing the standard prototype form used by the person where you invest your money. The fees are very small, usually $10 to $25 per year.

Then there is the **Employee Stock Option Plan (ESOP)** that gave a tax break to corporations, which allocated some stock to people besides management, which was truly revolutionary. Many large companies utilized the plan to involve employees in the future of the firm and also to increase shares of stock outstanding **capitalization**. The plans were **qualified plans** which means that they were pension or retirement-related...and regulated. Leverage by the corporation to buy shares provided an additional incentive to the plan that must be funded by the employer as a stock bonus or money purchase. Employees can convert their shares to cash inside the plan, reinvest dividends, have voting rights, and can take the plan with them when they leave.

Money purchase plans, also called cash-balance pensions, are plans paid entirely by the company. These plans were in great favor until ERISA tightened up the rules concerning corporate misconduct by the plan administrators. Furthermore, the **Multiemployer Pension Plan Amendments Act of 1980 (MPPAA)** created substantial penalties for employers closing out unfunded plans (especially during corporate takeovers). Finally, a 35% excise tax applied to corporations who mishandled the pension plans by taking money out of them for other purposes, a common practice with corporate buy-outs and takeovers (see your Wall Street movie for an example). The latest corporate maneuver is to replace defined benefit plans with money purchase plans because the payout rules are different. The defined benefit plan defines the benefit paid, which is based on the retiree's highest wages. The replacement plan adjusts benefits by different formulas, thus not top-loading it with larger guaranteed pensions.

Today, **401-K stock option plans** have replaced the wealth-to-the-top pension concept. The stock market has rewarded most executives very well. When the market slows down, there will be substitute plans for sure, or their compensation committee and outside accountants will all be fired. These plans allow employers to match employee contributions up to 6%. A very good deal!

Corporate pension plans fell into two general categories, the **defined benefit** that structured the amount of pension as a percentage of the individual employee's earnings. The other was the **defined contribution** that fixed the amount, usually a percentage of net profits, which must be funded annually. The profit contribution was considered a profit-sharing plan. These plans are complex requiring actuarial consultants and fiduciaries to track each employee. The employer cannot skip contributions for more than one year. Many pension plans today are a blend of money purchase and profit-sharing, which guarantees a contribution one way or another. This avoids the problem of what to do if there are no profits for two years in a row.

Savings plans were also incorporated into pension-related concepts with the **Deficit Reduction Act of 1984 (DEFRA) Deferred compensation 401K plans** were created and further refined to give employees more control over the investment from out-of-pocket salary contributions. The laundry list for pensions goes on and on with the **Omnibus Budget Reconciliation Act (OBRA) of 1987** the **Technical and Miscellaneous Revenue Act (TAMRA)of 1988**, and the **Retirement Equity Act (REA)of 1984** with annual changes until Congress runs out of strange acronym names for them.

Many firms and government agencies offer savings plans and deferred compensation plans. Again, these programs are subjected to pension laws for good control and thus offer restricted benefits. Many of the plans match savings with individuals to a small percentage of their salary. Both the deferred salary and matching funds are placed into a special retirement fund that usually gives the employee some say about where the money is invested. Mutual funds and insurance annuities are the usual investment vehicles for most of these plans because of the ease of administration by the investment advisors and institution). As a general rule, when an employee contributes his own money to a plan...any plan, he will have control over where the invested assets are placed. That is one reason the 401K rules have relaxed for first-time home mortgage loans, educational needs, and now IRAs as well.

Savings and loans became rechartered into federal credit unions after the big crash in the 1990s. They now have **National Credit Union Administration (NCUA)** $250,000 deposit insurance guarantees savings banks.

The **Pension Benefit Guaranty Corp (PBGC)** is charged with enforcing the above pensions by collecting some premiums for plan administration. They have the power to charge the corporate equity for failed plans or to pay benefits (with very little of their money) if all else fails. A decade ago, headlines were made in financial journals about the towering amount of unfunded pension plans in the US, and the inadequate role of the PBGC to cover, but the runaway stock market, fortunately, has erased that problem.

Almost all pension plans and IRAs can be rolled over into other qualified plans without adverse tax consequences. Insurance products, with the help of **IRS Code section 135**, go directly to other insurance plans. IRAs go to other IRAs (except Roth IRAs), but not pension plans. Pension plans are rolled over to other pension plans or IRAs, the statutory retirement age to avoid penalties for retiring too early, is still 59 ½. Early retirement poses a special problem from corporate downsizing and other economic reasons. A special rule for people aged at least 55 allows early retirees to **annuitize** their pension and draw on it for at least five years, to avoid penalties (It doesn't matter afterward because they will be the official retirement age then). Disability retirement waives penalties. Death cures all. Well, not really, because I recently saw a tax lien filed against an estate because the dead person had not filed a tax return after he died in January.

PLANNING TIPS

Investors must monitor their pension plans. ESOP plans can convert stocks, usually without broker fees, into cash should the company stock go south. IRA's, company 401-K plans, deferred compensation plans, and SEP plans are always open to reallocating the investment assets. Usually, only a telephone call is required to move things around. Keep the numbers handy.

The only plans which allow no investment flexibility are **insurance annuity plans**, but they can be rolled over, which might not be a good bet since they would both be insurance plans (see 1035 tax-free exchange). The best insurance plans are the GICs that companies use for pension reserves. **Corporate money purchase plans** may also offer no alternatives because the manager who puts the money into it for you has control over where it is working. Government Civil Service plans fit this category as well. Many government municipal pension funds are so underfunded that they are bankrupt. Chicago city is only 25% funded in 2020.

Many pensions became overfunded from good times in the stock market. It is not proper to back money out of them, especially when the contributions were deducted from taxable income and the rules are very tough about reversing contributions (like a Chinese finger pulling bamboo web). Congress loosened up and allowed the pension administrators to pay for the retirees' group medical insurance from these funds. This was an astute move. Now with medical insurance costs skyrocketing and the market about to slow down, it could create the reverse paradox of how to take back something that is not there now, when you couldn't take it out before, when it was.

TAXES

All pensions and money flowing from retirement-related accounts are taxable, even to your heirs. Pensions are taxed as ordinary income, except when taken from the plan prematurely. Any distribution received by an individual not the magic age of 59 ½ is subject to a 10% penalty on the federal tax returns. Many states have also enacted similar penalties with lesser percentages. Exceptions, of course, are a disability and a formal early retirement annuitized plan.

The **rollover provisions** provide that a direct rollover from one fiduciary to another is the easiest way. The other way is for you to receive the funds directly, which means it is now a distribution, not a rollover, and then deposit the money into another fiduciary (IRA) within 60 days. To cover the tax problem potential of the money being diverted instead of redeposited, there is a mandatory Federal 20% withholding provision. Now the rollover funds are 20% shy if you do decide to move them elsewhere else. One false ploy is to take them out and invest it into something for a killer return and then figure out how to move it back in the two-month period, if there is anything left.

Federal and state taxes of 50% on premature distributions are common because of the tax tables, penalties, and application of the same by most states. That is a terrible price to pay for the use of your hard-earned pension. There are many sources of funds, besides even credit cards, which are cheaper if available.

The tax ramifications of pensions confuse many people. The lowly experienced investment rep people in the Wal-Mart greeter position on the bank floor are oftentimes no help either. I do know of one client who had her insurance annuity penalties paid back by the bank when she changed her mind after the look-back inspection period had passed, and wanted all of her money back. They were afraid of the customer's bad news and complaints.

One thing is for sure. The rollover or distribution from the fund will have follow-up paperwork that will reach you by mail and the IRS by electronic means. If you drop the ball when completing your return, an SC2000 form will find you a year later with a bigger bill. Remember that the IRS created the computer or the computer was created for the IRS, whichever came first. This reminds me of my son's hounds on which he stated, "They will eat anything which doesn't eat them first."

Some of the older Employee Stock Ownership Plans (**ESOP)** had two kinds of distributions. The distribution split between pension (rolled over or taxed) and return of capital funds (contributions after taxes into the plan). Plan administrators have been diligent about the distribution statements so it is good news to cash one of them in or roll over the pension portion.

LEGAL COMPLIANCE

Retirement plans are an important part of financial planning. Licensing by broker-dealers is very important here. Usually, an insurance license (by state), **FINRA** security licenses, and some tax planning experience are required to do a good job. The shortcoming is that most sales reps are sales reps and lack the tax end of the business. The best guide for them is to reach for the telephone to talk to a supervisor or the people funding the plan. Every broker-dealer has an insurance department, and every mutual fund or insurance company has a retirement and tax specialist. Deadly is the quick wrong answer from inexperienced reps or insurance salespeople. However, it is possible to get a bank or broker to advise bad advice.

California now requires sales reps to include their insurance license number on all business cards, stationery, and advertising in case there are problems. Outside of ethical issues, retirement planning is the most complex area of finance.

Deferred compensation (403-B plans) are wage compensation that has been set aside tax-wise. When it is received upon retirement, and the funds flow through, the amount of the distribution will show up on a W-2 wage form. Don't be surprised if it was waged in the first place. The good news is that you paid Social Security taxes on it before it was set aside and invested.

SUCCESSFUL STRATEGIES

Successful retirement plan strategies include listing all of your assets (don't forget liabilities) including a current value for your pension plan.

Then schedule how much you can receive from the portfolio upon retirement age. Add Social Security benefits while factoring something in for inflation costs and future pension earnings. Social Security is indexed for low inflation rates, as if you can really believe you need to buy cheaper computers every year while medical, postage, fuel, insurance, transportation, utilities, taxes, and other costs go the other way. Social Security typically undercuts inflation at least a full point each year, which reduces benefits big time. Do not forget to have your tax guy tell you how much you will be paying to retire without wages. It is a whole new game and the withholding will never come out right, even if the plan will take taxes out for you. There will probably be a need for quarterly tax estimates for the first time in your life, which will reduce your savings as you go.

HORROR STORY - LUMP SUM DISTRIBUTION

This horror story is true. The tax client was building a new house. Because he was close to retirement age, he knew his pension was available without early withdrawal penalties. When he talked to the pension rep or clerk, he must have forgotten what he was doing or they were sound asleep, because he wanted to take his pension out to build the house. He was earning a good salary as a manager and already complaining about tax problems when he filed each year.

There are all kinds of financing for people who want to build new houses. This fellow had a general contractor's license and was aware of construction loans and permanent take-out loans, and all the costs and rates to do so. But no, he wanted a mortgage-free house to retire in, even if it ate his pension considerably.

Well, he took the lump-sum distribution and worked on the house until he retired the following year. Unfortunately, when he filed the tax returns the next year, he had very little income, because he had consumed most of his pension and his big wages were also gone. But he now had a huge tax problem from bad planning. The taxable pension was added on top of his wages and pushed his taxable income into new highs for the year. He is still trying to figure out what happened, and how to pay off both the state and the IRS. Perhaps a mortgage would help.

PROS & CONS OF PENSION PLANS

- Pension plans are second to none when financial planning is required. Find a professional to work with. Be sure that in addition to all the selling licenses, he knows something about taxes.

- Don't touch a pension or IRA distribution or rollover until you have investigated the distribution tax costs and consequences. These things are designed around the tax code, like a turtle's shell, and get you in trouble very easily if you remove the turtle contents.

- Review your pension or IRA data periodically. All fiduciary administrators issue paperwork at least quarterly or annually, if not more often, so pay attention to where the money is. If you reinvest dividends into a mutual fund IRA you will probably receive monthly statements that show you where the fund is going.

- Pensions and IRAs are investments and the principal can easily be changed or moved if it is not working right. Beware of people selling stuff. A telephone call to the administrator will move things from point A to B or the fallback position... money market cash account if required.

- You should not need to worry about your pension or IRA. If you do, then it is in the wrong place and you should do something about it.

- Above all, be conservative with pension money. Speculation is for other finances, which you may afford to lose, but the pension funds your lifestyle on retirement when wage income has ceased.

- Most pensions are now portable from job to job. Upon job change, there is also an opportunity to move it into a self-directed IRA without tax consequences. This is an opportunity to manage your own pension for the first time. If you are a sophisticated type, then do it. If not, let the new people manage it for you.

- The government has done a highly responsible job of creating an alphabet soup of tax code retirement and pension law changes. They are all for your benefit, so try to understand the parts that affect your personal situation.

- Stockbrokers are always trying to make you convert your traditional IRA into a Roth IRA. For most people, this makes no sense. Why pay a third of your IRA in taxes to invest it in something not taxable when you take it out. Only a dynamic investment portfolio could repay the lost tax money before earning the untaxed money. That is a risk. The real question is how many years does it take to make it up and the aggressive portfolio to accomplish it? Most rollover attempts are for retired people who have less years than when working. I personally think Roths were invented by broker-dealers to generate commissions, and have never done one.

CHAPTER 27: APPLICATION EXERCISES

1. Today, 401(k) stock option plans have replaced the wealth-to-the-top pension concept. ____ True ____ False

2. There are adverse tax consequences for rolling-over pension plans and IRAs into other qualified plans. ____ True ____ False

3. The Pension Benefit Guaranty Corp (PBGC) is charged with enforcing pensions by collecting premiums for plan administration. ____ True ____ False

4. The only plans which allow no investment flexibility are fixed insurance annuitized plans. ____ True ____ False

5. Deferred compensation (403-B) plans are wage compensation that has been set aside tax-wise, and when received upon retirement is reported on a W-2 wage form. ____ True ____ False

6. Money purchase plans, also called cash-balance pensions, are plans paid entirely by the company. ____ True ____ False

7. Employee Stock Ownership Plans (ESOP) can convert stocks, usually without broker fees, into cash should the company stock go south. ____ True ____ False

8. It's best to find a financial planner with an insurance license (by state), FINRA security license and some tax planning experience. ____ True ____ False

9. You should not need to worry about your pension or IRA. If you do, then it is in the wrong place and you should do something about it. ____ True ____ False

10. The government has done a highly responsible job of creating an alphabet soup of tax code retirement and pension law changes. ____ True ____ False

CHAPTER TWENTY-EIGHT

CORPORATE DEDUCTIONS, DIVIDEND EXCLUSION, PENSION COSTS, PRENUPTIAL-POSTNUPTIAL AGREEMENTS, MARRIAGE-DIVORCE, INSURANCE CONSIDERATIONS

Corporations have always had a tax-privileged position in the realm of taxpayer obligations. A small corporation is an orphan, although living the life of a separate legal entity; it has been treated as an extension of an individual tax situation. The lawyers are always trying to pierce the "corporate vale." An IRS auditor told me and my client, "a piggy bank for the owners," as she tore my client's successful small business into little taxable shreds. Larger corps, however, have perks such as chauffeured limousines, call girl credit card purchases, executive model secretaries (steno is out, but computers are in these days), and little jet airplanes to buzz around in. For the small business corporate president, however, the government would haggle over how many miles the businessperson drives to work daily in the company car, normally a non-deductible experience.

Big business is allowed certain legitimate deductions such as the cost of sales, endless marketing commercials, and the investment exclusion of 50% to 100% from the dividends received. The qualified dividend deduction is allowed because corporations tend to integrate with other corporations and would be paying taxes on their own dividends (double taxation) if there were not a proper exclusion. The dividends must, however, be received from domestic (USA) corporations.

Pension costs are also deductible but subject to top-heavy rules if they favor management too much. Remember that they also have the biggest salaries to base their fringe benefit costs on. Employee insurance is deductible but only the small cost of $50,000 of term insurance. Costs over that, which can be considerable, are taxed to the employee-manager.

Of course, that is a paltry amount of insurance, barely enough to cover the bar bills of some divorce lawyers I know who are trying to redeem their sins.

Medical insurance and reimbursement are limited since the IRS ruled that management must be treated the same as normal full-time employees, so now the bosses and family are no longer specially reimbursed by the company for all their miscellaneous medical expenses at year-end, like in the good old days. **Highly Compensated Employees (HCE** is the real IRS term) define execs as people earning over 125 grand annually during the preceding year or an officer earning over 45 grand (which is quite low), for discrimination purposes. And, you believed the govt. data that we had no inflation in the country! Another benefit was a one-time death benefit (you only die once) of an additional $5,000 in wages. This was disallowed several years ago to increase taxes on the business by disallowing the deduction (probably about the time the Social Security people dropped the paltry $155 death benefit).

The Executive stock options are the best fringe benefit at this time. Essentially, outside of job rewards, there are three executive areas of reimbursement, all chosen and hand tailored by the executive compensation committees, who are all handpicked by the executives themselves. Sort of like government where one hand washes the other. The first is wages, based on resume and friendship at the golf course clubhouse. The second is the management bonus, which is not always based on positive corporate results because it is a given to remain on the job. **CALPERS**, the huge **California State Employee Pensions**, recently found a voice for some clout after discovering pension administrators who approved blocks of loser stocks should be not rewarded annual handsome bonuses to pension executive investment advisors. Then there are the stock options that could grant an executive an option of 100,000 shares of stock at $10 per share exercised after one year if the market price of the stock is higher. Naturally, in this go-go market, the stock prices are always higher so if the executive says "yes" and the company buys and sells his stock that day, say $15, then he takes home a cool half-million in cash. There is no cash required from the employee who on paper has purchased and resold the shares of stock. Ordinary wages report to the IRS at year-end. Real cash must be disbursed for repurchasing or issuing more treasury stock shares, the shareholders say.

What if the stock is worth only $5 at the strike date? The management has a meeting and reprices the option at a different value, to reflect the bad performance or the bad market, say, only $2.50. Then the guy gets a smaller kick in the wallet. So, what is the purpose of the option? Just another way to give out a bonus, around the fair play tax rules and sometimes to avoid disclosing what is really happening to the outside shareholders, since it is really their money. The SEC has started coming down on corporate compensation recently by requiring limited disclosure about options and what happens to the shareholders. The next game will be to pay the bonuses from overseas earnings, which are not subject to domestic scrutiny.

All pension costs for administration, actuarial fees, contributions, and committee meetings to discuss all of this are deductible.

Dividends are not tax-deductible to any corporation, so published earnings are stated before dividends and before taxes. Earnings after taxes can actually increase if the corporation carries the losses back three years to get old tax money repaid. An important date is the ex-dividend date. Each quarter-end, the corporate BOD will meet to discuss the amount of dividends they will pay or will not pay. A date is determined, and the shareholders as of that declaration date will be paid. Stock prices tend to rise in anticipation of dividends to be paid and discounted after the date. The ex-dividend date is the day after the dividends are recorded.

Prenuptial considerations for individuals are important for all people with property who enter marriage. The correct name for prenuptial is **premarital agreement**. Naturally, there is a **Uniform Premarital Agreement Act,** strangely effective when Congress enacted the **Tax Reform Act of 1986** that altered all tax thoughts and matters for the next century. Essentially, the premarital segregates separate properties, especially in community property states, and set these property rights aside from commingled marital property. This is awfully important today when almost married couples meet the divorce lawyer sooner or later, an anticipated event almost as important as death itself (maybe a slow death after separation of property and for some, paying alimony). Also important is the right to set aside the benefit of these pre-marriage assets during the marriage, such as the market price increase, sale of these assets, or dividends from a stock portfolio if these funds can be separated tax-wise and not commingled in joint tax returns. It is important to note that not only can the property be set aside, but the economic benefit also be set aside and done properly. Qualifications for the agreement are to enter a legal marriage, that the property exists with full disclosure including liabilities, and that there is no coercion. Except for inheritances, all monies earned during a community property marriage become joint property unless defined otherwise. Dowries do not count anymore in the US. Only one wife or husband at a time is usually allowed. 'Till death do we part" is important for alimony unless its recipient (ex-partner) remarries.

A new event on the marital landscape is the postnuptial agreement. Sorry, I meant the post-marital agreement. This new lawyer-generated fee-earning session defines the property rights of a couple AFTER they have been married. It goes like this: Upon divorce, you get the dog, and I the nine cats, I get the mutual funds, you get the house, I get no alimony, you get the pension, I get the rock collection, you get to keep the children on your tax returns, etc. There is supposed to be no intimidation or "issue of unconscionability" but these agreements appear to be a predivorce settlement contract, not a postnuptial agreement. All of them are a sign of the times, when economies have become the most important issue in marriage.

About dependents: Aside from child care, payments and divorce agreements showing who gets the kids on the tax returns, the IRS deciding factor for depends is on who has the child physically in their case-custody from the days of the year, not the agreement.

Divorce is the death of a marriage. Lawyers have always been around funerals for various reasons, and there is no logic to suggest that they cannot badly handle marriages as well. One thing lawyers always fail to do is to define which spouse gets the tax deductions for the children... separate from the support issue, and another is to separate their billing for business or investment matters which is the only part of the expense and suffering which is tax-deductible. The IRS has finally made a ruling that regardless of the divorce agreement; the ex who has the children for one day more than ½ year gets the kids on the tax returns. And, the alimony, which used to be taxable to the recipient and deductible to the sender, is no longer material unless the divorce/alimony agreement dates prior to 01/01/2019. Alimony and spousal support are taxable to the recipient/deductible for the payor for the agreement signed before 12/31/18. Afterwards it is not taxable-deductible.

The community property states are Arizona, California, Idaho, Louisiana, Nevada, New Mexico, Texas, and Washington. This is almost as important as knowing the tax-free states such as Nevada, Florida, Washington, and Texas.

Insurance is important for generally two parties, the individual beneficiary, and the owner. A corporation can be both with a third party-the insured. They are never the same and an insurable interest must exist for a policy to be valid. The insurable interest part is important because it keeps people from insuring strangers and killing them the next day. The insurance would not normally become part of the prenuptial agreement since it would probably come in force, by insuring the spouses, after the marriage.

PLANNING TIPS

Planning a prenuptial or postnuptial event is like planning for the divorce. Sort of like perversely penciling out your estate tax returns in advance. They are for the few people with property who wish to keep property separate for estate or family purposes. Prior marriages and offspring can be a valid reason. Actually, the documentation is quite simple unless there is a great deal of property to identify. And it should reduce the murder and presumed suicide rates.

Taking title to ownership of property is highly important for planning your affairs. The definitions are as follows:

- **Sole ownership** can be a man or woman who is not married. An unmarried man or woman who is legally divorced. Or, a married man or woman as his or her sole and separate property.

- **Co-Ownership** can be **community property** acquired by spouses, or either during the marriage, otherwise, then by gift, bequest, devise, and descent or as the separate property is presumed community property. Co-Ownership can be by **joint tenancy** that is joint and equal interests in land owned by two or more individuals created under a single instrument with rights of survivorship. Co-Ownership can be a **tenancy in common** which undivided interests by co-owners are, but unlike joint tenancy, these interests need not be equal in quantity and may arise at different times. There is no right of survivorship; each tenant owns an interest that on his or her death vests in his or her heirs or devisee. Co-Ownership can also be in **trust** whereas the trustee of the trust holds title pursuant to the terms of the trust for the benefit of the trustor/beneficiary.

TAXES

Dividends are not deductible to a paying corporation; thus, the tax-avoiding (sometimes evading) issue of creating deductible expenses that individuals also face is a constant perpetual endeavor. Dividends received by a corporation can be 50%-100% excluded from corporate taxes if from a domestic corporation.

Legal expenses concerning business or investment assets is a deduction, even if part of the billing from a divorce proceeding. Get the lawyer to spell it out in his billing, although they are always reluctant to define their work. Defining business assets in a prenuptial agreement would also create a tax deduction.

Stock options are employment-related and create ordinary income for beneficiaries, not capital gains as with investment stock transactions. The IRS has made this quite clear and requires the gains to show up on a W-2 form at year-end for the recipient. This assures the highest tax rates for the beneficiary. It would be good if the broker firms would modify their portfolio tax statements accordingly instead of sharing a taxable event.

There are no special tax rates for capital gains earned by a corporation. There are restrictions on using capital losses, however (Losses can only offset capital gains with the balance carried forward forever). Corporations that deal with investments are called **holding companies** and face a barrage of special rules. Corporations sometimes buy liability insurance for the officers. I once had to testify in court over a wrongful death suit. The issue was "Did the corporation buy the murder weapon?"- <u>It did.</u>

A great corporate deduction is for qualified charitable contributions. The contributions are restricted to 10% of taxable income but are otherwise treated the same as an operating business expense. This violates the IRS's own "**ordinary and necessary doctrine'** but it works well for people who might otherwise take money out of the business to give it to the charity personally (after wages or dividends have been paid). Successful corporations have problems getting the cash out of the balance sheet because there are limits on officer's wages and other expenses. Dividends are paid from corporate reserves after taxes have been paid, so it is foolish to pay taxes then give the money away.

Prenuptial agreements or separate property interests that generate taxable income would require that tax returns be filed as "married filing separate" to keep the interests apart. Unfortunately, this usually exposes the parties to the old marriage penalty of higher tax rates and rules than if they had filed jointly.

The **Tax Cuts and Jobs Act of 2017** actually equalized the tax rates for married filing joint MFJ and filing separately MFS.

LEGAL COMPLIANCE

None of the above issues concern security sales. Insurance is mentioned with respect to insurable interests, which is an underwriting, not a selling issue. Stock options are handled internally by lawyers and the large brokerage houses that warehouse their client's security transactions. Lawyers handle divorces, some much better than others. More lawyers, the same people who want to divorce you when the time comes, also handle your prenups. The real issue here is finding a good lawyer when you need one. The easy part is finding them; the hard part is firing a bad one.

SUCCESSFUL STRATEGIES

The only successful strategy for the above **prenups** or **postnups** is employing good legal counsel. Of course, we are not discussing corporate matters but are examining the economic plea-bargaining part of a marriage. The best rule for finding good lawyers is that they live in a better part of town than you do (or in a better town). Referrals are good, but not always applicable. Paralegals can give good or bad advice but a lawyer is still required for all but for the simplest of marital legal matters.

HORROR STORY - DIVORCE

The greatest horror story is one where a divorcing couple cannot agree on anything. They hassle and haggle while revengeful or spiteful spouses run the lawyer bills ever higher and higher. Time in court and producing records and facing audits only prolong the agony and costs. The only goal of these arrangements is that they can impoverish, both economically and spiritually, both parties to the war. Unfortunately, the lawyers general the war to their gainful and hellish satisfaction. There are no winners to the end of this kind of destructive marriage, which was probably not worth anything, either.

PROS & CONS OF THE ABOVE

- Corporate stock options create a taxable windfall, but may not be exercisable in a flat or bear stock market.
- Corporate pension costs are a big part of compensation expenses that require very expensive legal and tax consulting experts, who must also consider all of the other fringe benefits as well.

- Small businesses are subjected to a much higher taxes in audits, than large corporations for the same types of deductions.

- Prenuptial and postnuptial arrangements are only to be considered when there are largely economic or family issues to be addressed.

- Separate tax returns may be required to keep marital agreement property and inheritances separate, especially in community property states.

- Small corporations must keep minute books current with annual meetings, etc. to maintain separate legal status from their owners.

- Contributions might best be paid from a corporate bank account, instead of individually.

- The title to assets, especially real estate, must be in clear title reflecting the current marital status and interests of all parties involved.

CHAPTER 28: APPLICATION EXERCISES

1. Corporate stock options create a taxable windfall, but may not be exercisable in a flat or bear stock market. ____ True ____ False

2. Small businesses are subjected too much higher taxes in audits than large corporations, for the same types of deductions.
____ True ____ False

3. Separate tax returns may be required to keep marital agreement property and inheritances separate, especially in community property states. ____ True ____ False

4. Prenuptial and postnuptial arrangements are only to be considered when there are largely economic or family issues to be addressed.
____ True ____ False

5. Qualified charitable contributions might best be paid from an individual account rather than from a corporate bank account.
____ True ____ False

6. Pension costs are tax deductible but subject to top-heavy rules if they favor management too much. ____ True ____ False

7. The IRS defines Highly Compensated Employees (HCE) as executives earning over $200,000 or more in compensation annually.
____ True ____ False

8. All costs for pension administration, actuarial fees, contributions, and committee meetings to discuss all of this are tax deductible.
____ True ____ False

9. The IRS has finally made a ruling that regardless of the divorce agreement; the ex who has the children for one day more than half year gets the kids on the tax returns. ____ True ____ False

10. Legal expenses concerning business or investment assets is a deduction, even if part of the billing from a divorce proceeding.
____ True ____ False

CHAPTER TWENTY-NINE

PASSIVE/ACTIVE INVESTOR PARTICIPATION, RENTAL REAL ESTATE, FOUNDATIONS, TAX AVOIDANCE SCHEMES, BUSINESS FORMS & CONSIDERATIONS

Somehow, every business book, except the ones telling you how to sell something and get rich, becomes a book about taxes. Investments involve business profit-making principles that can get stuck with solving and working around tax problems. In 1985, an accountant complained to somebody in the government that it was not fair that his client could write off his new $150,000 Rolls Royce car in three years as a business expense. That became the nucleus of the many **Tax Reform Act of 1986** changes afterward. Part of the changes were the active/passive investment activity rules which stated that passive losses from inactive investment activities could only be offset against passive earnings (**pigs & pals**) until the investment was disposed of (at which time the remaining losses could offset other income). This, of course, amounted to a revolution, not only of tax codification but also of the English language because it became so complicated.

Within this framework, residential rental properties are passive investments; although, their owners spend a great deal actively working and worrying about them. They were allocated a special active-passive status, with losses free to offset other income up to $25,000 except when other income exceeds $150,000 (then the loss is not allowable that year but can be carried forward) until the income has dropped below the $150,000 threshold or the underlying property is sold or disposed of.

Foundations and **tax avoidance schemes** go together. The first is legitimate, the other is not. The Internal Revenue Service must especially approve a foundation. It does not function as a local **tax-exempt charity 501C-3**. A tax-exempt charity spends the money it receives for operations. A **foundation** holds the money it receives (the **corpus**) and spends the income for very specific public needs. The rules are very strict for the foundation, which must also acquire corporate status from the state it resides in. This legal entity entails special fees and filing qualifications by the IRS, which can disallow it during the planning stages. Unfortunately, many famous charitable foundations spend all or most of their money advertising for more money and for administrative expenses, with little or nothing left over for the charitable cause.

Foundations create a tax deduction for the contributor, and because the numbers are large, accept property such as motor vehicles or real estate. Foundations are big-time and not for novice charities. They are sometimes incorporated into tax fraud schemes because the public has so little awareness of how they function. Form 990-PF (as in private foundation) must be filled out yearly if the annual receipts are more than 25,000. Because of their special tax status, they are subject to close review and audits by federal and state agencies. Income (donations received) and certain data are public information.

Business forms need to be discussed because they are an important part of the business world. The easiest is the **proprietorship**, which is a business with an individual owner. At year-end, he or she includes the business income and expenses in their individual tax returns. The forms are **1040 Schedule C**.

The next is the **general partnership**. This business holds all partners equally responsible for all acts. The business files a form 1065 partnership tax return. Profits or losses flow directly through to the partners. Partners cannot write off losses larger than their investment or loan obligations. The forms are **1065**.

AC (as in **Common**) **1120 corporation** issues stock for cash to its owners...making them shareholders, who are not responsible for corporate matters unless they are employed or engaged by the corp. The business files form 1120 corporate tax returns each year. Dividends paid are not a deduction for tax purposes; thus, corporate profits are taxed once at the corporate level, and then again at the shareholder level, a.k.a. double taxation. Corporate officers are generally immune from lawsuits unless the business is a professional corporation. Corporate shareholders are passive investors, but not in the **1120-S partnership** income/loss sharing relationship. A corporation with 75 or fewer shareholders can file a notice with the IRS to elect subchapter S status, which gives the shareholder's partnership tax status but retains corporate liability protection.

A **Limited Liability Company (LLC)** is a new hybrid business entity that acts tax-wise as a partnership but liability-wise as a corporation. It must register in the state of origin and pay fees, generally the same as a corporation. It files an annual **form 1065** federal partnership tax return. California extracts a minimum annual fee or larger fee based on sales income. A single-owner LLC must file as a proprietorship (who is his/her partner?) for federal tax returns but as an LLC partnership, for the state. He cannot be a limited partner tax-wise if he manages the company.

A limited partnership is an investment partnership with a general active partner and inactive passive investment partners. These businesses must be registered with the SEC and face many state and federal restrictions. The general partner is responsible for legal activities while the limited partners are immune from lawsuits. Gains and losses, which flow through to the limited partners, are severely restricted by the passive income-loss tax rules. Limited partners cannot be involved in the business for legal liability.

PLANNING TIPS

A local organization with good connections could create a large foundation to fill a public need without the usual government supervision or political restrictions. One service club, going far beyond the parameters of their parent organization, organized their own foundation. They gathered property and money from local influential citizens and raised over a million dollars. The foundation created scholarships for local high school kids and accomplished a great deal of good at a local level where the deed matches the need very efficiently.

Nonprofit organizations have fiduciary public responsibility to conservatively manage the donor assets. When Bernie Madoff's investment scheme collapsed in 2008, many foundations lost all their assets and closed with lawyers suing the trustees afterward for mismanagement.

An organization is only as good as the people who manage it. I once put together a foundation for my service club, using the above club as a model. An attorney member promised to send many customers to provide seed money after it started. The months of applications and filings were completed when a new club president decided he did not want to be bothered with it. He squashed it by withholding a small state filing fee. Meanwhile, the club was going nuts soliciting membership fees and surviving by collecting change from selling popcorn at public events. Several years later, I received a call from a state government official wanting to know whom to send the large tax bill to since the foundation reverted back an ordinary corporation (there were minimum but large annual fees owed) when the application process was killed. Fortunately, although I was no longer a member, I was able to find the home address of the club president, now ex-president. Unfortunately, the competitive club is earning $75,000 each year from its foundation to put kids through college, while this club's membership is still spending all of their time selling peanuts and popcorn.

TAXES

Many people join charitable organizations for the best altruistic purposes. They are social creatures, like most of us, who want to do some good, and to keep busy and have fun doing it. Joining the board of directors of any local charity is a very good deed. It is extremely important to keep in mind, however, that if anything goes wrong, you can be held responsible, along with the other board members. Tax-exempt organizations sometimes have **unrelated business income (UBI)** activities which are disallowed by the IRS code and the income is taxable.

One charitable organization fell behind filing payroll tax reports. Now, the IRS considers payroll taxes to be **trust fund** money, that is; public funds, not ordinary income taxes, because it has been taken from individual employee's paychecks. They will actually put people in jail for misappropriating these funds. The IRS called the organization on the rack because it is bad news not to file reports on time and another not to promptly pay the money owed with the reports. Since neither was done, a board meeting, which consisted of paid managers, and volunteers, was called to order with an **IRS revenue agent** present. I have met many revenue agents making house calls to collect those monies. He informed all present that they were individually liable for the taxes since they were responsible for the management of the organization. Then, he handed out financial forms for each member so they could give him their net worth and bank accounts for collection purposes. The penalties will double the amount of taxes assessed and the amount will never wash out in a bankruptcy.

The situation boiled down later on to hold the immediately responsible parties who signed checks and supervised payroll and all cash disbursement functions (no bills are more important than the payroll tax disbursements), including the executive director, personally responsible. Be sure, when volunteering to assist a local non-profit, that you know your responsibilities and feel good about the competence of the people you will work with. Some people, including myself, now avoid the trouble altogether.

Most small businesses which incorporate are subjected to the IRS **Code Section 1244** stock laws. These are very favorable laws concerning losses of capital from small business on dissolution or a qualified restricted stock loss sale. More often than not, most small businesses fail and this code section allows the incorporator to take ordinary loss treatment instead of limited capital loss treatment on his/her personal tax returns. Instead of capital gains treatment for the loss, which would be **Capital Gains &**

Losses, Schedule D, and the proper **Form 4797** for the Sale of Business property is used to show the loss which can offset ordinary income as an NOL. See a tax advisor for this one which is complicated to qualify. Most incorporating minute book minutes will attempt to spell it out as required.

When acquiring a business, sometimes a little luck is more important than due diligence and being a smart prudent investor. A fellow acquired a corporation that had been in business for many years. This business manufactured materials used in residential construction. The new owner paid for the outstanding stock and proceeded to run the business the same way as the previous owner.

One day, a state sales tax auditor arrived for a periodic audit. It had been many years since the business had been audited, because there were no audit records available. The new owner and his predecessor did not understand the sales tax rules. In California, residential construction materials are taxed when they are sold or delivered by the wholesaler or fabricator to the construction builder-user. The user then incorporates the materials into the house with his effort and labor but does not charge the new owner sales tax when the house is sold or completed. Otherwise, there would be a sales tax levy on every new or used house when sold.

There was a problem with the audit because the corporation had never charged sales tax to the contractors, but also had never paid sales tax on the materials it had purchased and used, either. Thus, sales tax was owed on all materials since the corporation had been in business. The prior owner had filed exempt sales tax forms with his suppliers and avoided taxes altogether. This increased his temporary profit margin considerably.

The auditor worked for a month on the case and presented a bill that was over $150,000 including penalties and interest. The new owner had to pay because the corporation, as a separate legal entity, was obligated regardless of who the shareholders were. Later the new owner, with threat of litigation, was able to recover by renegotiating the business purchase.

Sometimes a charitable-sounding organization will spring out of nowhere offering to take over your assets, yet still give you the use of them, while giving you the ultimate tax deductions everybody desires. Although there are some good charities, beware of the ones giving seminars that attract the people wearing suits & ties that work for the government.

The maximum charitable deduction for qualified charitable cash giving is 60% of income, with the unused balance carried forward. Special rules for the % and 60% carry forward. 100% is allowed for disaster relief but the money cannot be earmarked for a particular individual or family. There are varying amounts of deductions for lesser charities and appreciated the property. Anything given to a charity is not included in the gift tax reports or $15,000 individual annual exclusion. This is also a good way to keep money out of an estate where it can be counted for legal and executor fees, while providing for a good cause and saving taxes to do so.

Most of the wealth of this country is in real estate. The following rules dictate the tax aspects of investing in real estate: **Real Estate IRS Code Section 1250** gains and losses are considered long term for income taxes if they are held one year or longer. The sales price, which is usually supported by a 1099 form, must be shown (matched) in the proceeds part of the schedule 4797 Sale of Property gain or loss statement The purchase escrow costs are added to the amount paid plus improvements, with commissions and escrow costs from the sale to arrive at the cost basis figure. Then the accumulated depreciation is recaptured which increases the gain. The difference is the gain or loss.

All unused losses which were accumulated and not used (usually due to $150,000 gross income limitation) will now be expensed offsetting the other gains or losses. The above real estate rentals would be considered passive income. Note that cash and mortgages owed or not on the sold property do not affect the gain or loss. Many people assume the mortgage is somehow a part of the selling calculation in error.

An **Installment Sale IRS Section 453** can be considered which allows the seller, who takes back a note, to report the gain received annually, as a percent of the principal repaid. In other words, if there was a 10% gain on the sale of a property and the seller is holding a ten-year note, then 10% of the principal repaid each year would be reportable income in addition to the interest received. He/she can also elect to pay the taxes at the time of sale and not use this method of allocation gains to defer future taxes. These schedules can live in your tax returns for many years.

There are no taxes on **residential sales** if lived in as a residence two of the last five years. There are also no losses to be reported if it goes the other way. Cash makes no difference in gains or losses, otherwise paying cash for a property versus having a mortgage would completely upset the results. Outside of a pension plan, the home becomes the greatest leveraged asset gain a person may ever accomplish in a lifetime.

Real Estate Exchanges IRS Code Section 1031 rules that for like or same kind properties, any cash or mortgages that fall out of the property-for-property exchange is taxable. A special realtor facilitator is required to assure the timing and qualifying property requirements are met. These deals are very scarce because the match and the paperwork over the years is very hard to accomplish. Some deals are traded again and the outcome can get much obscured. Generally, only realtors become involved because real estate is their business. Residential real estate is not qualified, only business properties which can be equipment or real estate.

THERE ARE SPECIAL RULES FOR CHARITABLE TAX DEDUCTIONS

- The gift cannot have any strings attached. It must be free and clear for the recipient.
- The limit is 100% of the taxpayer's adjusted gross income.
- No future interest in property is allowed to qualify as an itemized deduction.
- The carryover (carryforwards) of unused qualified deductions are limited to five years. 60% of AGI. Non cash is less.
- Private charities and foundation contributions have a 30% annual limit.

- Capital gains property gifted to the private charities and foundations have a 20% limit.

- Contributions of $250 or more must be documented.

- Contributions of property (not cash) of $5,000 or more require a qualified appraisal.

- A residence can be gifted to a charity with the individual living in the property. The tax deduction is equal to the remainder value based on the life expectancy of the occupant. This is a remainder interest special clause.

- Other more complicated trusts and rules can be applied to charitable gifts for the proper attorney fees.

LEGAL COMPLIANCE

Due diligence is a highly important function of every broker-dealer. Every product sold by a firm through its people must be approved. The compliance department is responsible for reviewing every investment to be assured that it fits the licenses of the sales force, does not conflict with selling agreements for similar products, and is financially viable. Some large brokerage firms are quite creative in packaging their own investments for sale to their own clients, but the financial planning firms and smaller brokerages rely on outside products.

It would be quite easy for a firm to approve a mutual fund, if the firm is not crowding out established preferred funds; however, some investment products are quite complex with prospectuses several hundred pages long. The history and success of the people and firms packaging the investment must be considered, as well as the economic investment objectives. If the investment is a limited partnership (LP) or real estate investment trust (REIT), then the broker-dealer firm will send people out to examine the properties and gain a physical perspective of where the money will go.

Brokerage firms have elaborate annual meetings for their sales force, who might be from all over the country. They charge large fees, about $25,000 or more for investment firms to rent booth or table space to display their investment products and meet with the sales force. This money pays for the meetings that tend to run a half-week and can occupy full-time staff planning and organizing people for the entire year. Investment firms do not usually lobby their way past the due diligence process by buying booth space. I know of one firm whose investment product was under consideration at the time they bought their booth for the annual convention. After the conference, it was not approved.

Due diligence, in spite of detailed analysis and inspection, sometimes approves products that have problems afterward. This is par for the course. No paperwork in the world can change economics or changes in the marketplace. Sometimes a sixth sense is required; a look beyond the numbers and past the presentation. I have always visited the site for a new deal and have turned down many they approved. I have also never regretted it, because I am usually right for my clients.

SUCCESSFUL STRATEGIES

The successful strategy for this chapter is to keep the company of a good professional. In today's world, we are surrounded by information in abundance. Yet not always enough to make sophisticated decisions. The burden, unfortunately, lies with the informed investor to find reliable counsel and make intelligent decisions. Not all professionals are truly professional, any more than any other trades, and sometimes the information available is not what is required. Completely informed decisions may be impossible to make. Even Internet trading, information and technology which is a fluid thing changes from day to day. Simply find honest qualified people and believe in them.

HORROR STORY - CHAMBER OF COMMERCE

Business forms are confusing for some people. A fellow with a bookkeeping practice joined the local Chamber of Commerce to find new customers for his small business. Never one to turn business away, he volunteered to do the bookkeeping and tax work for the exempt corporation chamber. Unfortunately, he did not really understand that an exempt corporation is first incorporated as an ordinary corporation that is then allowed a tax exemption after it qualifies for charitable purposes

AND files the proper 990 year-end forms. Well, the bookkeeper forgot how to file the forms or ignored them for several years.

IRS and state-generated mails arrived and apparently, he did not get the message or ignored all the troubling signs. Some of the mail was sent certified, receipt requested, which means more trouble unless it is the big check they have been waiting for. Ignorance knows no bounds, and one day out of the blue, a tax lien for over $20,000 (a lifetime savings for the Chamber of Commerce) was suddenly extracted from the bank's operating account. Since the Chamber of Commerce was in the next town, I am not sure of the outcome except that it made great local newspaper copy for a while. Unfortunately, everybody except the Chamber of Commerce knew that the person did a lousy work.

PROS & CONS OF THE ABOVE INVESTMENT CONSIDERATIONS

- Business dealings are incredibly complex. Be sure your business form fits the situation and that you have good counsel. A Subchapter S Corporation brought in a new shareholder. When I told him that he had lost his tax status, when had brought in a corporate partner, a major customer for desperately needed cash and the business no longer qualified. It is that easy.

- Limited partnerships generate two problems: Liquidity, because they may be impossible to sell, and passive losses, which may be unusable tax-wise until the deal is closed out many years later. Some partnerships stretch out their closings for many extra years using the excuse that they are unable to liquidate the last of the assets. This is a ploy by some to defer the bad news that they did not make any money, or not let the cat out of the bag on how little money they did make. All to the detriment of the taxpayer client who could use the losses in his tax returns in the year when they close it out. Generally, the investor client loses track or interest in the partnership earnings or performance over the years because they are stretched out for so long.

- A suit for limited partnership losses can only be for the loss of capital, never earnings. A partnership may stretch out their final closing to keep the wolves (lawyers) away because the loss cannot be finalized until the investment deal is closed out. The best way to track partnership performance is to pay attention to the K-1 forms at year-end. They show cash returned to partners as the return of capital. When this amount has exceeded the original investment, the deal is in the profit zone. If it never reaches it, there will be a loss or a miracle at the end. Partnerships can shut down leasing operations but take years afterward to dispose of leased assets afterward.

- Foundations are big business if they are real. Do not partake in one unless you are on solid ground and have professional backing.

- Avoid business schemes that promise quick riches or tax-avoidance deals.

- Real estate partnerships once were everywhere. Then the tax rules dried up and leveraged deals became deadly deals. Avoid them if they are back in town. Now we have the 2008 crash to remember.

- Don't incorporate just to be an Inc. There should be a business need, based on liability, taxes or family continuation because they cost money to administer and have additional taxes, administration, and fuss. If you do incorporate the family business, do not make the mistake of incorporating in the nearest tax-free state because it doesn't work if your business is working elsewhere. You should be prepared to hire a professional accountant for a good set of books to match the business form as well.

- Charitable giving has tax breaks as well as providing for social good. For a good cause, it works all the way around.

CHAPTER 29: APPLICATION EXERCISES

1. A Limited Liability Company (LLC) is a new hybrid business entity that acts tax-wise as a partnership but liability-wise as a corporation.
   ___ True ___ False

2. Tax-exempt organizations sometimes have unrelated business income (UBI) activities which are permissible by the IRS code and the income is not taxable. ___ True ___ False

3. The maximum charitable deduction for qualified charitable cash giving is 40% of income, with the unused balance carried forward.
   ___ True ___ False

4. Charitable contributions of $250 or more must be documented.
   ___ True ___ False

5. Under a Charitable Remainder Trust, a residence can be gifted to a charity with the individual living in the property. ___ True ___ False

6. Because of their special tax status, Foundations are subject to close review and audits by federal and state agencies. ___ True ___ False

7. A business with an individual owner is a Proprietorship.
   ___ True ___ False

8. A corporation with 75 or fewer shareholders can file a notice with the IRS to elect subchapter S status, which gives the shareholder's partnership tax status but retains corporate liability protection.
   ___ True ___ False

9. A single-owner LLC can be a limited partner tax-wise if he manages the company. ___ True ___ False

10. There are no taxes within excludable $250,000/$500,000 if married amounts on residential sales if lived in as a residence two of the last five years. ___ True ___ False

PART SIX

DEATH & TAXES

Dying is a complicated business. Firsthand, there are gift taxes levied on property given away before the final day. Then, to avoid estate taxes very complex devices such as bypass spousal trusts are established to save more for the children and provide for other needs. Living trusts and wills are written and executed. Insurance policies are granted away when you know you have three or more year's life left, and complex trusts are set up to skip generations when you want to save something for the grandkids. Sane and competent executors are selected...usually beneficiaries to be rewarded one day with statutory fees equal to the attorney's charges for handling the estate. Pension taxes are finally accounted for by beneficiary, for all to rest in peace.

After that final day, individual, estate and fiduciary returns will keep accountants occupied and platoons of lawyers will be busy working with them. Out of state property creates ancillary probate extensions that can take as long as four years. Improper wills invite legal contests, probate, and many legal headaches. Will-substitutes can keep food on the table while time and the legal profession consumes the estate. We are working with the most complex part of the tax code because it was created for wealthy folks long before the Manhattan Project made the Bomb, and has been continually layered with new tax code since.

Finally, there is the **Uniform Determination of Death Act** to contend. This statute, which has been adopted by many states defines our demise as occurring officially when a person is brain dead, meaning the absence of brain waves, as well as the cessation of circulatory and respiratory functions. So, if somebody says you are brain dead, let us hope he is not serious!

CHAPTER THIRTY

GIFT & ESTATE TAXES, MARITAL EXEMPTION

Gift and estate taxes are the least understood part of the tax code by our citizens. It might be correct to say, they were never intended to be understood. Most professional people understand only little parts of it, which is probably the case. Just when you think you know how the system works, the word trust or fiduciary comes up and it all goes away again.

Gift taxes arrived to keep individuals from giving their estate away to escape estate taxes. After all, if the whole estate were dissipated, then there would be no estate taxes left to collect. Governments are designed mainly around collecting taxes, (and fight wars inside and outside of Congress) and the grease that keeps all the spending political wheels turning. In the early Colonial Era, all taxes were simply **duties on imported goods.** During the First World War, personal income taxes were instituted for the first time.

Now we have an automated millstone in the middle of all this effort and there are straps to hold the citizen taxpayer in place until the tax agents extract all the juices. The gift tax straps allow the taxpayer to give or gift up to $15,000 to anybody or everybody each year without encountering tax problems. The spouse can also double the ante without problems, as long as he/she officially agrees to in a process called **gift splitting**. The recipient always receives the money tax-free. The money gifted away is not tax-deductible, as some people would like to believe.

If more than $15,000 is given to an individual, the excess must be entered on a federal form 709 gift tax return at year-end. Now comes the catch. There are no taxes paid at this point unless you have given a great deal of money away. Then it ties to the estate tax tables. The estate also called transfer tax has an exclusion of $11,580,000 for the year 2020. If you gave somebody over $11,580,000 and the annual $15,000 exclusion amount during the year, the excess gift would be subject to estate taxes at 40% that would be paid with the return. The government allows you to give away the $15,000 each year but all amounts over that are allowed to offset the maximum estate tax exemption (think of it as the standard exemption on an individual tax return) until it is used up. Then there are tax problems, which is what estate planning is all about. What the system does is different from the individual tax returns because instead of starting at the minimum tax rate for the first taxable dollar after arriving at the taxable amount, you start in the middle of the tax tables for the first taxable dollar. In other words, you calculate the tax on the whole amount, then subtract the credit equal to the exemption. The tax tables up to the exemption amount, become a meaningless exercise.

THE ESTATE EXEMPTION EQUIVALENT AND UNIFIED CREDIT

Year	Exemption	Credit
2020	$11,580,000	$4,577,800
2019	$11,400,000	$4,505.800
2018	$11,180,000	$4,417,800
2017	$5,490.000	$2,141,800
2016	$5,450.000	$2,125,800
2015	$5,430.00	$2,117,800

These tables are applied as a credit, to offset tax calculations, which really get confusing. Like calculating your completed tax return and then going back to recalculating the taxes using the standard exemption and taking a credit for it. In practice, what really happens is that it sets the first taxable dollar at the 40% tax rate. Notice the regularity of the exemption increases.

The tax tables that apply before and after the exemption are as follows:

UNIFIED FEDERAL ESTATE AND GIFT TAX RATES

Taxable Amount			Tax rate %	Plus:	Equals Amount	Tax
$ up to:	$	10,000	18		$ -0-	
10,001	to	20,000	20		200	
20,001		40,000	22		600	
40,001		60,000	24		1,400	
60,001		80,000	26		2,600	
80,001		100,000	28		4,200	
100,001		150,000	30		6,200	
150,001		250,000	32		9,200	
250,001		500,000	34		14,200	
500,001		750,000	37		29,200	
750,001		1,000,000	39		44,200	
1,000,001		and over	40		54,200	

This brings us to the marital exemption. This exemption is a real plus for the married couple. This exemption allows the first-to-die spouse to avoid estate taxes by allowing his estate (half of the total estate) to shift to his remaining spouse on his death. This gives her complete control over the family assets until her death. The problem now is with her heirs because if the estate were not diminished before death, then the doubled-up estate, now appreciated, might pay more taxes. An example: The family estate is $19 million in the year 2019. The husband dies before year-end and because he has a proper will, which leaves half of the community property to his spouse, she now has the whole $19 million to account for. She dies the next year and now everything above her $11,400,000 exemption is taxed to her estate thus depriving her heirs of the taxes paid. If he had willed his property to the children, he would not have paid any taxes out of his estate because of his $11,400,000 exemption, and the surviving spouse would not have paid any taxes either. The way for her to keep all the estate and avoid taxes would be a trust arrangement, which is in the next chapter.

There is a provision in the estate 706 return where unused taxes on a spousal estate. Assume that ½ of the total estate is 10 million and his estate exemption is $1,580,000, the unused amount from his exemptions would advance to the spouse to increase her exemption when she passes away. There is also an unlimited provision to transfer assets from one spouse to another to avoid taxes on the first to die.

PLANNING TIPS

Nobody understands the gift and estate tax rules, unless it is their business. Do not try to guess your way through the estate planning process. Find an attorney who does nothing but estate planning (avoid the lawyer who wears too many hats), or if you can afford them, go to the big expensive law firm that has an estate tax specialist. Avoid paralegal or professional people who are not specialists. A Jack of all trades would be the master of your demise.

An amount less than the exemption (see the table because it is changes annually) is not subject to tax so this is not a problem for the person of small means. Just keep in mind that the first half of the estate is added to the second half estate (unless it goes to heirs and beneficiaries) after the funeral is over.

TAXES

Estates file a federal form 706 Estate Tax Return. This return is a very tough return. Accountants lose sleep at night worrying about the huge jigsaw puzzle that they must piece together to get it filed. Sometimes attorneys handle the returns, but the smarter ones give them away and save the gravy fees for themselves. Computers help, but the preparer must know what he/she is doing, unlike some of the individual tax work done in town for quickie refunds. I personally know of a law firm that filed a large return late without an extension, and received a $40,000 penalty from the IRS. It got very involved with our firm compiling the bad spending habits of one heir who spent more than her inheritance as executrix. This was part of another lawsuit against her from the other heirs. Because the trustee was a related heir, the probate court required her to be insured. Later after she dissipated most of the estate, a new lawyer had to sue the insurance company for restitution to the other heirs.

I filed my first 706 on a large estate, without a good computer program that makes everybody look good, and said my prayers. Several months later, a letter came in the mail from the IRS Atlanta. I opened the dreaded letter, believing that I was finally going out of business. The letter announced that the return had been audited and cleared. This was when I first learned that the IRS sends all estate returns to Atlanta to be audited. That is the same place where pension reports, the dreaded 5500 series documents are also reviewed and tabulated. To make matters worse, the audited "accepted" estate tax return letter is required by most states before they will formally close an estate probate. All the smart people must live near Atlanta. I was there and the people were very friendly. They have their Stone Mountain monument to remember. My broker-dealer was headquartered nearby.

An estate return is not required if the estate is less than the exemption amount and there have not been large taxable gifts. Remember that the individual estate is only ½ of the joint estate of a married couple. A Federal identification number may be required if there are undistributed assets earning interest, dividends, rents or other income during the probate period (**fiduciary (1041 forms)**). The return must be filed accordingly. Fiduciaries pay taxes on residual estate earnings.

An individual tax return is usually required to be filed for the year of death unless there is no income other than Social Security Benefits during that period.

If there is an estate return requirement, (even if the property all goes to the spouse or a trust) a Federal identification number must be applied for. This advises the government to expect a 706-estate tax return and perhaps a 1041 fiduciary return, with another federal identification number as well. Extensions are required if they cannot be filed in time; otherwise, there can be extra-large penalties.

PROBATE

If the deceased total assets exceed $150,000 and there is no will or living trust, probate by the court is required. The probate court can freeze assets until the estate distribution is settled.

The maximum statutory fees for administering probate is based on gross asset value, not reduced by mortgages, credit cards, or loans. These fees are:

GROSS ASSET VALUE ESTIMATED LEGAL/ OTHER REPRESENTATIVES

Gross Asset Value	Estimated Legal/ Other Representatives
$400,000	$22,000
$500,000	$26,000
$700,000	$34,000
$1,000,000	$46,000
$2,000,000	$66,000
$3,000,000	$86,000
$4,000.0000	$106,000

LEGAL COMPLIANCE

Some financial planners, paralegal, and independent stockbrokers have sold prepackaged estate plans. These are a set of forms that require an individual to fill in the blanks for name, date of birth, etc. The simple documents begin with the caveat that "an attorney will review and sign the documents". Most advice in the world is free but for anybody to take a fee to help create a will, a trust, or work with your estate except in the tax or investment capacity of a Registered Investment Advisor, they are actually giving legal advice.

In California, as with many states, a legal forms notary is required to create legal documents, usually under the direction of an attorney. With a million hungry lawyers swarming all over the country like wasps in the spring, there is no need to pay non-professionals to engage in this activity. It is bad enough to pay an attorney who is not a specialist to get involved in this complex area. Individuals involved with FINRA security or insurance, licenses are forbidden to engage in this work, especially establishing living trusts or wills and can be fired or sanctioned for giving legal advice for a fee. They should always advise you (without charge) to visit an attorney to complete the task. It would be their job to advise when you are in need of an attorney, and it should end there.

SUCCESSFUL STRATEGIES

The best strategy for estate planning is to review retirement plan documents and the tons of free information available from everywhere. The newspapers, television, Internet, Social Security Administration, associations, banks, current and past employment, all have printable information available to be reviewed and somehow digested. Avoid the people selling investments or advice on how to avoid taxes or get rich before you retire. Do not be pressured. Take your time and set up a filing system for your data. Take a little time off each month to review the stuff and talk it over with the spouse or financially-tuned next of kin. Do not be in a hurry to make decisions and always be well informed on important issues. Take notes and try to gain a broad understanding of your needs and where you need to go with your estate plan. Then find the right person to implement it.

Because of the complexity of the subject, many people attend seminars during which investment representatives and attorneys offer free lunches and expensive advice. There is a whole group of retired people who attend seminar after seminar because they have the time and desire to manage or at least understand their personal financial affairs. This is recommended because a lesson is not learned from flash exposure to a subject as complex and important as this. The chicken may be as hard to digest as the data.

A will is altered by filing a codicil which is an amendment. The original will be referred to but not physically altered. I saw a will which had been marked up and lined out by a demented elder. He actually invalidated the will and became intestate. Fortunately, his heirs went along with the scribbling and didn't throw the will out.

HORROR STORY - ESTATE PLANNING

After the surviving parent died, his 40-year-old daughter, who was the estate executrix, took over the large estate. There was a real estate to be sold, investments to be made, and she wanted to move from Texas to California to be near her boyfriend. She shared the estate with her brother, who had severe medical problems and never been self-supportive. He had been receiving state substance and considerable medical attention. The insurance money from the estate bought a residence, in her name, to house her brother. She planned to invest the family fortune in a much diversified portfolio with the focus on long-term income-producing investments. Before that was completed, the brother rejected his inheritance. By filing the disclaimer, none of the estate flowed to him. Instead, it went to his sister which guaranteed that he would continue to receive lifelong medical care and substance from the state agencies as an indigent citizen. No problems occurred because the family attorney, a reliable long-term associate of the deceased successful father, structured the plan.

The investments were divided into two separate portfolios, although they were both in the name of the sister. That way they could be tracked as if they were owned separately. At first, everything went well as the estate settled down. The sister moved to California with her brother and began to travel. The investments functioned as they should and there were no problems. Then the phone rang. She needed money wired to a bank where she was staying in Mexico. A month later, she needed money to buy a condo in Palm Springs. Then there was her new gambling school for card players, she started up. So, more and more investments were sold off to satisfy the large cash needs.

First, her money went to money market cash followed by the liquid investments. Penalties were lost to cancel insurance annuities. The phone kept ringing month after month from different places, and she was becoming as hard to find as Saddam Hussein. Finally, the brother's accounts in her name were victimized. One by one, they also disappeared. The school shut down and rumors had her working in a casino. The last investment to disappear was a limited partnership that took months to sell on the secondary market, at a great loss.

The client vanished with the completion of the spending binge. The boyfriend is in jail for nonviolent crimes. One must hope that the brother still has a roof over his head, even if it is now mortgaged or paid by chapter 8 funds.

PROS & CONS OF GIFT & ESTATE TAXES

- Gifts are never taxed to the recipient, but large gifts can be taxed to the giver.
- By gifting $15,000 annually to family members or other non-charitable loving friends, a large estate can be reduced substantially over the years, especially if the spouse doubles the ante.
- Small estates of less than the standard exemption (see the table) are not required to file estate tax returns, but may need to file a fiduciary tax return.
- A fiduciary tax return may be required for an estate that earns interest, dividends, rents, or other income before distribution to spouse or heirs. This is the estate supplemental tax return.
- Beware of quasi-legal professionals who will set up your living trust, do your will, or engage in other legal acts without the proper licenses or qualifications.
- Estate planning is the most complex area of the tax code and requires much research for individuals to understand their own affairs enough to engage professionals to complete their needs and wishes.
- The greatest asset of estate planning is the value of the marital exemption that avoids all taxes until the estate is either consumed or acted on by the death of the surviving spouse. Thus, all assets are available for the needs of the surviving spouse to continue the lifestyle she or he was accustomed to until these assets are not required any longer.
- It could be cheaper tax-wise to spin off some assets to heirs upon the death of the first spouse, to avoid taxation problems in the

future, even though the surviving spouse could assume the assets without immediate tax consequences.

- Because people live very long these times, it would be good planning to give assets to offspring and grandchildren while they are young enough to enjoy and use them.

- Many people die with large intact estates while their children have suffered financially for no reason.

- Old axiom, you can't take it with you, but assets could be put to bottom use.

- Wills must exclude all living trust assets because they are quasi-legal entities which act on death. Accordingly, for small simple estate, the living trusts when properly established, act as a will and thus, avoid probate. Think of it as a will substitute in these cases.

CHAPTER 30: APPLICATION EXERCISES

1. Gift taxes are allowed for by the IRS to keep individuals from giving their estate away to escape estate taxes. ____ True ____ False

2. If more than $15,000 is given to an individual, the excess must be entered on a Federal form 709 gift tax return at year end. ____ True ____ False

3. A fiduciary 1041 tax return may be required for an estate that earns interest, dividends, rents or other income before distribution to spouse or heirs. ____ True ____ False

4. It could be cheaper tax-wise to spin off some assets by Trust or Will to heirs upon the death of the first spouse, to avoid taxation problems in the future, even though the surviving spouse could assume the assets without immediate tax consequences. ____ True ____ False

5. Gifts are never taxed to the recipient, but large gifts can be taxed to the giver if they exceed the estate tax exemption. ____ True ____ False

6. In the early Colonial Era, all taxes were simply duties on imported goods. ____ True ____ False

7. Using a financial planner, paralegal or independent stockbroker to help you through the estate planning process is a good way to save money. ____ True ____ False

8. An individual tax return is usually required to be filed for the year of death, unless there is no income other than Social Security Benefits during that period. ____ True ____ False

9. If the total assets of the deceased exceed $150,000 and there is no will or living trust, probate by the court is required, which could freeze assets until the estate distribution is settled. ____ True ____ False

10. Individuals involved with FINRA security or insurance licenses are forbidden to engage in estate planning, especially establishing living trusts or wills and can be fired or sanctioned for giving legal advice for a fee. ____ True ____ False

CHAPTER THIRTY-ONE

LIVING TRUSTS, BYPASS TRUSTS, GRANTOR TRUSTS, GENERATION-SKIPPING DYNASTY TRUSTS, CHARITABLE REMAINDER TRUSTS

A great percentage of elderly people, and sophisticated people with financial means, now have living trusts. Also called family trusts, revocable trusts and grantor trusts, these documents provide an excellent opportunity to organize personal financial affairs, as well as providing for future estate planning matters. There are two phases in preparation of the **inter-vivos** living trusts. First, is to have an attorney prepare the trust, which can printed off his computer. The second is to review the value and disposition of all assets… are they working, do you need to change the distribution of the dividends or capital gains on some mutual funds, etc. Review the beneficiaries of insurance policies to assure that they do not benefit the wrong people such as ex-wives, and see what the cash value is at this time, for you will need to list it. Check the real estate titles (grant deeds) to make sure that they are recorded correctly in the trust name. Check signature cards at the bank to be sure your spouse or next of kin is there in case you become locked up in a Mexican jail and need a quick cash bond or you die and the husband/wife cannot buy groceries until the estate is settled.

If you do not have a trust then you may want a **Payable on Death (POD)** to make sure you or your spouse can get to your bank account when needed. This form is very important and available at your bank or credit union to transfer funds to your heirs or trustees without probate.

Check your auto insurance for enough coverage because additional liability coverage is cheap and you may have a really large estate now…enough for shysters to pursue. You may want to purchase a million-dollar personal liability clause. Also, review the home insurance policies to be sure you have the correct coverage because the value of the house may have increased and you may be underinsured (they never insure 100%, anyways) for replacement values. This is time to look at the pension plan and Social Security to be sure they are in place to do what you want. Locating the documents can be a real hassle, but do not throw the opportunity away by not filing them in a safe place after they are reorganized. Then, make a big list of all assets for the living trust final page.

A living trust defines property disposition according to the dictates of the will. It can set aside assets for the spouse with a marital deduction trust, set aside the spousal exemption trust, or establish a **Q-tip trust**, which allows the surviving spouse to receive all the income during life from assets that were **assigned** to other beneficiaries. It can have a **pour-over clause** to add unlisted assets to the trust, including a clause for a **durable power of attorney** for health or incompetence issues and it will define your executors and beneficiaries. An attorney should review living trusts, as well as wills, every five years because personal situations change, as well as the tax laws. Common sense dictates that a change of marital relationship or birth/death in the family would require some changes without delay.

A living trust avoids probate because it provides for the disposition of assets prior to the reading of the will. At the instant of death, the trust is legally activated and shorts out the courts in the probate process of distributing the assets of the estate. The living trust is auxiliary to the will and executes the demands of the will, which is part of the legal process. Although it supports the will, it does function without it if it is simple and the assets (especially real estate grant deeds) and financial accounts are in the trust name.

Trusts have different sections that perform different functions. The **A section** is the **Marital Trust** because it favors the surviving spouse by placing all his/her assets in this category for that usage. The **B section** is the **Bypass Trust** for property excluded (always the maximum amount) from the surviving spouse's taxable estate. The **C-section** is the **qualified Terminable Income Portion (Q-TIP)** or **Marital Trust** because the remaining spouse can elect to set property aside from current estate taxes while benefiting from the use and enjoyment of these assets which will be taxed upon the second death. This **C section** holds assets to be distributed by the wishes of the first decedent which are in excess of the marital deduction portion of the **B trust**.

The greatest value of the living trust is its flexibility to allow for the use of assets by the surviving spouse, yet setting them aside without taxation, for the future benefit of the heirs. Most importantly, it provides an opportunity for individuals to review their entire investment and retirement strategy and assign executors (besides the surviving spouse) for the will and beneficiaries for the future.

Do not expect the trust to create powers of attorney for the surviving spouse to handle financial affairs while both parties are still alive. A court order is required to give a person's affairs to another, even if married. A **Special Needs Trust** (A fiduciary) will need to be created for that legal event. The court will attempt to protect citizens in this way. There is a problem with many attorneys' generosity making themselves not only trustees of clients estates, but also as beneficiaries of the same and the court tries to halt this theft. Although probate is often times avoided with a living trust without a will, it is best to have a will if the estate is substantial. The **Will** directs the inheritance to the heirs while the trust holds them safely.

The living trust occupies a unique position in the tax laws which govern our lives. It exists on paper but does not act until a person (trustor) dies. Then the trust becomes a part of the deceased estate, a function of the will, and the basis of the estate tax return. The trust, which was inactive as an **inter-vivos revocable document** becomes a **testamentary trust** that is a legal entity. The testamentary trust is required to file fiduciary tax returns because it has been given legal existence. This event happens when there is no living survivor such a spouse who would jointly be still in the trust. Although probate is often times avoided with a living trust without a will, it is best to have a will if the estate is substantial. The will directs the inheritance to the heirs while the trust holds them safely.

A living trust is prepared in conjunction with a will. The will is more important than the trust because a person without a will is **intestate**, which means that the court will **probate** and decide the disposition of the estate by paying all claims and distributing all assets. The probate process requires public notice, the assignment of a court-appointed person, and numerous legal fees. The process is a lengthy period to go through. The legal function will then distribute the remaining estate assets instead of to whom the deceased might have desired. Never change a will by marking it up because that will invalidate it. Have a lawyer or legal person do a **codicil** that is an addendum to the will that will reference the original part to be changed and the changes made.

Because each succeeding generation of a family can be taxed on the same assets, a special provision of the law provides for a **generation-skipping trust**. This trust is entitled to a million-dollar exemption (after estate taxes have been paid) to distribute assets to younger generations. The 40% maximum estate transfer tax rate is paid on values over the million-dollar exemption. This is also called a **dynasty trust** because of its nature.

Charitable remainder trusts allow individuals to irrevocably fund a trust which will pay the individual an income (dividends from stocks or interest from bonds) for life with the principal going to a charity on his death. This trust creates a current income tax deduction for the remainder value of the property when it will be received by the charity. A charitable contribution, outside of tax planning, is always deductible as long as the charity is recognized and qualified as legitimate. This is important to high-income individuals who have tax problems. Charitable deductions, upon death, by force of the will, will also reduce a taxable estate.

Then there are the **grantor or rabbi trusts**. A living trust is a grantor trust. A Rabbi trust is a grantor trust with another misleading name. This legal term is used to describe a trust that will pay taxes the same as a living person. People have tried to package grantor trusts as tax shelters because people are not familiar with them. Probably the most important aspects of the living trust are title deeds, bank accounts, and the investment portfolio assets under the trust umbrella. If somebody says grantor trust and you are not in a tax seminar, run away before he empties your pockets and wallet or purse.

There are other complex trust variations designed to wrap around the gift or charitable rules, but the lawyers are well paid to discuss them further.

PLANNING TIPS

The whole chapter is about planning, which is to review your finances and organize your objectives with proper professional help. Because your finances are complex, it will require professional assistance and researching old records. Afterward, you will feel rewarded that you know where you are going and that your affairs are researched and detailed. The whole thing should flow together from the will to the trusts for reviewing all financial aspects of your present and future, which is now "the plan".

People selling investments always say they will make you money, but the above planning will save you money and properly organize your affairs. This chapter only skips across the water of estate taxation and only a professional can complete the immersion process. The most important thing is to be aware of the process and the interaction of your affairs. After all, it is your money and future.

TAXES

Living trusts do not file tax returns until they come into force upon the death of the grantor (or co-grantor spouse) as a **fiduciary 1041**. At that time the trust will file annual tax returns, unless all of the assets have been transferred to the living spouse as with a small non-taxable situation. The tax returns hold the property separate from the remaining spouse as a function to maintain the future tax status intended in the will and trust documents. We usually end up with the same grantor trust benefitting the living beneficiary. If there is a fiduciary trust (because there is no living party to sign escrow documents or account for other taxable income until settlement), then the income from the trust flows is paid by the trust or to the beneficiary who will pay taxes on it in their individual tax returns. The trust will deduct the income distributions flowing to the taxpayer to avoid double taxation (remember that the trust owns the assets because there was no spouse living).

Fiduciary trusts can also hold a property for limited times to dispose of in sale or timely distribution to heirs. The fiduciary trust will handle selling and disposing of assets, and issues a K-1 form, not unlike a partnership distribution document, which ties the individual to the trust activity at year-end. Grantor (living) trusts give great power to the surviving beneficiary, which enables the holder to use the assets.

LEGAL COMPLIANCE

I covered this subject in another chapter but must review it again because it is an abused area. Many financial advisors are in the legal business. They create or help create living trusts, advise people on will preparation, and engage in financial matters such as financing, which is not part of the broker-dealer relationship. No financial planner can bill for legal fees or work that appears to be legal in nature, unless he is an attorney. When giving advice he should advise you to seek legal help to properly complete the required work. Many financial planners are participating in living trust documentation. This is considered a legal matter and is bad news for any planner to be involved if his parent firm finds out.

Taking commissions for mortgage financing or any financial arranging is completely out of the scope of broker-dealer commitments. Receiving commissions based on financing is forbidden. Most broker-dealers are audited annually on outside income, and although some other passive-tax preparation income is considered non-threatening, most financial matters for fees, excluding tax preparation, are not allowed. The broker-dealer by lawful contract and FINRA supervision have control over all income from the sales executive. If a financial planner tries to bill for any of the above or to complete paperwork for any financing arrangements, it would be astute to place a call to his parent office to see if it is proper.

Gifts to a minor are the minor's property until he/she reaches the age of majority, which is 18. Because he/she is a minor, he/she cannot assume control of the funds that must remain under a guardian. **The Uniform Gift to Minors Act (UGMA)**, specifies the rules and who can act as a guardian (parents or court appointed). This is a contentious area for parents of movie star children or children who inherit money. The parents usually feel, not unjustly, that they deserve some of the funds. In any case, the funds cannot be used for the benefit of the parents or guardian, except for direct minor's benefit under strictly adhered principals of accountability. The **Uniform Transfers to Minors (UTMA) Act of 1986** replaced UGMA for further protections of the guardianship. A recent improvement was the **California Uniform Transfers to Minors Act (CUTMA)** of 1990, which amplified the Federal statute to include irrevocable gifts, fiduciary responsibilities, and extension of transferred property guardianship until age 25 for irrevocable trusts with specified age limits. This goes far beyond the checking accounts for minors who receive income as child actors or the $15,000 gift allowances against estates. It also allows a minor of age 14 or above to petition the courts to review his guardianship for abuse of funds which should be used only for his care and maintenance. Although the minor has ownership of a UGMA/UTMA account upon turning age 18 majority, many fiduciaries are instructed by will or trust to hold funds back from inheritance much longer to age 25 or even later.

SUCCESSFUL STRATEGIES

Unless you are wealthy and have used a large law firm, then you must find a reputable individual or team to prepare your will or trust. The will is necessary, unless you are a pauper. The trust works best if you have a spouse, and have enough assets to need control over their disposition and tax consequences.

The best strategy is to understand your financial position and study the planning suitable for your situation. Monitor the results and make your financial future your career. You will find that the better informed you are, the more successful your plans will be. Do not be surprised to find out that most middle-aged and senior people are doing the same.

Irrevocable charitable trusts or outright charitable gifting are good ways to convey assets to a good cause and receive a current tax benefit. The control over the asset must be relinquished completely for the transfer to be legal and tax beneficial. They also fit well into the will and create estate tax deductions on the death and final disposition of the estate. Best to give property away directly from a corporate business or appreciated property from your personal assets.

HORROR STORY - TRUST

A grantor trust is a term for a living trust in form but not substance. That is, it does not file tax returns while the grantor is alive, to become effective on death, is a temporary form as an entity that holds assets that create income for the recipient spouse, until death. In other words, all income is taxed to the holder trustee until death.

A very smart accountant-financial planner, working with bank clients, created a trust to avoid taxes. He contacted high-income people with a scheme to include all of their household assets, including the residence, into a trust which would have unlimited ability to control all income and expense the household assets as business assets. The trusts were named business trusts by him and converted personal property to business property.

"The lawyer who created these copyrighted trusts has never lost a case," he told his clients. The trust documents were extensive and contained a substantial reference to the Constitution and particularly to the intent of the founders of the Constitution and its amendments. In so many words, the trust declared itself to be freed of the income tax laws, as many tax protesters argue today. Nevertheless, the financial planner failed to tell his clients that Constitutional trusts were illegal because their sole purpose was to use Constitutional dialogue to evade taxes.

He continued to charge huge fees to set the trusts up, filed false tax returns, and handled other investments for these people as well. His mail-order Ph.D. was on the wall for all to see, an expert in taxes and all investment matters. In his favor was the fact that IRS in Atlanta handles all estate tax matters, and there were no local agents, even in the large Los Angeles office that knew anything about trusts. Business got so good that he enlisted the services of an attorney to set them up and provide credibility to the deal and an accounting clerk to handle the bookkeeping.

Everything went fine until the FBI showed up at the door on other matters, and the trust customers became incorporated into a huge class-action lawsuit over securities fraud. The trusts were completely fraudulent, and there were audits upon audits afterward. There were other lawsuits as well. He also had created a phony securities investment.

What about the lawyer who never lost a case? One of the defrauded trust owners called him and found that he probably never had any clients to go to court with because he sent out an exorbitant bill for the phone call. Nobody could afford him, even to defend his worthless case.

SECOND HORROR STORY - MARY LINCOLN

An example of how perverse the legal system could be would be the true story about Mary Lincoln, the wife of Abraham Lincoln. After the President was assassinated, her son reported to the authorities that his mother had gone mad and was spending his inheritance. In the absence of an estate trust, during the days when women had very little power, there was a competency trial, which resulted in her committal to an insane asylum. She had to suffer through the grief of Abraham while in an asylum for years before she was released. All because of the inheritance issue brought up by her son. Fortunately, the rules are more compassionate and logical (outside of the taxation issues) these days. Perhaps her experience had something to do with the beneficial changes in the law. Today a legal trust would need to be established by the courts, a Special Needs Trust to protect her.

PROS & CONS ABOUT THE ABOVE TRUSTS

- There is a great deal of fraud concerning trusts to save money during your lifetime, especially with grantor trusts. Outside of a charitable trust that would irrevocably give control of assets to a recognized charity, there is little a trust can do on an annual tax basis, that proper gifting cannot do.

- Gifting assets during your lifetime removes a property from your estate that saves taxes by not producing taxable income on an annual basis and saves estate taxes when you cash in your term on Earth.

- A living trust is recommended for married couples who have considerable assets or at least own a home.

- Avoid prepackaged living trusts sold by people who are not lawyers. The situation is simply not simple enough for non-professionals.

- When a person passes the fair market value of all property is determined when a residence is involved. Half of his/her share of the property (whoever dies first) goes to the spouse. Now the surviving spouse has a house with ½ fair market value from step up and value but ½ original cost. The living trust provides a unique solution of allowing a stepped-up basis for the whole house at this time.

- A will is an essential part of estate planning for large estates. You may not need a trust, but you do need a will. Both are best. You can get by with a living trust if the estate is simple and small.

- If you are thinking about setting up a living trust, use the opportunity to review all of your legal and investment documents, from fire insurance to pension, just to know where you are going and to understand what you have. Then buy a big safe to keep all important documents in. There was an article I read recently where somebody carried off the small safe a senior couple kept all their valuables in. Best safe is a huge gun safe on a small safe secured under a mat in a concrete-lined space under the closet carpet.

- It would be unusual for a person to review all of their documents during a financial planning session and not find a problem or something mistitled.

- Expect to pay at least $1,000 for a living trust-will combination from a reputable attorney.

- A trust can do more than manage money. It can be used as a vehicle for a durable health power of attorney for medical reasons. How about the non-resuscitate clause?

- The living trust, or revocable trust, or grantor trust, whatever you call it, is a living document that can be easily changed, which is why both trust and will should be reviewed every five years.

- Money gifted to a minor, who is a person less than 18 years old, must remain under guardianship until the person reaches the age of majority. That means the money is the property of the minor until he/she reaches 18 at which time, he/she can take complete control of the funds, unless they are under the control of a trust that can stretch it out a few years longer.

CHAPTER 31: APPLICATION EXERCISES

1. If you do not have a trust then you may want a Payable on Death (POD) statement at your banking institution to make sure you or your spouse can get into your bank account when needed.
    ____ True ____ False

2. A Q-tip trust allows the surviving spouse to receive all the income during life from assets that were assigned to other beneficiaries.
    ____ True ____ False

3. A living trust avoids probate because it provides for the disposition of assets outside the execution of the will. ____ True ____ False

4. A trust can only manage money and cannot be used as a durable health power of attorney for medical reasons. ____ True ____ False

5. You may not need a trust, but you do need a will. Both are best.
    ____ True ____ False

6. Living trusts are also called:
    ____ a.   Family Trusts
    ____ b.   Revocable Trusts
    ____ c.   Grantor Trusts
    ____ d.   Rabbi Trusts
    ____ e.   All of the above

7. A living trust creates powers of attorney for the surviving spouse to handle financial affairs while both parties are still alive.
    ____ True ____ False

8. Perhaps the most important aspects of the living trust are title deeds, bank accounts, and the investment portfolio assets under the trust umbrella. ____ True ____ False

9. Living trusts do not file tax returns until they come into force upon the death of the grantor (or co-grantor spouse) as a fiduciary 1041. At that time, the trust will file annual tax returns until all of the assets have been transferred to the living spouse or sold in a non-taxable situation. ____ True ____ False

10. Outside of a charitable trust that would irrevocably give control of assets to a recognized charity, there is little a trust can do on an annual tax basis that proper gifting cannot do. ____ True ____ False

CHAPTER THIRTY-TWO

FIDUCIARIES, EXECUTORS, WILLS, STATUTORY FEES, WILL SUBSTITUTES, GRANT DEEDS, TAX BASIS OF ASSETS, TITLING ASSETS, ANCILLARY PROBATE, REVERSE MORTGAGES

I am sure this is the hardest chapter in the book, because it is the most important. First, we need to define a fiduciary, which is an independent legal entity. An **Individual Taxpayer Identification Number (ITIN)** is required so the 1041 tax returns and K-1 forms can be filed. That number should be on all investments so the year-end forms are correct or the sale of a property is correct. The fiduciary is a conduit that may distribute income to a beneficiary, in which case the fiduciary is taxed on the remaining income, while the individual is taxed on non-taxed income received from the trust. No taxable income escapes the sharpened claws of the taxman.

Generally, there are two types of trusts; the first of which is the **irrevocable trust**, which is set up and funded while a person is alive or passed. The money placed into the trust is considered a gift from the corpus of the individual's estate and is accounted for inside the estate. For example, if a person had a million-dollar estate and gave half of it to fund a trust, the half-million would be considered a taxable gift and must be accounted for by filing a 709-gift tax return, which in turn relates to the remaining taxable future estate. A trust tax return is a fiduciary federal form 1041 that must be filed if the trust earns an income of $600 in a year or more.

The living trust is considered a simple **inter-vivos trust**, which is a conveyance of title or property made while the donor is living. This other fiduciary is a **revocable grantor trust**, which becomes a testamentary transfer upon death. That is, it is created as a document without power while the trustor is alive and exists only in the will (or living trust) until enforced upon the death of the creator. These are your living trusts, because they can be modified and changed while the creator is still alive. The grantor trust generally is tax-wise created at the death of a spouse, which leaves the control of the newly created trust under the control of the surviving spouse. The income earned by the survivor passes directly to the beneficiary for tax purposes, while the corpus or principal remains intact but now part of the remaining spouse's estate. Because all the income passes through to the surviving spouse, the fiduciary pays no taxes at all but the surviving spouse beneficiary pays taxes on the trust earnings, even if she or he does not receive it during the year. This is how a simple trust is created.

Any fiduciary other than the above would be a complex trust, which we will not discuss here because they are really complicated. The term fiduciary and trust are the same because "fiduciary" is a Latin word meaning trust (as "In God We Trust").

THE TAX TABLES FOR NONGRANTOR TRUSTS AND FIDUCIARIES FOR 2020 ARE:

Taxable income		% on + excess	Minus
$ -0-	$ 2,600	10%	$ -0-
2,601	9,450	24%	260
9,451	12,950	35%	1,904
12,751	And over	37%	3,129

The executor or executrix of an estate has the job of administering the will. An executor is a fiduciary, which is a person in a position of trust and confidence and who has the legal duty to act for the benefit of another as a personal representative. If the court appoints an executor (probate process from an intestate will or other problems), the executor is now the administrator, which means he/she reports to the court for his duties. The executor of your will need not be a family member; it can be an attorney or highly trusted individual. It should never be a family member who cannot be trusted to handle money, because there are sometimes terrible surprises in this most responsible area. An **alternate** individual should also be appointed in the will, in case the executor

predeceases the **testator** (creator and subject of the will). Because executors carry a large burden of responsibility, if the executor is not an officer of the court (a lawyer), a **surety bond** is usually required to ensure that the matters of the will are carried out properly. You do not need to see an old Alfred Hitchcock movie to know what people will do for money. Best, no matter what, that you never need to create a situation where the insurance bonding company comes into play, because before they payout, they say, "prove it is missing" and then, "sue us anyway."

The will is the central document of an estate. This true legal document is the focus of the entire estate. It must be properly signed and executed with copies held in the right places (remember the Howard Hughes problem of too many wills?). It can create testamentary trusts, distribute assets, set aside and allocate property, and give legal instructions to the probate court. It should include the contents of the estate, create clauses and provisions to pay taxes, lawyers and executors, prevent hang-ups that short out the **devisee** (heir) such as giving it all to a charity or the dog or cat that leads to **will contests** in court, etc. Dangerous mistakes, which should be dealt with before death, are those that lead to **ancillary probate.** This occurs when property, especially real estate, is located in another state that involves other state probate courts, tax returns, and new lawyers into focus to hang the estate up several years longer. An incorrect will causes the decedent to become **intestate,** that is to have no will at all, and matters are thrown into the **public jurisdiction** of the probate court judges.

If a married couple resides in a community property state, such as California, and there are many of these states now as English common law is modernized (except for the French State of Louisiana), no longer require a property to go into probate court if there is a surviving spouse. This simplifies the probate process unless there are headaches built into the will or out of state property.

A **will substitute** is property in a legal form which passes around the probate process, thus simplifying the estate settlement. These are deeds of title, **Joint Tenancy with Right of Survivorship (JTWROS)** in real or personal property, Joint Tenancy bank accounts, Payable on Death (POD) accounts which revert to another party on death, certain trusts, government savings bonds, life insurance proceeds, and living wills. There are many examples of individuals who married and forgot to change the title of the property or left bank accounts without the spouse's signature, thus leaving him/her without cash when it is needed the most. Insurance company beneficiaries also need to be reviewed, since most people outlive one or more marriages and children move away to follow the road to independence. Titling assets is a most important critical act that is one more reason you must have an attorney to handle these affairs.

The **tax basis** of inherited property is very important. The **step-up basis** is the **fair market value** at the time of death. This is the value used in the estate for estate tax purposes. But it is also the new cost figure (tax basis) for the heirs. Most important, though, is property jointly owned in a community property state. When the spouse dies, his/her half of the property is stepped up (or stepped down) in value. So, what happens to the other half of the surviving spouse? If the property deed is properly titled in both names as community property, then both halves, including the living spouse's half are stepped up. These matters are important because they provide the new cost basis for the property when sold or disposed of by the heirs.

Statutory fees are a great expense to an estate. They are allowable by the court and are automatically awarded without dispute for both the executor and the attorney. Because they are based on the gross amount of the estate, they can be enormous. The gross amount can include all property without regard to mortgages or liens, which means paying fees on liabilities. Having property not included in the estate, items gifted away previously or not requiring probate with living trusts, is a great saving device to keep the estate from getting devoured by legal fees.

These people, the attorney and the executor named in the will, will need to be paid in cash that is approved by the court as the probate proceeds. An executor can waive his fee, which is very important because it will become taxable income to him if he takes it. This also reduces the estate that can upset other family members in some cases. If the executor is also the prime heir of the estate, he could be converting tax-free inherited money to taxable monies by accepting the fees. Furthermore, all fees can be increased for additional extraordinary work. I know of one case where the attorney added a big lump because a residence was sold…even though the executor did all the work.

THE STATUTORY FEES APPROVED BY THE CALIFORNIA BAR ASSOCIATION ARE:

4% on the first $15,000
3% on the next $85,000
2% on the next $900,000
½% on the next $15,000,000
For all above $25,000,000 a reasonable amount to be determined by the court.

The fees are determined by the value of the estate accounted for by the personal representative is the total amount of the appraisal value of property in the inventory, plus gains over the appraisal value on sales, plus receipts, less losses from the appraisal value on sales, without reference to encumbrances or other obligations on estate property. Please note that if you loan of a million dollars against it, the fee is based on a million dollars.

There is a very concise listing of **California Probate Code Intestate Succession**. This list follows closest relatives to the deceased who didn't leave an estate. It ends with families of deceased children. That is how the Courts allocate assets by the law.

PLANNING TIPS

Living trusts and wills can be compiled with your own software, your own books, your own Internet connection, and the friendly person who will help you with them by filling in the blanks on his forms. What you really need is an attorney, because if these things were that simple and all boilerplate, then all humans on earth would look alike. What you need is a review of your personal financial and social situation and a competent professional to fit the pieces together in legal form. Financial advisors can tell you what works or not, and you can read books like this one, but somebody needs to review your needs in the legal sense and legitimatize the whole thing. The last thing you want, after your demise, is a will contest or probate to hang things up for years afterward because of mistakes or wrong intentions.

A fiduciary also can provide a legal signature to facilitate a sale of real estate after the owner has passed away. An attorney familiar with your affairs should supervise titling assets. I know of an elderly woman who changed the title to her home trust deed to include her sons. Several years later, one of the sons failed to file tax returns and pay his dues. The government, who peruses all property recordings as part of the collection process, promptly attached a lien to the property. When the property was sold later, after the lady passed away, the government took the amount owed, which was more than the son's share. The government has first lien priority over all other heirs on creditors.

Many senior citizens are outliving their savings and pensions but are no longer working. As we age, we don't want to move to lesser quarters with stress and different neighborhoods. Maybe the family doesn't want to take us in and privacy for all parties is a huge issue. Fortunately, the home is available not only as a source of equity but a place you can't afford. The solution is not a new loan because you lack the means to qualify or pay the new mortgage for it. What do you do, especially since our doctors and modern medicine keeps us alive so many years longer than in the past? In 1935 when Social Security started up as a fall back pension plan, the average person lived to be 48 years old. The full pension beginning date was based on you living to 65 to collect. That was 17 years after you statistically died. Ratchet forward and the numbers are reversed. The Bible implies that we will live to 70 and we are now exceeding that and Social Security which will soon begin paying pensions at 67 years. We will outlive all planned human obsolescence but survive with greater medical care and expenses than deemed possible. How do we recover our freedom and maintain a reserved but comfortable lifestyle?

The solution is simple. Because of the underlying economic inflation our property is usually worth more than we initially paid for it. If we were prudent and not refinancing and cashing out continually, there is a lot of equity or the place may even be paid off. After all, what a great investment it has been because we are paying for an appreciated property which cost less, with inflated dollars which are worth more. You are now ready for a reverse mortgage, not a mobile home with dogs and no lawn. A **reverse mortgage** a.k.a. **Home Equity Conversion Mortgage**, allows you to borrow against your home equity without making mortgage payments. You can, under certain terms, take money out to pay medical bills, get a new electric car, and visit the grandkids in the Ozarks on their annual vacation. The program was created by the **Federal Housing Authority (FHA)** and is a lifesaver for these times. The home value will also continue to appreciate as you continue residing in it over the years, while offsetting the forfeited mortgage payments. The math is beautiful. You will settle the mortgage only when you sell it or pass on. The only drawback is that the interest being credited against equity is not considered deductible by the IRS. But at 85 years old, it is unlikely you will ever need it with the over $10,000 standard deductions. Another great feature of this loan is that by not needing to move, your property taxes, which were based on your original purchase price, are stabilized and hopefully not marking to market with inflation. California Proposition 13 put a lid on leapfrogging real estate taxation by limiting the increases by 2% per year.

TAXES

All estates, unless insignificantly small, must file federal form 706 estate tax returns. The returns are sent to an IRS office in Atlanta, which is also a great place to live. The date of death is the focus of the estate tax returns. There is an interim period however, when investments and money in the estate will create income before distribution to the heirs. A fiduciary return, form 1041 is filed to account for taxable income before distribution to the heirs.

Like the estate, the fiduciary also requires an application for an identification number. This number alerts the IRS to look for the returns. Many banks have been filing ID applications for minor estates which are too small to file estate tax returns, thus creating filing problems for family members, especially when the savings accounts are left under the old taxpayer Social Security number. This causes the family to file a fiduciary tax return on income assigned to the deceased person's 1040 tax returns.

Lately, the IRS computers have been matching the fiduciary tax returns to the individual returns to assign the income properly. Yes, dead people file tax returns for their last partial year on earth. There have been instances where people have field for federal ID# numbers on living trusts which created huge problems for the owner.

All trusts, **irrevocable trusts** created during the life of the individual, and the grantor or other trusts created at death, must file 1041 fiduciary tax returns each year and pay any appropriate taxes before distributions, as directed in the will. A grantor trust will force the trust income back to the individual recipient's tax returns where the taxes are paid. Other trusts pay their own taxes. A trust is a legal entity and must be treated with caution. This is a complex area and expert legal and tax council is required but not always available at the proper time.

LEGAL COMPLIANCE

Stockbrokers and financial planners should not prepare wills or living trusts. They can advise you about aspects of your estate matters, but are not allowed to take money for giving legal advice. All stockbrokers (financial planners are also stockbrokers) must report all of their income from all sources to their supervising broker/dealer clearing firm, and receiving money for these activities would lead to termination.

Helping titling assets, reviewing all of the documents pertaining to your estate, and handling financial matters is within the domain of these financial people without selling legal advice. The Registered Financial Advisor will charge you for the time; the stockbroker will usually help as a professional courtesy as he sells you investments.

A financial person filed for a federal ID# for a living trust and somehow kept it alive until he passed. But they had also put his large pension under the trust instead of having it cashed in or willed to an heir. Accordingly, the broker-dealer would or could not change the ownership which resulted in the heir's inheritance going to the trust account, then taxed there, and finally not distributed back to the heir. Five years of useless 1041 tax returns were filed on a clerical error. Estate matters are so complex that many attorneys do not do a good job handling estate matters. The old saw applies, Jack of all trades is master of none. Remember the great movie Body Heat, where the lovely woman (Kathleen Turner) was smarter than the attorney, (William Hurt) who mishandled the will?

SUCCESSFUL STRATEGIES

The elderly woman died without immediate successors. This is a true story. While terminally ill at her apartment, she called on nearby cousins to take care of her, or at least visit, but they declined. Finally, she enlisted a woman friend at a nearby apartment to help as her incurable cancer continued its course. It was her decision to die at home, in the apartment where she, a retired secretary had lived a simple lifestyle for many years, because she had always independently determined her personal affairs. The trusty neighbor lady, who also had a disability, supported and helped her through the final stages when she was helpless and needy, until it was time to also administer the estate as the executrix.

The dying secretary had done her homework. She had gone to the library and researched all the books she could find on wills and estates. Then she had drafted a perfect **holographic will** four handwritten pages long, correctly witnessed and executed, newly listing her executrix neighbor, all of his/her assets which consisted of many hundreds of thousands of dollars in mutual funds, and the beneficiaries which were charities for homeless people in Los Angeles, and the Salvation Army. The executrix was surprised to learn the extent of the estate, which was barely small enough to escape estate taxes, because she and the cousins believed she (secretary) was impoverished from living so meagerly.

The little estate was probated for several years and the executrix was paid the unexpected statutory fee, which was considerable. There was also another gift for her kindness, the autographed picture of Rudolph Valentino, which had resided next to the secretary's bed for most of her life.

HORROR STORY - THE WILL

The will controls the testamentary trust, unless a trust is irrevocably created before death. That is the law. There can be no conflict between them. The tasks are joined as the will creates the flexible form while living, to create the fixed testamentary trust upon death.

The judge had a problem. One of his children, not the lawyer or daughter, but the handsome spoiled son, had a proclivity for gambling. There were always women hanging around him to help provide for his lifestyle as he gambled rather than work. The father (judge) tried to change his son's ways to no avail. Because he had worked very hard all his life, and created a large estate with his impeccable professional reputation, he did not want his son to waste it away gambling after he died, unless he could change his ways. He disowned the son who went his separate way. Therefore, the judge wrote into his will and large irrevocable trust that the son would not participate in the annual trust distribution, which was huge, unless he quit gambling and filed tax returns with real wages or employment. Otherwise, the documents read, the third portion would be split between the other son and daughter.

Year after year, the gambling son continued his ways, believing he was truly a "professional gambler". He worked the card games over the western state casinos while his wife worked hard to support him. The brother like his father, an attorney and the executor/trustee, and sister offered a hundred times to redistribute the third they received if only he could show that he, not his wife, had gainful employment.

Meanwhile, he continually pursued low-investment schemes to create income without work, always without results. Now in his early 50's, he continues without his legacy and I did not bother to return his last phone call for help from his brother administering the estate...

SECOND HORROR STORY - EXECUTRIX

When the single elderly doctor died, she left a considerable estate. The heirs were a large family consisting of her mature unsophisticated children to inherit her considerable wealth. The oldest daughter was the executrix and, like her sisters and brothers, was not used to handling money outside of her own modest living expenses. The daughter took charge of the checking and savings accounts, and reported directly, as required, to the attorney handling the estate. Then, she took a vacation overseas and began a shopping blitz.

Most states prudently require a bond to be purchased by larger estates to assure that the executor or executrix handles the matters in the best interest of all the heirs. One of the tenants of financial planning is to find a competent person to administer the will. In this case the attorney and doctor were dead wrong. Almost all of the money disappeared. The estate attorney looked the other way, as if that was the way things sometimes happen, without cause. He was incompetent himself, and lost his huge $40,000 statutory fee due to incompetently filing the estate tax returns.

Then, the heirs found out that the money was gone. Another attorney was hired to clear matters up. To make it harder, because the money was gone, there was a lack of money to pay the accountants to audit the banks and estate investments, and to pay new attorney's fees. Then the insurance company needed to be sued because the term "insurance bond" means, "sue me to collect" in insurance language.

The one thing the executrix did well was to make records disappear and convert money very cleverly, which left a lousy audit trail for my staff and the attorney. It took many years to settle and I do not know to this day how everyone made out.

PROS & CONS OF ALL THE ABOVE

- Will substitutes are an important part of planning. By having a co-signor on a bank account, properly titling assets to avoid probate (especially Joint Tenant with Right of Survivorship, JTWROS), and with life insurance policies, the many horrors of estate settlement can be avoided.

- Living Trusts also avoid probate although the above is part of the process as well.

- Out of state property, called ancillary property, can hang an estate up because each state will want a piece of the action. The solution is to sell it or give it to a member of the family to avoid hanging the estate up.

- Many states require a bond of the executor unless it is excluded in the will. This insurance bond must be renewed annually until the estate is settled. A probate estate, involved in litigation, or estate with the ancillary property will result in extra insurance invoices to be paid, especially if cash is short.

- Legal fees can be horrendous and hard to pay from an estate that may have a lot of real estate and little cash. If the property is encumbered, the gross estate will reflect only the amount of the property without regard for the liability, greatly increasing the amount of legal fees.

- An executor should consider waiving his fees, which can match the attorney's fees. By taking the expense money he is creating taxable income to himself while reducing his own estate distribution (especially if he is the primary beneficiary).

- A back-up or secondary executor should be considered for all wills because if both husband and wife or the executor predeceases the testator's choice, the will cannot be enforced without a probate action by the court (who will hang it up to find another executor).

- The executor should be a trusted person, preferably somebody who will not go mad at the sight of money.

- The estate and fiduciary process is involved and will require competent legal and financial counsel. Good luck!

CHAPTER 32: APPLICATION EXERCISES

1. A fiduciary does not have the power to sign legal documents to facilitate a sale of real estate after the owner has passed away.
   ____ True ____ False

2. A Fiduciary is an independent legal entity. ____ True ____ False

3. A back-up or secondary executor should be considered for all wills and trusts because if both husband and wife or the executor predeceases the testator's choice, the will cannot be enforced without a probate action by the court. ____ True ____ False

4. A reverse mortgage allows you to borrow against your home equity without making mortgage payments. ____ True ____ False

5. Because executors carry a large burden of responsibility, if the executor is not a lawyer a surety bond is usually required to ensure that the matters of the will are carried out properly. ____ True ____ False

6. If a married couple resides in a community property state, such as California, the state no longer requires a property to go into probate court if there is a surviving spouse. ____ True ____ False

7. If the executor is also the prime heir of the estate, he/she could be converting tax-free inherited money to taxable monies by accepting executor fees. ____ True ____ False

8. All irrevocable trusts created during the life of the individual, and the grantor or other trusts created at death, must file 1041 fiduciary tax returns each year and pay any appropriate taxes before distributions.
   ____ True ____ False

9. Out of state property, called ancillary property, can hang an estate up because each state will want a piece of the action. The solution is to sell it or gift it to a member of the family beforehand.
   ____ True ____ False

10. The estate and fiduciary process is involved and will require competent legal and financial counsel. ____ True ____ False

PART SEVEN
OTHER IMPORTANT FINANCIAL
CONSIDERATIONS

This is my favorite part, because it is where it all comes together. Therefore, "it is the beginning of the end," as Winston Churchill once said. A personal financial statement worksheet is provided so you can arrive at your net worth. Computer programs are available to help the more sophisticated individuals, while the rest of us do it the old-fashioned hard way…with a pencil and an eraser. Those of us who are recently divorced may wish to skip this section for hardship purposes, but it is really a good time to get it together again and see what is leftover.

Things to ponder will include Kiddie taxes especially for your minor children, Bankruptcies, FICO scores, how bad debts and collection agencies function, intestate succession, passport holds for past-due taxes, college savings 529 plans, and the SECURE ACT.

The rest of this section is to think about where we are going and how to get there. Not necessarily the usual death and taxes stuff, but practical considerations. "Why not give some of the estate to the grandkids before I die, instead of having the estate flow to the grown-up children who by then may also be retired?" Other issues are important as well, such as the practicality of a home mortgage when the deduction no longer saves taxes. It is a potpourri section without the dried flowers. The dominant theme is taxes again. After all, our complete legal existence is a tax event. Example: when we are born, we have created a tax exemption. When we die, we give it back.

CHAPTER THIRTY-THREE
BANKRUPTCIES, CREDIT SCORES, BAD DEBT, AUDITS, GOALS & ECONOMIC CONSIDERATIONS

Once, I met an old man in Bakersfield, California who was digging a bomb shelter under his house. This was in the mid-1960s after Khrushchev raised his fist at us and the Vietnam War was making mothers cry. Now, why would anybody want to nuke Bakersfield? Nobody who had ever been there, that is for sure. At least the new cellar-bomb shelter made a cool underground TV room for the man, because Bakersfield cooks at 115 degrees in the summer shade.

Recently, I ran into a fellow who has stocked his cave (food, water, gold coins, guns, and ammo) for the Grand Revolution coming up. He is convinced that society will come apart at the seams and he will be a fighting survivor. He is not of the Millennium group who believes the world will end for religious reasons, nor the Michel de Nostradamus and Edgar Cayce believers that the end is near. The fellow is a neighbor who is reflecting computer-induced panic.

Other computer panickers believe the monetary system will collapse and gold will be king again as the computer frustrated banks shut their doors. Better yet to worry about the panic on Wall Street, which could be a precipitation from the excess trading on Internet stocks or some other speculative calamity. The whole country of Holland went underwater financially because of tulip (yes, the flowers) speculation many years back. Be conservative and diversify by investing in the future, not the panic of the year.

Recently, the Scientific American Journal had an article about the multifractal geometric pattern that relates Wall Street performance to the patterns of galaxies. This use of quantitative mathematical modeling was considered more a positive predictor of market behavior than modern portfolio theory (which is assumed to mathematically predict stock market variations 95% of the time). This new theory appears to be the kind of boutique logic that led the hedge fund people to find winning and losing strategies in a new fashion. Remember that the market is driven by economic factors (war, economic expansion, contraction, changes in trade, weather, etc.) and emotional factors such as conservative or speculative motives. The prudent investor does not need a computer model to tell him what his economic expectations are if he is laid off his job, has a heart attack, or receives a big promotion.

About **FAIR, ISAAC, AND COMPANY (FICO) scores.** They are here whether or not you want them. The maximum Experian and other credit agency score is 850. All your financial activity, now including rents and utilities paid on time or not, is posted monthly on the payment due dates. Items benefitting your credit are length of installment loans and credit card applications to show stability and payment history. Offsetting the score are maxing out credit card limits, bad payment history, and legal matters.

A score above 620, the threshold line for subprime treatment, is usually required for an apartment lease while above 670 will buy you a car with a decent interest rate. A 740 score will reward you with the advertised favorable credit union interest rates and higher limits with no down payment auto loans. Above 800 is the best of all but the air is rarefied up there. Credit card companies also love the low risk scores and provide higher limits and usually better financing for balances (3-4% interest on advanced credit card limit on one-year loans.) Mortgages begin at 670 and the game begins. The bell curve on FICO scores parallel the intelligence of the general population with the bulk between 600 and 800.

A bankruptcy will cost you 35 points and live in the reports for ten years; However, the elements of the bankruptcy debt such as credit cards, installment loans, etc. will knock at least ten points off for each item and live on the credit report for exactly seven years. Different FICO scores are generated for different types of businesses, such as mortgage brokers, credit card banks, and auto loans. The FICO is like the moon, it is always there whether or not you can see it so you must always remember to take care of it. Being declined is an opportunity to get a free copy of the report that downed you. There is always an annual opportunity to obtain free credit reports from the three major agencies; Experian, Equifax, and TransUnion. Look up Free Credit Reports on Google and they will be there. Watch out for the people who want to be paid.

BANKRUPTCIES are a reorganization of your business or personal economic affairs by the Federal Bankruptcy Court under Title 11 of the US Code. The Court will document all your assets and liabilities with the help of your lawyer, and redistribute them, because your business has more liabilities than assets. The Court will assign a trustee, help arrange primary interim financing, generally control all affairs while creditors and their lawyers search for fraud, stashed, or misappropriated assets.

The first type of business bankruptcy is **CHAPTER 11 CORPORATE REORGANIZATION.** This requires debtor approval and results in complete control of the business by the Court and their trustees. Shareholders are first to lose everything while secured creditors can repossess the property and they will come out on top. Big corporate bankruptcies can find new primary lenders to carry them through the steps, especially if it is complex and drawn out (three to five-year terms to wind up affairs). These new lenders get first dibs on residual collections from the sale of assets and continuing business operations. Some corporations survive the restructuring and continue as ongoing businesses while others succumb to the rigors of business downfall or excessive debt. This is a good place to explain that all debt for taxes is at the top of the list to be paid. And on the top of the list are payroll taxes a.k.a. TRUST FUND taxes which result from employee withholding and related taxes. These are monies collected from individuals and not ever subjected to deletion or abolition by bankruptcy because they are held in trust for the government.

Chapter 13 is **INDIVIDUAL REORGANIZATION**, the equivalent of the above. It is a workout reorganization by the BK Court. The Court will allow three to five years to completely pay off debtors. Individuals are allowed to keep some assets, but all income and expenses are controlled by the trustee until completed. Only professional people with high income qualify for this treatment because they can cut living expenses, and not incur new ones, to equal things out. There are large trustee fees for maintenance as well. The **ABUSE PREVENTION AND CONSUMER PROTECTION ACT OF 2005** established new guidelines for means tests. The new disposable income test determines which Chapter the debtor belongs to.

Chapter 7 CORPORATE LIQUIDATION is for the business which is unable to pay its creditors. A trustee is appointed immediately on filing with broad powers to examine the business's financial affairs. If the business is slow to file, a creditor can initiate the filing on their own. Secured least risk creditors are paid first, shareholders of common stocks are paid last. A corporate case does not receive a BK discharge when the case is closed. This results in debts continuing to exist until statutory periods of limitations expire. In California, the Statute is good for four years.

Chapter 7 INDIVIDUAL BANKRUPTCY is a liquidation that has not passed the Chapter 13 means test. The trustee will sell all assets or return them to lienholders and pay debtors. An individual can usually reaffirm auto and mortgage liabilities by notifying the lender that he/she intends to continue making payments and has been diligent in the past. When the BK is finalized all involved parties are notified and a Fiduciary 1041 form is filed to close the matter. I have been in trials over bankruptcy proceedings where an ex-felon presented phony claims for liabilities and assets not existing (which is why the retired individual filed BK to get away from him). He and his unethical unscrupulous attorney would make the Democratic lawyers in Washington look like angels in comparison. A Chapter 7 or 13 BK is good for about 35 points off your FICO score for ten years until it vanishes from the credit reports. ALL the creditors listed in the BK, including credit cards and installment loans, are good for another negative ten points each for the seven years they will live in the credit reports. A person can always file for another bankruptcy in the future as well.

Bad debts that originate in California have a statutory four-year limitation from the last date billed. After four years, unscrupulous collection agencies will call and invite you coldly, without identifying themselves, to reaffirm the debt simply by admitting or answering that it was never paid. That resets the clock on payment and liability. Your mother was right, beware of strangers.

PLANNING TIPS

The old saw, buy low, sell high, does not work in practice. With the stock market at all-time highs, it appears that people are buying high so they can sell low later on. This is part of the human herding instinct that causes people to follow the crowd. A contrarian philosophy would be to buy low...what is low today, and sell high...what is selling high today. This appears to work for short-term bonds that have low-interest rates but are safe and many industrials or commodities that would be affected by the world slowdown.

TAXES

Tax planning is an individual function of personal finances. It would be prudent for a high-income taxpayer to sell losing stocks or other investments near year-end to pick up capital losses to offset other gains or the $3,000 other income offset. Be careful to wait at least a month to repurchase the same stock to avoid the wash-sale IRS rules that negate the trading activity as a tax sham.

Penalties for failing to take the **Required Minimum Distribution (RMD)** from a pension are 50% of the required distribution. This is designed to force people to move taxable funds from longer-term tax havens, whether retirees need it or not. The distribution age used to start at 70 1/2 but has been moved up to 72 effective for accounts beginning 01-01-2020. The penalty can be abated by appealing that elderly symptoms of forgetfulness, dementia, or general health caused the delays.

The **Setting Every Community Up for Retirement Enhancement (SECURE) Act** of 2019 made many changes. This act also extends IRA contributions after age 70 as long as there is earned income to qualify. The last item of the act is to change inheritance rules for Stretch IRAs which were IRAs that were to go to family, including children. Before,

IRAs could also be passed to trusts, spouses, and other beneficiaries. The new law clarifies that instead of beneficiaries benefiting from the tax advantages all their lives until age 72, they now have ten years to empty the account. Spouses are exempted from the ten-year rule and can roll over the other's IRA. Naturally, there is a laundry list of exemptions.

Another bit of planning is to contribute money to the **529 COLLEGE SAVINGS PLAN**. This acts like a ROTH IRA whereas the account does not create a tax exemption but the earnings are not taxable when qualified. A 529 can be contributed as a tax-free gift at the rate of the annual gift tax exclusion which is $15,000 annually at this time. Both spouses can contribute and it can go to children and grandchildren. It can also be front-loaded with five years contributions to jumpstart the account which would be $75,000 each kid from each spouse. These accounts are malleable and beneficiary students can be added or substituted. A gift tax return 709 is required because it is a reduction of the taxable estate.

There is a federal agency called **Financial Crimes Enforcement Network (FINCEN)**, an agency for financial matters which reports to the Treasury. After everybody looked the other way in September 2000 and the Twin Towers were smashed by terrorists, the government created money-laundering acts, mostly under the **Patriot Act**. This act was supposed to expose money laundering by having banks and other financial institutions report cash transactions of $10,000 or more. The person behind the teller window is supposed to help file a secret **SUSPICIOUS ACTIVITY REPORT (SAR)** directly to the Treasury. Uniquely, the bank client is not supposed to be advised at all and it is kept secret. Now, I have never heard of terrorists laundering money but we know the drug people and some business people do it. To make a long story short, I was on an IRS audit and the auditor asked about a $13,000 check the client had cashed. Yes, it turned out to be unreported income but the auditor was holding the highly confidential SAR report and a check photocopy, which had gone from the bank to the audit departments.

California has a special deal for **Net Operating Business Losses (NOL** for short), on your tax returns. You cannot carry them back for any years (the IRS will give you three) and it can be carried forward only to offset other earnings for only twenty more. The IRS will allow indefinite carryforwards.

California generally allows tax debt four years old to wash out in bankruptcy unless it is payroll tax money Trust Account debt. The IRS will do the same.

California's unpaid taxes will vanish off your ledger after 20 years, which is hard to outlive for some folks. The feds only keep it for ten years. Because of the Federal limit, we keep copies of tax returns and software on our computer for only ten years. Then we wash out all other copies because they become a liability in the computer for cyber theft. We also keep only the last four years of hard copy tax returns and client documents before we thoroughly micro-shred them for recycling (I have bad memories of the young Iranian women spreading out the shredded US Embassy documents on a big table). If you have refunds, you will receive them for only the last three calendar years. Four years or older refunds from amended returns go back to the treasuries. You will receive a thank you letter for the contribution which reminds of the statute of refunds limits. There is a three-year audit window for timely filed tax returns, which can be extended if the returns are fraudulent. Returns are required to be timely filed every year unless there is no taxable income.

The mysterious number on the Business tax returns, in response to "What kind of business activity is it?" is the Standard Industrial Classification, **SIC** from the US Department of Labor. This is the federal classification of work performed and is also used by insurance companies for Workmen's Compensation and many other needs. I once carried the little brown book around when I wrote business credit reports for Dun & Bradstreet. Uniquely, as expected, California has its own set of business codes as if tossing hamburgers deserves different classification than the Federal.

If you owe the IRS over $52,000 including penalties and interest, the IRS will send correspondence memo **CP 508C** to the Secretary of State, SOS. This is a notice to keep you from boarding the next ship or plane before settling accounts. That is not a huge number because a tax liability of $25,000 with penalties and interest can easily double in a few years.

Mutual funds also pose a tax angle, because internal trading gains are taxed each year to the shareholder, while losses are not recognized. Moving funds within the family of funds would create a sale and recognition of the stored losses. The wash-sale rules would not apply here, and the funds can move back, without commission expense, at any time.

Ongoing limited partnership losses cannot be recognized if passive income offsets are not available. At the end of the deal, when the final **K-1** form is filed, the losses that have accumulated over the years as passive losses in the individual tax returns can be finally expensed. Limited partners have no control over the activities of the partnership, but if a losing L/P is kept alive after the economic activity has slowed down, then it would be a good idea to bug the sales rep or people who sold the deal to you to remind them to shut it down for tax purposes.

Taxable income is another story. Installment sales make better sense than taking cash up front to close real estate or other tangible property deals. They will earn more money for you by deferring taxable gains, while creating an annuity with high, secured interest rates.

Rental real estate stores cause opposing problems. Rental losses accumulate from year to year if taxable income is over $150,000 while the accumulated depreciation that caused the losses becomes an opposite offset by reducing the basis when the property is sold. Clients are always surprised by the results, especially when they believe the cash from the sale is somehow taxable income. Best to keep these items in mind when selling a rental property because, with appreciation, deferred taxes appreciate as well.

There are thousands of different tax strategies, all dependent on the individual's tax and investment situation.

Last, but not least, from the Far Side Country of California. The new **AB 90 Loophole Closure** and **Small Business and Working Franchise**

Tax Relief Act of 2019, a.k.a. **LCSBWFTPA**, has passed. Nobody knows what it does because they cannot remember the name or acronym.

AUDITS

In both business and personal life, you must always be aware of the machinations of others, especially the armies employed to tax and take your hard-earned money. Always be diligent and defensible with your personal affairs and especially aware of what other people will do to you. Be scrupulous of the documents which today will bury you with computerized boilerplate and legalese. Think like a lawyer. Trust nobody. A holographic handwritten will is only half as valid as a written one but both would be suspects by the law. Be the law yourself and think like a lawyer when you conduct business affairs. In my first book, *American Independent Business*, the theme was to survive and defend the business, not to get rich. Everybody, especially the tax collector, is trying to extract your wealth in a million ways.

I received the new County real estate tax statement on a home I bought and saw the value being taxed was $50,000 more than I paid for the house. With a 2% annual tax levy that was a phony invoice for a thousand dollars a year as long as I lived there. I appealed and met the fools at the County by mail and phone. Appealed again to the next level. Finally, a year later they had to show them their job and won hands down. Be aware of all agencies and collectors for the King.

It seems the best employment must be with government agencies because I have only one employee but received an audit invitation recently from the California Employment Development, EDD people. They must have assumed I had dozens of people working out of their houses to handle my few accounts and was avoiding payroll taxes on the lot. The two auditors interrupted us for two weeks during our busiest time. They went through three years analyzing every entry and activity of my little business. Finally, I got their $10,000 bill in the mail. This would have paid their wages and overhead but they wouldn't answer my question, "Who sicced you on me?" Naturally, being a Scottish-English lion, I appealed and we started going round and round, item by item, document by document, to refute their outrageous bill. Wait, *Cook* for $5, is a magazine, not an off-record employee, was a typical item. For six months they recomputed and I re-appealed until the bill was down to a grand from my only employee working out of her house reconstructing records independently on a big tax fraud case. I could have appealed that one further, but they had worn me down and I had to give something to escape their claws. Later they commented that they never saw such detailed documentation but still wouldn't answer my question, "Who sicced you on me?" They were used to wearing people down and terrifying them into submission with outrageous claims.

Most audits are the result of the IRS, after receiving billions of computerized documents, comparing their data with your filed tax returns. Unless of course, you haven't filed, which is another serious matter. The material is sorted into separate computer categories. The first category is the **CP-XXX Communication Proposal** information letter, which tells the taxpayer that a difference has been found between filed return data and the computerized summary data in your IRS file. This letter will show a comparison with the tax return and a source document describing the missing income statement. The letter also computes a new liability tax due figure in case you do not respond. You are notified that you have 30 days to respond to the letter. If they are correct that you have missed some income or misstated some income then there is no need to respond. They will automatically send a determination letter showing the amount owed, penalties if any, and interest from April 15th of the tax year in question.

Your new CP letter will give you 20 days to pay. **Form 9465 Installment Agreement Request** can be filed, and they also take credit cards. A **form 843 Claim for Refund and Request for Abatement** can be filed to eliminate penalties, but not interest, for certain excuses. If you owe more than $10,000 but do not pay, the government will file **Tax Liens** on bank accounts and real estate. The installment Direct Debit (monthly payments directly from your bank account) agreement will halt the lien process at IRS but you need to file **form 12277** to shut down the legal process at the County level. If you owe more than $50,000 the IRS will request financial information from you to process an installment agreement. Lastly, a **form 4905 Offer in Compromise** is required with all your **financial data Forms 433A or F** to cut the amount of principal tax liabilities and penalties. The offer is a very time-consuming process and many misleading false ads have appeared offering false hope. They can be effective if done correctly and within strict guidelines of income vs expectations. All IRS collection agreements can extend out to six years.

If you feel they are wrong then you should immediately send a copy of the letter back with your response and documentation. **Transcripts** of your reported income or tax returns can be filed by contacting IRS.gov and finding the correct tab. You might call the 800-number provided to talk to an IRS person on the correspondence document but the hours-long wait on the phone to talk to someone who knows nothing about your problem is questionable. This person, if you can get through, can abate penalties over the phone if you agree to the assessment. The best person to contact is your tax preparer. He will request a **form 2848 Power of Attorney** for each of you and your spouse. If the IRS follow-up determination response letter disagrees with your information or you feel they are wrong, you have two remaining options. One is to file **form 911 Taxpayer Advocate** to explain to an outside party why you disagree. The other is to file a **Tax Court Petition** pro per (but this is usually for formal audit situations). To represent a taxpayer in any situation only Enrolled Agents of the Treasury, CPAs, and attorneys with the POA can represent you.

Always remember that all income filed into the IRS computer is considered taxable income. Therefore, any item missed or for a return not filed is taxed until you advise them otherwise or file the missing returns. Then, there is the other CP letter advising if you are being audited. This letter will give the year being audited (usually the middle year of the last three years that can be audited), the auditor's name, phone number, and the place of the audit. On the subsequent pages, they will detail the items they are looking at. This is a very specific detailed event which is better than in the past where they would audit every item in a business Schedule C or whatever page they were on. You must call the auditor to set a time and date. If you ignore the letter, you will get all kinds of mail advising you of your disallowed deductions and collection activities. There are two kinds of audits, however. The first was the old-fashioned face to face human audit. The other audit usually asks you to send your documents to the Holtsville, New York Regional office of IRS where someone unknown will review your response. The results were awful, but I do see an improvement where they can actually be reached on phone and will hold the audit open for further documents. You have the right of appeal within the audit office where the supervisor is required to review the audit on your written request. Beware though, that this is the same person who approved and signed off on the audit so the results are predictably poor.

If you have had bad results on either type of audit then you will receive a **90 Day Letter** which advises you to file a petition (not a form) in the **US Federal Tax Court** in Washington, DC by the date indicated. This is now in the realm of serious business, and a filing fee and registered mail will get it there. I have been in the Tax Court six times very successfully but also very well prepared. The tax court provides mediation one-on-one meetings to resolve tax issues to avoid a trial. They actually want to avoid a trial because of uncertain results and not to clog up the courts. This is the ultimate hearing and is always a pro per case unless it is truly large enough to pay for huge attorney fees. The mediators are the best and most experienced of the IRS tax audit staff, and I have always had good results with their handling of the cases. A statement from a mediator, "We like to resolve our cases to avoid the hazards and delays of court trial litigation." You will always, in audit or Federal Tax Court cases, be able to pick a venue nearest your residence. It always pays to have a good chance of winning and an experienced tax professional would not take on a frivolous or unreasonable case.

In past years, because of the IRS's poor computer software applications, the taxpayer would be required to bring audit year tax returns and returns from the prior and later years to the audit. That was because only the audit year was on the auditor's computer screen. Now, because of intensive worthwhile computer upgrades, all three years lie side by side on the auditor's new wide computer screen so the auditor can compare and review other activities (and audit all three years if profitable). At the end of the IRS audit, the auditor will advise the taxpayer/Enrolled Agent that if documentation during the audit was missing there will be an opportunity to hold the audit open further and that additional data can be submitted by mail. The two audit rules are, "no documentation equals no deduction, and that all business expenses must be reasonable and necessary." If the audit is reasonably concluded, the auditor will hit the print button on his/her computer and leave to go to the document printing room. Now is time for discussion with the client before the presentation of audit results.

It is important to know if the client wants to conclude the audit or appeal. The auditor will reappear with the printed documents, cite the bottom line, and ask for a signature and a check to conclude. The auditor really wants to get the thing off the desk for good at this critical moment. This is the time for the Enrolled Agent to ask the auditor to abate the penalties, if any, for a quick signature and conclusion. Most auditors will agree (unless they are retired Marine Corps Sergeants, hate the audited person because he/she gave the auditor a hard time, or is near retirement, etc.). The auditor is not empowered to waive interest charges. Wait for a bill in the mail, otherwise instead of writing the check, go through the steps for an appeal or Tax Court.

Examples of **Offers in Compromise** were two actual cases which went different ways. The first was a client who had experienced hardship from being out of work after the 2008 Great New Recession. We submitted an OIC for the elderly truck driver when he was back on his feet and working a lot of overtime. He owed substantial life-threatening taxes, penalties, and interest from not filing many years earlier. After several months, I received a call from the IRS at the Laguna Nigel pyramid building in California. The IRS agent informed me that the client didn't qualify for the deal due to income disqualifications. After asking for the details, I found that the overtime element of the client's wages had disqualified him for the terms we were seeking. The agent was nice enough to give me another day to contact my client who would update her on the situation. I called the client, who had recently cut back his overtime for health reasons; his wife immediately called the agent at IRS, informing her of the changes in financial status and the application was promptly approved. Afterwards, they were able to buy a small retirement dream home for life.

The other case was a brash outspoken online college instructor. He had severe tax problems from being out of work and couldn't get caught up. We did the OIC and several months later the phone rang. The IRS agent wanted to close the case as unqualified. I was able to squeeze the problem details from the reluctant IRS agent. Then the agent advised me to appeal and shut the case down, disapproved. He would not give the client a break to get back to save or review his application. I notified the client who contacted the agent without success the next day. The client decided to do his own appeal in the following month allowed. He lost. A difference in IRS personnel proved the real difference in both cases; although, the client should have retained me to try and turn it around. At least an appeal always gets to a better-qualified person. My motto is to always appeal.

For those most unfortunate to never show up for an audit and who have missed the Tax Court deadline, there is the Audit Reconsideration process. Using **form 12661 Disputed Issue Verification**, attach relevant documents, a letter explaining why you didn't appear at the audit, and a copy of the audit correspondence (so they can locate you in the computer). Be sure to detail why the enclosed materials are pertinent to the audit results. A month later, you will receive a letter stating that they received the documents and will get back to you. Then it may move across the country and you might receive several more letters over the next six months to a year until it is close for a regional auditor to contact you. That was for a difficult case, but simple cases are handled by correspondence and can still take six months to a year to be reviewed and settled without any human to human contact. In 2020 the current rate of interest is determined on a quarterly basis. For taxpayers the overpayment and underpayment rate is the federal short-term rate plus 3%.

I have been on hundreds of audits including six Tax Court Cases. I believed I won all the Tax Court cases firstly, because I had something winnable and secondly, because I met eyeball to eyeball with another entity to work the details out. The other cases were mostly from people who liked to do their own taxes and ended up losing their own audits. There are many stories here but the book must end somewhere. Yes, I did attend an audit for a client who passed away after he signed a Power of Attorney. The auditor, over the phone, wouldn't dismiss the audit, so I went to represent the client (or his estate) and it was settled. Death does not free us from our tax obligations. Of the last six recent IRS audits, I had over 50% no change audits.

LEGAL COMPLIANCE

Broker sales-rep fraud is a large problem, both for the broker-dealer firm and for the investors. During branch audits, the parent broker-dealer firm reviews the personal bank accounts of the audited firm or individual to be sure client funds do not get deposited. Investor money must never go anywhere outside the broker-dealer firm or directly to the investment. The sales rep can't receive cash or money orders, and that checks should be made out to him/her, or his/her branch business name, outside of the parent broker-dealer firm. The exceptions are for Registered Financial Advisors (still no cash) who manage funds and are independently responsible and audited by their state and SEC, because they are legally acting as a broker-dealer in a sense.

The other danger of sales-rep fraud is selling-away, which is investing your money in an investment not approved by the broker-dealer firm. This is very dangerous for the investor, because the deal can be selling snowballs to Eskimos and nobody of authority is reviewing the deal.

The final area of caution is discretionary trading. For this, you must really love your sales-rep, because you are placing your money in his/her control to do as he/she sees. The only control you have over his activities if you are this trusting, is to review cash balances and match cost and sales trades to see if he/she is churning the stocks for commissions. If you are not sophisticated enough to follow through, have a trusted person look out for you.

SUCCESSFUL STRATEGIES

Some people have so much integrity that they would exhibit a golden halo if one could be seen. I was fortunate enough to have such a client. This fellow, together with his family, operated a small construction company in town. Then, he decided to retire and leave the desert for a cooler northern state where the trees grew without a monthly water bill. The laid-back fellow, whose role model is the virtuous John Wayne, always followed a simple life, completely obtuse to the material desires of most consumer-oriented Americans. When he and his family retired, he was only forty years old, and planned to live forever on his savings and proceeds from selling the small construction business. Then, several years later, the baby granddaughter got sick and did not improve.

The family traveled back again to stay at the child's bedside, taking turns to watch and give support every minute of every day for over a month. Finally, the child recovered and a lifestyle change occurred again for the family who then decided to buy the business back from the new owners who were not as successful as he had been. They dug in and grew the business again, happy to be closer to their family, and extended family that grew into the business as well.

This conservative non-sophisticated client owns dividend-rich mutual funds in his corporation, to avoid taxes on surplus cash earnings. His personal portfolio receives an insurance annuity pension monthly check from the business, since he has retired again. He has extensive cash, real estate, and tax-free mutual funds. His savings still grows, because he has always been able to pay cash for everything and has no liabilities except for some investment real estate mortgages.

He can still be seen at the office or shop, a guy who looks like John Wayne without the hat or gun. The office is saturated with John Wayne pictures and memorabilia, and the granddaughter, who recently married, will promptly pick up the phone if you call.

HORROR STORY - REALTOR

The fellow was articulate, well dressed, and spoke professionally about real estate investments. He would procure foreclosed houses through his special connections with various lenders, and everybody would make tons of money. He was very convincing, many people invested money, some of them thousands of dollars in small bills from lifelong savings, and the fellow proceeded to buy properties by the dozen. The game plan was buying foreclosed properties to rent the highly leveraged (mortgaged) properties for several years as they appreciated and when the local slow real estate market improved, he would sell them at a huge profit since they were bought cheap, to begin with. After the deal warmed up, his contractor friend was hired for a handsome salary to manage the properties, which all needed repairs to be rented out.

Flaws began to show up in the plan, almost from the beginning. **Comps,** the market evaluation of the properties compared to other properties, somehow failed to arrive after much-heated verbalization. The next was that the highly paid maintenance and leasing manager always needed more money for extensive repairs. Later, there was the death wish Christmas card received by the realtor from one of his former clients. The minor repair list grew as leaking roofs needed complete replacement, tenants quit paying rent and had to be evicted, while the investor's cash flow gushed outward until it dried up.

Finally, the day of reckoning arrived with the properties all placed for sale with a broker while the realtor, who talked and performed like a real politician, disappeared into the sunset for his next bad deal. All of the properties, except one foreclosure and another for a very small profit, were sold at a loss, because they were bought wrong…above market, in the beginning. Then the truth came out; that he had bought all of the troubled properties for above market prices without proper appraisal from a secondary real estate lender who had foreclosed on them. He took their trashy garbage properties off their hands at premium prices. Only a small amount of the investor money was ever returned.

Some people, like the above realtor, can talk up a great show while presenting a lucid game plan of perfect economic intentions, but are incapable of prudent action after they get their deal together. Unfortunately, these dangerous people are not usually discovered until the investment is already moving ahead to its doom. He is probably moved to Washington now to follow his calling.

SECOND HORROR STORY - INCARCERATION

Most people have an opportunity for jail time. It can be drag racing as a teen-ager, speeding, theft, fraud, assault, drunken driving with injuries, family violence, tax evasion, murder, or the many unsociable things people can do to others. On the business side of the coin, there is a requirement that tax returns must be completed before being locked up. I can't imagine what the punishment would be if they were not completed (maybe the criminal-to-be can't afford to pay for it) or maybe they would be let him/her free for incomplete paperwork (no way, Jose). The other requirement is that fines, levies, and making victims whole again can require restitution from someone who has just mortgaged his house to pay for a criminal lawyer. This usually leads to a jailhouse bankruptcy to clear the slate. The US Bankruptcy Code provides forms and instructions online for this event. I imagine that a person writing a best-selling book afterward about the crime would probably get to keep the proceeds, although O. J. Simpson had repercussions from his civil suit (and his publisher).

Being in jail is not good and can ruin your life, even if you get out afterward. I visited a client once in the old Riverside County courthouse jail. We emptied our pockets first and weren't allowed to carry anything in, except for the guy carrying the stack of Bibles, and I'm sure those weren't the Gideon Bibles for travelers. Then there was the window of one-inch thick glass and a telephone receiver next to it. The reception was awful. "That's because they're taping the conversation for evidence," my client reported. Sure enough, later they introduced a tape of his wife's visit when he threatened her over the phone. My murderous client was attempting to sell his business and all financial statement documents needed to be unbound and loose (spiral binders are used for prison murders and worse)... It was just an awful experience for all involved. Especially because being in the dungeon, even for securities exam fingerprints, leaves one with the cold taste of being treated like the guys on the other side of the bars. After all, we are all equal.

Sometimes the tables get turned, and you can visit the place without an invitation, like Johnny Cash. One evening a friend, who had been in a fight with his unhappy spouse, arrived on my doorstep. He had huge scratches on his left cheek which were turning from blood red to black, from his spouse plowing his face with four nicely manicured colored nails. I received a call from this distressed spouse as the victim was drowning his sorrow with vodka. She was blaming him for causing the event. Then she announced that she was going to call the police. "Lady, please don't," I advised as a neutral friend of both parties. Ten minutes later, as the now unsober, unhappy, almost innocent spouse was backing out of my driveway, a police car pulled up blocking the way. Inside they made their notes in response to her call. "How did you get the injury to your face," an officer asked the intoxicated victim. After a collective moment, he responded that his spouse did it and that is why he left home. The officers made more notes, then left. I convinced him to stay in my house until he sobered up. Later as he was sleeping, the phone rang and it was his wife calling from the County Jail where they had given her a new number and a place to stay on assault charges. He went home to his children and later to a bond broker.

THE FINAL HORROR STORY - GERMAN RESTAURANTEUR

An elderly man of German origin owned and managed a German Food Restaurant with two senior Deutsch affluent women. Every town and city has a German Restaurant because where else can you get a Wiener schnitzel on rye? The restaurant was in an older part of town and declining as new housing was all out of town where the shopping centers sprung up. The restaurant did well to keep the owners fed, if not economically well nourished. These hardy people would never retire or give up their lifelong self-employment.

The man would visit our office monthly with his financial work and talk about the Good Old Days and when he was a pilot on a Fokker Bi-winged fabric plane during the Great World War, which was named because it was the first war that encompassed the whole world. He was flying over No Man's Land and the trenches when a British plane came out of nowhere with the pilot spraying his plane until the Lewis machine gun emptied. His machine gunner in front of him in the open cockpit was killed along with the engine. The restaurateur was shot through the legs and managed to glide the plane to a landing. He was in the British sector and whisked off to a field hospital and later to a concentration camp in England until the war ended. There he quickly learned some English and a desire to go to the U.S. after the war, which he did.

This elderly man, now in his eighties, showed me the scars on his legs and was very contented, surviving the war and being in America with his little business and a bit of Germany. His future was the business and he never planned retirement, as people do today, as long as he was alive. He spoke very little of his personal life, a wife if there ever was one, and may have been living in the business location. He never had a bad word to say.

One day a female associate visited with the news. "He was killed by a hit and run driver outside the business last night, " she sorrowfully said, pausing for tears. After a lifelong struggle through a World War and economic survival in the wrong side of town, he was suddenly gone with an unnatural death. The Deutsch Fraus would keep the declining business going for another year before closing.

The message here is that planning for both your physical and economic future will avoid many things, but there is always the unknown factor which is simply an unexpected demise. The unseen fighter plane that takes you away unexpectedly.

PROS & CONS ABOUT THE ABOVE CONSIDERATIONS

- Sometimes, the best deals can be flawed, and there is no way to know until problems flow from it. Even the best intending people, with the help of your money, can turn out to be fools.
- Integrity is the most important asset or tool for operating a business. A business is the biggest investment a person can have.
- Never give cash to an investment rep. The same goes that any checks should be made out directly to the investment or broker-dealer firm (usually a corporation).

- Keeping out of debt is the best investment that can be made. Interest payments are "spending the seed corn of investment".

- High risk and speculation can promise great above-average returns... or great losses.

- Trust nobody. One of my tax clients came to me after his tax preparer phonied many tax returns and had the refund go to his bank account. After the preparer got out of prison, he called his old clients back for another round.

CHAPTER 33: APPLICATION EXERCISES

1. Chapter 11 Corporate Reorganization is a type of business bankruptcy that requires debtor approval and results in complete control of the business by the Court and their trustees. ____ True ____ False

2. The maximum Experian and other credit agency score is 800. ____ True ____ False

3. Most audits are the result of the IRS comparing their audited data with your filed tax returns. ____ True ____ False

4. Keeping out of debt is the best investment that can be made. ____ True ____ False

5. A bankruptcy will cost you up to 35 points on your FICO score and live in the reports for ten years. ____ True ____ False

6. Different FICO scores are generated for different types of businesses, such as mortgage brokers, credit card banks, and auto loans. ____ True ____ False

7. Penalties for failing to take the Required Minimum Distribution (RMD) from a pension at age 72+ are 50% of the required distribution, which is designed to force people to move taxable funds from pensions. ____ True ____ False

8. The Setting Every Community Up for Retirement Enhancement (SECURE) Act of 2019 extends IRA contributions after age 70 as long as there is earned income to qualify. ____ True ____ False

9. Both the IRS and California will generally allow tax debt four years old to wash out in bankruptcy, unless it is payroll tax trust account debt. ____ True ____ False

10. If you owe the IRS over $52,000 including penalties and interest, the IRS will send correspondence memo CP 508C to the Secretary of State. The State Department may revoke your passport to keep you from boarding the next ship or plane before settling accounts. ____ True ____ False

PICTURE APPENDICES

APPENDIX A: STOCK CERTIFICATES

APPENDIX B: GERMAN CURRENCY

APPENDIX C: BONDS

The following photos are from the author's personal collection of stock certificates, currency, and bonds.

APPENDIX A

STOCK CERTIFICATES

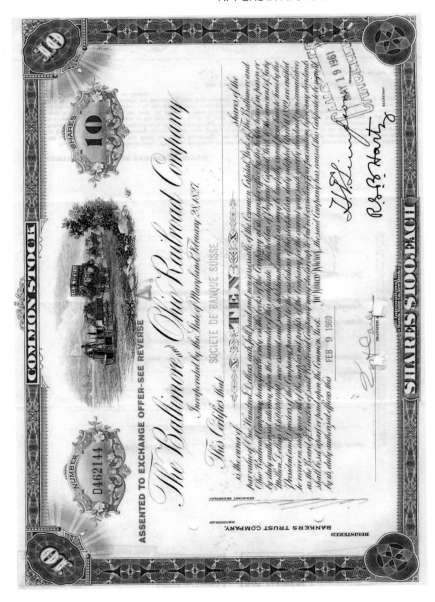

Image 1: Stock certificate for the Baltimore and Ohio Railroad Company previously owned by a Swiss bank issued 1960.

Image 1: Back side

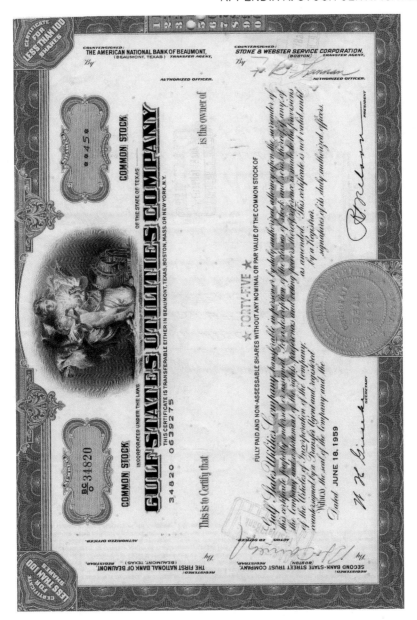

Image 2: Stock certificate for Gulf States Utilities Company issued 1959.

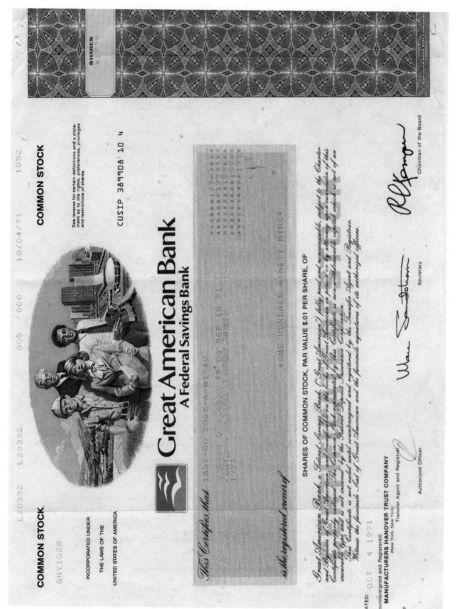

Image 3: Great American Bank stock certificate issued 1991.

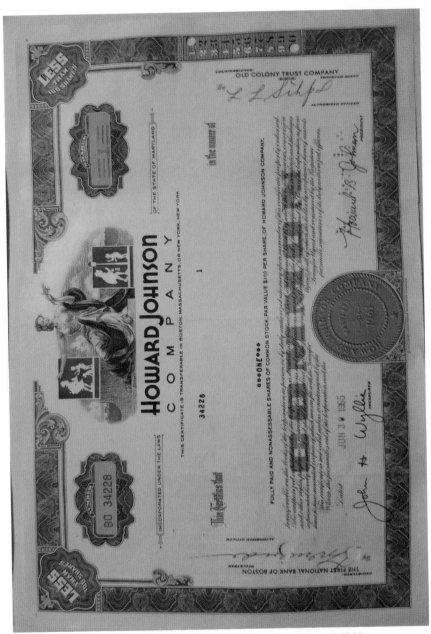

Image 4: Howard Johnson common stock certificate issued 1965.

Image 5: On the book cover. Pan American World Airways, Inc stock certificate issued 1976.

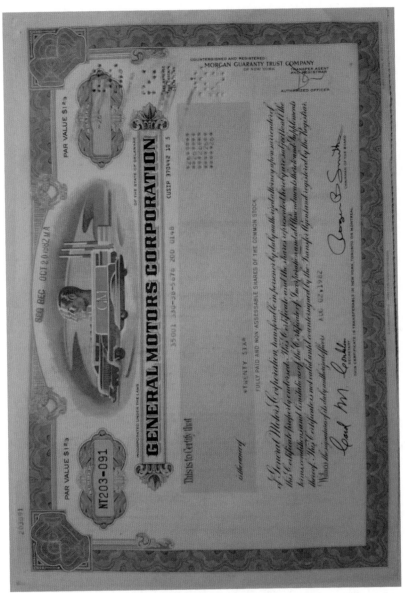

Image 6: On the Cover. General Motors Corporation stock certificate issued 1982.

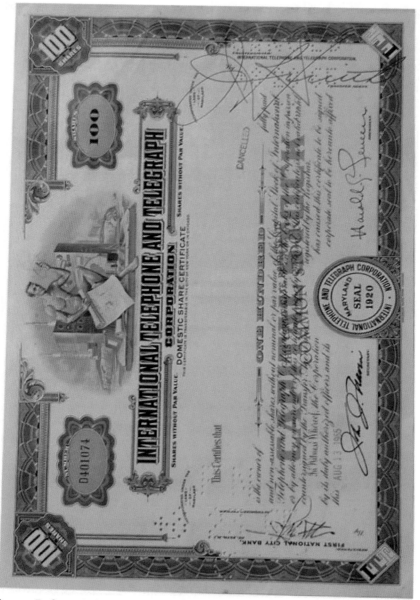

Image 7: Canceled stock certificate for International Telephone and Telegraph issued 1965.

Image 8: Standard Brands Paint Company stock certificate issued 1972.

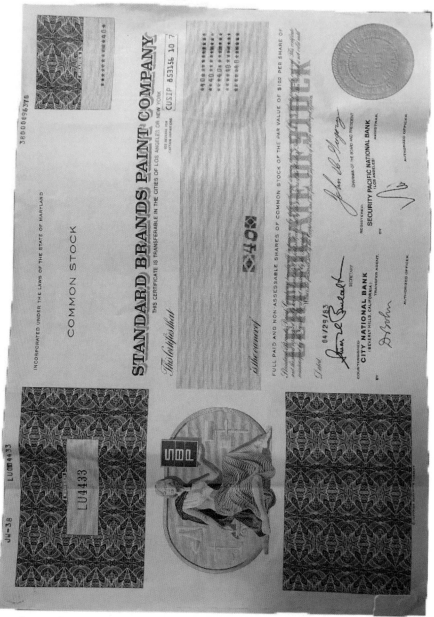

Image 9: Standard Brands Paint Company stock certificate issued 1983.

APPENDIX B

GERMAN CURRENCY

Image 10: 50-million-German mark bill WW 1 Repatriations Debt Financial Collapse of 1923.

Image 11: Front and Back of 1908 100-German mark bill.

APPENDIX C

BONDS

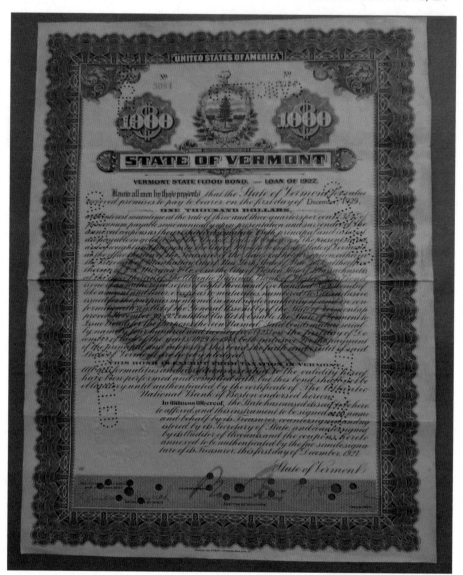

Image 12: Vermont State Gold Flood Bond $1,000 loan of 1927 paying 3 3/4% interest.

Image 13: Louisiana State Port Commission $1000 Serial Gold Bond issue of 1914 paying 5% interest.

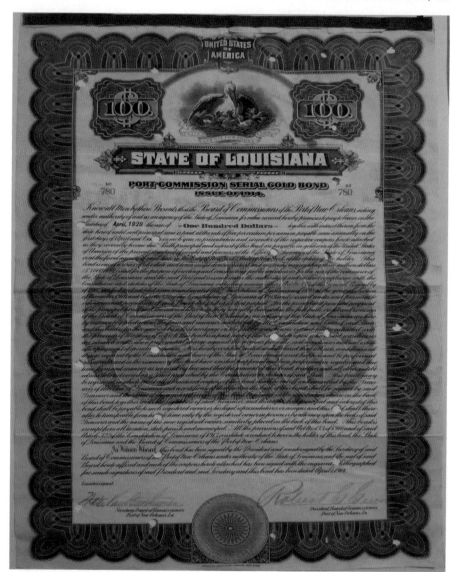

Image 14: Louisiana Port Commission $100 Serial Gold Bond issue of 1914 paying 5% interest.

Image 15: Back Cover Catskill Cement Company $1000 Gold coupon bond of 1902 paying 6% interest.

GLOSSARY OF INVESTMENT TERMS

ADR: American Depository Receipt is an exchange instrument, which allows foreign stocks to be traded through American exchanges. Shares of these foreign companies are held on deposit in U.S. banks for trading purposes.

ADV: The disclosure or Advisory statement given to Registered Investment Advisory clients when they sign the contract for fee or management services. This statement includes the professional licensing, education and experience of the principal advisor and others in his organization, as well as the securities trading and fees structure of his firm.

ANCILLARY PROBATE: An estate problem which results in part of an estate to be settled in the probate court of a foreign state because of real estate owned in two or more places.

ANNUITY: An insurance product with tax advantages that is sold as an investment. The earnings are not generally taxed until accumulated values exceed premiums paid.

ARBITRAGE: High-risk trading which is usually highly leveraged. Investments purchased in one market for sale in another at a higher price.

ARBITRATION AGREEMENT: One page of every new client application, which obligates the client and firm to meet outside the courtroom to settle differences. This FINRA function can strip a broker of his license and levy heavy fines with restitution for illegal acts. They can also eliminate nuisance complaints without the expense and delays of a courtroom trial, and are disdained by the local Bar Association.

ASSET ALLOCATION: The distribution or reallocation of a portfolio on a percentage basis.

ASSETS-EQUITY: Is the ratio of corporate total assets compared to shareholder's equity.

BAILOUT CLAUSE: A minimum earnings percentage which is a part of all annuities, if not met, allows the participant policyholder to cash the policy in or transfer it without penalty.

BALANCED FUNDS: Investment funds, which are invested in both stocks and bonds.

BASIS POINTS: Are used to define bond commissions and interest rates based on 100 points to equal one percent.

BEAR MARKET: A stock market, which is trending down with decreasing prices. Officially, when prices fall 20% or more in a major index.

BEARER BONDS: Unregistered bonds that pay to the party in possession as owner. A dollar bill could be considered a bearer bond because it could be exchanged without purchase, sale or recordation.

BETA: A complex five-year formula to determine stock and mutual fund investment risk. A Beta of 1.0 is neutral, a 1.1 is low risk, and a .9 is a higher risk.

BLACKOUT PERIOD: The period between early retirement and being old enough to qualify for Social Security benefits. This is especially hard on non-employed spouses who lose a husband or wife prematurely.

BLUE SKY: A term used for individual state qualification of a security after the FINRA approves it. Also used for the initial ad, which precedes the offer.

BOILER ROOM: A broker/dealer telemarketing place where salespeople hype up the values and deals of various stocks and orchestrate manipulations, oftentimes entirely fraudulent and misleading.

BOND RATINGS: A rating system by both Moody's and Standard & Poor's that consider Aaa or AAA bonds the highest rating, A for adequate, and Baa or BBB are poor.

BOOK VALUE: Is the tangible value of a business's total assets.

BOTTOM FISHER: A bargain hunter who buys stocks during low cycles in the market.

BRAIN DEAD: An official position of the Uniform Determination of Death Act, that with the absence of brain waves, it's officially over.

BREAK POINTS: The division between sales charge reductions on mutual fund purchases, which includes all purchases made over an 18-month period.

BULL MARKET: A stock market which is trending upward with increasing prices.

BUSINESS FUNDAMENTALS: A broker term used to establish comparative historic market data from broad business stock prices or indexes during normal market conditions to establish basic conditions for reference points during bear markets. IE; another way to sell stocks when the market is going south.

BUYER'S REMORSE: The stockbroker's nightmare as a result from the client discussing their recent investments with uninformed equally ignorant neighbors or the unscrupulous competition.

CALLABLE BONDS: Mortgage bonds or other financial instruments that could be paid off before maturity due to market changes in interest rates or other conditions.

CAPITAL GAINS TAX: Special federal individual tax rates for long-term gains on an investment property held over one year or more before the sale. The capital gains rate for property held more than 18 months is 20%, unless the individual is in the 15% tax bracket, in which case it would be 10%. For assets held more than one year but less than 18 months, the rate is 28% except for individuals in the 15% tax bracket, then it is reduced to 15%. For property held less than one year, the tax rate is the same as for ordinary income, but can offset all capital losses. Capital losses in excess of capital gains are limited to offsetting other taxable income by only $3,000 each year with the excess carried forward to the next tax year.

CAPITALIZATION: The sum of the debt and stocks issued by a corporation.

CBOE: The Chicago Board of Exchange, because they are located in the Midwest, is the commodity exchange of the country, although they also maintain a separate stock trading exchange.

C CORP: Any ordinary corporation that is not a non-profit, S-Corp, or other type.

CD: Certificates of Deposit savings certificates are issued by banks and savings & loans for terms of three months to ten years with interest penalties charged for early withdraw. They are insured by FDIC or other government agencies up to $100,000.

CFP: A Certified Financial Planner is an individual who has survived various investment and planning exams given by the College of Financial Planning.

CHURNING: Excessive illegal stock trading by brokers to generate commissions.

CLOSE CORP: A small, closely held corporation of 35 or fewer shareholders, which cannot publicly sell shares of stock.

CMO: A Collateralized Mortgage Obligation consists of a bundle (tranche) of government agency insured mortgages by common term and interest rates.

COMMODITIES: Precious metals, oil, and, agricultural products offered through a special exchange such as the Chicago Board of Exchange. (CBOE).

COMPLIANCE: A broad term used by the FINRA to determine that their rules are being followed correctly.

CONSUMER CONFIDENCE INDEX: A monthly survey of public retail purchasing wishes. The wide range is from zero to 200, with over 90 considered positive. The trends, as well as the numeric score, are viewed as an indicator of economic contraction or expansion.

CONTRARIAN: A contrarian bets that the market has peaked by selling when others are buying and bidding prices up.

CORE BUSINESS: The basic corporate business, separated from non-related acquired businesses that distract from historic product mix.

COUPONS: Historic term for interest-bearing coupons attached to bonds which could be clipped off and cashed in quarterly or when due.

CPI: The consumer price index is an annual comparison of consumer goods compared to a base cost. The index is used as an indicator of price inflation or deflation. It is also an important index used to increase Social Security benefits and for salary-wage negotiations and economic comparisons. The October index was 164% of the 1982-4 base (of 100%). The 1982 base was a devaluation of the prior base when the percentage became too big a political embarrassment.

CREDIT WATCH: A bank or institution alert indicating corporate problems, which could lead to a downgrading of bonds or other lending.

CURRENCY EXCHANGE: The New York exchange which handles only international currencies shown in US dollar equivalents.

DAX 100 INDEX: This is a total rate of return index of the 100 most highly capitalized stocks traded on the Frankfurt Stock Exchange. The index base value was 500 on 12/31/1987.

DAY TRADER: A full-time or heavily committed speculator who trades in and out of the market on a daily (more like hourly) basis at a terminal in the office of a brokerage firm or with his own computer in his own office or residence.

DEBENTURES: A corporate unsecured loan, which makes the lender a general creditor.

DEBT-EQUITY RATIO: Is the ratio of long-term corporate liabilities to total assets.

DEFERRED CONTINGENT CHARGES: Sales charges or load, which are not charged directly against sales at the time of purchase. The implied sales charge is reduced by one point each year over five or six years until it is zeroed out, but results in a charge to the investor if the fund is sold before the term is completed.

DELISTED STOCKS: Securities that are no longer shown in the trading listings in the financial journals, because the value has fallen below $1 or the minimum exchange qualifications.

DERIVATIVES: Financial instruments called repurchase agreements-certificates, swaps, of bonds, packaged or bundled to take advantage of market changes in interest rates. Also, highly leveraged global bets of hybrid investments and swaps. Contracts whose values are linked to or derived from those of underlying assets, such as bonds, stocks or commodities.

DILUTED SHARES: Are calculations of values based on present stock prices which represent numbers of shares increased by stock splits, not original issue or book value.

DIRECT STOCK PURCHASE PLANS: Allow shareholders to buy additional shares of stocks by reinvesting their dividends. This also saves commission expense to the shareholder.

DISCOUNT: Bonds sold for less than face value due to the stated interest rate being under market relative to current interest rates or other risks.

DISTRIBUTION: Cash proceeds from mutual funds, not necessarily earnings.

DIVERSIFICATION: A portfolio with investments in many different areas to reduce risk from concentration in any single area.

DIVIDEND YIELD: The percent of dividends compared to the price on an annual basis.

DOGS OF THE DOW: Stocks, which have a high yield (low price to earnings), compared to price, which is used as an indicator that they are priced low relative to the market. Also, part of a low-five strategy of concentrating portfolios, especially unit trusts, by buying the lowest five "dogs".

DOW JONES INDUSTRIAL AVERAGE: Is an index of price-weighted stocks based on the average market price of 30 Blue Chip stocks. It has been continually adjusted for stock splits, stock dividends, and substitutions of stocks.

DOW JONES INTERNET INDEX: A new 40 company index of Internet companies listed in the NASDAQ.

DOW JONES TRANSPORTATION AVERAGE: An index representing the average market capitalization of the largest 20 transportation companies.

DOW JONES UTILITY AVERAGE: Is a price-weighted average of 15 electricity-producing utility companies that are listed on the New York Exchange. The average began on 1/2/1929.

DUE DILIGENCE: The qualifying investigation and review of a security before it is offered by the BD firm.

EARNINGS PER SHARE: Is the net income at year-end divided by a number of outstanding shares.

ECONOMIC REALITY TEST: A dastardly audit means test used by the Internal Revenue Service whereas the audit victim's living standards are compared to a chart showing what his actual income should be. The test, used mostly on the self-employed, is used to "find" hidden income which is not shown on tax returns to pay for the lifestyle.

ELECTRONIC COMMUNICATIONS NETWORK (ECN): An Internet institutional trading network for stock trades.

EQUITIES: Stocks traded over the major exchanges or over the counter.

ERISA: The Pension Reform Act of 1974 created standards for company pension funding, policies, employee vesting, and diversifying a portfolio.

ESOP: Employee Stock Option Plans are employee pension plans that consist entirely of shares of stock from the employing corporation. Like all pension plans, they are required to be administered by an independent trustee or administrator. These plans are not protected during the bankruptcy of the underlying company.

ESTATE TAX EXEMPTION: A large exemption adjusted for inflation occurring after 2011, increased to $11,400,000 for 2019.

ESTATE TRUST: A fiduciary which accounts for taxes on investment earnings during the period an estate is created (death) and the final distribution to heirs.

EXECUTOR/EXECUTRIX: Are the individuals or agents appointed by a will, trust, or the court to administer estates, minor's investments or other financial affairs.

FEDERAL RESERVE BOARD: An independent federal agency of banks with great power over interest rates, the money supply, and subsequently, the economy.

FINRA: The National Association of Security Dealers, which is responsible, under the SEC, for the conduct and licensing of individuals and firms of the securities industry. The FINRA can be reached at 301-590-6500 or finra.org.

FIRST CALL: An organization that collects corporate data and projects corporate profits quarterly.

FIRST PRINCIPLES OF ARISTOTLE: Actively questioning every assumption made about a problem and rethinking a solution from scratch. Essentially, it's thinking like a scientist or engineer and not making assumptions without proving it. James Dyson and Elon Musk are visionaries who all used this regime to build their businesses and change the world.

FLIPPING: A brokerage or institutional firm practice of buying blocks of new IPO shares at the issue price and immediately selling them over the secondary (open) market at a huge profit instead of holding them.

FREELOOK PERIOD: The period of one week to a month (for the elderly) from policy delivery, during which an insurance product buyer can return the policy for cancellation and full refund.

FSE 100: A capitalization-weighted index of the 100 most highly capitalized companies traded on the London Stock Exchange. The index base level was 1,000 on 1/3/1984.

FUTURES: Options for commodity trading sometimes highly leveraged and used by speculators and large firms desiring firm future prices for manufacturing needs.

GENERAL SECURITIES REPRESENTATIVE: A registered securities salesperson who can sell most securities including stocks and bonds.

GENERATION-SKIPPING TRUST: A trust, which allows special estate tax rules to come into play by allocating trust assets to a family with a generation removed. It is also sometimes called a dynasty trust.

GDP: The sum of the national annual output of goods and services. This complex formula is used as an economic indicator to measure the size and growth, or decline, of the economy. The inclusion of government employee pension contributions as individual savings helped boost the nation's personal savings rate after it dipped underwater before recalculation during late 1999.

GICs: Guaranteed Investment Contracts are a blend of investment-grade securities sold as a bond-like IOU by banks or insurance companies to large retirement plans for a stable predictable value.

GIFT TAXES: Are assessed on annual gifts over $10,000 per individual recipient, not including the spouse. These gifts in excess of $10,000 are first applied against the estate tax unified credit and then taxed according to the estate tax tables.

GIFT TAX EXEMPTIONS: Are few, mainly the spouse, education, medical, and charity.

GOVERNMENT BONDS: Short...less than one year or long-term...up to 30 years, general obligation debt bonds issued by the federal government. They are sold in dollars and 32nds.

HAIRCUT: A small charge or commission charged by an investment advisor or fund.

HEDGE FUNDS: Extremely risky, highly leveraged investments for rich investors with club membership requirements of one million dollars net worth or income of $200,000 annually.

HERDING: Institutions or individuals following or imitating each other when trading.

HIGH YIELD BONDS: Risky, in comparison with government bonds, corporate short-term financing for takeovers paying high-interest rates. As of late, speculative investments in third world countries.

HOLOGRAPHIC WILL: A handwritten will.

IMPUTED INCOME: An interesting term directly from the Internal Revenue Service, which means taxable income not included in normal compensation. An example is employer-paid insurance coverage that exceeds the cost for $50,000 of term coverage. The difference appears as an inclusion in the employee's taxable W-2 wages.

INDEX ARBITRAGE: Computer trading programs, which automatically trade on price changes between stock and bond futures.

INDEX FUNDS: Broad portfolios of many stocks representing a buy and hold passive portfolio strategy.

INFLATION/DEFLATION INDEX: Another name for the Consumer Price Index.

INSIDER INFORMATION: Confidential information which, if leaked or used for securities trading, would result in illegal profiting by inside principals.

INTELLECTUAL CANNIBALISM: The self-destructive social acts committed by state and federal governments to create more complex tax rules during the perpetual process of raising taxes.

INTEREST RATE YIELD: The actual yield reflects the annual average of the interest rate modified by the original cost difference above or below par value. The reverse would be true for interest rate cost, especially for mortgages that have high up-front costs.

INTERNAL RATE OF RETURN (IRR): This is not the usually reported net or taxable earnings, but the real earnings within a firm.

INTERNAL REVENUE CODE SECTION 79: This Code section allows a corporation to deduct the cost of $50,000 face value of term insurance for each employee. All insurance with a face value in excess of that amount is taxed as a fringe benefit to the employee.

INTERNAL REVENUE CODE SECTION 1035: This Code section allows an insurance policy to be transferred to another new insurance policy without taxation (deferred) of the accumulated taxable earnings.

INTERNET INDEX: A recently compiled index of active Internet stocks.

INTESTATE: Dying without a will creates a probate situation where the courts must administer the distribution of estate assets. This is a lengthy process, which involves lawyers, which always reduces one's estate considerably.

INVESTMENT OBJECTIVES: A financial planning term used to summarize the resources and goals of an individual investor.

IPO: Initial Public Offering is the first step for a corporation to sell shares of stock to the public for expansion venture capital.

IRA: Individual Retirement Act offers a reduction of taxable income for a qualified contribution to a retirement account of up to $2,000 annually.

IRREVOCABLE TRUSTS: Trusts which are established by gifting the property to a formal legal trust which will file fiduciary returns and pay taxes as a separate legal entity.

JUMBO CD: A Certificate of Deposit for $100,000, which is also the threshold amount for FDIC and SLDIC deposit insurance.

KEY MAN INSURANCE: Large life insurance policies on key executives paid and owned by corporations. The insurance is to compensate the corporation for financial loss from the employee's demise.

LIMITED PARTNERSHIP: A long-term passive investment, which is managed by a non-investor general partner but limits liability and active participation of the investor-partners.

LIPPER BOND INDEX: A weekly and year-to-date index of the largest bond mutual funds showing the changes in value. Located in the daily financial journals.

LIPPER BOND RATING: A quarterly ranking of bond mutual funds based on the quality of the portfolio and performance of the fund.

LIPPER EQUITY INDEX: A weekly and year-to-date index of the largest mutual funds showing the changes in value. Located in the daily financial journals.

LIPPER PARTNERSHIP INDEX: A quarterly ranking based on the quality and performance of limited partnerships.

LIVING TRUST: An inactive revocable trust, which is activated on the death of the owner and sometimes functions as a grantor trust fiduciary (Bypass Trust) afterward.

LONG: A trading position held by investor or brokerage house owning and possessing the securities being sold.

LOOK-BACK PERIOD: The three-year period during which life insurance proceeds, after the policy has been given away, can be taxed to an estate.

LOW-INCOME HOUSING CREDITS: Are federal income tax credits based on large housing buildings or projects, which are rented to low-income individuals. Uniquely sold to investors with a promise of no cash back but tax refunds larger than the contribution.

MANAGED ACCOUNT: An account managed by a Registered Investment Advisor for fees based on the value of invested assets in the portfolio. Unlike a typical stockbroker portfolio that is charged sales fees per transaction.

MARGIN ACCOUNT: Extension of credit, currently up to 50% of secured securities, for stock trading by individuals. The money is borrowed from banks by B/D firms and loaned out to investment clients at a higher rate. The Federal Reserve Board determines these credit limits, which are more conservative than in 1929 when they were considered the major reason for the big sell-off that precipitated the Great Stock Market Crash.

MARGIN CALL: An offer by the broker to sell your securities for you when the market value has fallen enough to threaten the amount loaned on margin.

MARKET CAP: A formula consisting of basic shares outstanding multiplied by share price which gives the total market value of the company's stock.

MARKET TIMERS: Financial advisors who move mutual funds back and forth to cash whenever the stock market dips or changes course.

MICROCAP: Penny stock and small-cap stocks that are highly speculated because small changes in value can create large gains or losses from small amounts invested.

MONEY MARKET FUNDS: Are funds holding short-term financial assets with a maturity of less than one year. The share price is always $1.

MONEY PURCHASE PENSION: A pension plan, no longer in common usage, which required corporate contributions and control with long vesting periods for employees. They usually purchased only corporate stock in the same company and were top-heavy in favor of management.

MORNINGSTAR RATINGS: Are used for three, five and ten-year periods to rate mutual fund performance relative to the other funds in the same field. The ratings look like the bell-curve IQ scale on a graph with the premium 5-star rating the top 10%, 4-star is 22.5%, the 3-star median is 35%, lower 2-star is 22.5% and the remaining 1-star is 10% which means sell now! There are also equity style box ratings that rank funds by small to large size and undervalued to growth characteristics, and fixed-income boxes which categorize bond funds from low to high risk and short to long term.

MORTALITY CHARGES: A surprisingly small annual fee charged internally to an insurance or annuity policy based on actuary calculations. These are the actual death insurance annual costs assigned to the insurance policy.

MSCI EAFE: Is an index of 1,000 companies representing the stock markets of 18 countries including Australia, Austria, Belgium, Denmark, Finland, France, Germany, Italy, Netherlands, Norway, Spain, Sweden, Switzerland, and the United Kingdom.

MUNICIPAL BONDS: Infrastructure financing by state and local municipalities resulting in individual federal and state tax-exempt interest earnings.

MUTUAL FUND: A large publicly traded fund, which is managed by Advisors and professional managers. Mutual funds are open-ended investment companies that vary the number of shares outstanding, which are bought and sold directly by the fund.

NAPM INDEX: National Association Purchasing Index represents future orders based on a 2% sample of the Gross Domestic Product. This important economic indicator is neutral at 50%, a 51% index would indicate a growing economy, and a 49% figure a decline.

NASDAQ COMPOSITE: This is a market-weighted index of all common stocks traded over the counter that is included in the NASDAQ quotation system. It excludes those listed on an exchange and those with only one market maker. It is a total return index of predominantly smaller capitalization companies with dividends reinvested.

NAV: Net Asset Value is the closing value of one mutual fund share at the end of the day's trading, based on the value of the portfolio divided by the number of shares outstanding. It is also the trading price used for all shares bought and sold during the day.

NIKKI-DOW/NIKKI 225: This is a price-weighted index of 225 top-rated Japanese companies listed in the first section of the Tokyo Stock Exchange. This average was first published on 5/16/1949.

NON-PERFORMING ASSET: A security or other asset that is not earning a market rate of return. A company in liquidation, notes in default, a company not making a profit or paying dividends.

ORIGINAL ISSUE: The first of successive security offerings.

OSJ: Office of Supervisory Jurisdiction is a term for a branch manager who supervises trading and conduct of sales reps. He also hires and fires these individuals, and is subjected to an annual audit by his B/D firm for his branch sales activities.

OTHER HIGH-RISK OBJECTIVES: The term applied at the end of the investment objective listing for many mutual funds, which authorizes the advisor to invest in "other" risky financial instruments too dangerous to describe.

OVER-THE-COUNTER-BULLETIN-BOARD: A special section of the NASDAQ Stock Market where small issues and troubled stocks are traded.

PAR: Face value of financial instrument.

PARADIGM: An unpronounceable term used by financial analysts to confuse ordinary people.

PAY TO PLAY: A corrupt process practiced by brokerage firms and financial institutions buying the business by paying campaign contributions to politically oriented public officials who head public pension plans or are connected to lucrative municipal bond deals.

P-E RATIO: The price-earnings ratio is the relationship or percentage of the current stock price to earnings. A low ratio is most desirable in determining the real economic value of the stock or the market in general. The S & P 500 index was 24 times earnings before the Crash in 1929. During 1998, the P-E varied from 26 to 30.

PERCEIVED INCOME: A unique taxing concept pioneered by California, whereas a person holding any professional license is taxed on imaginary income if he does not file a tax return (even if he is retired or not working). In 1998 the net taxable income presumption for a realtor was $25,000 and insurance agent $35,000.

PERSONAL HOLDING COMPANY: Another IRS Code section 541 item which taxes undistributed corporate income, which acts as "incorporated pocketbooks" for personal or passive investment income.

PHANTOM STOCK PLAN: A management incentive system for non-public corporations. While stock option plans are based on publicly traded prices for stock shares, phantom plans rely on other internal growth indicators such as cash assets and equity from reinvested profits.

PINK SHEETS: A penny stock listing place for losers and bankrupt firms.

PONZI SCHEME: A term used for fraud, named after Charles Ponzi, a creative salesperson who sold up to 23 house lots per acre of Florida real estate in the 1920s.

POP: Public Offering Price is the mutual fund total return performance after allowing a reduction for Class A commission charges and assuming all distributions are reinvested.

PREMIUM: An amount paid in excess of face value for a bond, which has a higher interest rate than the current market.

PRICE-SALES RATIO: The ratio of share price to sales.

PRIME INTEREST RATE: A base loan rate charged banks, based on the Federal Reserve Board discount rate plus three points.

PRINCIPAL: An individual holding both general security and supervisory licenses. He/she is usually a branch manager (OSJ) who approves trading of individual brokers and has hiring & firing responsibilities.

PRIVITATION OR GOING PRIVATE: Is the act of withdrawing or buying public shares back by the corporation to delist the business and conduct business privately.

PROSPECTUS: A document containing financial information on new mutual funds or other financial issues, which must be approved by the SEC before presentation to the public. All clients must be given a current prospectus at the time a security is sold.

PUMP-AND-DUMP: An insider trading scheme during which a B/D firm hypes a stock they hold a position in and dumps the stock after the value is pumped up. The increased activity can cause the SEC to notice and shut down illegal trading.

PUTS: An option to buy stocks for a fixed price. The option, which is sold for a fee, can be exercised if the value rises above that certain amount.

Q-TIP TRUST: A Qualified Terminable Interest Property Trust is created on the death of a spouse and allows the amount above the estate tax deduction to shift into a special grantor trust for the benefit of the surviving spouse, and then his/her surviving heirs without further estate taxes.

QUARTERS: Corporate fiscal three-month financial periods are expressed as Q1, Q2, Q3, and Q4 (year-end).

REBALANCING PORTFOLIO: A periodic review of investments to redistribute concentration of investments due to changing risk and earnings.

RED HERRING: The preliminary prospectus of a security (bond) offering, prior to approval, used to advise prospective buyers of the new issue.

REGISTERED INVESTMENT ADVISOR: An individual or firm who, for a fee, manages funds for clients or consults with them about their investments. The individual or firm is required to pass both FINRA principal exams and other advisory exams.

REGISTERED REPRESENTATIVE: Another name for a stockbroker who is registered by the FINRA licensing process.

REGULATION T: A SEC ruling that requires all security trades to be cleared within three days from the trade date (T+3).

REINSURANCE: A cooperative effort between insurance companies to allocate large policy investment and risk between firms (one company would sell a large $5,000,000 policy, keeping a million-dollar portion which might be their retention limit, and farm the remainder out to other insurance companies to spread or share the risk).

REIT: Real Estate Investment Trusts hold a special corporate charter, which allows the business to pay dividends directly to shareholders without first paying corporate taxes.

REMIC: Real Estate Mortgage Insured Callable notes such as Federal Housing loans which are bundled for an average term. If any of the underlying mortgages are canceled or paid off, that part of the loan is considered called.

REPURCHASE: The purchase of outstanding stock by the issuing corporation. The repurchased stock then becomes Treasury Stock.

RESTRICTED STOCK: Is the unregistered stock of a close-held corporation, usually a small family business, which cannot be traded publicly. Restricted stocks are subject to the SEC section 144 ruling that established tough sales guidelines, which severely limit trading.

RETIREMENT PLAN IRS CODE SECTION 401-K: An employer-sponsored pension plan which gives employees investment control and also provides for corporate matching contributions and immediate vesting.

REVENUE PER EMPLOYEE: Total corporate income divided by the number of employees.

REVERSE STOCK SPLIT: The reduction of the numbers of shares outstanding by reissuing fewer shares of stocks for the number issued. The reverse of the usual stock split. Sometimes done as a desperate measure to increase share price when the values have fallen enough to become delisted on an exchange.

RIA: The Registered Investment Advisor is the highest licensed and regulated investment professional. An individual must be qualified by the SEC to speak or act publicly about investments, as well as manage funds for fees.

ROE: Return On Equity is the percentage of net income divided by common stock to determine the performance of the investment.

ROTH IRA: A special retirement account, which does not offer a tax deduction for the initial deposit, but allows the earnings and principal to remain untaxed on distribution.

RULE 12b-1: Annual fees, usually about 1% charged investors, based on portfolio value, by mutual fund Advisors.

RUSSELL 2000: This is an index comprised of the smallest 2,000 companies in the Russell 3,000 index, which represents approximately 11% of the total market capitalization. The index base value of 135 was developed on 12/31/1986.

SAFE HAVEN: An investment unaffected by investment volatility in other areas. A cash account in a mutual fund would be considered a safe haven.

SALLIE MAE: Is the huge government agency (SLM Holdings Corp.) responsible for issuing debt to support student loans.

SCALPING: A broker-dealer event that calls for highly promoting a stock they hold (making the market) while marking it up for unsuspecting clients to earn unrealistic profits.

S CORP: A small corporation of 35 shareholders or less, which has elected and qualified as S Corp status from IRS that allows net income to be distributed as taxable partnership income. This avoids corporate taxes and allows some shareholders to utilize the corporate veil of liability.

SEC: The Securities Exchange Commission is responsible for the regulation of all nongovernmental securities.

SECONDARY MARKET: The resale market for any security after the initial issue and purchase.

SEED CAPITAL: Initial venture capital investment to develop a small company from the early concept or idea stage.

SELLING AWAY: Trading securities or any other investments that are not approved by the sales rep's firm.

SHORT: A trading position, or sale, conducted without actual ownership of the securities. The sold shares are borrowed for a future purchase to cover the position, hopefully at a cheaper price.

SINKING FUND: Funds set aside to pay off notes or debt.

SNAIL MAIL: The US Post office vs electronic means.

SPENDING DOWN: The process of reducing an individual's estate to income and asset levels low enough to qualify for state aid to pay for nursing home care.

SPLIT DOLLAR LIFE INSURANCE: A plan or arrangement between an employer and an employee whereas the employer pays the amount equal to the cash value increases in the policy with the employee paying the difference. Upon death, the employer is paid back the cash value portion of the policy with the difference going to the employee's estate.

SPOUSAL EXEMPTION: An estate tax rule allowing the decedent's estate to remain untaxed while the other spouse is alive (afterward it all gets taxed).

SRO: A Self-Regulatory Organization, such as the FINRA, acts as a policeman, judge and jury to enforce regulation of its peers and members.

STANDARD & POOR 500: This is an index consisting of 500 widely held common stocks in the four broad sectors: industrials, utilities, financial, and transportation. Each stock affects the total return index in proportion to its market value, which includes dividends reinvested.

STANDARD & POOR STAR RANKINGS: 5-star is a buy, 4-star means to accumulate, 3-star for hold, 2-star to avoid, and 1-star is sold.

STATUTORY ESTATE ATTORNEY FEES: These fees, which are based on the size of the estate, can be paid to the executor and executrix (which creates a tax problem) as well as the lawyer, unless waived. They are: 4% on the first $15,000, 3% on the next $85,000, 2% on the next $900,000, 1% on the next $9,000,000, ½% on the next $15,000,000, and a court determined fee for amount above $25,000,000 along with additional compensation for extraordinary services, such as the legal imagination will allow. Statutory is the legal term that takes the negotiation out of the deal.

STOCK OPTIONS: A management inducement based on the price of the stock increasing in the future. The option has no cost because it is only exercised when it is sold, unless the stock price declines.

STOCK TRADING SHARE PRICES: Are expressed in even dollars and sixteenth fractions. A stock selling for five and eight/sixteenth dollars would be $5½, or $5.50.

STOCK EXCHANGES: New York in the US; Nikkei in Tokyo, Japan; Hang Seng in Hong Kong, China; Xetra Dax in Frankfurt, Germany; CAC in Paris, France; and FTSE in London, England.

STRATEGIC ALLIANCE: A synergetic combination of companies in different, but complementary businesses.

SUITABILITY TEST: A matching of risk preferences between investors and investment products.

TAX REFORM ACT OF 1986: The purpose of the Act was to serve as a simplistic version of the federal income tax code. It failed!

TEENY: A small uptick on a stock, usually $1/16^{th}$ point. A minimal amount but enough to cause waves of trading by day traders buying and selling large blocks of cheap stocks.

TELEPHONE REDEMPTION: A privilege offered mutual fund clients whereas a fund can be sold or transferred directly through a telephone conversation, after proper identification.

THE STREET.COM: A company that compiles an Internet sector index.

TIPS: Treasury inflation-protected securities are a ten year-coupon-paying bond that has a principal adjustment to even out inflation values over the term (because the coupon is unchanged). The yield is about 4% over the inflation index, which makes it a good deal for the owner-holder.

TOMBSTONE: The initial public announcement, usually in a financial newspaper, of a new security offering.

TREASURY STRIPS: Treasury bonds with maturity dates that coincide with calendar quarters to assure quarterly dividends.

TRUSTEE: The individual or organization that has the legal authority to act for or administer a trust.

UNDERWRITING FEES: Investment firm charges for the legal and administrative charges for handing new issues of stocks or bonds.

UNIFORM GIFT TO MINORS ACT: Otherwise known as UGMA, this law codified the treatment of funds gifted, earned, or inherited by minors. Generally, it places the control of the child's funds under a guardian who must adhere to strict laws of accountability until the minor reaches age 18, which is the age of majority.

UNIT TRUSTS: A bundling of securities in a specific sector, sometimes mixed with zero coupons or strip treasury bonds, and sold in unit shares to investors. These are closed-end trusts, which are composed of a specific number of shares and trade on the securities exchanges after the issue is sold out.

UNIVERSAL INSURANCE: An insurance investment product, which combines insurance and investment monies.

UNSUITABLE: A term feared by securities salespeople, which means the sale shouldn't have been made because of a mismatching of client and product.

VARIABLE ANNUITY: An insurance product, which combines insurance with various securities that are managed by outside Investment Advisors.

VENTURE CAPITAL: Initial seed and growth capital for new entrepreneurial early-stage companies, before the IPO, that is sought from individuals, partnerships, or syndicates, all of which participate in the ownership of the emerging firm.

VENTURE CAPITAL MOVES: Business-to-business which are related business mergers, e-commerce which are electronic superstores, and vertical portals which means absorbing required components of a business (vertical integration).

VIATICAL SETTLEMENT: An arrangement to advance cash by assigning life insurance proceeds in anticipation of death within two years, usually by terminally ill AIDS victims. The investor usually buys the policy by irrevocably making himself the owner and beneficiary for a 35% discount from the face value of the policy.

VULTURE CAPITAL: Nonperforming bonds that are sold at distressed prices by high-yield bond mutual funds and other investors to vulture investors (hedge funds). The vultures hope by buying large blocks, to take control of the company by pressuring shareholders into a restructuring bankruptcy which would give them a debt trade for an equity position.

WILL: The most important part of any estate because it defines who gets what and puts the economic estate in order. An attorney must compile and keep it updated because it is such an important legal document that would result in will-contest litigation or probate if not perfect.

WILTSHIRE 5000: This is a market value-weighted index of over 5,000 securities. The capital value of the index is composed of approximately 86% of New York Stock Exchange issues, 3% of the American Stock Exchange, and 11% of NASDAQ over the counter issues. It is a total return index with dividends reinvested.

WORM FARM: An investment product for fools.

WRAP FEES: Money management charges on the investor's total portfolio.

YEAR TWO-GRAND: The point in time whence all economic activity and human existence was predicted to cease. An economic and social millennium.

YIELD BURNING: Excessive markups charged on municipal bond issues by investment bankers, which reduce the investor's yield by increasing the cost.

YIELD TO MATURITY: The true annual percentage earned on bonds after considering discounts, premiums, and commissions.

ZERO COUPON BOND: A bond that does not pay interest until it is sold or matures. An example is the small $25 government Series E savings bond which initially costs $12.50.

ZILLIONS: This is a term used for incomprehensible large numbers such as the US national debt, or the number of barrels of oil in the Mid-East. Quadrillion is four times as many.

References

Newspaper:

Burns, J. (2008, March 5). SEC proposes faster ETF path to market. *The Wall Street Journal.*

Chung, J. & Banerji (2019, November 22). Bridgewater makes $1.5 billion options bet on falling market. *The Wall Street Journal.*

Faucon, B. & Said, Summer, S. (2020, March 8). Saudis instigate oil-price clash with Russia. *The Wall Street Journal.*

Higgins, T. (2020, March 20). Musk, striking a defiant tone, resisted pressure to halt TESLAs

Hodari, D. (2019, February 10). Thieves mine catalytic converters for metal more valuable than gold. *The Wall Street Journal.*

Iosebashvili, A. & Ramkumar, A. (2017, October 23). Palladium prices soar in sign of global growth and auto demand. *The Wall Street Journal.*

Isaac, A. & Ostroff, C. (2020, January 23). Central banks warm to issuing currencies. *The Wall Street Journal.*

Jungle, J. & Mclaughlin, K. (2020, February 21). Changes for veterans loans. *The Wall Street Journal.*

Krouse, S. & Hagerty, J. (2020, February 8-9). Fall of the worldcom CEO spurred legal changes. *The Wall Street Journal.*

Loder, A. (2019, July 9). Investing in funds & ETFS. *The Wall Street Journal.*

Mackintosh, J. (2010, August 31-September 1). How investors can best utilize ETFs. *The Wall Street Journal.*

Michaels, D. (2019, September 26). Washington gives exchange traded funds fast lane to market. *The Wall Street Journal.*

Michaels, D. (2020, February 5). SEC alleges startup's coin skirts safeguards for investors. The *Wall Street Journal.*

Ramkumar, A. (2020, January 13). Oil falls as bullish wagers decline.

The Wall Street Journal.

Ramkumar, A. (2019, December 5). Higher emissions standards help extend booking palladium Rally. *The Wall Street Journal.*

Ravo, N. (2020, March 9). Drips survive in a no-fee world. *The Wall Street Journal.*

Shroeder, M. (2020, January 10). Glass-Steagall compromise. *The Wall Street Journal.*

Tergesen, A. (2020, February 14). Making sense of the new savings-plan rules. *The Wall Street Journal.*

Verlaine, J. (2020, March 9). Short-term loan sector worries banks. *The Wall Street Journal.*

Wexler, A. (2019, November 30). De Beers diamonds reflect a changing market. *The Wall Street Journal.*

Wigglesworth, R. (2019, November 1). The man who solved the market-how Jim Simons built a moneymaking machine. *The Wall Street Journal.*

Zuckerman, G. & Rubin, R. (2019, December 18). Renaissance employees could face clawbacks over hedge fund's tax maneuver. *The Wall Street Journal.*

Webpage

Galante, M. (1989, July 25). Karchers settle insider case with fine. Retrieved from https://www.latimes.com/archives/la-xpm-1989-07-25-mn-305-story.html

Carlson, B. (2020, January 28). More questions and answers about   the secure act. Retrieved from https://www.forbes.com/sites/bobcarlson/2020/01/28/more-questions-and-answers-about-the-secure-act/#4dde22386486

Stroud, F. Cryptocurrency mining. Retrieved from https://www.webopedia.com/TERM/C/cryptocurrency-mining.html

Kramer, L. (2020, March 23). An overview of bull and bear markets. Retrieved from https://www.investopedia.com/insights/digging-deeper-bull-and-bear-markets/

U.S. silver coins: when they ended and what they're worth.   Retrieved from https://coinsite.com/us-silver-coins-when-they-ended-and-what-theyre-worth/

Mutual fund fees and expenses. (2017, January 01). Retrieved from
https://www.ally.com/do-it-right/investing/fees-and-expenses-for-mutual-funds/

Dollarhide, M. (2020, April 12). Chapter 11. Retrieved from
https://www.investopedia.com/terms/c/chapter11.asp

Chapter 13-Bancruptcy (2020, January 21). Retrieved from
https://www.uscourts.gov/services-forms/bankruptcy/bankruptcy-basics/chapter-13-bankruptcy-basics

Daugherty, G. (2020, April 27). How is the social security trust fund invested?
Retrieved from
https://www.investopedia.com/ask/answers/110614/how-social-security-trust-fund-invested.asp

California legislative information uploaded. (2020, March 15). Retrieved from
https://leginfo.legislature.ca.gov/

Elon Musk (2020, March 22). Retrieved on March 22, 2020, from
https://en.wikipedia.org/wiki/Elon

Madoff investment scandal. In *Wikipedia*. Retrieved on March 22, 2020, from
https://en.wikipedia.org/wiki/Madoff_investment_scandal

Baer, J. (2020, February 5). Bernie Madoff says he's dying, requests early release
from prison. Retrieved from
https://www.wsj.com/articles/bernie-madoff-says-hes-dying-requests-early-release-from-prison-11580945272

Kenton, W. (2020, March 27). Section 1202. Retrieved from
https://www.investopedia.com/terms/s/section-1202.asp

Block, J. (2020, December 19). Will you get a tax break if you donate closely held
stock? Retrieved from
https://www.accountingweb.com/tax/irs/will-you-get-a-tax-break-if-you-donate-closely-held-stock

Virtual Currencies. Retrieved on January 12, 2020, from
https://www.irs.gov/businesses/small-businesses-self-employed/virtual-currencies

Probate code –Prob division 6 wills and intestate succession.
Retrieved on February 2, 2020, from
https://leginfo.legislature.ca.gov/faces/codesdisplayexpandedbranchxhtml?tocCode=PROB&division=6,&title=part=chapter=&article

Erb, K. Tax extenders bring back some – but not all – popular deductions Retrieved on December 18, 2019, from https://www.forbes.com/sites/kellyphillipserb/2019/12/17/tax-deductions/#4ff81fa57ef7

What is a good FICO score? Retrieved on January 22, 2020, from https://www.experian.com/blogs/ask-experian/credit-education/score-basics/what-is-a-good-credit-score/

Market volatility regulations. Retrieved on March 10, 2020, from https://personal.vanguard.com

Ramkumar, A. (2020, January 13). Unwind of bullish oil bets could limit crude-price gains. Retrieved from https://www.wsj.com/articles/unwind-of-bullish-oil-bets-could-limit-crude-price-gains-11578930716

Kagan, J. (2019, September 29). What Is a Section 1244 stock? Retrieved from https://www.investopedia.com/terms/s/section-1244-stock.asp

Hayes, A. (2020, April 7). Federal call. Retrieved from https://www.investopedia.com/terms/f/federal-call.asp

Wood, R. IRS intensifies hunt for crypto tax cheats. Retrieved on January 30, 2020, from https://www.forbes.com/sites/robertwood/2020/01/29/irs-intensifies-hunt-for-crypto-tax-cheats/#5e76b4913cee

Chapter 13- Bankruptcy basics. Retrieved on January 21, 2020, from https://www.uscourts.gov/services-forms/bankruptcy/bankruptcy-basics/chapter-13-bankruptcy-basics

Associated Press. (1998, November 3). Nasdaq completes its merger with Amex. Retrieved from https://www.nytimes.com/1998/11/03/business/nasdaq-completes-its-merger-with-amex.html

Mutual fund fees and expenses. (2017, January 01). Retrieved from https://www.ally.com/do-it-right/investing/fees-and-expenses for-mutual-funds/

Book:

Nolo Law for All. (2019) Quicken WillMaker

The Tax Book De Luxe Edition Plus Tax Year 2019

INDEX

T

MORE ABOUT THE AUTHOR

Phillip Bruce Chute, EA is a businessman-writer. He lives with Nenita Lariosa, a retired educator, and is currently a tax and financial advisor with a consulting practice in Temecula, California. He has been an Enrolled Agent of the U.S. Treasury since 1976. While a professional tax expert, he practiced financial planning, stockbroker investments, and financial management for the clientele of his large tax practice. For 20 years he was a NASD licensed Registered Series 7, Registered Principal OSJ Series 24, and Financial Advisor Series 63. He currently holds California insurance licenses Fire & Casualty, Life & Disability, and Investment Annuities.

Phillip served as a paratrooper in the 82nd Airborne Division in the States and Europe during the Cold War. His financial career began when the State of California awarded him Private Investigator license #5912 as a business credit reporter for Dun & Bradstreet. Afterwards he worked as an accountant in various businesses until buying several practices in Riverside, California. The business evolved into a financial practice with a securities branch in Orange County, California.

Phillip has several other published works, including: *The Silver Thread of Life, The Metric Clock, Rock and Roll Murders,* and *American Independent Business.* He has also published articles for the *Nova Scotia* periodical, *The Shore News.*

THE AUTHOR'S OTHER WORKS

The Silver Thread of Life: Real accounts of spiritual encounters by the author and others.

American Independent Business: Sold 5,000 copies and used as a college textbook and reference for business entrepreneurs.

Rock & Roll Murders: Fiction, based on a true story about the KOLA radio station-Fred Cote Murder-One trials and conviction in Riverside in 1990.

The Metric Clock: Coming of Age Older Teen Fiction set in the mid-1940s New England.

Trust Me: An upcoming True story of a Con Man

Hazardous Business: An upcoming Fictional Story